T0230113

Lecture Notes in Artificial Intelligence   1224

Subseries of Lecture Notes in Computer Science
Edited by J. G. Carbonell and J. Siekmann

Lecture Notes in Computer Science

Edited by G. Goos, J. Hartmanis and J. van Leeuwen

Springer
Berlin
Heidelberg
New York
Barcelona
Budapest
Hong Kong
London
Milan
Paris
Santa Clara
Singapore
Tokyo

Maarten van Someren   Gerhard Widmer (Eds.)

Machine Learning: ECML-97

9th European Conference on Machine Learning
Prague, Czech Republic, April 23-25, 1997
Proceedings

Springer

Series Editors
Jaime G. Carbonell, Carnegie Mellon University, Pittsburgh, PA, USA
Jörg Siekmann, University of Saarland, Saarbrücken, Germany

Volume Editors

Maarten van Someren
Universiteit van Amsterdam, Faculteit der Psychologie
Roetersstraat 15, 1018 WB Amsterdam, The Netherlands
E-mail: maarten@swi.psy.uva.nl

Gerhard Widmer
University of Vienna
Department of Medical Cybernetics and Artificial Intelligence
and
Austrian Research Institute for Artificial Intelligence
Schottengasse 3, A-1010 Vienna, Austria
E-mail: gerhard@ai.univie.ac.at

Cataloging-in-Publication Data applied for

Die Deutsche Bibliothek - CIP-Einheitsaufnahme

Machine learning : proceedings / ECML-97, 9th European
Conference on Machine Learning, Prague, Czech Republic, April 23 -
25, 1997. Maarten van Someren ; Gerhard Widmer (ed.). - Berlin ;
Heidelberg ; New York ; Barcelona ; Budapest ; Hong Kong ;
London ; Milan ; Paris ; Santa Clara ; Singapore ; Tokyo : Springer,
1997
   (Lecture notes in computer science ; Vol. 1224 : Lecture notes in
   artificial intelligence)
   ISBN 3-540-62858-4 kart.

CR Subject Classification (1991): I.2, F.2.2

ISBN 3-540-62858-4 Springer-Verlag Berlin Heidelberg New York

© Springer-Verlag Berlin Heidelberg 1997
Printed in Germany

Typesetting: Camera ready by author
SPIN 10549593   06/3142 – 5 4 3 2 1 0   Printed on acid-free paper

Foreword

The Ninth European Conference on Machine Learning (ECML-97), held in Prague, Czech Republic, April 23–25, 1997, continues the tradition of earlier EWSL and ECML conferences as the major European forum for the presentation and discussion of research in machine learning.

The scientific programme of ECML-97 consisted of three invited talks (by Stuart Russell, Luc Steels, and Paul Vitányi), plenary paper presentations, and a poster session, and was followed by a day of specialized workshops organized by MLNet, the European Network of Excellence in Machine Learning.

There were two kinds of plenary paper presentations: long comprehensive papers (30-minute presentations, up to 16 pages in the proceedings) and short papers (15 minutes, 8 pages). The selection of papers was based on at least two reviews per submission. Of the 73 papers submitted to ECML-97, 26 were finally accepted for publication in the proceedings (13 long and 13 short papers), giving an acceptance rate of about 35%.

This proceedings volume contains papers relating to the invited talks (Part 1) and the 26 papers presented at the conference (Part 2). A major goal of the four post-conference MLNet workshops was to explore new aspects of machine learning. The organizers of these workshops wrote short papers introducing the topic of their workshop and articulating the main issues. These articles are collected in Part 3. The proceedings of the workshops appear as technical reports of the University of Economics, Prague.

Our thanks go first to all the authors who submitted their work and thus made the conference possible. Thanks also to the members of the programme committee and the reviewers for their efforts and input, and to the invited speakers for sharing their ideas and visions with us. ECML-97 was organized by the University of Economics, Prague (Faculty of Informatics and Statistics), in cooperation with the Czech Technical University (Faculty of Electrical Engineering) and the Center for Theoretical Study (Charles University & Academy of Sciences). Our gratitude goes to the Local Chair, Radim Jiroušek, and the members of the organizing committee. We would also like to thank all the sponsors who made the organization of ECML-97 possible.

February 1997

Maarten van Someren
Gerhard Widmer

Programme Chairs

Maarten van Someren, University of Amsterdam, The Netherlands
Gerhard Widmer, University of Vienna and Austrian Research Institute for
Artificial Intelligence, Vienna, Austria

Local Chair

Radim Jiroušek, University of Economics, Prague, Czech Republic

Programme Committee

David W. Aha (USA)
Ivan Bratko (Slovenia)
Ken De Jong (USA)
Sašo Džeroski (Slovenia)
Yves Kodratoff (France)
Ramon Lopez de Mantaras (Spain)
Stan Matwin (Canada)
Gholamreza Nakhaeizadeh (Germany)
Lorenza Saitta (Italy)
Derek Sleeman (UK)
Stefan Wrobel (Germany)

Francesco Bergadano (Italy)
Pavel Brazdil (Portugal)
Luc De Raedt (Belgium)
Werner Emde (Germany)
Nada Lavrač (Slovenia)
Heikki Mannila (Finland)
Katharina Morik (Germany)
Céline Rouveirol (France)
Jürgen Schmidhuber (Switzerland)
Paul Vitányi (Netherlands)

Organizing Institutions

University of Economics, Prague (Faculty of Informatics and Statistics)
Czech Technical University (Faculty of Electrical Engineering)
Center for Theoretical Study (Charles University & Academy of Sciences)

Organizing Committee

Petr Berka, Ivan M. Havel, Lenka Lhotská, Vojtěch Svátek, Olga Štěpánková,
Lucie Váchová, Jan Vyšehradský, Milena Zeithamlová.

Sponsors

The European Network of Excellence in Machine Learning (MLNet)
Komerční banka, a.s.
MŠMT Grant No. PR 96291
AXIOM, s.r.o.

Additional Reviewers

Cristina Baroglio
Peter Brockhausen
Bogdan Filipič
João Gama
Aram Karalič
Igor Kononenko
Claire Nedellec
Enric Plaza
Anke Rieger
Rafał Sałustowicz
Michèle Sebag
Marco Wiering
Jieyu Zhao

Stefan Bell
Claudio Carpineto
Peter Flach
Matjaz Gams
Jörg-Uwe Kietz
Miroslav Kubat
Filippo Neri
Uroš Pompe
Marko Robnik Šikonja
Thomas Schneckenburger
Luís Torgo
Mark Winter
Zijian Zheng

Marko Bohanec
Antoine Cornuéjols
Johannes Fürnkranz
Daniele Gunetti
Volker Klingspor
Fraser Mitchell
Johann Petrak
Thomas Reinartz
Giancarlo Ruffo
Nicol Schraudolph
Simon White
Rüdiger Wirth

Table of Contents

III Workshop Position Papers

Part I:

Invited Papers

Uncertain Learning Agents

Stuart Russell

Computer Science Division
University of California, Berkeley
russell@cs.berkeley.edu

Abstract. The nature of the task environment in which an intelligent agent must operate has a profound effect on its design. It can be argued that AI has only recently begun to take seriously the problem of partial observability of the environment, despite the fact that this is perhaps the primary reason why intelligent agents need memory and internal representations. In complex environments, partial observability goes hand in hand with uncertainty, and necessitates the development of new tools for representation, inference, decision making, and learning. I will describe work in progress on a suite of such tools, including methods for learning complex models of a partially observable, stochastic environment, methods for using such models to keep track of what's happening in the environment; and methods for reinforcement learning with hierarchical behaviour descriptions.

Constructing and Sharing Perceptual Distinctions

Luc Steels

VUB Artificial Intelligence Laboratory
Pleinlaan 2 1050 Brussels
email: steels@arti.vub.ac.be and
Sony Computer Science Laboratory
6 Rue Amyot
F-75005 Paris, France

The paper describes a mechanism whereby agents generate perceptual distinctions through a series of adaptive discrimination games and share these distinctions through adaptive language games. Results from computer simulations as well as experiments on robotic agents are presented.

1 Introduction

Machine learning research on concept formation has mostly concentrated on inducing definitions of concepts from examples (see e.g. [3] It is assumed that the necessary conceptualisations have been performed by a teacher and that the learning system gets positive and negative examples of the concepts to be learned. There are however many situations where examples are not available. Indeed, it could be argued that as long as the examples are supplied by a teacher, the intelligence resides in the teacher and does not originate in the learner.

This paper focuses on how an autonomous agent might be able to *construct* appropriate conceptualisations himself. It investigates how an agent may construct new distinctions relevant for discriminating objects in its environment. The construction process is based on the random generation of a variety of distinctions which then undergo selectionist pressure based on how well they discriminate. The system is open in the sense that new objects may always enter into the environment forcing the agent to refine or expand the available repertoire of distinctions.

But if every agent creates his own distinctions, we are confronted with the problem how there could ever arise coherence in a group of agents. The second part of the paper addresses this question. It is proposed that language plays a critical role in establishing a shared set of perceptual distinctions. A mechanism is therefore proposed whereby distinctions are lexicalised and used in language-based interactions. As part of an interaction (further called a language game) the agents adapt their lexicon so as to maximise communicative success in future games. The agents thus not only construct their own distinctions but their own language for verbalising these distinctions as well, all without the intervention of a teacher.

Our work has proceeded in two steps. First software simulations have been constructed to explore possible mechanisms for the creation of distinctions and the formation of a language for communicating these distinctions in a group of agents. The resulting algorithms have then been ported to physical robotic agents to demonstrate that the perceptual distinctions can be grounded in real-world sensing and actuation.

The paper is in four parts. The first section reports the algorithm for the creation of perceptual distinctions. The second section reports on the language games. Then results on coupling the two mechanisms are described. Finally some robotic experiments for the development of grounded concepts are discussed. The paper builds further on earlier results reported in [5], [6] and [7]. These papers should be consulted for additional technical detail.

2 Creating perceptual distinctions through discrimination games

2.1 Principles

Let us assume that there is a set of objects, or more generally situations, which have characteristics that are sensed through sensory channels. The datastream on a sensory channel is either the direct output of a sensor (e.g. infrared or visible light) or is the result of a low-level perceptual routine. A sensory channel yields a value in the continuous range between 1.0 and 0.0.

A discrimination tree is associated with each sensory channel. The tree divides the continuous domain into subdomains and thus maps the sensory channel into a discrete set of categories represented as features. A feature consists of an attribute value pair. The attribute expresses a path in the discrimination tree and the value the end point of the path.

The goal of the learning process is to construct the appropriate discrimination trees starting from scratch. Which discrimination trees are appropriate depends on the task and the environment. In this paper, we focus on discrimination tasks. The agent must develop an adequate repertoire of features for discriminating between the objects present in its environment. For example, if one object can be distinguished from the other objects because it has a different color, then it is necessary to have enough color distinctions. If all objects in the context have the same color but different sizes, it is necessary to make use of size-distinctions, etc.

We propose that an agent engages in adaptive discrimination games. Each game involves the following steps:

1. A context is determined or presents itself. The context consists of a set of objects and some or all sensory channels have values for each of these objects.
2. One object in this context is chosen as the topic, i.e. the object to be discriminated from the others.
3. All available discrimination trees are used to construct the features for each object.

4. A distinctive feature set is computed. It consists of the minimal set of features that distinguish the topic from the other objects in the context.

The last step may fail because there may not be enough distinctions available. In that case, a channel is picked randomly from the channels for which the topic has a value, and the discrimination tree associated with this channel is extended by subdividing the range and thus creating a new distinction. There is no guarantee that this distinction will be adequate for discriminating the object - that remains to be seen in future discrimination games.

It is also possible that there is more than one possible set of discriminating features. In this case a choice is made based on the following criteria:

1. The smallest set is preferred. Thus the least number of features are used.
2. In case of equal size, it is the set in which the features imply the smallest number of segmentations. Thus the most abstract features are chosen.
3. In case of equal depth of segmentation, it is the set of which the features have been used the most. This ensures that a minimal set of features develops.

A forgetting mechanism could be implemented that eliminates superfluous distinctions, although this is not yet done in the current implementation.

The algorithm is adaptive in the sense that an agent changes its internal structure to be more successful in future discrimination games. It is top-down because the most general distinctions are created before refinements are made. It is selectionist because distinctions are created and then subjected to selection pressure coming from success in discrimination. In this respect the proposed system is related to Edelman's proposals [1] except that selection comes from discrimination and not classification. It is adaptive because it keeps expanding to cope with the steady stream of new objects entering the environment, and thus not settle into an equilibrium like a Kohonen network for example [2].

2.2 Implementation Results

The discrimination games described above has been implemented and encapsulated in (software) agents. A set of sensory channels is created and an initial set of objects is randomly generated with arbitrary values for some of the sensory channels. Then the agent starts discrimination games based on random selection of a subset of objects as context and one of its members as topic. A typical sample output of the program is as follows:

```
a-5: o-0 <-> {o-8 o-1 }
Topic:
   o-0: ((s-3 v-1)(s-4 v-1)(s-5 v-0))
Context:
   o-8: ((s-0 v-1)(s-1 v-0)(s-3 v-1)
         (s-4 v-0)(s-5 v-0))
   o-1: ((s-0 v-1)(s-3 v-0)(s-4 v-1))
No distinctive features but refinements possible.
Refining attribute: s-5 => s-5-0, s-5-1
```

Agent $a5$ tries to distinguish object $o0$ from $o8$ and $o1$. There are already some features available. For example $o0$, which acts as the topic, has the features $((s3\ v1)(s4\ v1)(s5\ v0))$. None of the features is however sufficient. Because $(s3\ v1)$ is shared by $o8$, $(s4\ v1)$ by $o1$ and $(s5\ v0)$ by $o8$. As a consequence of this failure, a new refinement is created by a further distinction on channel 5.

Figure 1. shows two snapshots of the progressive buildup of the discrimination trees by a single agent.

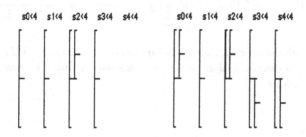

Fig 1. Two snapshots of discrimination trees for one agent (a-4) at different consecutive time points. One can see that on the left no tree has been made yet for channel 4, whereas on the right such a tree exists. The trees are drawn with the top node to the left.

It can be shown experimentally that an agent will develop all the discriminations needed to distinguish between a set of objects. Figure 2. shows the decreasing *failure* in discrimination for a set of 5 objects. It starts from 1.0 (complete failure) and rapidly reaches 0.

3 Language games

We now turn to the question how different agents, which each create their own distinctions based on the adaptive mechanism described above, are capable to share distinctions. Some degree of sharing already happens because the agents are in the same environment. The feature repertoire is determined by the kinds of objects that are encountered, and therefore agents arrive at similar discriminations. However to encourage further congruence and to be able to share information, a lexicon formation mechanism has been implemented. This mechanism allows a group of distributed agents to develop a common lexicon through a series of adaptive language games.

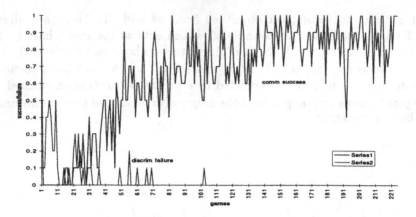

Figure 2. Graph showing the average failure in discrimination (series 2 on y-axis) against the number of discrimination games (x-axis - scale 1/10). The communicative success is shown as series 1.

3.1 Principles

Let a word be a sequence of letters drawn from a finite shared alphabet. An expression is a set of words. In the experiments reported here, word order does not play a role. A lexicon L is a relation between feature sets and words. A single word can have several associated feature sets and a given feature set can have several associated words. For each word-meaning pair, the use and success in use is recorded. Words that are used more and have more success are prefered. This establishes a positive feedback loop pushing the group towards coherence.

Each agent $a \in A$ is assumed to have a single lexicon L_a which is initially empty. A feature set of a word in L is denoted as $F_{w,L}$. The following functions can be defined:

- $cover(F, L)$ defines a set of expressions U such that $\forall u \in U, \{f \mid f \in F_{w,L} \text{ and } w \in u\}$
- $uncover(u, L)$ defines a feature set F such that $F = \{f \mid f \in F_{w,L} \text{ and } w \in u\}$.

A language game involves a dialog between two agents, a speaker and a hearer, within a particular contextual setting which consists of objects of which one is chosen as the topic. The agents perceive these objects through the sensory channels and construct features through the discrimination trees discussed earlier.

The scenario for a language game is as follows:

1. A speaker and hearer as well as a context consisting of a set of objects is randomly identified.
2. The speaker selects one object as the topic and points to this object so that the hearer shares the topic.

3. Both speaker and hearer identify possible distinctive feature sets using the perceptions on the sensory channels and the discrimination trees.
4. If there is at least one set of discriminating features, the speaker selects such a set and translates it to words using the cover function. Words that have been used the most and have been most successful in use are prefered. An important additional criterion for selecting the set of possible discriminating features is that those sets are preferred which can be expressed in language. This causes those features to be preferred that have been lexicalised and establishes a positive feedback loop pushing the agents towards coherence both for the lexicon and for the feature repertoire.
5. The hearer interprets this expression using the uncover function and compares it with his expectations.

As a side effect of such a language game, various language formation steps take place:

1. *No differentiation possible* (step 3 fails): In this case new features are created as discussed in the previous section.
2. *The speaker does not have a word* (step 4 fails): In this case at least one distinctive feature set S is detected but the speaker s has no word(s) yet to express it. The language game obviously fails. However the speaker may create a new word (with a probability $p_w = 0.05$) and associate it in his lexicon with S.
3. *The hearer does not have a word*: At least one distinctive feature set S is detected and the speaker s can construct an expression to express it, i.e. $cover(S, L_s) = W$. However, the hearer does not know the word. Because the hearer has a hypothesis about possible feature sets that might be used, he is able to extend his lexicon to create associations between the word used and each possible feature set. If there is more than one possibility, the hearer cannot disambiguate the word and the ambiguity is retained in the lexicon.
4. *The speaker and the hearer know the word*: In this case there are two possible outcomes:
    (a) *The meanings are compatible with the situation*: The dialog is a success and both speaker and hearer achieve communicative success. Note that it is possible that the speaker and the hearer use different feature sets, but because the communication is a success there is no way to know this. Semantic incoherences persist until new distinctions become important and disambiguate.
    (b) *The meanings are not compatible with the situation*: The same situation as before may arise, except that the feature set uncovered by the hearer is not one of the feature sets expected to be distinctive. In this case, there is no communicative success, neither for the speaker or the hearer.

3.2 Implementation Results

The language games described above have been implemented and encapsulated in software agents. The simulation experiments consistently show that a common repertoire of word-meaning pairs develops conjointly with the development of a feature repertoire. A typical language game is the following:

```
LANGUAGE GAME 878.
   Speaker: a53.
   Hearer: a49
   Topic: o-8
   Context: {o-3 o-7 o-1 o-4 o-9 o-6 }
   Speaker expresses: [(a53-s4 v0)]
   Hearer expects: [(a49-s4 v0)]
  a53: [(a53-s4 v0)] => ((G U))
  a49: => [(a49-s4 v0)]
success
```

Agent *a*54 converses with *a*49 about *o*8. Both speaker and hearer have identified the same distinctive feature set. It is translated into the expression '((G U))' by the speaker which matches the expected distinctive feature uncovered from this expression by the hearer. The language game therefore ends in success.

Figure 2 shows for a group of agents both the decreasing failure in discrimination (which evolves towards 0.0) and the increased success in communication (which evolves towards 1.0). Figure 3. shows the discrimination trees developed by agents operating in the same environment. Some interesting observations can be made: We see that there are on the one hand strong similarities between the agents. For example, the discrimination trees for channel 4 look almost identical At the same time we see that there are differences. For example, for channel 2 we see that agent 3 has an elaborate discrimination tree whereas agent 2 has almost no distinctions. Also when we inspect the lexicons of the different agents we see important similarities (how else could there be complete communicative success) but at the same time we see differences. These differences are maintained because the environment allows multiple possibilities for discrimination and the same word may therefore be associated with different features without being noticed. New objects coming into the environment may disambiguate words or may cause some of the agents to develop distinctions shared by others.

Both the feature formation and language formation processes are open. The (distributed) lexicon adapts itself when new features are created. New words are created and sentences become more complex. The system is also open with respect to the number of agents: New agents may enter at any time in the population. The new agent will gradually take over words already present but is also a new source of novelty.

4 Grounding experiments

In our laboratory, we are conducting various experiments in sensory-motor intelligence with robotic agents. The agents are small Lego-vehicles which have a variety of sensors (infrared, visible light, sound, touch, etc.), actuators for moving around in the environment, batteries, and on board processors. The robots operate in a physical ecosystem in which they have opportunities to recharge

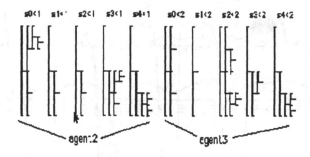

Figure 3. Overview of different discrimination trees for two different agents.

their batteries but also competitors which have to be countered by performing work [4]. Experiments are going on to carry to port the mechanisms reported in this paper onto the physical robots operating in this ecosystem (see [7] for a more extended discussion). The various mechanisms described in the present paper are mapped on a physical counterpart as follows.

The sensory channels contain the real world data obtained from the physical sensors. An example of such data is given in figure 4. The sensors are always located on the body in pairs, for example left infrared and right infrared sensor, left and right visible light sensing, etc., so that the robot has a center of perception (as most animals). An object is in this center of perception when the left and right sensory data cross over. Thus if the robot turns left towards the visible light emitted by the charging station, it will be centered on the charging station when the left visible light peak decreases and crosses the increasing right visible light peak. The sensory values at these crossing points act as input to the discrimination games.

The protocol for engaging in language games has been implemented by a combination of physical gestures and communications through a radio link between the robots. Two robots engage in a communication when both are facing each other. Then each robot makes a 360 degree turn to develop a panoramic sensory view of the environment. The pointing is implemented by a gesture: The speaking robot emits 4 infrared beams whilte moving towards the topic, so that the other robot can observe in which direction it moves. The speaking robot halts when it is facing the object that it wants to see as the topic of the conversation. The listening robot detects the topic by consulting its own sensory map. Then the language game starts as described above.

Although many technical problems still remain to be resolved to enable larger scale experiments, the experiments so far have been successful in showing that the proposed mechanisms do indeed lead to an adequate repertoire of perceptually grounded distinctions and a shared language for using these distinctions to identify objects in the environments.

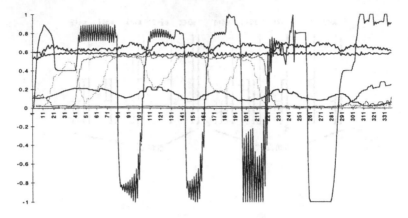

Figure 4. Sensory data streams taken from physical robot. The channels include left and right infrared and visible light sensing and motor speeds.

5 Conclusions

This paper has proposed a mechanism for creating perceptually grounded distinctions driven by adaptive discrimination games. It has also proposed a mechanism for creating a shared set of words to express the features resulting from perception and thus to share the perceptual categories in a group of distributed agents. Both mechanisms are selectionist: There is a way to create variation (by the expansion of discrimination trees or the introduction of a new word-meaning pair) and to select appropriate variations based on their use (success in discrimination or communication).

The proposed mechanisms have two interesting characteristics from a machine learning point of view. First of all there is no distinction between the construction of new distinctions or new word-meaning pairs and the learning of distinctions/words. The agent always constructs and then tests whether the distinctions or word-meaning pairs have the desired effect. Thus the agents are not only capable to acquire existing distinctions or lexicalisations but also to create new ones. We can therefore explain both the origin *and* acquisition of concepts and words by the same mechanism. This contrasts with most inductive learning algorithms which require a teacher to make prior conceptualisations or lexicalisations.

Second, although the proposed mechanisms are selectionist they are not genetic (as in the case of genetic algorithms). Agents do not have to reproduce in order to induce a change. The selectionist forces do not operate on the agents but on the structures inside agents. The result is nevertheless an evolutionary process but it is a cultural as opposed to genetic evolution.

6 Acknowledgement

The author's research, including the simulation experiments reported in the paper, were financed by the Sony Computer Science Laboratory in Tokyo and Paris. Many people have contributed to realise the physical grounding experiments. Robot builders at the VUB AI Lab (soft and hardware) include Andreas Birk, Tony Belpaeme, Peter Stuer and Danny Vereertbrugghe. Ruth was the first one to try the grounding experiment on real robots during a short term visit to the laboratory. These experiments were continued by Paul Vogt, a masters student from the university of Groningen, visiting the Brussels laboratory.

References

1. Edelman, G.M. 1987. *Neural Darwinism: The Theory of Neuronal Group Selection.* New York: Basic Books.
2. Kohonen, T. (1988) *Self-Organization and Associative Memory.* Springer Series in Information Sciences. Vol 8. Springer Verlag, Berlin.
3. Langley, P. (1987) Machine Learning and Concept Formation. *Machine Learning Journal* 2, pp. 99-102.
4. Steels, L. (1994) The Artificial Life Roots of Artificial Intelligence. *Artificial Life Journal* 1(1), pp. 89-125.
5. Steels, L. (1996a) Emergent Adaptive Lexicons. In: Maes, P. (ed.) (1996) From Animals to Animats 4: Proceedings of the Fourth International Conference On Simulation of Adaptive Behavior, The MIT Press, Cambridge Ma.
6. Perceptually grounded meaning creation. In: Tokoro, M. (ed.) (1996) Proceedings of the International Conference on Multi-Agent Systems. The MIT Press, Cambridge Ma.
7. Steels, L. and P. Vogt (1997) Grounding language games in robotic agents. (to appear)

On Prediction by Data Compression*

Paul Vitányi[1] and Ming Li[2]

[1] CWI, Kruislaan 413, 1098 SJ Amsterdam, The Netherlands. Email: paulv@cwi.nl
[2] Department of Computer Science, City University of Hong Kong, Kowloon, Hong Kong. Email: mli@cs.cityu.edu.hk

Abstract. Traditional wisdom has it that the better a theory compresses the learning data concerning some phenomenon under investigation, the better we learn, generalize, and the better the theory predicts unknown data. This belief is vindicated in practice but apparently has not been rigorously proved in a general setting. Making these ideas rigorous involves the length of the shortest effective description of an individual object: its Kolmogorov complexity. In a previous paper we have shown that optimal compression is almost always a best strategy in hypotheses identification (an ideal form of the minimum description length (MDL) principle). Whereas the single best hypothesis does not necessarily give the best prediction, we demonstrate that nonetheless compression is almost always the best strategy in prediction methods in the style of R. Solomonoff.

1 Introduction

Given a body of data concerning some phenomenon under investigation, we want to select the most plausible hypothesis from among all appropriate hypotheses, or predict future data. 'Occam's razor' tells us that, all other things being equal, the simplest explanation is the most likely one. Interpreting 'simplest' as 'having shortest description', the most likely hypothesis is the most compressed one. Traditional wisdom says that improved compression of the learning data samples leads to better generalization properties and better prediction on unseen data. The length of the shortest effective description of some object is its Kolmogorov complexity. The argument says that among all "appropriate" hypotheses the one of least Kolmogorov complexity is the most likely one. In [8] we have rigorously demonstrated that this piece of traditional wisdom is "almost always" valid. This shows that compression is good for hypothesis selection. But is it also good for prediction?

* Paul Vitányi is also affiliated with the University of Amsterdam. He was supported by NSERC through International Scientific Exchange Award ISE0125663, and by the European Union through NeuroCOLT ESPRIT Working Group Nr. 8556, and by NWO through NFI Project ALADDIN under Contract number NF 62-376. Ming Li was supported in part by NSERC operating grant OGP-046506, ITRC, and a CGAT grant and the Steacie Fellowship. On sabbatical leave from: Department of Computer Science, University of Waterloo; Email: mli@math.uwaterloo.ca.

The best single hypothesis does not necessarily give the best prediction. For example, consider a situation where we are given a coin of unknown bias p of coming up "heads" which is either $p_1 = \frac{1}{3}$ or $p_2 = \frac{2}{3}$. Suppose we have determined that there is probability $\frac{2}{3}$ that $p = p_1$ and probability $\frac{1}{3}$ that $p = p_2$. Then the "best" hypothesis is the most likely one: $p = p_1$ which predicts a next outcome "heads" as having probability $\frac{1}{3}$. Yet the best prediction is that this probability is the expectation of throwing "heads" which is

$$\frac{2}{3}p_1 + \frac{1}{3}p_2 = \frac{4}{9}.$$

Thus, the fact that compression is good for hypothesis identification problems does not imply that compression is good for prediction. We analyse the relation between compression of the data sample and prediction in the very general setting of R. Solomonoff [14, 15]. We explain Solomonoff's prediction method using the universal distribution. We show that this method is not equivalent to the use of shortest descriptions. Nonetheless, we demonstrate that compression of descriptions almost always gives optimal prediction.

1.1 Background and Previous Work

The classical method for induction is Bayes's rule. The problem with applying Bayes's rule is that one requires the prior probabilities of the hypotheses first. Unfortunately, it is often impossible to obtain these. In the unlikely case that we possess the true prior distribution, in practice the data tend to be noisy due to the measuring process or other causes. The latter confuses Bayes's rule into overfitting the hypothesis by adding random features while trying to fit the data.

One way out of the conundrum of *a priori* probabilities is to require prediction or inference of hypotheses to be completely or primarily data driven. For prediction this was achieved using the Kolmogorov complexity based universal distribution, [14, 15], and for hypothesis identification by the minimum description length (MDL or MML) approach, [10, 11, 19, 20]

Ideally, the description lengths involved should be the shortest effective description lengths. (We use 'effective' in the sense of 'Turing computable', [16].) Shortest effective description length is asymptotically unique and objective and known as the *Kolmogorov complexity* of the object being described. Such shortest effective descriptions are 'effective' in the sense that we can compute the described objects from them. Unfortunately, it can be shown, see [6], that one cannot compute the length of a shortest description from the object being described. This obviously impedes actual use. Instead, one needs to consider computable approximations to shortest descriptions, for example by restricting the allowable approximation time. This course is followed in one sense or another in the practical incarnations such as MML and MDL. There one often uses simply the Shannon-Fano code, which assigns prefix code length $-\log P(x)$ to x irrespective of the regularities in x. If $P(x) = 2^{-l(x)}$ for every $x \in \{0,1\}^n$, then the code word length of an all-zero x equals the code word length of a truly irregular x. While the Shannon-Fano code gives an expected code word length close to the entropy, it does not distinguish the regular elements of a probability ensemble from the random ones.

The code of the shortest effective descriptions, with the Kolmogorov complexities as the code word length set, also gives an expected code word length close to the entropy yet compresses the regular objects until all regularity is squeezed out. All shortest effective descriptions are completely random themselves, without any regularity whatsoever. Kolmogorov complexity can be used to develop a theory of (idealized) minimum description length reasoning. In particular, shortest effective descriptions enable us to rigorously analyse the relation between shortest description length reasoning and Bayesianism. This provides a theoretical basis for, and gives confidence in, practical uses of the various forms of minimum description length reasoning mentioned.

In [7, 8] we rigorously derived and justify this Kolmogorov complexity based form of minimum description length, 'Ideal MDL', via the Bayesian approach using a particular prior distribution over the hypotheses (the so-called 'universal distribution'). This leads to a mathematical explanation of correspondences and differences between Ideal MDL and Bayesian reasoning, and in particular it gives some evidence under what conditions the latter is prone to overfitting while the former isn't. Namely, for hypothesis identification Ideal MDL using Kolmogorov complexity can be reduced to the Bayesian approach using the universal prior distribution, provided the minimum description length is reached for those hypotheses with respect to which the data sample is *individually random* in the sense of Martin-Löf, [9]. Under those conditions Ideal MDL, Bayesianism, MDL, and MML, select pretty much the same hypothesis. These conditions hold for almost all combinations of hypothesis and data sample. Consequently, we showed that the hypothesis that compresses the data sample most is almost always the "best" hypothesis.

2 Roots of Kolmogorov Complexity

2.1 A Lacuna of Classical Probability Theory

An adversary claims to have a true random coin and invites us to bet on the outcome. The coin produces a hundred heads in a row. We say that the coin cannot be fair. The adversary, however, appeals to probability theory which says that each sequence of outcomes of a hundred coin flips is equally likely, $1/2^{100}$, and one sequence had to come up.

Probability theory gives us no basis to challenge an outcome *after* it has happened. We could only exclude unfairness in advance by putting a penalty side-bet on an outcome of 100 heads. But what about 1010...? What about an initial segment of the binary expansion of π?

Regular sequence $\Pr(00000000000000000000000000) = \frac{1}{2^{26}}$,
Regular sequence $\Pr(01000110110000010100111001) = \frac{1}{2^{26}}$,
Random sequence $\Pr(10010011011000111011010000) = \frac{1}{2^{26}}$.

The first sequence is regular, but what is the distinction of the second sequence and the third? The third sequence was generated by flipping a quarter. The second sequence is very regular: $0, 1, 00, 01, \ldots$. The third sequence will pass (pseudo-)randomness tests.

In fact, classical probability theory cannot express the notion of *randomness of an individual sequence*. It can only express expectations of properties of outcomes of random processes, that is, the expectations of properties of the total set of sequences under some distribution.

Only relatively recently, this problem has found a satisfactory resolution by combining notions of computability and statistics to express the complexity of a finite object. This complexity is the length of the shortest binary program from which the object can be effectively reconstructed. It may be called the *algorithmic information content* of the object. This quantity turns out to be an attribute of the object alone, and absolute (in the technical sense of being recursively invariant). It is the *Kolmogorov complexity* of the object.

2.2   A Lacuna of Information Theory

Shannon's classical information theory assigns a quantity of information to an ensemble of possible messages. All messages in the ensemble being equally probable, this quantity is the number of bits needed to count all possibilities. This expresses the fact that each message in the ensemble can be communicated using this number of bits. However, it does not say anything about the number of bits needed to convey any individual message in the ensemble. To illustrate this, consider the ensemble consisting of all binary strings of length 9999999999999999.

By Shannon's measure, we require 9999999999999999 bits on the average to encode a string in such an ensemble. However, the string consisting of 999999999-9999999 1's can be encoded in about 55 bits by expressing 9999999999999999 in binary and adding the repeated pattern '1'. A requirement for this to work is that we have agreed on an algorithm that decodes the encoded string. We can compress the string still further when we note that 9999999999999999 equals $3^2 \times 1111111111111111$, and that 1111111111111111 consists of 2^4 1's.

Thus, we have discovered an interesting phenomenon: the description of some strings can be compressed considerably, provided they exhibit enough regularity. This observation, of course, is the basis of all systems to express very large numbers and was exploited early on by Archimedes in his treatise *The Sand Reckoner*, in which he proposes a system to name very large numbers:

> "There are some, King Golon, who think that the number of sand is infinite in multitude [... or] that no number has been named which is great enough to exceed its multitude.[...] But I will try to show you, by geometrical proofs, which you will be able to follow, that, of the numbers named by me [...] some exceed not only the mass of sand equal in magnitude to the earth filled up in the way described, but also that of a mass equal in magnitude to the universe."

However, if regularity is lacking, it becomes more cumbersome to express large numbers. For instance, it seems easier to compress the number 'one billion,' than the number 'one billion seven hundred thirty-five million two hundred sixty-eight thousand and three hundred ninety-four,' even though they are of the same order of magnitude.

2.3 Lacuna in Randomness

In the context of the above discussion, random sequences are sequences that cannot be compressed. Now let us compare this with the common notions of mathematical randomness. To measure randomness, criteria have been developed that certify this quality. Yet, in recognition that they do not measure 'true' randomness, we call these criteria 'pseudo' randomness tests. For instance, statistical surveys of initial sequences of decimal digits of π have failed to disclose any significant deviations from randomness. But clearly, this sequence is so regular that it can be described by a simple program to compute it, and this program can be expressed in a few bits.

The notion of randomness of individual objects has a long history which goes back to the initial attempts by von Mises, [17], to formulate the principles of application of the calculus of probabilities to real-world phenomena. Classical probability theory cannot even express the notion of 'randomness of individual objects'. Following almost half a century of unsuccessful attempts, the theory of Kolmogorov complexity, [4], and Martin-Löf tests for randomness, [9], finally succeeded in formally expressing the novel notion of individual randomness in a correct manner, see [6]. Objects which are random in this sense will satisfy *all* effective tests for randomness properties—those which are known and those which are yet unknown alike.

3   Kolmogorov Complexity

The Kolmogorov complexity, [4, 22, 6], of x is simply *the length of the shortest effective binary description of x*. Formally, this is defined as follows. Let $x, y, z \in \mathcal{N}$, where $\mathcal{N}$ denotes the natural numbers and we identify $\mathcal{N}$ and $\{0,1\}^*$ according to the correspondence

$$(0, \epsilon), (1, 0), (2, 1), (3, 00), (4, 01), \ldots$$

Here ϵ denotes the *empty word* '' with no letters. The *length* $l(x)$ of x is the number of bits in the binary string x. For example, $l(010) = 3$ and $l(\epsilon) = 0$.

The emphasis is on binary sequences only for convenience; observations in any alphabet can be so encoded in a way that is 'theory neutral'.

A binary string x is a *proper prefix* of a binary string y if we can write $x = yz$ for $z \neq \epsilon$. A set $\{x, y, \ldots\} \subseteq \{0,1\}^*$ is *prefix-free* if for any pair of distinct elements in the set neither is a proper prefix of the other. A prefix-free set is also called a *prefix code*. Each binary string $x = x_1 x_2 \ldots x_n$ has a special type of prefix code, called a *self-delimiting code*,

$$\bar{x} = x_1 x_1 x_2 x_2 \ldots x_n \neg x_n,$$

where $\neg x_n = 0$ if $x_n = 1$ and $\neg x_n = 1$ otherwise. This code is self-delimiting because we can determine where the code word $\bar{x}$ ends by reading it from left to right without backing up. Using this code we define the standard self-delimiting code for x to be $x' = \bar{l(x)}x$. It is easy to check that $l(\bar{x}) = 2n$ and $l(x') = n + 2\log n$.

Let $T_1, T_2, \ldots$ be a standard enumeration of all Turing machines, and let $\phi_1, \phi_2, \ldots$ be the enumeration of corresponding functions which are computed by the respective Turing machines. That is, T_i computes ϕ_i. These functions are the *partial recursive* functions or *computable* functions. The Kolmogorov complexity $C(x)$ of x is the length of the shortest binary program from which x is computed. Formally, we define this as follows.

Definition 1. The *Kolmogorov complexity* of x given y (for free on a special input tape) is

$$C(x|y) = \min_{p,i}\{l(i'p) : \phi_i(p, y) = x, p \in \{0,1\}^*, i \in \mathcal{N}\}.$$

Define $C(x) = C(x|\epsilon)$.

The Kolmogorov complexity is absolute in the sense of being recursively invariant by Church's Thesis and the ability of universal machines to simulate one another, [6]. For technical reasons we also need a variant of complexity, so-called prefix complexity, which associated with Turing machines for which the set of programs resulting in a halting computation is prefix free. We can realize this by equiping the Turing machine with a one-way input tape, a separate work tape, and a one-way output tape. Such Turing machines are called prefix machines since the halting programs for anyone of them form a prefix free set. Taking the universal prefix machine U we can define the prefix complexity analogously with the plain Kolmogorov complexity. If x^* is the first shortest program for x then the set $\{x^* : U(x^*) = x, x \in \{0,1\}^*\}$ is a *prefix code*. That is, each x^* is a code word for some x, and if x^* and y^* are code words for x and y with $x \neq y$ then x^* is not a prefix of x.

Let $\langle \cdot \rangle$ be a standard invertible effective one-one encoding from $\mathcal{N} \times \mathcal{N}$ to prefix-free recursive subset of $\mathcal{N}$. For example, we can set $\langle x, y \rangle = x'y'$. We insist on prefix-freeness and recursiveness because we want a universal Turing machine to be able to read an image under $\langle \cdot \rangle$ from left to right and determine where it ends.

Definition 2. The *prefix Kolmogorov complexity* of x given y (for free) is

$$K(x|y) = \min_{p,i}\{l(\langle p, i \rangle) : \phi_i(\langle p, y \rangle) = x, p \in \{0,1\}^*, i \in \mathcal{N}\}.$$

Define $K(x) = K(x|\epsilon)$.

The nice thing about $K(x)$ is that we can interpret $2^{-K(x)}$ as a probability distribution. Namely, $K(x)$ is the length of a shortest prefix-free program for x. By the fundamental Kraft's inequality, see for example [6], we know that if $l_1, l_2, \ldots$ are the code-word lengths of a prefix code, then $\sum_x 2^{-l_x} \leq 1$. This leads to the notion of universal distribution—a rigorous form of Occam's razor–below.

4 Universal Distribution

A Turing machine T computes a function on the natural numbers. However, we can also consider the computation of real valued functions. For this purpose we consider both the argument of ϕ and the value of ϕ as a pair of natural numbers according to the standard pairing function $\langle \cdot \rangle$. We define a function from $\mathcal{N}$ to the reals $\mathcal{R}$ by a Turing machine T computing a function ϕ as follows. Interpret the computation $\phi(\langle x, t \rangle) = \langle p, q \rangle$ to mean that the quotient p/q is the rational valued tth approxmation of $f(x)$.

Definition 3. A function $f : \mathcal{N} \rightarrow \mathcal{R}$ is *enumerable* if there is a Turing machine T computing a total function ϕ such that $\phi(x, t+1) \geq \phi(x, t)$ and $\lim_{t\to\infty} \phi(x, t) = f(x)$. This means that f can be computably approximated from below. If f can also be computably approximated from above then we call f *recursive*.

A function $P : \mathcal{N} \rightarrow [0, 1]$ is a *probability distribution* if $\sum_{x \in \mathcal{N}} P(x) \leq 1$. (The inequality is a technical convenience. We can consider the surplus probability to be concentrated on the undefined element $u \notin \mathcal{N}$).

Consider the family $\mathcal{EP}$ of *enumerable* probability distributions on the sample space $\mathcal{N}$ (equivalently, $\{0,1\}^*$). It is known, [6], that $\mathcal{EP}$ contains an element $\mathbf{m}$ that multiplicatively dominates all elements of $\mathcal{EP}$. That is, for each $P \in \mathcal{EP}$ there is a constant c such that $c\,\mathbf{m}(x) > P(x)$ for all $x \in \mathcal{N}$. We call $\mathbf{m}$ a *universal distribution*.

The family $\mathcal{EP}$ contains all distributions with computable parameters which have a name, or in which we could conceivably be interested, or which have ever been considered. The dominating property means that $\mathbf{m}$ assigns at least as much probability to each object as any other distribution in the family $\mathcal{EP}$ does. In this sense it is a universal *a priori* by accounting for maximal ignorance. It turns out that if the true *a priori* distribution in Bayes's Rule is recursive, then using the single distribution $\mathbf{m}$, or its continuous analogue the measure $\mathbf{M}$ on the sample space $\{0, 1\}^\infty$ (defined later), is provably as good as using the true *a priori* distribution.

We also know, [6], that

Lemma 4.
$$-\log \mathbf{m}(x) = K(x) \pm O(1). \tag{1}$$

That means that $\mathbf{m}$ assigns high probability to simple objects and low probability to complex or random objects. For example, for $x = 00\ldots0$ (n 0's) we have $K(x) = K(n) + O(1) \leq \log n + 2\log\log n + O(1)$ since the program

$$\texttt{print } n\_\texttt{times a `0'}$$

prints x. (The additional $2\log\log n$ term is the penalty term for a self-delimiting encoding.) Then, $1/(n\log^2 n) = O(\mathbf{m}(x))$. But if we flip a coin to obtain a string y of n bits, then with overwhelming probability $K(y) \geq n - O(1)$ (because y does not contain effective regularities which allow compression), and hence $\mathbf{m}(y) = O(1/2^n)$.

4.1 Example: Betting Against a Crooked Player

Let us apply this to the betting problem on a not-known-to-be false coin we identified in Section 2.1 as a lacuna in probability theory.

Alice, walking down the street, comes across Bob, who is tossing a coin. He is offering odds to all passers-by on whether the next toss will be heads or tails. The pitch is this: he'll pay you two dollars if the next toss is heads; you pay him one dollar if the next toss is tails. Should she take the bet? If Bob is tossing a fair coin, it's a great bet. Probably she'll win money in the long run. After all, she would expect that half Bob's tosses would come up heads and half tails. Giving up only one dollar on each heads toss and getting two for each tails—why in a while she'd be rich!

Of course, to assume that a street hustler is tossing a fair coin is a bit of a stretch, and Alice is no dummy. So she watches for a while, recording how the c oin comes up for other betters, writing down a '1' for 'heads' and a '0' for 'ta ils'. After a while she has written 01010101010101. This doesn't look good. So Alice makes the following offer.

Alice pays Bob $1 first and proposes that Bob pays her $2^{1000-K(x)}$ dollars. and x is the binary sequence of the 1,000 coin flip results. This is fair since Bob is only expected to pay her

$$\sum_{|x|=1000} 2^{-1000} 2^{1000-K(x)} \leq \$1,$$

by Kraft's inequality. So Bob should be happy to accept the proposal. But if Bob cheats, then, for example, Alice gets $2^{1000-\log 1000}$ dollars for a sequence like 0101010101...!

In the 1 versus 2 dollars scheme, Alice can propose to add this as an extra bonus pay. This way, she is guaranteed to win big: either polynomially increase her money (when Bob does not cheat) or exponentially increase her money (when Bob cheats).

5 Randomness Tests

One can consider those objects as nonrandom in which one can find sufficiently many regularities. In other words, we would like to identify 'incompressibility' with 'randomness'. This is proper if the sequences that are incompressible can be shown to possess the various properties of randomness (stochasticity) known from the theory of probability. That this is possible is the substance of the celebrated theory developed by the Swedish mathematician Per Martin-Löf.

There are many properties known which probability theory attributes to random objects. To give an example, consider sequences of n tosses with a fair coin. Each sequence of n zeros and ones is equiprobable as an outcome: its probability is 2^{-n}. If such a sequence is to be random in the sense of a proposed new definition, then the number of ones in x should be near to $n/2$, the number of occurrences of blocks '00' should be close to $n/4$, and so on.

It is not difficult to show that each such single property separately holds for all incompressible binary strings. But we want to demonstrate that incompressibility implies all conceivable effectively testable properties of randomness (both the known ones and the as yet unknown ones). This way, the various theorems in probability theory about random sequences carry over automatically to incompressible sequences. We do not develop the theory here but refer to the exhaustive treatment in [6] instead. We shall use the properties required in the sequel of this paper.

6 Bayesian Reasoning

Consider a situation in which one has a set of observations of some phenomenon, and also a finite or countably infinite set of hypotheses which are candidates to explain the phenomenon. For example, we are given a coin and we flip it 1000 times. We want to identify the probability that the coin has outcome 'head' in a single coin flip. That is, we want to find the bias of the coin. The set of possible hypotheses is uncountably infinite if we allow each real bias in $[0, 1]$, and countably infinite if we allow each rational bias in $[0, 1]$.

For each hypothesis H we would like to assess the probability that H is the 'true' hypothesis, given the observation of D. This quantity, $\Pr(H|D)$, can be described and manipulated formally in the following way.

Consider a sample space Ω. Let D denote a sample of outcomes, say experimental data concerning a phenomenon under investigation. Let $H_1, H_2, \ldots$ be an enumeration of countably many hypotheses concerning this phenomenon, say each H_i is a probability distribution over Ω. The list $\mathcal{H} = \{H_1, H_2, \ldots\}$ is called the *hypothesis space*. The hypotheses H_i are exhaustive and mutually exclusive.

For example, say the hypotheses enumerate the possible rational (or computable) biases of the coin. As another possibility there may be only two possible hypotheses: hypothesis H_1 which says the coin has bias 0.2, and hypothesis H_2 which puts the bias at 0.8.

Suppose we have *a priori* a distribution of the probabilities $P(H)$ of the various possible hypotheses in $\mathcal{H}$ which means that $\sum_{H \in \mathcal{H}} P(H) = 1$. Assume furthermore that for all $H \in \mathcal{H}$ we can compute the probability $\Pr(D|H)$ that sample D arises if H is the case. Then we can also compute (or approximate in case the number of hypotheses with nonzero probability is infinite) the probability $\Pr(D)$ that sample D arises at all

$$\Pr(D) = \sum_{H \in \mathcal{H}} \Pr(D|H)P(H).$$

From the definition of conditional probability it is easy to derive **Bayes's formula**[3]

$$\Pr(H|D) = \frac{\Pr(D|H)P(H)}{\Pr(D)}. \qquad (2)$$

---

[3] Some Bayesians prefer replacing $\Pr(D|H)P(H)$ by a joint probability of data and hypotheses together, the prior $P(D, H) = \Pr(D|H)P(H)$.

The prior probability $P(H)$ is often considered as the learner's *initial degree of belief* in hypothesis H. In essence Bayes's rule is a mapping from *a priori* probability $P(H)$ to *a posteriori* probability $\Pr(H|D)$ determined by data D.

Continuing to obtain more and more data, this way the total inferred probability will concentrate more and more on the 'true' hypothesis. We can draw the same conclusion of course, using more examples, by the law of large numbers. In general, the problem is not so much that in the limit the inferred probability would not concentrate on the true hypothesis, but that the inferred probability gives as much information as possible about the possible hypotheses from only a limited number of data. Given the prior probability of the hypotheses, it is easy to obtain the inferred probability, and therefore to make informed decisions. However, in general we don't know the prior probabilities. The following MDL approach in some sense replaces an unknown prior probability by a fixed 'universal' probability.

7 Prediction by Compression

Theoretically the idea of predicting time sequences using shortest effective descriptions was first formulated by R. Solomonoff, [14]. He uses Bayes's formula equipped with a fixed 'universal' prior distribution. In accordance with Occam's dictum, it tells us to go for the explanation that compresses the data the most— but not quite as we shall show.

The aim is to *predict* outcomes concerning a phenomenon μ under investigation. In this case we have some prior evidence (prior distribution over the hypotheses, experimental data) and we want to predict future events. This situation can be modelled by considering a sample space S of one-way infinite sequences of basic elements B defined by $S = B^{\infty}$. We assume a prior distribution μ over S with $\mu(x)$ denoting the probability of a sequence starting with x. Here $\mu(\cdot)$ is a *semimeasure*[4] satisfying

$$\mu(\epsilon) \leq 1$$
$$\mu(x) \geq \sum_{a \in B} \mu(xa).$$

Given a previously observed data string x, the inference problem is to predict the next symbol in the output sequence, that is, to extrapolate the sequence x. In terms of the variables in formula 2, H_{xy} is the hypothesis that the sequence starts with initial segment xy. Data D_x consists of the fact that the sequence starts with initial segment x. Then, $\Pr(D_x|H_{xy}) = 1$, that is, the data is forced by the hypothesis, or $\Pr(D_z|H_{xy}) = 0$ for z is not a prefix of xy, that is, the hypothesis contradicts the data. For $P(H_{xy})$ and $\Pr(D_x)$ in formula 2 we substitute $\mu(xy)$ and $\mu(x)$, respectively. For $P(H_{xy}|D_x)$ we substitute $\mu(y|x)$. This

---

[4] Traditional notation is '$\mu(\Gamma_x)$' instead of '$\mu(x)$' where *cylinder* $\Gamma_x = \{\omega \in S : \omega$ starts with $x\}$. We use '$\mu(x)$' for convenience. μ is a *measure* if equalities hold.

way the formula is rewritten as

$$\mu(y|x) = \frac{\mu(xy)}{\mu(x)}.$$ (3)

The final probability $\mu(y|x)$ is the probability of the next symbol string being y, given the initial string x. Obviously we now only need the prior probability μ to evaluate $\mu(y|x)$. The goal of inductive inference in general is to be able to either (i) predict, or extrapolate, the next element after x or (ii) to infer an underlying effective process that generated x, and hence to be able to predict the next symbol. In the most general deterministic case such an effective process is a Turing machine, but it can also be a probabilistic Turing machine or, say, a Markov process (which makes its brief and single appearance here). The central task of inductive inference is to find a universally valid approximation to μ which is good at estimating the conditional probability that a given segment x will be followed by a segment y.

In general this is impossible. But suppose we restrict the class of priors μ to the *recursive* semimeasures and restrict the set of basic elements $\mathcal{B}$ to $\{0, 1\}$. Under this relatively mild restriction on the admissible semimeasures μ, it turns out that we can use the single universal semimeasure $\mathbf{M}$ as a 'universal prior' (replacing the real prior μ) for prediction. The notion of universal semimeasure $\mathbf{M}$ is a continuous version of $\mathbf{m}$ we saw before, and which is explained in [6]. defined with respect to a special type Turing machine called *monotone* Turing machine. The universal semimeasure $\mathbf{M}$ multiplicatively dominates all enumerable (computable from below) semimeasures. If we flip a fair coin to generate the successive bits on the input tape of the universal reference monotone Turing machine, then the probability that it outputs $x\alpha$ (x followed by something) is $\mathbf{M}(x)$.

It can be shown that the universal distribution *itself* is directly suited for prediction. The universal distribution combines a weighted version of the predictions of all enumerable semimeasures, including the prediction of the semimeasure with the shortest program. It is not a priori clear that the shortest program dominates in all cases—and as we shall see it does not. However, we show that in the overwhelming majority of cases—the typical cases—the shortest program dominates sufficiently to validate the approach that only uses shortest programs for prediction. The properties of $\mathbf{M}(x)$ allow us to demonstrate that a minimum description length procedure is almost always optimal for prediction.

Given a semimeasure on $\{0, 1\}^{\infty}$ and an initial binary string x our goal is to find the most probable extrapolation of x. That is, taking the negative logarithm on both sides of Equation 3, we want to determine y with $l(y) = n$ that minimizes

$$-\log\mu(y|x) = -\log\mu(xy) + \log\mu(x).$$

We assume that μ be a *recursive* semimeasure.

This theory of the *universal semimeasure* $\mathbf{M}$, the analogue in the sample space $\{0, 1\}^{\infty}$ of $\mathbf{m}$ in the sample space $\{0, 1\}^{*}$ equivalent to $\mathcal{N}$, is developed in [6], Chapter 4, and Chapter 5. A celebrated result of Solomonoff, [15], says that

M is very suitable for prediction. Let S_n be the μ-expected value of the square of the difference in μ-probability and M-probability of 0 occurring at the nth prediction

$$S_n = \sum_{l(x)=n-1} \mu(x)(\mathbf{M}(0|x) - \mu(0|x))^2.$$

We may call S_n the *expected squared error at the nth prediction.*

Theorem 5. *Let μ be a recursive semimeasure. Using the notation above, $\sum_n S_n \le k/2$ with $k = K(\mu)\ln 2$. (Hence, S_n converges to 0 faster than $1/n$.)*

A proof using Kulback-Leibler divergence is given in [6]. There it is additionally demonstrated that for almost all unbounded x the conditional probability of **M** converges to the conditional probability of μ. Note that while the following Theorem *does* imply the convergence of the conditional probabilities similarly to Theorem 5, it *does not* imply the speed of convergence estimate. Conversely, Theorem 5 does not imply the following.

Theorem 6. *Let μ be a positive recursive measure If the length of y is fixed and the length of x grows to infinity, then*

$$\frac{\mathbf{M}(y|x)}{\mu(y|x)} \to 1,$$

with μ-probability one. In infinite sequences ω with prefixes x satisfying the displayed asymptotics are precisely the μ-random sequences.

Proof. We use an approach based on the Submartingale Convergence Theorem, [1] pp. 324–325, which states that the following property holds for each sequence of random variables $\omega_1, \omega_2, \ldots$. If $f(\omega_{1:n})$ is a μ-submartingale, and the μ-expectation $\mathbf{E}|f(\omega_{1:n})| < \infty$, then it follows that $\lim_{n\to\infty} f(\omega_{1:n})$ exists with μ-probability one.

In our case,

$$t(\omega_{1:n}|\mu) = \frac{\mathbf{M}(\omega_{1:n})}{\mu(\omega_{1:n})}$$

is a μ-submartingale, and the μ-expectation $\mathbf{E}t(\omega_{1:n}|\mu) \le 1$. Therefore, there is a set $A \subseteq B^\infty$ with $\mu(A) = 1$, such that for each $\omega \in A$ the limit $\lim_{n\to\infty} t(\omega_{1:n}|\mu) < \infty$. These are the μ-random ω's by Corollary 4.8 in [6]. Consequently, for fixed m, for each ω in A, we have

$$\lim_{n\to\infty} \frac{\mathbf{M}(\omega_{1:n+m})/\mu(\omega_{1:n+m})}{\mathbf{M}(\omega_{1:n})/\mu(\omega_{1:n})} = 1,$$

provided the limit of the denominator is not zero. The latter fact is guarantied by the universality of **M**: for each $x \in B^*$ we have $\mathbf{M}(x)/\mu(x) \ge 2^{-K(\mu)}$ by Theorem 4.4 and Equation 4.10 in [6].

Example 1. Suppose we are given an infinite decimal sequence ω. The even positions contain the subsequent digits of $\pi = 3.1415\ldots$, and the odd positions contain uniformly distributed, independently drawn random decimal digits. Then, $\mathbf{M}(a|\omega_{1:2i}) \to 1/10$ for $a = 0, 1, \ldots, 9$, while $\mathbf{M}(a|\omega_{1:2i+1}) \to 1$ if a is the ith digit of π, and to 0 otherwise.

There are two possibilities to associate complexities with machines. The first possibility is to take the length of the shortest program, while the second possibility is to take the negative logarithm of the universal probability. In the discrete case, using prefix machines, these turned out to be the same by the Coding Theorem 4. In the continuous case, using monotone machines, it turns out they are different.

Definition 7. The complexity KM is defined as

$$KM(x) = -\log \mathbf{M}(x).$$

In contrast with C and K complexities, in the above definition the greatest prefix-free subset of *all* programs which produce output starting with x on the reference monotone machine U are weighed.

Definition 8. Let U be the reference monotone machine. The complexity Km, called *monotone complexity*, is defined as

$$Km(x) = \min\{l(p) : U(p) = x\omega, \omega \in S_{\mathcal{B}}\}.$$

We omit the Invariance Theorems for KM complexity and Km complexity, stated and proven completely analogous to the Theorems with respect to the C and K varieties. By definition, $KM(x) \leq Km(x)$. In fact, all proper complexities coincide up to a logarithmic additive term. It has been shown that equality does not hold: the difference between $KM(x)$ $(= -\log \mathbf{M}(x))$ and $Km(x)$ is very small, but still rises unboundedly. This contrasts with the equality between $-\log \mathbf{m}(x)$ and $K(x)$ in Theorem 4. Intuitively, this phenomenon is justified by exposing the relation between $\mathbf{M}$ and $\mathbf{m}$.

The Coding Theorem 4 states that $K(x) = -\log \mathbf{m}(x) + O(1)$. L.A. Levin, [5], conjectured that the analogue would hold for the unrestricted continuous version. But it has been shown, [3], that

$$\sup_{x \in \mathcal{B}^*} |KM(x) - Km(x)| = \infty,$$

There it is shown that the exact relation is (for each particular choice of basis $\mathcal{B}$ such as $\mathcal{B} = \mathcal{N}$, the natural numbers, or $\mathcal{B} = \{0, 1\}$)

Lemma 9.

$$KM(x) \leq Km(x) \leq KM(x) + Km(l(x)) + O(1). \tag{4}$$

This shows that the differences between $Km(x)$ and $KM(x)$ must in some sense be very small. The next question to ask is whether the quantities involved are usually different, or whether this is a rare occurrence. In other words, whether for *a priori* almost all infinite sequences x, the difference between Km and KM is bounded by a constant. The following facts have been proven, [3].

Lemma 10. *(i) For random strings $x \in \mathcal{B}^*$ we have $Km(x) - KM(x) = O(1)$.*

(ii) There exists a function $f(n)$ which goes to infinity with $n \to \infty$ such that $Km(x) - KM(x) \geq f(l(x))$, for infinitely many x. If x is a finite binary string ($\mathcal{B} = \{0,1\}$), then we can choose $f(n)$ as the inverse of some version of Ackermann's function

An infinite binary sequence ω is μ-random iff

$$\sup_n \mathbf{M}(\omega_1 \ldots \omega_n)/\mu(\omega_1 \ldots \omega_n) < \infty,$$

and the set of μ-random sequences has μ-measure one, see [6], Chapter 4. Let ω be a μ-random infinite binary sequence and xy be a finite prefix of ω. For $l(x)$ grows unboundedly with $l(y)$ fixed, we have by Theorem 6

$$\lim_{l(x)\to\infty} \log \mu(y|x) - \log \mathbf{M}(y|x) = 0. \tag{5}$$

Therefore, if x and y satisfy above conditions, then maximizing $\mu(y|x)$ over y means minimizing $-\log \mathbf{M}(y|x)$. It is shown in Lemma 10 that $-\log \mathbf{M}(x)$ is slightly smaller than $Km(x)$, the length of the shortest program for x on the reference universal monotonic machine. For binary programs this difference is very small, Lemma 9, but can be unboundedly in the length of x.

Together this shows the following. Given xy that is a prefix of a (possibly not μ-random) ω, optimal prediction of fixed length extrapolation y from an unboundedly growing prefix x of ω need not necessarily be reached by the shortest programs for xy and x minimizing $Km(xy) - Km(x)$, but is reached by considering the weighted version of all programs for xy and x which is represented by

$$-\log \mathbf{M}(xy) + \log \mathbf{M}(x) = (Km(xy) - g(xy)) - (Km(x) - g(x)).$$

Here $g(x)$ is a function which can rise to in between the inverse of the Ackermann function and $Km(l(x)) \leq \log\log x$—but only in case x is not μ-random.

Therefore, for certain x and y which are *not* μ-random, optimization using the minimum length programs may result in very incorrect predictions. However, for μ-random x we have that $-\log \mathbf{M}(x)$ and $Km(x)$ coincide up to an additional constant independent of x, that is, $g(xy) = g(x) = O(1)$, Lemma 10. Hence, together with Equation 5, we find the following.

Theorem 11. *Let μ be a recursive semimeasure, and let ω be a μ-random infinite binary sequence and xy be a finite prefix of ω. For $l(x)$ grows unboundedly and $l(y)$ fixed,*

$$\lim_{l(x)\to\infty} -\log \mu(y|x) = Km(xy) - Km(x) \pm O(1) < \infty,$$

where $Km(xy)$ and $Km(x)$ grow unboundedly.

By its definition Km is monotone in the sense that always $Km(xy) - Km(x) \geq 0$. The closer this difference is to zero, the better the shortest effective monotone program for x is also a shortest effective monotone program for xy and hence predicts y given x. Therefore, for all large enough μ-random x, predicting by determining y which minimizes the difference of the minimum program lengths of xy and x gives a good prediction. Here y should be preferably large enough to eliminate the influence of the $O(1)$ term.

Corollary 12 Prediction by Data Compression. *Assume the conditions of Theorem 11. With μ-probability going to one as $l(x)$ grows unboundedly, a fixed-length y extrapolation from x maximizes $\mu(y|x)$ iff y can be maximally compressed with respect to x in the sense that it minimizes $Km(xy) - Km(x)$. That is, y is the string that minimizes the length difference between the shortest program that outputs $xy \ldots$ and the shortest program that outputs $x \ldots$.*

7.1 Hypothesis Identification and Compression

We briefly mention the related work on hypothesis identification and compression. The so-called minimum description length principle is an algorithmic paradigm that is widely applied. That is, it is widely applied at least in spirit; to apply it literally may run in computation difficulties since it involves finding an optimum in a exponentially large set of candidates as noted for example in [6]. Yet in some cases one can approximate this optimum, [18, 21]. For the theoretical case where the minimum description lengths involved are the Kolmogorov complexities, we mathematically derived the minimum description length paradigm from first principles, that is, Bayes's rule, [6, 7, 8]. To do so we needed auxiliary notions of *universal distribution* and *Martin-Löf tests* for *randomness of individual objects*.

Before proceeding it is useful to point out that the idea of a two-part code for a body of data D is natural from the perspective of Kolmogorov complexity. If D does not contain any regularities at all, then it consists of purely random data and there is no hypothesis to identify. Assume that the body of data D contains regularities. With help of a description of those regularities (a model) we can describe the data compactly. Assuming that the regularities can be represented in an effective manner (that is, by a Turing machine), we encode the data as a program for that machine. Squeezing all effective regularity out of the data, we end up with a Turing machine representing the meaningful regular information in the data together with a program for that Turing machine representing the remaining meaningless randomness of the data. This is the intuition, which finds its basis in the Definitions 1 and 2. However, it is difficult to find a valid mathematical way to force a sensible division of the information at hand in a meaningful part and a meaningless part. One way to proceed is suggested by the analysis below.

A practice oriented theory like MDL, although often lacking in justification, apparently works and is used by practitioners. The MDL principle is very easy to use in some loose sense, but it is hard to justify. A user of the MDL principle does not need to *prove* that the concept class concerned is learnable, rather he needs to choose a concept that can be described shortly and without causing too many errors (and he needs to balance these two things).

In various forms aimed at practical applications the idea of doing induction or data modelling in statistical hypothesis identification or prediction was proposed by C. Wallace and co-authors [19, 20], who formulated the *Minimum Message Length (MML)* principle and J. Rissanen [10, 11] who formulated the *Minimum Description Length (MDL)* principle. Here we abstract away from epistemological and technical differences between MML and MDL, and other variants, and their concessions to reality in the name of feasibility and practicability. We focus only on the following central ideal version involved. Indeed, we do not even care about whether we deal with statistical or deterministic hypotheses. All effectively describable hypotheses are involved.

Definition 13. Given a sample of data, and an effective enumeration of models, *ideal MDL* selects the model which minimizes the sum of

- the length, in bits, of an effective description of the model; and
- the length, in bits, of an effective description of the data when encoded with the help of the model.

Intuitively, with a more complex description of the hypothesis H, it may fit the data better and therefore decreases the misclassified data. If H describes all the data, then it does not allow for measuring errors. A simpler description of H may be penalized by increasing the number of misclassified data. If H is a trivial hypothesis that contains nothing, then all data are described literally and there is no generalization. The rationale of the method is that a balance in between seems required. Similarly to the analysis of prediction above, in [7, 8] we have shown that in almost all cases maximal compression finds the best hypotehsis.

8 Conclusion

The analysis of both hypothesis identification by Ideal MDL and prediction shows that maximally compressed descriptions give good results on the data samples which are random with respect to probabilistic hypotheses. These data samples form the overwhelming majority and occur with probability going to one when the length of the data sample grows unboundedly.

References

1. J.L. Doob, *Stochastic Processes* , Wiley, 1953.
2. P. Gács, On the symmetry of algorithmic information, *Soviet Math. Dokl.*, 15 (1974) 1477-1480. Correction: ibid., 15 (1974) 1480.
3. P. Gács, On the relation between descriptional complexity and algorithmic probability, *Theoret. Comput. Sci.*, 22(1983), 71-93.

4. A.N. Kolmogorov, Three approaches to the quantitative definition of information, *Problems Inform. Transmission* 1:1 (1965) 1-7.
5. L.A. Levin, On the notion of a random sequence, *Soviet Math. Dokl.*, 14(1973), 1413-1416.
6. M. Li and P.M.B. Vitányi, *An Introduction to Kolmogorov Complexity and its Applications*, Springer-Verlag, New York, 1993.
7. M. Li and P.M.B. Vitanyi, Computational Machine Learning in Theory and Praxis. In: 'Computer Science Today', J. van Leeuwen, Ed., Lecture Notes in Computer Science, Vol. 1000, Springer-Verlag, Heidelberg, 1995, 518-535.
8. P.M.B. Vitanyi and M. Li, Ideal MDL and Its Relation To Bayesianism, 'Proc. ISIS: Information, Statistics and Induction in Science', World Scientific, Singapore, 1996, 282-291.
9. P. Martin-Löf, The definition of random sequences, *Inform. Contr.*, 9(1966), 602-619.
10. J.J. Rissanen, Modeling by the shortest data description, *Automatica-J.IFAC* 14 (1978) 465-471.
11. J.J. Rissanen, *Stochastic Complexity and Statistical Inquiry*, World Scientific Publishers, 1989.
12. J.J. Rissanen, Fisher information and stochastic complexity, *IEEE Trans. Inform. Theory*, IT-42:1(1996), 40-47.
13. J. Segen, *Pattern-Directed Signal Analysis*, PhD Thesis, Carnegie-Mellon University, Pittsburgh, 1980.
14. R.J. Solomonoff, A formal theory of inductive inference, Part 1 and Part 2, *Inform. Contr.*, 7(1964), 1-22, 224-254.
15. R.J. Solomonoff, Complexity-based induction systems: comparisons and convergence theorems, *IEEE Trans. Inform. Theory* IT-24 (1978) 422-432.
16. A.M. Turing, On computable numbers with an application to the Entscheidungsproblem, *Proc. London Math. Soc.*, *Ser. 2*, 42(1936), 230-265; Correction, Ibid, 43(1937), 544-546.
17. R. von Mises, Grundlagen der Wahrscheinlichkeitsrechnung, *Mathemat. Zeitsch.*, 5(1919), 52-99.
18. V. Vovk, Minimum description length estimators under the universal coding scheme, in: P. Vitányi (Ed.), *Computational Learning Theory*, Proc. 2nd European Conf. (EuroCOLT '95), Lecture Notes in Artificial Intelligence, Vol. 904, Springer-Verlag, Heidelberg, 1995, pp. 237-251; Learning about the parameter of the Bernoulli model, *J. Comput. System Sci.*, to appear.
19. C.S. Wallace and D.M. Boulton, An information measure for classification, *Computing Journal* 11 (1968) 185-195.
20. C.S. Wallace and P.R. Freeman, Estimation and inference by compact coding, *J. Royal Stat. Soc.*, *Series B*, 49 (1987) 240-251. Discussion: ibid.,252-265.
21. K. Yamanishi, A Randomized Approximation of the MDL for Stochastic Models with Hidden Variables, *Proc. 9th ACM Comput. Learning Conference*, ACM Press, 1996.
22. A.K. Zvonkin and L.A. Levin, The complexity of finite objects and the development of the concepts of information and randomness by means of the theory of algorithms, *Russian Math. Surveys* 25:6 (1970) 83-124.

Part II:
Regular Papers

Induction of Feature Terms With INDIE

Eva Armengol and Enric Plaza

IIIA - Institut d'Investigació en Intel·ligència Artificial
CSIC - Spanish Council for Scientific Research
Campus UAB, 08193 Bellaterra, Catalonia, Spain.
Vox: +34-3-5809570, Fax: +34-3-5809661
{eva,enric}@iiia.csic.es
http://www.iiia.csic.es

Abstract. The aim of relational learning is to develop methods for the induction of descriptions in representation formalisms that are more expressive than attribute-value representation. Feature terms have been studied to formalize object-centered representation in declarative languages and can be seen as a subset of first-order logic. We present a representation formalism based on feature terms and we show how induction can be performed in a natural way using a notion of subsumption based on an informational ordering. Moreover feature terms also allow to specify incomplete information in a natural way. An example of such inductive methods, INDIE, is presented. INDIE performs bottom-up heuristic search on the subsumption lattice of the feature term space. Results of this method on several domains are explained.

1 Introduction

The aim of relational learning is to develop methods for the induction of descriptions in representation formalisms that are more expressive than attribute-value representation. Relational learning research is thus biased by the representation formalism used. Most work on ILP (inductive logic programming) has been focused on induction in subsets of first order logic like Horn or Datalog clauses. We think ML research can also profit from exploring other representation formalisms that allow the expressive power of relations but are different subsets of fist order logic.

In this paper we present a representation formalism based on feature terms and INDIE, a bottom up learning method that induces class descriptions in the form of feature term from positive and negative examples. Feature terms (also called feature structures or ψ-terms) are a generalization of first-order terms that have been introduced in theoretical computer science in order to formalize object-oriented capabilities into declarative languages. Feature term formalisms have a family resemblance with—but are different from—unification grammars and description logics (KL-One-like languages) [1, 5].

An advantage of feature terms is that they allow a natural way to describe incomplete information [1]. Incomplete information arises the so-called problem of "unknown values" in ML and, specially in attribute-value representation, the problem of irrelevant attributes. For instance, in § 4 we present the induction of class descriptions for the identification of marine sponges using INDIE. It turns out that depending on the kind of skeleton a sponge may have (*fiber* or *spiculate*) a collection of attributes is irrelevant to the description of the sponge. Sorts (types) in feature terms solve this problem by relating each predicate (attribute) to the sort to which it is relevant. Following our example, the *spicarch* predicate is relevant to skeletons of sort *spiculate* but not to skeletons of sort *fiber*.

Feature terms form a lattice by means of the subsumption relationship. From subsumption (equivalent to the *more general than* relation in ML) it is natural to define the operations of unification and anti-unification (AU) in which INDIE is based (see §2). While the generalization relation is the natural one for induction, and has been used extensively in classical ML methods, most relational learners based on Horn clauses are based on some notions of inversion deduction (resolution, entailment, etc). In these ILP approaches the generalization relation has to be derived from deduction and, since there are several ways in which this can be done, the generalization relation has been a focus of research and debate—see [4] for a thorough summary of the different proposals.

The structure of the paper is the following. First, feature terms are formally described and then subsumption and AU operations are defined. Then §3 presents an inductive method for feature terms INDIE, based on the subsumption and AU operations. § 4 shows the results of INDIE in several domains—including standard ML data sets. Finally, related work and our final conclusions are discussed.

2 Feature Terms

Feature terms are a way to construct terms. The difference between feature terms and first order terms is the following: a first order term, e. g. $f(x, g(x, y), z)$, can be formally described as a tree and a fixed tree traversal order—in other words, variables are identified by position. The intuition behind a feature term is that it can be described as a labeled graph—in other words, variables are identified by name (regardless of order or position). This difference allows to represent partial knowledge.

Feature terms are just terms and require to be integrated into a representation formalism to be used in representation, reasoning and learning. We will presently introduce the role of feature terms in the reflective object-centered representation language Noos [2]. Noos was designed to support the integration of learning methods into knowledge modeling frameworks and here we will merely present the subset needed to explain induction of descriptions from examples. Intuitively, Noos extends the formalisms of [1, 5] allowing the values of features to be *sets of values*.

2.1 Feature Terms in Noos

Our approach to formalize Noos is related to the research based on ψ-*terms* [1, 5], and extensible records [7] that propose formalisms to model object-oriented programming constructs. **Noos** is an object-centered representation language based on *feature terms*. *Feature terms* are record-like data structures embodying a collection of *features*.

We describe the **Noos** signature Σ as the tuple $\langle S, \mathcal{F}, \leq \rangle$ such that:

- S is a set of *sort symbols* including $\bot, \top$;
- $\mathcal{F}$ is a set of *feature symbols*;
- $\leq$ is a decidable partial order on S such that $\bot$ is the least element and $\top$ is the greatest element.

We define an interpretation $\mathcal{I}$ over the signature $\langle S, \mathcal{F}, \leq \rangle$ as the structure

$$\mathcal{I} = \langle \mathcal{D}^{\mathcal{I}}, (f^{\mathcal{I}})_{f \in S}, (\ell^{\mathcal{I}})_{\ell \in \mathcal{F}} \rangle$$

such that:

- $\mathcal{D}^{\mathcal{I}}$ is a non-empty set, called *domain* of $\mathcal{I}$ (or, universe);
- for each symbol s in S, $s^{\mathcal{I}}$ is a subset of the domain; in particular, $\top^{\mathcal{I}} = \mathcal{D}^{\mathcal{I}}$ and $\bot^{\mathcal{I}} = \emptyset$;
- for each feature ℓ in $\mathcal{F}$, $\ell^{\mathcal{I}}$ is a total unary function $\ell^{\mathcal{I}} : \mathcal{D}^{\mathcal{I}} \mapsto \mathcal{P}(\mathcal{D}^{\mathcal{I}})$. When the mapping is not defined it is assumed to have value $\top$.

Given the signature Σ and a set $\mathcal{V}$ of variables, we define feature terms as:

Definition 1. A feature term ψ is an expression of the form:

$$\psi \quad ::= \quad X : s\,[f_1 \doteq \Psi_1 \cdots f_n \doteq \Psi_n]$$

where X is a variable in $\mathcal{V}$, s is a sort in S, $f_1, \cdots, f_n$ are features in $\mathcal{F}$, $n \geq 0$, and each Ψ_i is either a feature term or a set of feature terms. We also identify a feature term with the singleton set of that feature term.

Note that when $n = 0$ we are defining only a sorted variable $(X : s)$. We call the variable X in the above feature term the *root* of ψ, and say that X is *sorted* by the sort s (noted $Sort(\psi)$) and has features $f_1, \cdots, f_n$.

Using this syntax for feature terms, the following expression (named ψ_1)

$$\psi_1 = X : Person \begin{bmatrix} last\_name \doteq Smith \\ drives \quad \doteq Y : Car \begin{bmatrix} owner \doteq X \\ model \doteq Z : Ibiza \end{bmatrix} \end{bmatrix}$$

is an example of a feature term denoting persons whose last_name is Smith, who drive an Ibiza-model car of which she/he is also the owner.

A feature term is a syntactic expression that denotes sets of elements in some appropriate domain of interpretation ($[\![\psi]\!]^{\mathcal{I}} \subset \mathcal{D}^{\mathcal{I}}$). Thus, given the previously defined interpretation $\mathcal{I}$, the denotation $[\![\psi]\!]^{\mathcal{I}}$ of a feature term ψ, under a valuation $\alpha : \mathcal{V} \mapsto \mathcal{D}^{\mathcal{I}}$ is given inductively by:

$$\llbracket \psi \rrbracket^{\mathcal{I}} = \llbracket X : s[f_1 \doteq \psi_1 \cdots f_n \doteq \psi_n] \rrbracket^{\mathcal{I}} = \{\alpha(X)\} \cap s^{\mathcal{I}} \bigcap_{1 \leq i \leq n} (\ell_i^{\mathcal{I}})^{-1}(\llbracket \psi_i \rrbracket^{\mathcal{I}})$$

where $F^{-1}(S)$, when F is a function and S is a set, stands for $\{x | \exists S' \supset S$ such that $F(x) = S'\}$; i.e., denotes the set of all elements whose images by F contains at least S.

Using this semantical interpretation of feature terms, it is legitimate to establish a relation order between terms. Given two terms ψ and ψ', we will be interested in determine when $\llbracket \psi \rrbracket^{\mathcal{I}} \subset \llbracket \psi' \rrbracket^{\mathcal{I}}$.

2.2   Subsumption

The semantical interpretation of feature terms brings an ordering relation among feature terms (also called *descriptions* in **Noos**). We call this ordering relation *subsumption*. The intuitive meaning of subsumption is that of *informational ordering*. We say that a feature term ψ subsumes another feature term ψ' ($\psi \sqsubseteq \psi'$) when all information in ψ is also contained in ψ'—i. e. corresponds to the semantical relation of $\llbracket \psi' \rrbracket^{\mathcal{I}} \subset \llbracket \psi \rrbracket^{\mathcal{I}}$.

Definition 2. (Subsumption)
Given two feature terms ψ and ψ', ψ subsumes ψ', $\psi \sqsubseteq \psi'$, when :

1. $Sort(\psi) \leq Sort(\psi')$, and
2. for every $f_i \doteq \Psi_i$ defined in ψ then f_i has to be defined in ψ' as $f_i \doteq \Psi_i'$ and exists a total injective function $h : \Psi_i \to \Psi_i'$ such that $\forall \psi_k \in \Psi_i \ \psi_k \sqsubseteq h(\psi_k)$.

For instance, consider the previous presented example of a feature term (ψ_1) and the following one (ψ_2) denoting persons driving a car with an owner and any car model:

$$\psi_2 = X : Person \left[drives \doteq Y : Car \begin{bmatrix} owner \doteq V : Person \\ model \doteq Z : Car\_model \end{bmatrix} \right]$$

Clearly $\psi_2 \sqsubseteq \psi_1$, i. e. this term subsumes the previous one. Notice here that **owner** in ψ_2 has variable V different from X—an equality that was enforced in ψ_1 since both had the same variable X. In other words, ψ_1 has more constraints (more information) than ψ_2 but also all information in ψ_2—thus the subsumption holds.

Finally, we introduce the notion of *equivalence* among feature terms:

Definition 3. (Equivalence) Given two feature terms ψ and ψ', we say that they are syntactic variants if and only if $\psi \sqsubseteq \psi'$ and $\psi' \sqsubseteq \psi$.

Anti-unification (AU) in feature terms is defined in the classical way (as the "least common subsumer" or "most specific generalization") over the subsumption lattice as follows.

Definition 4. (Anti-unification) The anti-unification of two terms $\psi \sqcap \psi'$ is an upper lower bound with respect to the subsumption ($\sqsubseteq$) ordering.

Notice that the upper lower bound of two terms need not be unique—i. e. there may be several terms that are an upper lower bound and are not equivalent. An algorithmic definition of AU is given in § 3. Moreover AU can also be used in Case-based Reasoning for establishing a symbolic representation of similitude and reasoning about similitudes [11].

2.3 Understanding Feature Terms as Clauses

There a several syntaxes amenable to represent feature terms. We have used up to now a record-like syntax, but graphs and clausal syntaxes can also be used. Using labeled graphs (1) arcs are labeled with predicates symbols, (2) nodes stand for sorted variables where the sort symbol is the node label, and (3) path[1] equality is tantamount to variable symbol equality. An example is the induced description of a class of marine sponges as shown at Figure 5 (notice that feature *size* has a set value with two elements *Megas* and *Micros* but no path equality appears).

Feature terms can be also understood as conjunctions of clauses[2]. This clausal representation is useful and more usual for ML methods. There are two kinds of atomic clauses: sort clauses $(X : s)$ and feature clauses $(f(X, Y))$. A given feature term can be represented also as a conjunction of these two kind of atomic clauses. Thus, for a term $\psi = X : s[f_1 \doteq \psi_1 \cdots f_n \doteq \psi_n]$, a clausal form $\phi(\psi)$ is built as follows $\phi(\psi) = X : s \wedge f_1(X, Y_1) \wedge \phi(\psi_1) \wedge \cdots \wedge f_n(X, Y_n) \wedge \phi(\psi_n)$, where $Y_1, \cdots, Y_n$ are roots of $\psi_1, \cdots, \psi_n$ respectively.

For instance, the first example of feature term (ψ_1) is represented in clausal form as follows:

$$X : Person \wedge \quad lastname(X, \text{Smith}) \quad \wedge \quad drives(X, Y)$$
$$\wedge \quad Y : Car \quad \wedge \quad owner(Y, X) \quad \wedge \quad model(Y, Z) \wedge Z : Ibiza$$

2.4 The Inductive Setting

The process of induction over feature terms with the goal of finding a *discriminant description* can be specified as follows:

Given
1. a set of positive E^+ and negative E^- examples.
2. a notion of *subsumption*
3. Background knowledge B in the form of domain methods

---

[1] A path is a sequence of arcs.
[2] The reader interested in the precise mapping among the different representations (and the semantic consistency of the subsumption lattice across these mappings) is referred to [1].

Find a feature term (description) ψ such that $\forall\, e^+ \in E^+ : \psi \sqsubseteq e^+$ and $\forall\, e^- \in E^- : \psi \not\sqsubseteq e^-$.

Notice that AU of positive examples provides a way for achieving the first condition $e^+_{AU} = e^+_1 \sqcap e^+_2 \ldots \sqcap e^+_n \Rightarrow e^+_{AU} \sqsubseteq e^+ : \forall\, e^+ \in E^+$, namely the least general generalization of E^+ subsumes all positive examples but it may also subsume some negative example. Next section describes the heuristic strategy used by INDIE for exploiting the AU operation to search for a discriminant description in the subsumption lattice of feature terms.

In the inductive setting presented here we have included a given (3), namely background knowledge B, that will be now summarily explained. Background knowledge is expressed in **Noos** by means of methods that infer the values of features. A feature term is *closed* when all methods had inferred values for the features. The AU of two feature terms requires them to be closed, so the **Noos** AU method forces the domain methods to be applied in a lazy on-demand way. Method definition has not been included in the syntax introduced in this section for reasons of space and because it is not needed for the domains shown in §4 (but see [2]). A recension of feature term induction with background knowledge is to wait for another article.

3 The Inductive Method INDIE

INDIE is a heuristic bottom-up inductive learning method that obtains a most specific generalization subsuming a set of positive examples. The main contribution of INDIE is handling objects represented as feature terms. INDIE can work either on positive examples only or on positive and negative examples. Working on positive examples only requires AU and it allows to solve the characterization task (also called discovery or description problem), useful in KDD and Data-Mining. Working on positive and negative examples allows to perform the discrimination task (also called prediction problem or concept learning) that is the usual in most ML applications. In the following we describe INDIE in the discrimination task.

3.1 Description of the Method

Given a set of training examples $E = \{e_1, ..., e_m\}$ and a set of solution classes $C = \{C_1, ..., C_n\}$, the goal of INDIE is to obtain a discriminant description D_k for each solution class C_k. Each example e_i is a feature term having a subset of features $A_i = \{A_{i1}, ..., A_{ik} | A_{ij} \in \mathcal{F}\}$. Training examples can have a different subset of legal features in $\mathcal{F}$. Each feature A_i has as values a set of objects O_i where each $o_{ij} \in O_i$ is a feature term that can have, in turn, a set of features.

A description $D_k = \{d_{jk}\}$ represents a disjunction of feature term descriptions for the current solution class C_k. Each d_{jk} subsumes a subset of positive examples of C_k and does not subsume negative examples. In a discriminant task, negative examples of a solution class C_k are all those training examples that do not belong to C_k.

<u>Function</u> INDIE (E^+, E^-)
   $D = \emptyset$
   $D_k = $ **Anti-unification** (E^+) ; most specific generalization
  <u>if</u> $D_k \sqsubseteq e$ for some $e \in E^-$
     <u>then</u> $A_l = \{A_i |$ features in D_k chosen according to leaf bias$\}$
        $P_N = $ **Discriminant-partition** (A_l, E^+, E^-)
        <u>for</u> each set $S_i \in P_N$ <u>do</u>
           $D_i = $ INDIE(S_i, E^-)
           Add D_i to D
       <u>end-for</u>
    <u>else</u> Add D_k to D
  <u>end-if</u>
  Eliminate any $d \in D$ such that $d \sqsubseteq d' \in D$
  <u>return</u> D
<u>end-function</u>

Fig. 1. INDIE obtains a disjunction of descriptions D_k that do not subsume negative examples for the current class.

Given a set of positive examples E^+ for a solution class C_k the INDIE algorithm (Fig. 1) obtains, using the AU operation, a most specific generalization D_k subsuming all the examples in E^+. If the description D_k does not subsume negative examples then D_k is a correct description for C_k. Because the value of a feature can be a set, several most specific generalizations subsuming all the positive examples can be built. This means that if one of the most specific generalizations D_k subsumes some negative example there is two options to solve this situation: 1) to search for another most specific generalization D_j that does not subsume negative examples, or 2) to specialize D_k until no negative examples are subsumed. Using the first option all the possible most specific generalizations are tested searching for a description D_k that does not subsume negative examples. If all the descriptions D_k subsume negative examples, the second option has to be taken. The second option assumes that the only way to describe the current solution class C_k is using a disjunction of descriptions.

The next question is, how many descriptions are necessary to describe C_k? To answer this question a heuristic approach is taken. INDIE selects the most relevant feature A_d (using the *discriminant − partition* function explained later) that generates a partition P_N of E^+ in N classes, where N is the number of different values that A_d takes in E^+. Thus, if D_k subsumes some negative examples there is at most a disjunct of N descriptions for C_k, i.e., $D_k = \{d_{jk}\}$ for $j = 1$ to N. The new specialized description is a disjunction $D_k = \{d_{jk}\}$ recursively obtained by applying the INDIE algorithm to each set of the partition P_N. This process is repeated until D_k does not subsume negative examples or all the features have been used. If there are two descriptions d_{1k} and d_{2k} in D_k such that $d_{1k} \sqsubseteq d_{2k}$

<u>Function</u> AU2 (E_1, E_2, D)
    Let D be a new term with $Sort(D) = Sort(E_1) \sqcap Sort(E_2)$
    $A = \{A_i | \text{ common attributes to } E_1 \text{ and } E_2\}$
    <u>for</u> each $A_i \in A$ <u>do</u>
        $V_i = (v_{i1}, v_{i2})$ where $v_{i1} = E_1.A_i$ and $v_{i2} = E_2.A_i$
        <u>if</u> $v_{i1} = v_{i2}$
            <u>then</u> add-feature (D, A_i, v_{i1})
            <u>else</u> <u>if</u> there is a $p \in *paths*$ such that $p = (V_i, d_i)$
                <u>then</u> add-feature (D, A_i, d_i)
                <u>else</u> Let d_i be a new term with $Sort(d_i) = Sort(v_{i1}) \sqcap Sort(v_{i2})$
                    add (V_i, d_i) to *paths*
                    <u>if</u> v_{i1} and v_{i2} have zero features
                        <u>then</u> add-feature (D, A_i, d_i)
                        <u>else</u> add-feature $(D, A_i,$ AU2 $(v_{i1}, v_{i2}))$
        <u>endif</u> <u>endif</u> <u>endif</u>
    <u>end for</u>
<u>end function</u>

Fig. 2. Anti-unification operation that constructs the most specific generalization covering a given set of positive examples. $Add - feature(d, a, v)$ is a function that adds the feature a with value v to the description d.

then d_{2k} can be eliminated and the disjunct is simplified.

    In the next sections, we explain the main steps of INDIE, i.e. how to construct a most specific generalization (AU operation), which bias is used to select the set of features that allow the to define a partition over the positive examples and how the most discriminant partition is selected (discriminant-partition operation).

3.2 Anti-unification

The goal of the anti-unification (AU) operation is to construct a most specific generalization D from a set of positive examples E^+ of the current solution class C_k. Figure 2 shows the algorithm AU2 used to obtain a most specific generalization of two examples E_1 and E_2. The first step is to obtain the set of features that are common to both E_1 and E_2. We will explain AU2 assuming the attributes have only one value, and later we will explain the case when the values of an attribute are sets. For each common attribute A_i, let us consider the pair $V_i = (v_{i1}, v_{i2})$, where $v_{i1} = E_1.A_i$ (the value taken by the A_i in the example E_1) and $v_{i2} = E_2.A_i$. Each pair V_i has associated an object d_i that is the description obtained from the AU of the values contained in V_i. All the pairs (V_i, d_i) are stored in the *paths* variable (see Figure 2) in order to detect if a particular combination of values has already been anti-unified. Whenever the algorithm founds a pair (v_{i1}, v_{i2}) already contained in *paths*, its associated object d_i is the value for $D.A_i$. This process assures path equality. When the pair $V_i = (v_{i1}, v_{i2})$ has not previously appeared, the values v_{i1} and v_{i2} have to be anti-unified.

Feature terms in Noos, as we saw, are set-valued. Let us suppose that $S_{i1} = E_1.A_i$ and $S_{i2} = E_2.A_i$ are sets of values. The AU of S_1 and S_2 has to find a set of values S such that: 1) $Card(S) = min\{Card(S_{i1}), Card(S_{i2})\}$, and 2) each $s_i \in S$ is obtained from the AU of two different values $v_j \in S_1$ and $v_k \in S_2$. The AU2 algorithm is applied to each possible pair (v_j, v_k) where $v_j \in S_1$ and $v_k \in S_2$, obtaining a set $\{g_p\}$ containing $Card(S_1) \times Card(S_2)$ descriptions. From this set, a most specific combination[3] of $Card(S)$ elements has to be taken as the value set of the attribute A_i. Note that can exist several incomparable combinations that are maximally specific. AU2 randomly chooses one of them. The AU of n examples $E_1, ..., E_n$ consists of applying the AU2 algorithm $n-1$ times, starting by computing $D_1 = AU2(E_1, E_2)$ and iterating $AU2(D_{i-2}, E_i)$ over $i = 3 ... n$.

3.3 Bias and Partitioning the Set of Positive Examples

The discriminant-partition function (see Figure 3) determines the most discriminant feature A_d (among those features belonging to $\mathcal{F}$).We consider as candidates to be the most discriminant feature only those features appearing in D_k. This bias reduces the set of candidates to those features appearing in all the positive examples. In a structured representation two kinds of features can be distinguished: leaf features and intermediate features (those belonging to intermediate levels of the structured representation). For example, in the sponge shown in Figure 4, some leaf features are *axis* or *grow* and some intermediate features are *size* or *micros*. Usually, existing inductive learning methods select one predicate at time to specialize a clause. If we select an intermediate feature as the most discriminant, its value is a subterm and this means that the description D_k is specialized according the type of that subterm. This situation is equivalent to specialize a clause introducing several predicates at time. The selection of only one predicate is achieved in feature terms by selecting a leaf feature. Therefore, our bias is to consider as candidates to be the most discriminant feature the set of leaf features of D_k. In practice, the selection of an intermediate feature to specialize the description D_k tends to produce descriptions too specific (in the sense that it quickly reaches a disjunction of M descriptions, where M is the number of positive examples). In principle, we are interested in a description of a solution class using the least number of descriptions.

To select the most discriminant feature we take the minimum distance between partitions—using the López de Mántaras distance [8]. Given two partitions P_A and P_B of a set S, the distance among them is computed as follows:

$$d_N(P_A, P_B) = 2 - \frac{I(P_A) + I(P_B)}{I(P_A \cap P_B)}$$

---

[3] A most specific combination is such that is not subsumed (in the sense of definition 2) by any other combination.

Function DISCRIMINANT-PARTITION (A_l, E^+, E^-)
    $Dist = \emptyset$
    while $A_l \neq \emptyset$ do
        $P_c = ((E^+)(E^-))$;; the correct partition
        for $A_i \in A_l$ do
            $P_i = \{S_i \subset E \mid \forall v_i \in S_i \text{ and } \forall v_j \in S_j : Sort(v_i) \neq Sort(v_j)\}$
opez de M $D_i = D(P_c, P_i)$;; L
           Add D_i to $Dist$
        end-for
    end-while
    useful-attribute = false
    while $Dist \neq \emptyset$ and (useful-attribute = false) do
        $d_{min} = min\{D_i \in Dist\}$
        Let A_{min} and P_{min} the attribute and the partition associated to d_{min}
        $P_d = \{S_i' \mid S_i' = S_i - E^- : S_i \in P_{min}\}$
        if P_d has only one non-empty S_i'
           then Remove d_{min} from $Dist$
           else useful-attribute = true
        end-if
    end-while
    if $Dist = \emptyset$ then return E^+
             else return P_d
    end-if
end-function

Fig. 3. Discriminant-partition function selects the most useful attribute in a description leaf using the López de Mántaras distance. The set of relevant attributes is given in A_l by algorithm in Fig. 1

where $I(P)$ is the information of a partition P and $I(P_A \cap P_B)$ is the mutual information of two partitions.

In our case, the distance measure is applied to compute the distance among a partition generated by a feature and the correct partition. The correct partition P_c has two classes, one containing the positive examples (examples in C_k) and the other containing the negative examples (those not in C_k). Thus, for each feature $A_i \in A_l$ in a description leaf of the current description, the set of training examples $E = E^+ \cup E^-$ is partitioned according the sorts of the values of A_i generating a partition P_i. Each partition P_i is compared with the correct partition P_c using the López de Mántaras distance. The most discriminant feature A_d is that producing a partition P_d having the minimum distance $D_d(P_d, P_c)$ to the correct partition P_c.

Generalization Post-process After applying INDIE, an optional post-processing step can be used. Since D_k is a most specific generalization for a solution class C_k, it can be generalized (in principle) without subsuming any negative example. The post-process consists of eliminating features as far as no negative examples are subsumed For each description $d_{jk} \in D_k$, the algorithm for post-processing uses the López de Mántaras distance to rank all the features belonging to d_{jk}. The features are considered from the least discriminant to the most discriminant.

4 Experiments with INDIE

In this section we show the results of applying INDIE to several domains: robots, drugs, marine sponges, and lymphographies. We have chosen these datasets to show and evaluate different aspects of this feature term induction method. In the following subsections the results of these experiments are explained.

4.1 Concept Learning using INDIE

The robots domain [10] consists of a description of six robots that belongs to two solution classes: *friendly* and *unfriendly*. The robots are described using an attribute-value representation. However, using the feature term formalism obtains a relational definition for the *friendly* class:

$$\text{Friendly} = X : robot \begin{bmatrix} body\_shape \doteq Y : shape \\ head\_shape \doteq Y : shape \end{bmatrix}$$

i. e. the robots that have the same shape of body and of head belong to the *friendly* class.

The drugs domain consists in a description of several drugs and is used by the KLUSTER system [9] . From these descriptions KLUSTER can obtain several classifications, i.e. what is an active substance, what is a monodrug, when a substance is sedative, etc. To represent the domain objects KLUSTER uses a representation language based on KL-ONE. In INDIE we have represented the domain objects as feature terms and the goal is to obtain a description for the solution classes *monodrug*, *combidrug* and *placebo*. The obtained descriptions for these classes are similar to those obtained by the KLUSTER system. The following are descriptions obtained by INDIE for the *monodrug, combidrug* classes.

$$\text{Monodrug} = X : drug \begin{bmatrix} effects \doteq Y : drug\_effect \\ contains \doteq Z : active\_substance \left[affects \doteq W : symptom \right] \end{bmatrix}$$

$$\text{Combidrug} = X : drug \left[contains \doteq \begin{matrix} Y : active\_substance \\ Z : active\_substance \end{matrix} \right]$$

The differences are due to the different representation (see §5 for a comparison of it with INDIE). Notice that the main difference between both classes is using one active substance (*monodrug*) and more than one active substance (*combidrug*). This fact derives from the definition of subsumption, namely that any example

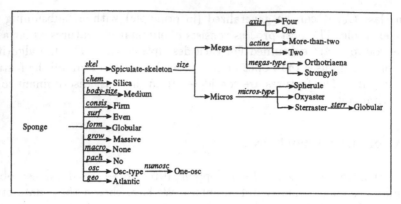

Fig. 4. A *graph* description of a feature term for a specimen of marine sponge (of the *Erylus discophorus* species).

subsumed by the *Combidrug* description above, needs to have (at least) two active substances for feature *contains*. These examples would also be subsumed by *Monodrug* description (they also have *one* active substance) except that they do not satisfy the other two features (*effects* and *affects*) .

We have employed INDIE in the multistrategy learning system for marine sponge identification SPIN. Marine sponges offer a good test bed for the capability of feature terms for dealing with incomplete descriptions, since marine sponges variability involves that certain properties are relevant only for certain types and/or certain subcomponents of them. Given a set of sponges correctly classified INDIE has been capable to obtain a description for the different taxa. Sponges are represented as feature terms. See an example of a marine sponge in Figure 4 using the graph syntax for feature terms. Marine sponges can be described by a great variety of features and they form a domain where partial descriptions ("incomplete information") are commonplace. For example, a marine sponge of the *Erylus discophorus* species may be described by the skeleton, the geographic localization, the form and the color whereas other sponge only may be described by the skeleton. Figure 5 shows the descriptions obtained by INDIE for the *Erylus* taxon.

Also of interest are the results of INDIE in the family relations domain. Notice that INDIE infers descriptions (e. g. of persons that are uncles or mothers) and not rules to compute the relations uncle or mother. For this concepts, INDIE finds a correct and discriminating description with AU only, and the discriminating stage is not used. In this situation, INDIE's anti-unification (AU) stage is closer to the characterization task—discovering regularities as found in data mining or in the so-called description problem—indeed AU finds by definition *all* those common to a set of (positive) examples. Let us consider those persons that are mothers and those that are uncles in the family relations dataset. In the both cases INDIE finds using AU a description that subsumes only positive examples

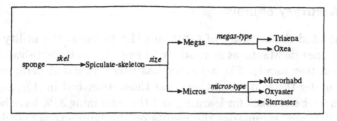

Fig. 5. A *graph* description of a feature term for the description of the *Erylus* genus).

and no negative examples (those persons that are not, respectively, mothers or uncles). In the case of the mother description, AU finds the following term:

$$
X : female
\begin{bmatrix}
son & \doteq Y : male &
\begin{bmatrix}
father & \doteq W \\
mother & \doteq X \\
sister & \doteq Z
\end{bmatrix} \\[2ex]
daughter \doteq Z : female &
\begin{bmatrix}
father & \doteq W \\
mother & \doteq X \\
brother & \doteq Y
\end{bmatrix} \\[2ex]
husband \doteq W : male &
\begin{bmatrix}
son & \doteq Y \\
daughter & \doteq Z \\
wife & \doteq Y
\end{bmatrix}
\end{bmatrix}
$$

All this regularities hold for all the involved persons in the dataset. After the optional generalization postprocess only one of the regularities remains, namely

$$X : female \left[husband \doteq W : male \left[son \doteq Y : male \right] \right]$$

that clearly is correct—but other regularities that have very similar heuristic values have been eliminated, so they could have equally been chosen (like having a son or a daughter).

The uncles description also induces a number of regularities by AU, for instance, the niece X has the following relation with the uncle Z:

$$X : female \left[mother \doteq Y : female \left[brother \doteq Z : male \right] \right]$$

and also the following one, expressed in clausal form:

$$
\begin{aligned}
&X : female \quad \wedge \quad father(X, Y) \quad \wedge \quad Y : male \quad \wedge \quad sister(Y, W) \quad \wedge \\
&W : female \quad \wedge \quad husband(W, Z) \quad \wedge \quad Z : male \quad \wedge \quad uncle(X, Z) \ .
\end{aligned}
$$

While ILP systems are more biased to single predicate learning, this example shows that feature term induction is biased toward "multiple predicate learning"—in the example above, a description of niece has been found in relationship to the uncle description. After the simplification postprocess the only following regularity remains:

$$X : male \left[wife \doteq Y : female \left[niece \doteq Z \right] \right]$$

4.2 The Accuracy of INDIE

We have evaluated the accuracy of INDIE in order to assess the utility for INDIE of using the López de Mántaras heuristic with respect to attribute-value learners of the decision tree family. The accuracy has been evaluated performing some experiments under the same conditions that those described in [12], i.e. the 67% of the cases have been taken for learning and the remaining 33% have been taken for test. We will now summarize the results on the lymphographies data set of the Irvine ML Repository. The accuracy for C4.5, CN2 and PIK are respectively 76.4, 81.7/76.5 (corresponding to two parameter setting), and 77.2.

A main difference of INDIE is that it can provide multiple solutions, situation that may be useful in some domains (i.e. for the sponge classification) or not. If we consider that multiple solutions including the correct one is a correct solution then the accuracy of INDIE is 81.4. However if we consider that a multiple solution is incorrect even if it contains the correct solution then the accuracy of INDIE is 76.63.

5 Discussion

There has been relatively few work on induction on "structured representations" compared to the intensive research performed on Horn clause representations. The KLUSTER system [9] and the LCSLearn algorithm [6] work on some description logics (a KL-One-like language). As we said of description logics, these formalisms are related to but different from feature terms. A main semantic difference is that feature terms provide a *uniform* representation while description logics are *hybrid*—there are two different formalisms, one for the describing concepts (T-box) and another one for describing instances (A-box).

KLUSTER searches for a most specific generalization MSG from positive examples. If MSG covers negative examples KLUSTER follows a particular algorithm to specialize the MSG by means of introducing new **at-most** and **at-least** predicates in the feature descriptions. INDIE uses AU to find a most specific description that subsumes positive examples (similarly to KLUSTER since both follow a bottom-up strategy) and then to specialize the description INDIE introduces disjunction of descriptions following a distance-based heuristic. KLUSTER has been applied only to the drugs domain we showed in §4.

The LCSLearn algorithm is a bottom up inductive method for C-Classic, a subset of the Classic description logic language that has all Classic constructors except for the **same-as** constructor, that is roughly equivalent to *path equality* in feature logics. Since feature logics and INDIE depend heavily on the notion of path equality, both LCSLearn and INDIE seem complementary in studying formalisms that embody different useful subsets of first order logic. However, the LCSLearn is comparable only to the AU step in INDIE —the LCSLearnDisj algorithm, the disjunctive induction version of LCSLearn, is more akin to INDIE in that it is able to induce a disjunction of description. While LCSLearn is shown to be pac-learnable, nothing is said in [6] about LCSLearnDisj. While INDIE uses a distance-based heuristic to select how to split a description into a disjunction of descriptions, LCSLearnDisj essentially chooses positive and negative examples in a random way until a disjunctive discriminant description is reached.

Subsumption is a natural way to relate to induction. Classical ML methods did so while ILP methods have to deal with deductive relations—from which a generalization relation has to be defined. Although the relation of the expressiveness of feature term formalisms and Horn clauses formalism is an open issue in the current research literature, it is possible that the first can be a subset of the latter. If that would be the case, the less expressive formalism of feature terms—closer to object-oriented representations—could be more appropriate for application domains that do not require the full induction of logic programs since they can work on the well defined subsumption lattice of feature terms.

The formalization introduced here has to be enriched to include domain methods in **Noos** performing inference. INDIE is already applicable since it requires *closed* feature terms and the AU operation forces method evaluation generating the closed feature terms. Future experimental work on several application domain is needed to show learning of feature terms with background knowledge.

Incomplete information has a natural representation in feature terms that base the subsumption relation in the notion of information ordering. A subsumed description is a *refined* term—a description with more refined (more specific sorts) or additional (new features) information.

The explanation of the framework for combining multiple learning methods in SPIN is left out for lack of space but the reader is referred to [3] for such an explanation regarding the multistrategy learning system CHROMA. The SPIN system currently combines INDIE with CRASS, a lazy learning method that uses an entropy-based measure to estimate the better example to perform an sponge identification by case-based reasoning [11].

Future work includes finishing a formal study of subsumption and AU complexity. Currently we know complexity stems from set-valued features —in fact, subsumption in feature terms without set values is lineal with the number of nodes and features [5]. We know that subsumption is much more costly only when we have embedded set-values. That is, if $D_1.A_i = S$ where S is a set, and there is a term $D_2 \in S$ that also has a set valued attribute, say $D_2.A_j = S'$, then we say S' is an embedded set-value at depth one. We estimate the complexity of dealing with embedded set-values in subsumption to be $O(n^k)$ where n is the maximum cardinality of a set and k is the embedding depth. In practice this means that while representing some application domain a user can have a clear idea of the expected complexity just looking at the level of embedding.

Related to complexity two aspects of INDIE are currently being developed. One is the effect of using a weaker form of subsumption—roughly, one that does not require in set subsumption that the subsumed elements are different. This weaker form decreases the language expressiveness, since the constraint on a minimum set cardinality (as used in the drugs domain) is dropped, but may also decrease complexity. A second aspect is parameterizing INDIE with a maximum node number to be considered during AU—equivalent to a maximum number of variables to be considered. Other options are also to limit the depth or number of features; the relationship of this bias to ij-determinacy in Horn clauses induction is also interesting. Lastly, we are developing a second inductive method using a declarative bias mechanism constraining the form of feature terms to be searched during induction.

Acknowledgments The authors thank Josep-Lluís Arcos and Ramon López de Mántaras for the discussions and the support he provided in this and other closely related work. The research reported on this paper has been developed at the IIIA inside the SMASH Project funded by Spanish CICYT grant TIC-96-1038, and a CICYT fellowship. Information about this and updated results will be posted at http://www.iiia.csic.es/Projects/learning.html.

References

1. H. Aït-Kaci and A. Podelski. Towards a meaning of LIFE. *J. Logic Programming*, 16:195–234, 1993.
2. J. L. Arcos and E. Plaza. Inference and reflection in the object-centered representation language Noos. *Journal of Future Generation Computer Systems*, 12:173–188, 1996.
3. E. Armengol and E. Plaza. Integrating induction in a case-based reasoner. In J. P. Haton, M. Keane, and M. Manago, editors, *Advances in Case-Based Reasoning*, number 984 in Lecture Notes in Artificial Intelligence, pages 3–17. Springer-Verlag, 1994.
4. F. Bergadano and D. Gunetti. *Inductive Logic Programming. From Machine Learning to Software Engineering.* The MIT Press, 1995.
5. B. Carpenter. *The Logic of Typed Feature Structures.* Tracts in theoretical Computer Science. Cambridge University Press, Cambridge, UK, 1992.
6. W. W. Cohen and H. Hirsh. Learning the classic description logic: Theoretical and experimental results. In *Principles of Knowledge Representation and Reasoning: Proceedings of the Fourth International Conference*, 1994.
7. L. Dami. *Software Composition: Towards an Integration of Functional and Object-Oriented Approaches.* PhD thesis, University of Geneva, 1994.
8. R. López de Mántaras. A distance-based attribute selection measure for decision tree induction. *Machine Learning*, 6:81–92, 1991.
9. J.-U. Kietz and K. Morik. Polynomial induction of structural knowledge. *Machine Learning*, 14:193–217, 1994.
10. N. Lavrac and S. Dzeroski. *Inductive Logic Programming: Tecniques and applications.* Ellis Horwood, 1940.
11. E. Plaza, R. López de Mántaras, and E. Armengol. On the importance of similitude: An entropy-based assessment. In Boi Faltings et al, editor, *Case-Based Reasoning, EWCBR-96*, Lecture Notes in Artificial Intelligence. Springer-Verlag, 1996.
12. X. M. Zhou and T. S. Dillon. Theoretical and practical considerations of uncertainty and complexity in automated knowledge acquisition. *IEEE Trans. Knowledge and Data Engineering*, 7:699–712, 1995.

Exploiting Qualitative Knowledge to Enhance Skill Acquisition

Cristina Baroglio
baroglio@di.unito.it
tel. +39-11-7429229 fax +39-11-751603

Dip. di Informatica, Università degli Studi
c.so Svizzera 185, I-10149, Torino, Italy

Abstract. One of the most interesting problems faced by Artificial Intelligence researchers is to reproduce a capability typical of living beings: that of learning to perform motor tasks, a problem known as *skill acquisition*. A very difficult purpose because the overwhole behavior of an agent is the result of quite a complex activity, involving sensory, planning and motor processing. In this paper, I present a novel approach for acquiring new skills, named *Soft Teaching*, that is characterized by a learning by experience process, in which an agent exploits a symbolic, qualitative description of the task to perform, that cannot, however, be used directly for control purposes. A specific Soft Teaching technique, named *Symmetries*, was implemented and tested against a continuous-domained version of well-known pole-balancing.

Keywords: skill acquisition, knowledge-based feedback, adaptive agents.

1 Introduction

In this work we consider a framework where an *artificial agent* interacts with its environment by executing actions. Our *aim* is to have the agent performing a specific *task* by generating a proper control device. Generally speaking, the controller can be built in many ways (from direct encoding to the use of AI techniques); in this paper we are interested in the approaches that exploit *on-line learning methods*. The reason is that using learning methods less information is to be supplied explicitly to the agent, its lack being balanced by the capability of acquiring it autonomously, which simplifies the controller's production.

In the literature, learning rules have already been used to acquire control knowledge either from examples, e.g. [13], or from the agent's experience, e.g. [14, 6]; this latter solution is known as *adaption*. In order to have adaption, one must find a form of *feedback*, that can be "processed" by the agent's learning rule. Typically, adaption is obtained by means of *Reinforcement Learning* (RL). As the name suggests, however, the feedback returned in this case is quite poor: in fact, it is a scalar value, corresponding to a reward when the agent satisfies the goal condition or to a punishment when it enters a failure state. Then, in RL the focus of attention is mostly posed on how to learn a policy given that the states of the underlying model are known, a hypothesis that does not hold in most real-world tasks. To overcome this limit, RL was applied to agents implemented as *neural networks*, but so, convergence cannot be guaranteed anymore [12].

One feature that is often overlooked when dealing with adaption is that live agents (such as us) exploit a lot of *knowledge* to help their learning. We do not know how this knowledge is "encoded" in the brains but we know that we use it to monitor our behavior, to recover from errors, to describe in words a task we want to have accomplished and use such simple descriptions to guide its execution. This is the focus of interest of this work.

2 Soft Teaching

The *Soft Teaching* methodology is based on a particular use of knowledge that can be observed in our everyday experience. Let's see it with an example. Supposing a human teacher has to explain the pole-balancing task to a human learner, (s)he would probably say something like "Manouver the cart, moving it left or right, so to keep the pole on it vertical". Note that this description does not contain any suggestion of what to do, "moving it left or right" is just the list of the possible actions that can be taken. We say that this description is *non-operational* because the learner still has to find a policy that allows him/her to achieve the goal. By using the above knowledge, however, the learner can criticize his/her behavior during training. We call such a mechanism the *Human-Teacher-Human-Learner* (or HTHL) interaction scheme: since the teacher cannot transfer his/her skill to the learner, it transfers some information that (1) makes the learner *aware* of what is to be achieved and (2) allows him/her to *start* and *bias* a learning process that leads to building some new actuative knowledge.

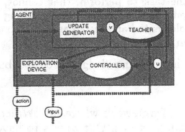

Fig. 1. The proposed architecture.

The architecture presented here (Fig. 1) is based on the HTHL scheme: the adaptive agent owns some *qualitative knowledge* (given in a *symbolic* notation) about the task and the domain, that can be turned into a very precise evaluator. The knowledge is supplied by a human teacher, who does not take part to the learning process, and is *non-operational*. The module that handles the qualitative knowledge is called *teacher* or *teacher-on-line* It is the "trait d'union" between the *symbolic* level, to which knowledge belongs, and the *analogical* level of the controller. In this framework, an adaptive agent can be trained by producing different kinds of *feedback signals* and/or using different *training algorithms*.

Indirect Supervised Learning In particular, this work introduces a subset of Soft Teaching methods called *Indirect Supervised Learning* (or simply ISL) methods. A training technique belongs to the ISL family if (1) it exploits a *supervised* learning rule and (2) the error is computed as a function of the difference between the action built by the controller and an alternative action generated by the *teacher-on-line*. This latter feature allows training to be performed *on-line*, keeping, on one hand, the advantages related to learning by interaction (of classical RL) and, on the other, overcoming some of the limits of the approaches to teaching that are already in the literature (Section 4). *Indirect Supervised Learning* is, then, a new learning paradigm in which the teacher returns *suggestions* in addition to reinforcements. The approach is somewhat similar to the one proposed by Clouse and Utgoff [4] (see Section 4), the difference is that in our case the decision of *when* and *what to suggest* is taken *automatically* instead than by a human teacher (that is what "indirect" stands for).

From an abstract perspective, the ISL *teacher architecture* is made of three main modules: a *strategy generation module*, a *strategy evaluation module*, and a *model of the world*. The main loop of the ISL algorithm is as follows:

1. given a world situation and current controller, build a strategy S;
2. produce a set of alternative strategies to the one built in step 1;
3. evaluate each strategy using the model and the teaching knowledge;
4. apply the best scoring strategy S';
5. if the effects are as those predicted by the model, update the controller exploiting the applied strategy S' and the original strategy S; otherwise, update the model in a supervised way;
6. if the trial is not over go to step 1.

The idea of exploiting a world model is not new in control applications (see [10]), the real novelty stands in the way strategies are evaluated. All the strategies taken into account in the learning process are built in one of the two following ways. The first consists in getting a situation from the world, using the current controller to produce a first action and, at last, entering a loop in which, first, the next situation is predicted by the model, then, the controller is used to generate next action according to the prediction. Strategy's length is defined by the human teacher. The model of the world is intended to be a *learning* module. So far, however, in order to study the effect of ISL in skill acquisition avoiding any additional complication, a *perfect* model was used. Once a strategy is available, it is possible to produce a set of alternatives by modifying it so to investigate the surroundings of the search space. Of course, different methods can be applied to this aim. In the implementation, random variants were used.

Symmetries *Symmetries* is an ISL method, used to better exploit the information contained in the best-scoring strategy. The idea is simple: in tasks like pole-balancing the domain is naturally symmetric, i.e. in absolute values, what the controller should do when the pole falls at its right is exactly what it should do when it falls at its left. A human learner realizes such a structure in the domain and exploits it. The same should happen in artificial learners.

Symmetries goes beyond the current perceptions of the agent, elaborating its experience. Such an elaboration is to be done *on-line* because the only alternative is to accumulate long traces of execution to post-process. The method developed alternates experience to *hypothetical reasoning*: once S' was applied and the controller updated, a subset of the points that are symmetric (w.r.t. 0) to the state that caused S''s generation are built (in the experiments on pole-balancing only x and θ signs are changed). The strategy that the agent would apply starting from each of them is built together with a proper symmetric version S'_i of S'. Both are evaluated by the teacher-on-line: if S'_i scores better than the strategy produced by the controller, it is used as a desired target by the update rule. The check is necessary because the current controller is not bound to be symmetric.

Strategy evaluation Strategies are evaluated by means of the teacher's *knowledge*. The first step is to give it a *spatial interpretation* so to allow *scalar* evaluations. A thorough description of this process can be found in [1]. Then, a single action can be evaluated by mapping on this space the input situations before and after the action was applied. Given an input $x1$ and a predicate P with a fuzzy semantics, we define P's *distance from truth* as follows: distFromTruth($P(x1)$) is 0 if $P(x1)$ *is* true, the distance between $x1$ and the truth set of P otherwise. For a better understanding let's consider predicate *closeToEnd*, whose semantics is as follows: $closeToEnd(x) \Leftrightarrow distance(x, END) < threshold$. $closeToEnd(x1)$ returns $threshold - distance(x1, END)$, where END is a given constant. Distance from truth can be extended to conjunctions of predicates by using a Euclidean-like distance measure, e.g., if $goal = P_1 \&\& ... \&\& P_n$, $distFromTruth(goal(x1))$ will be $\sum_{i=1,...,n} distFromTruth(P_i(x1))^2$. When the sum returns a value different than 0 (condition not satisfied) the *translated sigmoid function* $(1 + exp^{-\alpha x})^{-1} - 1$ is used to map it on the range $[-1, 0]$. The negative interval accounts for the fact that the evaluations can be used directly as negative reinforcements. Last, if the direction of movement is different than the desired one, the evaluation is discounted.

In order to evaluate a strategy the evaluations of each single step are combined by means of a discounted sum $eval_n = goodness(a_n) + \gamma\ eval_{n-1}$ where a_n is the action taken at time-step n and $\gamma \in [0, 1]$ is a discount factor.

The learner In the experiments, the learner was implemented as a Neural Network: this choice does not restrict the set of functions that can be approximated because it is well-known [7] that a three-layered neural network can approximate any function. Different models were tried; the ones that gave the best results belong to the *Locally Receptive Fields* family (or LRFNs, see [2]). They perform a piecewise approximation, being each hidden neuron's activation region a closed area of the input space. Then, every update has a *local* effect, leaving the knowledge acquired for situations far from the current one unchanged. This *locality* turned out to be very important to overcome *unlearning*, to find conditions that allow to check if the hidden neurons number is sufficient to represent the desired control function, and to dynamically grow the network during the learning process (see [10, 5]). The networks were implemented by means of the Fuzzy-Neural system already described in [2]: a same network topology allows to implement, alternatively, *Fuzzy Controllers* (FCs) and *Radial Basis Function Networks* (RBFNs). A network can be interpreted as a fuzzy knowledge base and the learning process preserves the rules' structure. In all experiments the same initial controller, made of 25 random rules, was used.

```
[region]
      test1        = (THETA > 0);
      goal         = (inclination() == 0);
      failure      = ((THETA > 0.2094384) || (X >= 2.4));
[context1]
      X            = any;
      THETA        = less;
[static-cond1]
      fluxpipe     = (vertical() && keep - off());
```

3 Experimental results

The method described in this paper was tested against *pole-balancing* [1]. The reason is that it is one of the most classical RL testbeds; it is well understood and allows comparisons with other techniques. Furthermore, although it is simpler than most real-world tasks, it allows to face many of the difficulties shown by continuous-domained control problems. The pole-balancing simulator is, depending on the experiment, exactly the one made freely available by Rich Sutton[1] (we will call it RS, for short) or a variant of it that can handle continuous actions. In all experiments the controller has the same four inputs $\langle X, \dot{X}, \theta, \dot{\theta} \rangle$: the position of the cart, its time derivative, the inclination of the pole, and its time derivative. The goal is to keep the pole balanced for 100,000 timesteps. For each experiment, the generalization ability of the learned controllers was checked by starting part of the trials in situations different than those used during training. Generalization tests are extremely interesting because interacting with the world, the experience is limited to the portion of the input space directly faced during the exploration. As we will see, using *Simmetries* it is possible to increase the speed of learning allowing a neural approximator to learn a continuous pole-balancing control function in *half* the number of training trials required by RS to learn a policy in which only *two* alternative actions are allowed. The learned controllers also show *very good* generalization performances. The domain knowledge is reported above. It is a coding of: *the goal is to keep the pole balanced; if you bump against the ends of the track or the pole's inclination is greater than a certain angle you fail.* It is encoded by keywords GOAL and FAILURE. The other sections are used to give more information about the behavior desired when the agent is in a particular context (see [1] for details). For the sake of simplicity only the case (THETA>0) is reported (the other being symmetric).

Experiments in the RL framework. Different experiments were carried on using a traditional reinforcement function. They were done for comparison purposes. First of all, RS was tried. The reinforcement function used by this system returns -1 in case of failure and 0 otherwise. The state space is divided in 162 boxes; for each input situation the box containing it is selected and an action is produced according to this selection (see [3]). In RS all the experiments start from situation $\langle 0, 0, 0, 0 \rangle$ and training stops after 100 trials if the goal is not reached. RS learned to balance the pole in a number of trails $n \in [58, 79]$.

Then, I checked if two classical reinforcement functions (one returning -1 for failures and 0 otherwise and the other returning -1 for failure, 1 for success and 0 otherwise) could guide a LRFN in learning to balance a pole *without* using any particular RL technique, i.e. simply using it instead of a teacher. The task is much more difficult than before because a *continuous* function is to be acquired. In both cases the LRFN shows *no* learning performance.

Last and due to the fact that in most of the experimens below the initial situation is different than $\langle 0, 0, 0, 0 \rangle$, RS was started in situations respectively equal to $\langle 0, 0, r, 0 \rangle$ and $\langle r, 0, r, 0 \rangle$, where r stands for a random value. Strangely enough, in case $\langle 0, 0, r, 0 \rangle$ the agent is not able to keep the pole balanced for more than the initial timestep. In the other case, instead, learning takes place but it takes over 100 trials two attempts out of three. At the third attempt it learns in 72 trials.

Experiments in the ISL framework. Due to strategy random generation, typical of the ISL framework, each experiment was repeated up to 5 times. In all experiments the same teaching knowledge and the same initial LRFN were used. However, depending on the antecedent composition rule chosen, the net could be either a FC or a RBFN. A few words are, now, to be spent about the

---

[1] ftp.gte.com.

distribution of the initial situations faced during training and test. Depending on how close a situation is to satisfying the failure condition, we can characterize initial situations by their degree of *difficulty*. Random generation affects only two input variables: x, the cart's position and θ, the pole's inclination. Since θ value is always very close to 0, the difficulty mostly depends on x. Then, for a better evaluation of the results we must take into account the distribution of the initial situations produced w.r.t. this feature.

Table 1. Symmetries off. The columns report: the parameter values (strategy length and γ); the (avg.) first successful trial; the (avg.) successful test trials starting in $\langle 0, 0, r, 0 \rangle$; the (avg.) successful test trials starting in $\langle r, 0, r, 0 \rangle$.

configuration	first success	$\langle 0, 0, r, 0 \rangle$	$\langle r, 0, r, 0 \rangle$
1 step $\gamma = 0.9$	392	0 out of 10	0 out of 10
5 steps $\gamma = 0.9$	114	4.33 out of 10	0.33 out of 10
10 steps $\gamma = 0$	308	4.5 out of 10	1 out of 10
$\gamma = 0.1$	311	0.25 out of 10	0 out of 10
$\gamma = 0.4$	348	0 out of 10	0.66 out of 10
$\gamma = 0.5$	398	8.75 out of 10	2.5 out of 10
$\gamma = 0.9$	304	7.66 out of 10	2 out of 10

To this aim, the domain $[-2.4, 2.4]$ was split in three ranges: $peril = [-2.4, -2.0] \cup [2.0, 2.4]$ $semiperil = [-2.0, -1.6] \cup [1.6, 2.0]$, and $safe = [-1.6, 1.6]$, ordered from the closest to the farthest from failure. The distribution is as follows: 73% of initial situations belong to $safe$, 16% belong to $semiperil$, and the last 11% to $peril$. Since a situation belonging to $peril$ can be non-recoverable (pole falling towards the end of the track), in the worst case (all $peril$ situations non-recoverable) the maximum performance expected is 89%; more frequently, when half of the $peril$ situations cannot be recovered a maximum 94.5% performance can be obtained. However, when the starting situation is of the same type as during training ($\langle 0, 0, r, 0 \rangle$), a 100% performance is expected.

Simmetries was applied both to RBFNs and to FCs. In both cases, the number of trials required dropped considerably w.r.t. training without Symmetries but RBFNs showed a *stabler* performance, i.e. the speed of learning of the same initial controller in different trials all configured in the same way did not vary too much. This is why most of the experiments were done on RBFNs. Their learning behavior was incredibly good. First of all, the speed of learning was always much higher than without Symmetries dropping from about 300 trials (see Table 1) to a value in between the 20th and the 40th trial. Note that these speeds are even higher than those of RS (and let's recall that RS's learning problem is easier and that the number of rules it uses is 162 vs. the 25 rules used here). The second nice feature of the learning process was that in the case in question the pole's oscillation was always reduced very quickly to an almost unperceivable movement. During tests, the controllers did from 9 to 10 successful trials out of 10 in $\langle 0, 0, r, 0 \rangle$ and (in the average) 6 trials out of 10 in $\langle r, 0, r, 0 \rangle$, for an overall 96% of success in $\langle 0, 0, r, 0 \rangle$ and 60% otherwise.

However, using RBFNs one must pay attention to limit the update to the

Table 2. Test performances of the set of controllers saved every 20,000 timesteps.

cntr. saved at timestep	avg. perf. in trial $\langle 0, 0, r, 0 \rangle$	avg. perf. in trial $\langle r, 0, r, 0 \rangle$
30,000	418	397
50,000	397	606
70,000	356	211
90,000	380	280

rules whose activation is high, otherwise *unlearning* may occur. The results reported above were obtained updating rules whose activation was higher than 0.4 but when the threshold is decreased things change. Table 2 shows what happens using a threshold equal to 0.2: during the first successful trial of the training phase, the controller was saved at fixed time intervals obtaining a set of different controllers that were, then, tested as in the previous experiments. All the controllers up to the 10,000th time-step show the same good performances. However, when training passes the 10,000th timestep, the controllers obtained are *no more* able to balance the pole for a long enough time and the average performance decreases a little bit as the time passes (seeTable 2). The cause is *over-fitting*: during the first successful trial, the controller specializes to return lower and lower forces as the oscillation diminishes forgetting what to do when the oscillation is greater. Note, however, that increasing the threshold too much (0.6 in the experiments) prevents the controller from learning because rules are never updated.

4 Related work

In the literature, there are few examples of teaching applied to learning skills. The first and most common way of teaching a task to an agent is to produce a learning set made of examples of good execution *recorded* by a skilled human operator. Each recorded trace is a sequence of pairs $\langle x^t, a^t \rangle$ where x^t is the input situation at time step t, and a^t is the correspondent action applied by the operator. Afterwards, a learning algorithm is applied off-line to induce a skill. This approach is commonly followed when the agent is implemented as a *neural network*. Teaching by examples has explicitly been used in the work by Kaiser [9, 8], and in the Fuzzy Neural methodology [2] and has also been applied in RL by Lin [11]. The main difference w.r.t. the aforementioned approach, is that here each sequence of pairs ends with a reinforcement value. The learner is shown the sequences backwards and uses a RL rule to update an approximation of the value function. Learning by examples shows, however, a couple of drawbacks. The first is that, due to the existing learning rules (such as gradient descent), as long as the learner works on recorded examples only, it is very difficult for it to *outperform* its teacher. Unfortunately, there are applications, especially industrial tasks, in which on one hand, it is not possible to generate examples of *optimal* behavior (the human operator is not a perfect operator); on the other, often it is not even possible to produce enough examples. An alternative consists in giving *hints* to the learner when necessary, as done by Clouse and Utgoff [4]: in the work developed so far, the teacher is supposed to be a *human operator* who monitors the learning process, which, in turn, exploits RL techniques. When the agent is stuck in a situation it is not able to solve the teacher gives it a hint, i.e.

(s)he suggests what to do. The agent applies the action and learning goes on. However, in many tasks a human expert cannot monitor the learning process of the agent because a continuous stream of inputs at a very low perceptive level (forces, speeds, ...) is to be handled quickly.

5 Conclusions

In this paper a novel approach to skill acquisition, named *Soft Teaching*, is proposed; its main characteristic is that, differently than what can be found in the literature, the teaching process is performed in a fully *automatic* way, exploiting some *qualitative knowledge* about both the goal and the domain. Such knowledge is non-operational, i.e. it cannot be used to directly control the agent, but can be used to evaluate the agent's behavior. In this sense, Soft Teaching is inspired by the described HTHL scheme. Among the many different architectures that can be developed within Soft Teaching, the focus is posed on *Indirect Supervised Learning* methods, in which Soft Teaching is used jointly with a supervised learning rule. In particular, a specific ISL technique, named *Symmetries*, was implemented and tested against pole-balancing. Experimental comparisons show that Symmetries allows to obtain very good performances reducing the number of trials necessary to learn a controller of one order of magnitude.

References

1. C. Baroglio. Teaching by shaping. In *the ICML Workshop on learning by induction vs. learning by demonstration*, Tahoe City, CA, USA, 1995.
2. C. Baroglio, A. Giordana, M. Kaiser., M. Nuttin, and R. Piola. Learning controllers for industrial robots. *Machine Learning, Spec. Iss. on Learning Robots*, (23), 1996.
3. A.G. Barto, R.S. Sutton, and C.W. Anderson. Neuronlike adaptive elements that can solve difficult learning prolems. *IEEE Trans. on SMC*, SMC-13:834–836, 1986.
4. J.A. Clouse and P.E. Utgoff. A teaching method for reinforcement learning. In *Proc. of the Machine Learning Conference MLC-92*, pages 92–101, 1992.
5. B. Fritzke. Growing Cell Structures – a self-organized network for unsupervised and supervised learning. *Neural Networks*, 7(9), 1994.
6. V. Gullapalli. A stochastic reinforcement learning algorithm for learning real valued functions. *Neural Networks*, 3:671–692, 1990.
7. K. Hornik, M. Stinchcombe, and H. White. Multilayer feed-forward networks are universal approximators. *Neural Networks*, 2:359–366, 1989.
8. M. Kaiser and J. Kreuziger. Integration of symbolic and connectionist processing to ease robot programming and control. In *ECAI'94 Workshop on Combining Symbolic and Connectionist Processing*, pages 20 – 29, 1994.
9. M. Kaiser and F. Wallner. Using machine learning for enhancing mobile robots' skills. In *IRTICS-93*, 1993.
10. P. Katenkamp. Constructing controllers from examples. Master Thesis, Univ. of Karlsruhe, Germany, 1995.
11. L.J. Lin. Self-improving reactive agents based on reinforcement learning, p lanning and teaching. *Machine Learning*, 8:293–321, 1992.
12. M.A.F. McDonald. Approximate discounted dynamic programming is unreliable. Technical Report 94/6, Dept. of Comp. Sci., Univ. of Western Australia, Oct. 1994.
13. L.X. Wang and J.M. Mendel. Generating fuzzy rules by learning from examples. *IEEE Trans. on SMC*, SMC-22(6):1414–1427, November 1992.
14. C.J.C.H. Watkins and P. Dayan. Technical note: Q-learning. *Machine Learning*, 8:279–292, May 1992.

Integrated Learning and Planning Based on Truncating Temporal Differences

Paweł Cichosz

Institute of Electronics Fundamentals
Warsaw University of Technology
Nowowiejska 15/19, 00-665 Warsaw, Poland
phone: +48-22/660-77-18, fax: +48-22/25-23-00
cichosz@ipe.pw.edu.pl
http://www.ipe.pw.edu.pl/~cichosz

Abstract. Reinforcement learning systems learn to act in an uncertain environment by executing actions and observing their long-term effects. A large number of time steps may be required before this trial-and-error process converges to a satisfactory policy. It is highly desirable that the number of experiences needed by the system to learn to perform its task be minimized, particularly if making errors costs much. One approach to achieve this goal is to use hypothetical experiences, which requires some additional computation, but may reduce the necessary number of much more costly real experiences. This well-known idea of augmenting reinforcement learning by planning is revisited in this paper in the context of truncated TD(λ), or TTD, a simple computational technique which allows reinforcement learning algorithms based on the methods of temporal differences to learn considerably faster with essentially no additional computational expense. Two different ways of combining TTD with planning are proposed which make it possible to benefit from $\lambda > 0$ in both the learning and planning processes. The algorithms are evaluated experimentally on a family of grid path-finding tasks and shown to indeed yield a considerable reduction of the number of real interactions with the environment necessary to converge, as well as an improvement of scaling properties.

1 Introduction

A *reinforcement learning* (RL) system at each step of discrete time observes the current *state* of its environment and executes an *action*. Then it receives a *reinforcement*, or reward value, and a state transition takes place. Reinforcement values provide a measure of the quality of actions executed by the system. The objective of learning is to identify a *decision policy* (i.e., a state-action mapping) that maximizes the reinforcement values received by the learner *in the long term*. A typical performance measure is the expected total discounted sum of reinforcement it receives during its lifetime in continuous learning tasks, or during a trial in episodic tasks. Rewards from subsequent time steps are multiplied by the subsequent powers of a *discount factor* $0 \leq \gamma \leq 1$, which, for positive γ, makes the learner take into account not only the immediate, but also the delayed consequences of its actions, and, for $\gamma < 1$, to consider the rewards received soon more important that those from the far future. This involves the temporal credit assignment problem, commonly solved using algorithms based on the methods of *temporal differences* (TD) [11].

The key problem with the existing reinforcement learning algorithms is that they usually converge slowly, especially for tasks with large state spaces. A considerable part of current RL research is devoted to various possible ways of overcoming this painful deficiency. Of those, it is particularly worthwhile to mention state generalization by the use of function approximators [13,3], hierarchical RL architectures [7,6], and integrating learning with planning [12,9]. The last approach is investigated in this paper in a new, promising context. Novel hybrid learning and planning algorithms are proposed, obtained by combining the frameworks of the Dyna architecture [12] and of the TTD procedure [2]. These two are briefly described in the next section.

2 Background

The Dyna architecture is a generic instantiation of the idea of combining reinforcement learning with planning by means of learning from hypothetical experiences. The TTD procedure is a simple computational technique that allows one to efficiently implement TD-based reinforcement learning algorithms in their $TD(\lambda > 0)$ versions, which usually converge faster than the simplest $TD(0)$ ones. The discussion of these two foundations for this work is limited to the most essential points. The reader may refer to the cited literature for more details.

2.1 Dyna Architecture

The basic idea of Sutton's Dyna framework [12] is that one can reduce the number of interactions with the "real world" necessary to learn an acceptable policy by introducing a number of hypothetical interactions with a model, which predicts the consequences of the learner's actions in different states. The model is usually not known *a priori* and thus it is learned during the regular operation of the learning system. Hypothetical experiences are processed by essentially the same reinforcement learning algorithm as real ones. Learning from experiences generated by the model is referred to as planning.

The generic Dyna algorithm is shown in Figure 1, as a sequence of operations performed at each time step. The current real experience, $\langle x_t, a_t, r_t, x_{t+1} \rangle$, is used to update the model in Step 4 and then passed to the underlying reinforcement learning algorithm, referred to as $\mathbb{RL}$. Additionally, a number of hypothetical experiences are processed, generated by applying a (forwards) model to different state-action pairs.

The operation written as $\mathbb{FM}(x, a)$ is intended to return a pair (r, x') such that executing action a in state x is predicted to result in a transition to state x' and a reinforcement value of r. Of course a model must be sufficiently accurate to

---

At each time step t:

1. observe current state x_t;
2. $a_t := \text{select\_action}(x_t)$;
3. perform action a_t; observe new state x_{t+1} and immediate reinforcement r_t;
4. $\text{update\_model}(x_t, a_t, r_t, x_{t+1})$;
5. $\text{RL}(x_t, a_t, r_t, x_{t+1})$;
6. repeat K times
   (a) choose a hypothetical state x;
   (b) $a := \text{select\_action}(x)$;
   (c) $(r, x') := \text{FM}(x, a)$;
   (d) $\text{RL}(x, a, r, x')$.

Fig. 1. The generic Dyna algorithm.

be useful, and a very poor model may be harmful. The learner may be supplied with some initial model as a part of its background "innate" knowledge. Each real experience may be used to update the model and to verify its reliability. Planning should be performed only if the current model is found to be reliable—in a practical implementation of the algorithm from Figure 1, Step 6 should be probably conditioned by the reliability status of the model.

In order to instantiate the Dyna architecture, one has to select its three major components: model representation and learning algorithms, a strategy for choosing hypothetical experiences, and a reinforcement learning algorithm. The task of learning a model is a typical *supervised learning* task and there are several methods that can be applied to accomplish it. The proper choice of one of them depends, first of all, on the state and action representation. Peng and Williams [9], and independently Moore and Atkeson [8] developed heuristic planning strategies for deciding which hypothetical experiences are most promising and should be presented to the learner. The essential idea of these heuristics is to assign a priority number to each of candidate experiences, based on the magnitude of the reinforcement learning error value recently used to update some of its possible successor states, and to maintain a priority queue of experiences. Then each time when a planning step is to be performed, a promising hypothetical experience may be extracted from the queue. This simple idea is reused by one of the algorithms proposed later in this paper.

2.2 Q-Learning

The Q-learning algorithm [14] is currently the most popular TD-based reinforcement learning algorithm, used also in this work. It learns a Q-function, assigning to each state-action pair (x, a) an estimate of the cumulative discounted sum of future rewards received after executing action a in state x and performing optimally thereafter. The Q-learning update rule, in its generic TD(0) version, may be written as follows:

$$\text{update}^{\beta}\left(Q,\ x_t, a_t,\ r_t + \gamma \max_a Q(x_{t+1}, a) - Q(x_t, a_t)\right), \tag{1}$$

which is the notation used throughout this paper to express that $Q(x_t, a_t)$ is updated using an error value of $r_t + \gamma \max_a Q(x_{t+1}, a) - Q(x_t, a_t)$, to a degree controlled by a step-size parameter β.

The implementation of the update operation given by Equation 1 depends on the function representation method used. For a simple look-up table representation, used in this paper, it simply consists in adding $\beta \Delta$, where Δ is the error value, to the value stored in the appropriate table entry.

Another issue that needs more specification in a practical implementation is how actions to perform at each time step are selected. In the experiments presented in this paper a standard Boltzmann distribution-based stochastic strategy is used, with the selection probability of action a in state x proportional to $\exp(Q(x, a)/T)$, where $T > 0$ is a temperature parameter, adjusting the amount of randomness. This action selection mechanism is known not to perform very well in many cases, but it keeps the algorithms experimented with as generic as possible.

2.3 TTD Procedure

The TTD procedure [2,4] allows one to implement TD-based reinforcement learning algorithms in their TD($\lambda > 0$) versions without conceptually appealing, but computationally demanding eligibility traces [1,10,4]. Only its particular instantiation for the Q-learning algorithm is discussed below, but modifications for other RL algorithms are straightforward [2].

TTD relies on applying, at time t, the following update operation to the state and action from time $t - m + 1$:

$$\text{update}^{\beta}\left(Q,\ x_{t-m+1}, a_{t-m+1},\ z_{t-m+1}^{\lambda,m} - Q(x_{t-m+1}, a_{t-m+1})\right), \tag{2}$$

where $z_t^{\lambda,m}$ is the TTD(λ, m) return for time t, defined as

$$z_t^{\lambda,m} = \sum_{k=0}^{m-2} (\gamma\lambda)^k \left[r_{t+k} + \gamma(1 - \lambda) \max_a Q(x_{t+k+1}, a)\right]$$
$$+ (\gamma\lambda)^{m-1} \left[r_{t+m-1} + \gamma \max_a Q(x_{t+m}, a)\right]. \tag{3}$$

This can be implemented by maintaining an m-step experience buffer, at time t storing records of x_{t-k}, a_{t-k}, r_{t-k}, and $\max_a Q(x_{t-k+1}, a)$ for $k = 0, 1, \ldots, m - 1$. For convenience, the corresponding buffer elements are designated by $x_{[k]}$, $a_{[k]}$, $r_{[k]}$, and $u_{[k]}$, respectively. Under this notational convention, the Q-learning version of the TTD(λ, m) procedure is presented in Figure 2, as a sequence of operations performed to process an experience $\langle x, a, r, x' \rangle$. A pair of square brackets appears as an additional argument of the procedure to indicate the indexing mechanism used to access the experience buffer.

---

ttd_procedure$^{\lambda,m}(x, a, r, x', [\,])$:

1. $x_{[0]} := x$; $a_{[0]} := a$; $r_{[0]} := r$; $u_{[0]} := \max_{a'} Q(x', a')$;
2. $z := \text{ttd\_return}^\lambda([m-1])$;
3. update$^\beta \left(Q, \; x_{[m-1]}, a_{[m-1]}, \; z - Q(x_{[m-1]}, a_{[m-1]})\right)$;
4. shift the indices of the experience buffer;
5. return z.

Fig. 2. The TTD procedure.

The operation of Step 2, written as ttd_return$^\lambda([m-1])$, computes the
TTD(λ, m) return for time $t - m + 1$, i.e., for the least recent experience stored
in the buffer (designated by $[m-1]$). This can be performed either iteratively,
based directly on the definition of TTD returns, or in an incremental manner,
which is particularly efficient. The appropriate algorithms are described in detail
in the existing TTD literature [2,4].

3 Combination of TTD and Dyna

The generic Dyna architecture, as presented in Figure 1, does not make any
explicit assumptions about the reinforcement learning algorithm used, except
that it performs updates based on quadruples consisting of a state, an action,
a resulting reward value, and a successor state. In particular, the architecture
might be used in the same way for TD-based algorithms, regardless of whether
they learn with TD(0) or TD($\lambda > 0$). However, while the learning process may
benefit from positive λ as usual, it does not have any effect for the planning
process, since hypothetical experiences do not form a temporal sequence. This
section presents simple modifications of Dyna, based on preliminary ideas first
formulated in [5], which use sequences of hypothetical experiences, and thus
allow the planning process to benefit from $\lambda > 0$. They rely on applying the
TTD procedure to hypothetical experiences similarly as it is applied to real
ones.

3.1 Forwards and Backwards Planning with TTD

The most straightforward approach to applying TTD effectively to hypothetical
experiences, if they form a temporal sequence, is to process them in exactly the
same way as real experiences, using a separate n-element hypothetical experience
buffer. Similarly as in the generic Dyna architecture, a forwards model is used to
predict for a state-action pair a corresponding reward value and successor state.
Another way of combining Dyna with TTD is to use for planning the TTD
returns computed during the regular operation of the procedure (when running
for real experiences), rather than maintain a separate experience buffer and perform TTD for hypothetical experiences separately. When, during regular TTD

learning at time t, the TTD return for time $t - m + 1$ is computed, it contains meaningful information not only for x_{t-m+1}, but for its possible predecessors, their predecessors, etc. For this idea to be practically useful, a backwards model is needed, that would return for a state x' a triple of $\langle x, a, r \rangle$ such that performing action a in state x is predicted to result in a reinforcement value of r and a successor state x'. The operation of such a model will be referred to as $\mathbb{BM}(x')$.

3.2 TTDyna Algorithm

The two ideas outlined above may be applied together, using two models, a forwards and a backwards one (or a single model providing the functionality of both). The resulting algorithm, called TTDyna, performs one regular TTD update for the current real experiences at each time step, and afterwards it processes several hypothetical experiences in the forwards planning and backwards planning mode. Figure 3 presents the details.

At each time step t:

1. observe current state x_t;
2. $a_t := \text{select\_action}(x_t)$;
3. perform action a_t; observe new state x_{t+1} and immediate reinforcement r_t;
4. $\text{update\_model}(x_t, a_t, r_t, x_{t+1})$;
5. $z := \text{ttd\_procedure}^{\lambda, m}(x_t, a_t, r_t, x_{t+1}, [\,])$;
6. $F := 0$; while $F < N_f$ do
   (a) $F := F + 1$; if $t = 0$ or $f > n_f$ then $f := 0$;
   (b) if $f = 0$ then
       choose a hypothetical state x;
   (c) $a := \text{select\_action}(x)$;
   (d) if $(r, x') := \mathbb{FM}(x, a)$ then
          i. $\text{ttd\_procedure}^{\lambda, n}(x, a, r, x', \{\,\})$;
          ii. $x := x'$; $f := f + 1$;
       else $f := 0$.
7. $B := 0$; $b := 0$; while $B < N_b$ do
   (a) $B := B + 1$; if $b > n_b$ then $b := 0$;
   (b) if $b = 0$ then
       $z' := z$; $x' := x_{[m-1]}$;
   (c) if $(x, a, r) := \mathbb{BM}(x')$ then
          i. $u' := \max_{a'} Q(x', a')$; $z' := r + \gamma(\lambda z' + (1 - \lambda)u')$;
          ii. $\text{update}^{\beta}\left(Q, x, a, z' - Q(x, a)\right)$;
          iii. $x' := x$;
       else $b := 0$.

Fig. 3. The TTDyna algorithm.

Steps 5 and 6(d)i refer to the basic TTD algorithm presented in Figure 2, the former for the current real experience, and the latter for a hypothetical experience from the currently processed sequence. As already said above, TTD uses a separate experience buffer for hypothetical experiences, which is denoted using curly braces { } instead of square brackets [ ]. The forwards planning process is controlled by two parameters: N_f is the maximum number of hypothetical experiences to use at a time step, and n_f is the maximum length of a hypothetical experience sequence. If $n_f < N_f$, more than one hypothetical sequence is used at one time step. The sequence started at time t may be continued at subsequent time steps.

The actual number of hypothetical experiences processed during forwards planning and the length of individual sequences may be different from N_f and n_f, respectively, depending on whether the model succeeds at predicting the consequences of state-action pairs it is requested to. The $\mathrm{FM}(x, a)$ operation is assumed to return false whenever the model is unable to give a reliable prediction of a reward and successor state resulting from performing action a in state x. On success, the model is assumed to return a (possibly different on each call) reward and successor state for a given state-action pair. A simple implementation of such a model, used in the experiments presented later in this paper, will be described in Section 3.3.

The backwards planning part of the algorithm performs at each time step a maximum of N_b updates for hypothetical experiences, which may form a sequence with the maximum length $n_b \leq N_b$. Each sequence starts from the (just updated) state $x_{[m-1]}$ and goes backwards in time, along its possible predecessors. Given the TTD return for $x_{[m-1]}$ (assumed to be returned by the call to the TTD procedure in Step 5), their TTD returns may be computed iteratively, as demonstrated by Step 7(c)i. The backwards model is assumed to return false when it is unable to produce a new reliable prediction, and on success to return a (possibly different on each call) state-action-reward triple for the hypothetical successor state for which it is invoked.

3.3 Model Implementation

The algorithm described above strongly depends on model implementation. This in turn is a hard problem itself and deserves separate, extensive studies, which are beyond the scope of this preliminary work. In the experiments presented in this chapter, similarly as for function representation, we use a look-up table model representation, although it may be hypothesized that some generalizing function approximators that have proved themselves useful for the former purpose, may turn out to be useful for the latter as well.

For a forward model, a separate look-up table is used for every action, assuming a discrete action space. Each table entry corresponds to one environment state and stores a predicted reward value r and an estimate p of the occurrence likelihood of each state as a successor state (which also assumes a discrete state space). The operation of model update:

$$\mathrm{update\_model}(x, a, r, x') \tag{4}$$

may be then implemented by

$$FM_a[x].r := (1 - \alpha)FM_a[x].r + \alpha r \qquad (5)$$

and

$$FM_a[x].p_y := \begin{cases} (1 - \alpha)FM_a[x].p_y + \alpha & \text{if } y = x' \\ (1 - \alpha)FM_a[x].p_y & \text{otherwise,} \end{cases} \qquad (6)$$

where α is a step-size parameter, FM_a denotes the look-up table corresponding to action a, brackets are used to indicate for which state the table entry is referred to, and dots to designate access to the two components of each entry. The successor state x', returned by $FM(x, a)$, may be then chosen based on $FM_a[x].p$ either deterministically, as $\arg\max_y FM_a[x].p_y$ (this is the approach adopted in the experiments presented later in this paper), or stochastically, which may be appropriate if there are multiple possible successor states for a given state-action pair.

To predict backwards, a single look-up table may be used, containing, for every state, the corresponding likelihood estimates for the predecessor state and action, and a reward value. The update operations for states and rewards are analogous to those presented above for a forwards model:

$$BM[x'].p_y := \begin{cases} (1 - \alpha)BM[x'].p_y + \alpha & \text{if } y = x \\ (1 - \alpha)BM[x'].p_y & \text{otherwise,} \end{cases} \qquad (7)$$

and

$$BM[x'].r := (1 - \alpha)BM[x].r + \alpha r. \qquad (8)$$

For actions the update operation is a straightforward analog of Equation 6:

$$BM[x'].q_b := \begin{cases} (1 - \alpha)BM[x'].q_b + \alpha & \text{if } b = a \\ (1 - \alpha)BM[x'].q_b & \text{otherwise,} \end{cases} \qquad (9)$$

where q is an estimate of the occurrence likelihood of each action in a preceding experience.

This is indeed a very simple approach to model learning and it has many obvious deficiencies. First, similarly as a tabular function representation, it is only applicable to relatively small tasks. Second, and maybe even more important, in the backwards case it provides no clear way of dealing with states for which there may be multiple predecessor state-action pairs. While a forwards model with such a limitation is still sufficiently powerful for deterministic tasks, for a backwards model it is much more painful. There are some relatively simple possibilities of overcoming these drawbacks, at least in part. One could deal with continuous states by applying the ideas which have already shown themselves useful for function representation in reinforcement learning, i.e., by replacing look-up tables with some kinds of function approximators. In particular, it looks possible to use CMAC-like sparse coarse-coded look-up tables to implement continuous-state models. To allow multiple predecessor state-action pairs for a given state x' in a backwards model, it might be reasonable to first select (e.g., stochastically) a predecessor state x, based on the estimated probability distribution $BM[x'].p$, and then select an action that, if executed in state x, can be predicted to cause a transition to x'. If there are relatively few actions, which is often the case, one could simply make a forward prediction for x and each possible action, to see whether it can bring the system to state x'. These possible extensions have been, however, postponed for future work, so that this work focuses exclusively on the usefulness of a particular way of using models for reinforcement learning rather than on the usefulness of particular models themselves.

4 TTD Sweeping

Unlike the two TTDyna algorithms, the approach described in this section is intended not to require any models, except for the very simplest one: the memory of a number of past real experiences. This eliminates the problem of choosing an appropriate model representation and learning method and thus may be sometimes more attractive, if it turned out to give similarly good performance.

The basic idea of TTD sweeping, or TTD-SW for short, is to store a relatively large number M of past experiences in the TTD experience buffer, which is made much longer than m, say, several thousand steps instead of one or two dozens. The TTD procedure still operates as usual, on a fraction of the buffer corresponding to the most recent m experiences, but additionally *TTD sweeps* are performed for some other regions of the buffer. A sweep for a buffer region delimited by $k_1 < k_2$ consists in performing sequentially updates for experiences $[k]$, $k = k_1, k_1 + 1, \ldots, k_2$, according to:

$$\text{update}^\beta \left(Q, \; x_{[k]}, a_{[k]}, \; z_{[k]}^{\lambda, k-k_1+1} - Q(x_{[k]}, a_{[k]}) \right), \tag{10}$$

where $z^{\lambda, k-k_1+1}$ denotes the $(k - k_1 + 1)$-step TTD return for experience $[k]$. Figure 4 shows how this process is exactly organized.

Whenever an update of the Q-function for experience $[k]$ is performed, either during regular learning or sweeping, two additional operations take place. First, $u_{[k+1]}$ is updated to reflect the new Q-values for $x_{[k]}$. Second, experience $[k + \mu]$ (which must have been observed μ time steps before experience $[k]$) becomes a candidate for sweeping and its index is inserted into a queue, possibly with some priority value, e.g., depending on the magnitude of the error value used for the update. The maximum queue length, designated by q, limits the number of high-priority experiments which are candidates for further updates.

At each time step a maximum of N_s sweeps are performed, for buffer regions determined as follows. An experience $[s]$ is taken out from the queue. We still assume that the buffer's indices are shifted appropriately at each time step, so

At each time step t:

1. observe current state x_t;
2. $a_t := \text{select\_action}(x_t)$;
3. perform action a_t; observe new state x_{t+1} and immediate reinforcement r_t;
4. $\text{ttd\_procedure}^{\lambda,m}(x_t, a_t, r_t, x_{t+1}, [\ ])$;
5. $u_{[m]} := \max_a Q(x_{[m-1]}, a)$;
6. $\text{to\_queue}([m - 1 + \mu])$;
7. repeat N_s times
   (a) $[s] := \text{from\_queue}()$; $\hat{\mu} := \text{correct}(\mu)$;
   (b) $z := u_{[s-\hat{\mu}+1]}$;
   (c) for $k = s - \hat{\mu} + 1, s - \hat{\mu} + 2, \ldots, s$ do
      i. $z := r_{[k]} + \gamma(\lambda z + (1 - \lambda)u_{[k]})$;
      ii. $\text{update}^{\beta}(Q, x_{[k]}, a_{[k]}, z - Q(x_{[k]}, a_{[k]}))$;
      iii. $u_{[k+1]} := \max_a Q(x_{[k]}, a)$;
      iv. $\text{to\_queue}([k + \mu])$.

Fig. 4. The TTD sweeping algorithm.

that [0] always refers to the current real experience. Therefore the implementation must provide an appropriate index translation mechanism, to ensure that the index value retrieved from the queue points to the same experience buffer element which was pointed to when the corresponding entry was inserted to the queue. The maximum sweep length is μ, but it may be reduced, which is written $\hat{\mu} = \text{correct}(\mu)$, to ensure that experiences $[s - \hat{\mu}]$ through $[s]$ do belong to the same sequence and that sweeping does not interfere with the regular TTD operation, which involves the first m buffer elements, i.e., $s - \hat{\mu} + 1 \geq m$. Then a sweep is performed for a buffer region delimited by $s - \hat{\mu} + 1$ and s.

5 Experimental Results

In this section the results of preliminary experiments with the algorithms proposed above are presented, designed so as to verify the usefulness of their most generic versions. The performance of the TTDyna and TTD sweeping approaches to planning are compared to each other, as well to the performance of their TD(0) versions and of TD(0) and TTD($\lambda > 0$) without planning.

5.1 Learning Tasks

Three simple grid path-finding tasks, differing in the grid size, are used for the experiments. Figure 5 illustrates the 10×10 grid world which is the basis for these tasks. The state representation supplied to the learning agent is simply the number of the cell it is currently in. At each step the agent can choose any of the four allowed actions of going North, South, East, or West. At the beginning of each trial the agent is placed in its fixed initial location. A trial ends when the agent reaches the goal location. The agent receives a reinforcement value of −1 at all steps except when it enters the goal cell, when the reinforcement is 0.

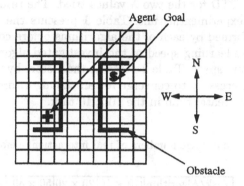

Fig. 5. The grid environment.

Apart from the basic 10 × 10 task, more difficult 20 × 20 and 50 × 50 tasks are used, obtained by dividing each cell (including the barrier and goal cells) of the environment shown in Figure 5 into, respectively, $2^2 = 4$ and $5^2 = 25$ equal smaller cells. The agent's starting location is at $(2, 6)$ for the 10 × 10 task, at $(4, 12)$ for the 20 × 20 task, and at $(12, 32)$ for the 50 × 50 task, assuming that the coordinates count from 0 and start from the left upper corner. The shortest path to any goal cell for the three tasks consists, respectively, of 20 steps, 36 steps, and 84 steps.

5.2 Experimental Design and Results

The following algorithms were applied to each of the three grid tasks:

- the TTD procedure with $\lambda = 0$ and $\lambda = 0.5$,
- TTDyna with $\lambda = 0$ and $\lambda = 0.5$,
- TTD sweeping with $\lambda = 0$ and $\lambda = 0.5$.

The TTD procedure used $m = 25$. For all algorithms γ was set to 0.95 and T to 0.01. These values appeared reasonable based on prior work with TTD [2,4]. Additionally, for TTDyna we used $N_f = 10$, $n_f = 5$, and $N_b = n_b = 5$, and for TTD sweeping $M = 500$, $N_s = 3$, $\mu = 8$, and a priority queue of length $q = 25$. A number of preliminary runs with different settings of these planning parameters were carried out and the above were found to be roughly best, but not crucial for successful performance. Both the algorithms performed similarly for a wide range of parameter values. The step-size parameters used for updating the Q-function were equal 0.5 for $\lambda = 0$ and 0.125 for $\lambda = 0.5$, the values optimized in a series of preliminary runs. Twice larger or smaller β appeared to yield only slightly worse results. Model update operations for TTDyna, implemented according to

Equations 5 and 6, used $\alpha = 1$, which is a natural choice for deterministic tasks. The Q-values were initialized to -5 for the 10×10 task, -7 for the 20×20 task, and -10 for the 50×50 task, to provide a reliable initial guess.

Figure 6 compares the learning curves obtained by using TTDyna, TTD-SW, and "pure" TTD for the two λ values tried. The results are averaged over 25 independent experimental runs. Table 1 presents the total number of real interactions performed by each of the algorithms before convergence. To better illustrate how the learning speed of the investigated algorithms scales up with the size of the state space, Table 2 presents the factors by which the numbers of steps and trials necessary to converge for all the algorithms in the 20×20 and 50×50 tasks are greater than in the 10×10 task.

Table 1. The average numbers of real interactions before convergence.

Task/Algorithm	10×10	20×20	50×50 task
TTD(0)	22,381	132,971	1,938,440
TTD(0.5)	18,626	114,651	1,821,950
TTDyna(0)	2753	18,964	264,970
TTDyna(0.5)	3303	20,063	247,705
TTD-SW(0)	7404	52,470	716,453
TTD-SW(0.5)	9885	59,039	667,253

Table 2. The factors by which the numbers of steps and trials before convergence for the 20×20 and 50×50 tasks are greater than for the 10×10 task.

Task/Algorithm	20×20		50×50	
	Steps	Trials	Steps	Trials
TTD(0)	5.95	3.15	86.5	22.0
TTD(0.5)	6.2	2.45	98.0	16.0
TTDyna(0)	6.9	2.8	97.5	18.0
TTDyna(0.5)	6.05	1.65	75.5	8.3
TTD-SW(0)	7.05	2.75	98.0	16.5
TTD-SW(0.5)	5.95	2.2	67.0	12.0

We can observe that

- without planning, $\lambda > 0$ considerably improves convergence speed,
- for $\lambda = 0$, both TTDyna and TTD-SW result in much faster learning than for "pure" TD(0),
- $\lambda > 0$ gives a significant further learning speed improvement for TTD-SW,
- unlike in the 10×10 task, for the larger tasks the learning speed of TTDyna improves for positive λ,

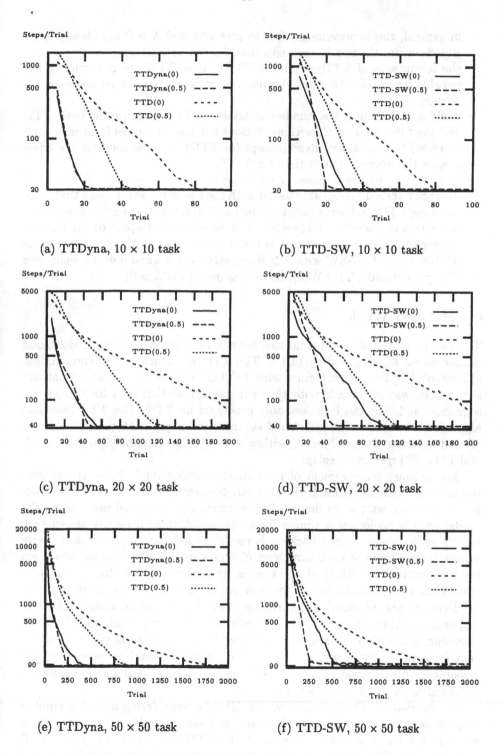

(a) TTDyna, 10 × 10 task

(b) TTD-SW, 10 × 10 task

(c) TTDyna, 20 × 20 task

(d) TTD-SW, 20 × 20 task

(e) TTDyna, 50 × 50 task

(f) TTD-SW, 50 × 50 task

Fig. 6. Learning curves for TTD, TTDyna, and TTD-SW.

- in general, the improvements due to planning and $\lambda > 0$ are clearly more significant for the two larger tasks than for the 10×10 one,
- the advantages of TTDyna and TTD-SW over TTD are particularly noticeable when one compares the number of (real) time steps necessary to converge,
- while $\lambda > 0$ reduces the number of trials until convergence for both TTD and the two planning algorithms, it does not always reduce (and may even increase) the number of steps (except for TTD), because the first few trials are, on the average, longer than for $\lambda = 0$,
- with respect to the number of trials necessary to converge, TTDyna and TTD-SW scale up noticeably better with the size of the state space than non-planning TTD, and using positive λ further improves their scaling properties,
- the effects of planning and positive λ on scaling with respect to the number of steps necessary to converge is not quite clear, but the combination of TTDyna and TTD-SW with $\lambda > 0$ appears to give some improvement over TTDyna(0) and TTD-SW(0), as well as over TTD($\lambda > 0$).

6 Related Work

The two presented algorithms borrow heavily from prior work on model-based reinforcement learning and on TD(λ). The TTDyna algorithm is a combination of Sutton's [12] Dyna architecture with TTD [2]. Its novelty consists essentially in a special way of using hypothetical experiences, so that they form temporal sequences and thus can be reasonably processed by TTD. The TTD sweeping algorithm is related to the *prioritized sweeping* technique of Moore and Atkeson [8] and a similar *Queue-Dyna* algorithm of Peng and Williams [9] on one hand, and Lin's [6] *experience replay*.

The primary improvement of prioritized sweeping (and Queue-Dyna) over the original Dyna algorithm is that hypothetical experiences to process are chosen in a special way, according to their heuristically estimated usefulness. The model used is no longer a simple forwards model: it additionally stores each state's predecessors, as in a backwards model. States have also certain priority values assigned and at each time step K states with the highest priorities are used to generate hypothetical experiences by applying the model. Whenever a state's utility is updated with a large error value, the priorities of its possible predecessors are increased appropriately (to a degree proportional to the corresponding estimated transition probabilities). This idea is adopted by TTD sweeping, although used in a very simplified form: no model is maintained, except for a memory of a number of past time steps. It would be interesting and possibly useful to extend the TTD-SW algorithm, so that it handles multiple potential predecessors of each state as well.

In experience replay, as used by Lin [6], after completing a trial a number of past experiences are processed in the reversed chronological order. This is actually the same as a single sweep of the TTD-SW algorithm. Thus, TTD sweeping is in effect a combination of experience replay with a Dyna-like control strategy, which determines which experiences it is most useful to replay.

7 Conclusion

This paper investigated some possible ways of implementing the well-known idea of augmenting reinforcement learning by model-based planning in a more effective way. The motivation was to make the planning process benefit from $TD(\lambda > 0)$ in a similar way as learning. The TTD procedure, which implements $TD(\lambda)$ without eligibility traces, was found particularly useful for this purpose.

The presented experimental results show that the two proposed techniques indeed reduce the necessary number of real experiences necessary of converge by a large factor, at least several times. TTDyna appeared to perform better than TTD-SW, though an attractive feature of the latter is that it does not need any explicit models. However, given more carefully designed and reliable models than the simple ones used in the experiments, the advantages of TTDyna are likely to be even more evident.

The learning speed improvement due to TTDyna and TTD-SW is particularly noticeable in comparison to $TD(0)$ without planning. It is apparently less spectacular in comparison to $TD(\lambda > 0)$ without planning, because $\lambda > 0$ alone gives much faster learning. However, when one compares the number of (real) time steps before convergence rather than the number of trials, it turns out that the effects of planning are definitely more significant than the effects of positive λ. For the planning using $\lambda > 0$ appeared not to give any further reduction of the number of steps necessary to converge, because the first few trials, before any meaningful Q-values have been learned, were relatively longer than for $\lambda = 0$, which is certainly somewhat disappointing. This effect may be due to the rather *ad hoc* settings of other parameters and the primitive action selection mechanism, and thus there is a chance that it will be eventually overcome. Positive λ was found to be still useful for the planning process anyway, as it may give some further reduction of the necessary number of trials, particularly for large tasks. In many cases minimizing the number of trials may be equally or more important as minimizing the number of steps. It is therefore important to note that, with respect to the number of trials necessary to converge, the proposed algorithms appear to scale better with the size of the state space than TTD without planning, particularly for $\lambda > 0$.

It must be stressed that the reported results have been obtained by using the most generic versions of the algorithms. It seems likely that much greater performance gain can be obtained by using better model representation methods for TTDyna and better TTD sweeping heuristics. This is what should be verified by future work.

Acknowledgements

The author gratefully acknowledges the financial support from the Polish Committee for Scientific Research under Grant 8 T11C 04611 and from the Foundation for Polish Science.

72

References

1. A. G. Barto, R. S. Sutton, and C. W. Anderson. Neuronlike adaptive elements that can solve difficult learning control problems. *IEEE Transactions on Systems, Man, and Cybernetics*, 13:835–846, 1983.
2. P. Cichosz. Truncating temporal differences: On the efficient implementation of TD(λ) for reinforcement learning. *Journal of Artificial Intelligence Research*, 2:287–318, 1995.
3. P. Cichosz. Truncated temporal differences with function approximation: Successful examples using CMAC. In *Proceedings of the Thirteenth European Symposium on Cybernetics and Systems Research (EMCSR-96)*, 1996.
4. P. Cichosz and J. J. Mulawka. Fast and efficient reinforcement learning with truncated temporal differences. In *Proceedings of the Twelfth International Conference on Machine Learning (ML-95)*. Morgan Kaufmann, 1995.
5. P. Cichosz and J. J. Mulawka. Integrated architectures for learning, planning, and reacting based on approximating TD(λ). In *Proceedings of the First International Workshop on Intelligent Adaptive Systems (IAS-95)*, 1995.
6. Long-Ji Lin. *Reinforcement Learning for Robots Using Neural Networks*. PhD thesis, School of Computer Science, Carnegie-Mellon University, January 1993.
7. S. Mahadevan and J. Connell. Automatic programming of behavior-based robots using reinforcement learning. *Artificial Intelligence*, 55:311–365, 1992.
8. A. W. Moore and C. G. Atkeson. Prioritized sweeping: Reinforcement learning with less memory and less time. *Machine Learning*, 13:103–130, 1993.
9. J. Peng and R. J. Williams. Efficient learning and planning within the Dyna framework. In *Proceedings of the Second International Conference on Simulation of Adaptive Behavior*. The MIT Press, 1993.
10. R. S. Sutton. *Temporal Credit Assignment in Reinforcement Learning*. PhD thesis, Department of Computer and Information Science, University of Massachusetts, 1984.
11. R. S. Sutton. Learning to predict by the methods of temporal differences. *Machine Learning*, 3:9–44, 1988.
12. R. S. Sutton. Integrated architectures for learning, planning, and reacting based on approximating dynamic programming. In *Proceedings of the Seventh International Conference on Machine Learning (ML-90)*. Morgan Kaufmann, 1990.
13. R. S. Sutton. Generalization in reinforcement learning: Successful examples using sparse coarse coding. In *Advances in Neural Information Processing Systems 8*. Morgan Kaufmann, 1996.
14. C. J. C. H. Watkins. *Learning from Delayed Rewards*. PhD thesis, King's College, Cambridge, 1989.

θ-subsumption for Structural Matching

Luc De Raedt[1] and Peter Idestam-Almquist[2] and Gunther Sablon[1]

[1] Department of Computer Science, Katholieke Universiteit Leuven
Celestijnenlaan 200A, B-3001 Heverlee, Belgium
[2] Department of Computer and Systems Sciences, Stockholm University
Electrum 230, S-164 40 Kista, Sweden

Abstract. Structural matching, originally introduced by Steven Vere, implements and formalizes the notion of a "most specific generalisation" of two productions, possibly in the presence of a background theory. Despite various studies in the mid-seventies and early eighties, several problems remained. These include the use of background knowledge, the non-uniqueness of most specific generalisations, and handling in-equalities. We show how Gordon Plotkin's notions of "least general generalisation" and "relative least general generalisation" defined on clauses can be adapted for use in structural matching such that the remaining problems disappear. Defining clauses as universally quantified disjunctions of literals and productions as existentially quantified conjunctions of literals, it is shown that the lattice on clauses imposed by θ-subsumption is order-isomorphic to the lattice on productions needed for structural matching.

1   Introduction

In the early seventies, Gordon Plotkin [18, 19], introduced a notion of θ-subsumption between different clauses (i.e., universally quantified disjunctions of literals). In 1971, Plotkin [20] extended θ-subsumption into relative θ-subsumption with regard to a background theory. Now, θ-subsumption and relative θ-subsumption are the basic notions of generality employed by many inductive logic programming (ILP) systems, cf., e.g., Golem [16], Claudien [3], FOIL [21].

In the mid seventies, inspired by Plotkin, Steven Vere [23] studied the problem of generality between productions (i.e., existentially quantified conjunctions of literals). More specificially, he analyzed the issues involved in computing maximally specific generalizations of productions. In later work [24, 25], this notion was extended in order to enable the use of background knowledge. The notion of a maximally specific generalization is of central importance to the field of concept-learning, as many concept-learning systems repeatedly compute the maximally specific generalizations of their examples. Despite the fact that the popular field of inductive logic programming employs clauses (and Vere employs productions), we believe that productions are still a powerfull and interesting representation for concept-learning. This is confirmed by the fact that several recent learning systems still employ productions (e.g. [1, 7]). Furthermore, the inductive logic programming setting known under the name of *learning from interpretations* [5, 4] seems closely related to using productions.

Vere's work was important and influential, as it was continued by many other researchers such as [6, 26, 7, 8]. Nevertheless, there are at least two remaining problems:

First, there is the open question as to how this line of research on structural matching is related to the earlier work on least general generalisation by Gordon Plotkin. Our first contribution is to answer this open question by showing that these two approaches are actually each others duals. This is realized by adapting Plotkin's original notions of θ-subsumption and relative θ-subsumption for use to Vere's problem. In particular, we explicitly give an isomorphism between Plotkin's approach and structural matching. This in turn shows — for the first time — how the field of inductive logic programming relates to that of structural matching.

Secondly, there were several limitations of Vere's work and that of his followers, that are not present in Plotkin's work: One limitation is that Vere only considered constants and variables in productions, and not the more general functors, hence, Vere considered only a subset of first order logic. Another major problem with Vere's work and that of his followers is that the maximally specific generalization of two productions is not necessary unique[3]. Vere [23] formulates this control problem as follows :

Because a generalization replaces just two products, and a number of distinct generalizations may exist, there remains the question of strategies in the application of the induction procedure in an iterative manner to a large number of positive products.

To see that this is problematic from an efficiency point of view, consider the classical concept-learning task where the aim is to find a single production that generalizes a given set of positive and negative examples. In order to decide whether a solution exists to this problem one has to consider all alternative maximally specific generalizations of the set of positive examples and to test whether these are consistent with the negatives. If the maximally specific generalizations are not unique, this corresponds to testing (in the worst case) an exponential number of alternative generalizations. If on the other hand, the maximally specific generalization of any two productions is unique, only a single generalization needs to be computed and tested. This should be much more efficient.

As an immediate consequence of this problem, the programs developed by Vere and his followers all included a number of heuristics to choose among competing maximally specific generalizations. These heuristics were often mixed with the logical aspects of generalization (as e.g. in [6], who use the number of variables in a production as a heuristic). In contrast, our work will allow to seperate the logical from the control (or heuristic) aspects of generalization.

---

[3] The main reason for this is that rather than using normal subsitutions to define generality, Vere employs inverse substitutions. Within inductive logic programming, it is well-known that inverse substitutions are much harder to deal with than the classical deductive substitutions, mainly because of their non-uniqueness.

At a more general level, the mapping between the representations and operations employed in structural matching and ILP makes the relation between these two techniques — for the first time — explicit. From this point of view, our work can be regarded as a rational reconstruction of structural matching in (inductive) logic programming terminology.

The paper is organised as follows: in Section 2, we introduce the logical concepts needed; in Section 3, we briefly summarize the main characteristics of θ-subsumption and "least general generalisation"; in Section 4, we outline how this notion can be mapped onto structural matching; in Sections 5 and 6, we generalize the results of Sections 5 and 6 to relative θ-subsumption and "relative least generalisation"; finally, in Section 7, we conclude.

2 Logic programming concepts

We first outline some standard logic programming concepts.

A first-order alphabet is a set of variables, functor symbols, and predicate symbols. An atom $p(t_1, \ldots, t_n)$ is a predicate symbol p followed by a bracketed n-tuple of terms. A positive literal is an atom, a negative literal is a negated atom. A term t is a variable V or a functor symbol $f(t_1, \ldots, t_n)$ immediately followed by a bracketed n-tuple of terms. Constants are functor symbols of arity 0.

Definition 1. A *clause* is a finite disjunction of literals closed under universal quantification $\forall(l_1 \vee \ldots \vee l_n)$. The *clausal language* $\mathcal{D}_\mathcal{A}$ given by a first-order alphabet $\mathcal{A}$ consists of the set of all clauses that can be constructed from the symbols in $\mathcal{A}$.

An example clause D_1 is, e.g., $\forall X(\neg block(X) \vee black(X))$, stating that all blocks are black.

Definition 2. A *production* is a finite conjunction of literals closed under existential quantification $\exists(l_1 \wedge \ldots \wedge l_n)$. The *production language* $\mathcal{C}_\mathcal{A}$ given by a first-order alphabet $\mathcal{A}$ consists of the set of all productions that can be constructed from the symbols in $\mathcal{A}$.

An example production C_1 is, e.g., $\exists X(block(X) \wedge \neg black(X))$, stating that there is a block which is not black. The results and discussion in this paper will be independent of the choice of first-order alphabet $\mathcal{A}$, and we will therefore for simplicity in the following write $\mathcal{D}$ and $\mathcal{C}$ instead of $\mathcal{D}_\mathcal{A}$ and $\mathcal{C}_\mathcal{A}$.

For the purposes of this paper, a *formula* F will be a production or a clause. We will denote the set of literals in a formula F by $set(F)$. E.g., the example clause D_1 above corresponds to the set $set(D_1) = \{\neg block(X), black(X)\}$.

Also, we introduce two one-to-one mappings, which will be used further on.

Definition 3. The mapping $\mathcal{F}_\mathcal{C} : \mathcal{C} \mapsto \mathcal{D}$ maps every production in $\mathcal{C}$ to its negation in $\mathcal{D}$. The mapping $\mathcal{F}_\mathcal{D} : \mathcal{D} \mapsto \mathcal{C}$ maps every clause in $\mathcal{D}$ to its negation in $\mathcal{C}$.

This means that

$$\mathcal{F}_C(\exists(l_1 \wedge \ldots \wedge l_n)) = \forall(\neg l_1 \vee \ldots \vee \neg l_n),$$

and

$$\mathcal{F}_D(\forall(l_1 \vee \ldots \vee l_n)) = \exists(\neg l_1 \wedge \ldots \wedge \neg l_n).$$

The reader may notice that $\mathcal{F}_C^{-1} = \mathcal{F}_D$ and $\mathcal{F}_D^{-1} = \mathcal{F}_C$, since $\neg\neg l = l$ for any literal l. Furthermore, $\mathcal{F}_C(c) = \neg c$ and $\mathcal{F}_D(d) = \neg d$

A substitution $\theta = \{V_1/t_1, \ldots, V_n/t_n\}$ is an assignment of terms to variables. Applying a substitution θ to a term, literal, or formula F yields the instantiated term, literal, or formula $F\theta$, where, for every $1 \le i \le n$, all occurences of the variables V_i in F are simultaneously replaced by the corresponding terms t_i.

3 θ-subsumption

Let us now introduce Plotkin's notion of θ-subsumption.

Definition 4. A clause D_1 θ-subsumes a clause D_2 if and only if there exists a substitution θ such that $set(D_1)\theta \subseteq set(D_2)$. We write $D_1 \preceq_D D_2$ to denote that D_1 θ-subsumes D_2.

For example, $father(X,Y) \vee \neg\ parent(X,Y) \vee \neg\ male(X)$ θ-subsumes $father(jef,paul) \vee \neg\ parent(jef,paul) \vee \neg\ parent(jef,ann) \vee \neg\ male(jef) \vee \neg\ female(ann)$ with $\theta = \{X\ /\ jef,\ Y\ /\ paul\ \}$.

The notion of least general generalisation of a set of clauses is then defined as follows:

Definition 5. A clause G is a *generalisation* of a set of clauses $S = \{D_1, \ldots, D_n\}$ if and only if, for every $1 \le i \le n$, $G \preceq_D D_i$. A generalisation G of a set of clauses S is a *least general generalisation* (lgg_D) of S if and only if, for every generalisation G' of S, $G' \preceq_D G$.

The operation of computing an lgg_D underlies many ILP systems. Plotkin [18] has investigated the structure imposed by θ-subsumption. He has proven the following key properties (cf. [13]):

Implication. If D_1 θ-subsumes D_2, then $D_1 \models D_2$. The opposite does not hold for self-recursive clauses: let $D_1 = p(f(X)) \vee \neg p(X)$ and $D_2 = p(f(f(Y))) \vee \neg p(Y)$; then $D_1 \models D_2$ but D_1 does not θ-subsume D_2. Therefore deduction using θ-subsumption is not equivalent to implication among clauses. This also motivated research on inverting implication by Idestam-Almquist [9], Muggleton[14], Lapointe and Matwin [11].

This property also shows that θ-subsumption is a meaningful structure on $\mathcal{D}$ for ILP systems. Indeed, typical ILP systems employ a set of positive examples P (represented by ground clauses) and aim at deriving a hypothesis H (represented by a *set* of clauses) that implies the facts, i.e., $H \models P$. Because of the implication property, this aim will be fulfilled when all clauses in P are θ-subsumed by clauses in H.

Equivalence. There exist different clauses that are equivalent under θ-subsumption, e.g., $parent(X,Y) \vee \neg \; mother(X,Y) \vee \neg \; mother(X,Z) \; \theta$-subsumes $parent(X,Y) \vee \neg \; mother(X,Y)$ and vice versa. Because two clauses equivalent under θ-subsumption are also logically equivalent (i.e., by implication), learning systems should generate at most one clause of each equivalence class. For an extended discussion of equivalence, see Maher [12].

Reduction. To get around this problem, Plotkin defined equivalence classes of clauses, and showed that there is a unique representative (up to variable renamings) of each equivalence class, which he named the *reduced* clause. A clause D is reduced if and only if there exists no literal l such that $(D - \{l\})$ and D are equivalent under θ-subsumption. Learning systems can get around the problem of equivalent clauses when working with reduced clauses only. An algorithm to reduce clauses directly follows from the definition of a reduced clause: repeatedly delete a literal from a clause and check whether the resulting clause is θ-subsumed by the original clause; if it is, apply the corresponding substitution, omit duplicate literals, and repeat the procedure; if no literal can be deleted in this way, conclude that the clause is reduced.

Lattice. The set of reduced clauses forms a lattice, i.e., any two reduced clauses have a unique $lub_{\mathcal{D}}$ (least upper bound, which is the $lgg_{\mathcal{D}}$) and a unique $glb_{\mathcal{D}}$ (greatest lower bound).The least general generalisation operator is the basic operation of many specific to general ILP systems, e.g., Golem [16], Clint [2], ITVS [22] applied on ILP.

Plotkin has also given a procedure to compute the $lgg_{\mathcal{D}}$ of two clauses: the $lgg_{\mathcal{D}}$ of the terms $f(s_1, \ldots, s_n)$ and $f(t_1, \ldots, t_n)$ is $f(lgg_{\mathcal{D}}(s_1, t_1), \ldots, lgg_{\mathcal{D}}(s_n, t_n))$. The $lgg_{\mathcal{D}}$ of the terms $f(s_1, \ldots, s_n)$ and $g(t_1, \ldots, t_m)$, with $f \neq g$, is the variable v, where v represents this pair of terms throughout. The $lgg_{\mathcal{D}}$ of two atoms $p(s_1, \ldots, s_n)$ and $p(t_1, \ldots, t_n)$ is $p(lgg_{\mathcal{D}}(s_1, t_1), \ldots, lgg_{\mathcal{D}}(s_n, t_n))$, the $lgg_{\mathcal{D}}$ being undefined when the sign or the predicate symbols are unequal. Finally, the $lgg_{\mathcal{D}}$ of two clauses D_1 and D_2 is then

$$\bigvee_{l_1 \in set(D_1)} \bigvee_{l_2 \in set(D_2)} lgg_{\mathcal{D}}(l_1, l_2).$$

For example, the $lgg_{\mathcal{D}}$ of $father(tom, ann) \vee \neg \; parent(tom, ann) \vee \neg \; male(tom) \vee \neg \; female(ann)$ and $father(jef, paul) \vee \neg \; parent(jef, paul) \vee \neg \; male(jef) \vee \neg \; male(paul)$ is $father(X,Y) \vee \neg \; parent(X,Y) \vee \neg \; male(X) \vee \neg \; male(Z)$. The equivalent reduced clause is $father(X,Y) \vee \neg \; parent(X,Y) \vee \neg \; male(X)$.

Infinite Ascending Chains. There exist infinite strictly ascending chains in the above lattice, e.g.,

$h(X_1) \vee \neg \; p(X_1, X_2)$
$h(X_1) \vee \neg \; p(X_1, X_2) \vee \neg \; p(X_2, X_3)$
$h(X_1) \vee \neg \; p(X_1, X_2) \vee \neg \; p(X_2, X_3) \vee \neg \; p(X_3, X_4)$
...

Infinite Descending Chains. There also exist infinite strictly descending chains in the lattice, e.g.,

$h(X_1) \vee \neg p(X_1, X_2) \vee \neg p(X_2, X_1)$
$h(X_1) \vee \neg p(X_1, X_2) \vee \neg p(X_2, X_3) \vee \neg p(X_3, X_4) \vee \neg p(X_4, X_1)$
$h(X_1) \vee \neg p(X_1, X_2) \vee \neg p(X_2, X_3) \vee \neg p(X_3, X_4) \vee \neg p(X_4, X_5) \vee \neg$
$p(X_5, X_6) \vee \neg p(X_6, X_7) \vee \neg p(X_7, X_8) \vee \neg p(X_8, X_1)$
...

All clauses in both these infinite series θ-subsume the clause $h(X) \vee \neg p(X,X)$ and are θ-subsumed by the clause $h(X) \vee \neg p(X,Y)$.

4 Structural matching

In this section, we map Plotkin's notion of θ-subsumption onto productions. We will show that the resulting structure is order-isomorphic to θ-subsumption on clauses. As a result the algorithms and results by Plotkin can be directly mapped to productions.

Definition 6. A production C_1 *θ-subsumes* a production C_2 if and only if there exists a substitution θ such that $set(C_1)\theta \subseteq set(C_2)$. We will write $C_1 \preceq_C C_2$ to denote that C_1 θ-subsumes C_2.

For example, $\exists X, Y(circle(X) \wedge red(X) \wedge circle(Y) \wedge large(Y))$ θ-subsumes $circle(a) \wedge red(a) \wedge large(a)$ with substitution $\theta = \{X/a, Y/a\}$.

Vere employed a different notion of generalization. More specifically, according to Vere, a production C_2 is more specific than a production C_1 if there is an inverse substitution θ^{-1} such that $set(C_2)\theta^{-1} \subseteq set(C_1)$. An inverse substitution maps terms *at specified places* onto more general terms (or variables). Within the inductive logic programming literature, it is well-known that inverse substitutions are much harder to use and reason about than classical deductive substitutions [17].

A straightforward property of $\preceq_C$, which could be used as an alternative definition, is:

Lemma 7. Let C_1 and C_2 be two productions. Then, $C_1 \preceq_C C_2$ if and only if $\mathcal{F}_C(C_1) \preceq_D \mathcal{F}_C(C_2)$.

Let us now show that θ-subsumption imposes a meaningful structure on $\mathcal{C}$. This follows from :

Lemma 8. Let C_1 and C_2 be two productions. If $C_1 \preceq_C C_2$, then $C_2 \models C_1$.

Proof. This will be proven as a special case of Lemma 14. $\qquad\square$

In structural matching examples are ground (i.e.,variable free) productions. Ground productions closely correspond to logical interpretations (which can also be represented by a conjuction of true and false ground facts). When using examples that are interpretations, Lemma 8 shows that θ-subsumption is doing precisely what is expected: all interpretations that are a model for a production C_2 (i.e., that are *covered* by C_2) are also a model for every production C_1 that θ-subsumes C_2. Thus, θ-subsumption provides a genuine generality relation on $\mathcal{C}$.

It is straightforward to see that the structure imposed by θ-subsumption on $\mathcal{C}$ is exactly the same as that imposed on $\mathcal{D}$. This is because both productions and clauses are mapped to sets of literals when reasoning about θ-subsumption.

Formally, we have:

Theorem 9. *The ordered set* $(\mathcal{C}, \preceq_{\mathcal{C}})$ *is order-isomorphic to the ordered set* $(\mathcal{D}, \preceq_{\mathcal{D}})$.

Proof: We have to show that there is a one-to-one mapping from $\mathcal{C}$ to $\mathcal{D}$, which is monotone. The mapping $\mathcal{F}_{\mathcal{C}}$ clearly is one-to-one. It is monotone because for any productions C_1 and C_2, $C_1 \preceq_{\mathcal{C}} C_2$ if and only if $\mathcal{F}_{\mathcal{C}}(C_1) \preceq_{\mathcal{D}} \mathcal{F}_{\mathcal{C}}(C_2)$ (Lemma 7). □

As a consequence, all results proven by Plotkin and all algorithms on clauses apply to productions as well. For learning algorithms the most important results are concerned with reduced descriptions and least general generalisations.

We do not provide detailed descriptions of the resulting algorithms as they are essentially the same as Plotkin's, due to the uniform set representation. However, we can now easily define $lgg_{\mathcal{C}}$ in terms of $lgg_{\mathcal{D}}$ and the mappings $\mathcal{F}_{\mathcal{C}}$ and $\mathcal{F}_{\mathcal{D}}$ because of Theorem 9.

Corollary 10. *Let* C_1 *and* C_2 *be two productions. Then,*

$$lgg_{\mathcal{C}}(C_1, C_2) = \mathcal{F}_{\mathcal{D}}(lgg_{\mathcal{D}}(\mathcal{F}_{\mathcal{C}}(C_1), \mathcal{F}_{\mathcal{C}}(C_2))).$$

Let us also illustrate that the resulting structure on the search space solves some of the remaining problems with structural matching.

Example 1. Consider the following descriptions of scenes (from [8]).

$C_1 = circle(a) \wedge red(a) \wedge large(a)$
$C_2 = circle(b) \wedge circle(c) \wedge red(b) \wedge green(c) \wedge small(b) \wedge large(c)$

$G_1 = \exists X (circle(X) \wedge red(X))$
$G_2 = \exists X (circle(X) \wedge large(X))$
$G = \exists X, Y (circle(X) \wedge large(X) \wedge circle(Y) \wedge red(Y))$

Hayes-Roth and McDermott's algorithm would return both G_1 and G_2 as maximally specific generalisations of C_1 and C_2. As a consequence, their system has to explore two different paths through the search space. Similar problems exist for the framework of Steven Vere [23]. In contrast, according to our notion of generality G is the unique least general generalisation of C_1 and C_2. Furthermore, G is reduced.

Another problem solved adopting the ordered set $(\mathcal{C}, \preceq_{\mathcal{C}})$ is that it enables to handle function symbols.

5 Relative θ-subsumption

Plotkin [20] extended the notion of θ-subsumption to θ-subsumption relative to a theory (i.e., a finite set of clauses).

Definition 11. A clause D_1 *θ-subsumes* a clause D_2 *relative* to a theory T, denoted $D_1 \preceq_{\mathcal{D},T} D_2$, if and only if there exists a C-derivation of a clause R from D_1 and T such that $R \preceq_{\mathcal{D}} D_2$.

A C-derivation of R from D_1 and T is a resolution derivation of R from D_1 and T in which the clause D_1 is used exactly once. Our definition slightly differs from Plotkin's definition; in Plotkin's definition a resolution derivation is a C-derivation if and only if the clause D_1 is used *at most* once. Hence, our notion of relative θ-subsumption differs from Plotkin's w.r.t. clauses that logically follow from the theory only. With our definition a clause is a *lgg$_{\mathcal{D}}$* of a set of clauses if and only if it is a *rlgg$_{\mathcal{D}}$* of this set of clauses w.r.t. the empty theory. This is not the case with Plotkin's definition. However, the difference between the two definitions is not important since clauses that follow from the theory only are usually not considered in inductive learning.

Note that if a clause D_1 θ-subsumes a clause D_2, then it also θ-subsumes D_2 w.r.t. a theory T, by choosing $R = D_1$.

Definition 12. A clause G is a *relative generalisation* of a set of clauses $S = \{D_1, \ldots, D_n\}$ w.r.t. a theory T if and only if, for every $1 \leq i \leq n$, $G \preceq_{\mathcal{D},T} D_i$. A relative generalisation G of a set of clauses S w.r.t. a theory T is a *relative least general generalisation (rlgg$_{\mathcal{D},T}$)* of S if and only if, for every relative generalisation G' of S, $G' \preceq_{\mathcal{D},T} G$.

The idea of relative θ-subsumption is that one can take into account a background theory when learning. Relative θ-subsumption has similar properties as θ-subsumption.

Implication. If a clause D_1 θ-subsumes a clause D_2 relative to a theory T, then $T \cup \{D_1\} \models D_2$.
This property shows that relative θ-subsumption imposes a meaningful structure on $\mathcal{D}$ for ILP systems in the presence of a background theory. Indeed, typical ILP systems employ a set P of positive examples (represented by ground definite clauses) and a theory T, and aim at deriving a hypothesis H that implies the clauses , i.e., $T \cup H \models P$. Because of the implication property, the aim of ILP will be fulfilled when all clauses in P are θ-subsumed by clauses in H relative to T.

Equivalence, Reduction and Lattice. Because relative θ-subsumption is directly derived from θ-subsumption, the structure $(\mathcal{D}, \preceq_{\mathcal{D},T})$ is very similar to $(\mathcal{D}, \preceq_{\mathcal{D}})$. Indeed, Plotkin [20] also defines notions of equivalence, reduction, and relative least general generalisation w.r.t. a theory T. Unfortunately, the theoretical results for generalisation relative to a theory are not as good as for generalisation without respect to a theory. In particular, in general there does not exist an $rlgg_{D,T}$ of a set of clauses w.r.t. a theory. This is due to the fact that a clause by definition is a finite disjunction of literals, while a relative least general generalisation may include an infinite number of literals. However, whenever there exists an $rlgg_{D,T}$ it is unique up to equivalence. The $rlgg_{D,T}$ of a set of definite clauses $\{D_1, \ldots, D_n\}$ w.r.t. a theory T can be computed in the following way [15, 10] For each clause D_i $(1 \leq i \leq n)$ collect all ground unit clauses that are derivable from T and the complement $\overline{D_i}$ of D_i, and construct a clause D_i' that is the complement of this set of unit clauses. Then the $rlgg_{D,T}$ of $\{D_1, \ldots, D_n\}$ w.r.t. T can be found by computing the lgg_D of $\{D_1', \ldots, D_n'\}$.

6 Relative Structural Matching

Kodratoff and Ganascia [6], and Vrain [26] have all given definitions of structurally matching two productions in the presence of background knowledge, thereby building on Vere's original framework. However, similarly as Vere's original framework, these techniques suffer from a number of problems, which include the fact that there may be multiple relative most specific generalisations, and difficulties in handling functors. The question thus arises as to whether it is possible to map Plotkin's structure of relative θ-subsumptions onto the set of productions.

One way to define relative subsumption for productions would be to map Plotkin's definition directly onto productions. As this would involve modifying the proof-procedure, this would be rather complicated. Therefore, we will rather upgrade the alternative definition of θ-subsumption for production given in Lemma 7. This results in the following definition :

Definition 13. A production C_1 θ-subsumes a production C_2 relative to a theory T, denoted $C_1 \preceq_{C,T} C_2$, if and only if $\mathcal{F}_C(C_1) \preceq_{D,T} \mathcal{F}_C(C_2)$.

First note that in this definition T is also a clausal theory. Second, if T is empty, this definition again reduces to θ-subsumption for productions.

Let us again show that this structure is meaningful for concept-learning when using interpretations or ground productions as examples and a clausal background theory:

Lemma 14. Let C_1 and C_2 be productions and T a theory. If $C_1 \preceq_{C,T} C_2$ then $T \wedge C_1 \models C_2$.

Proof. $C_1 \preceq_{C,T} C_2$ iff
$\mathcal{F}_C(C_1) \preceq_{D,T} \mathcal{F}_C(C_2)$ only if (because of the relation of $\preceq_{D,T}$ to implication)
$T \wedge \mathcal{F}_C(C_1) \models \mathcal{F}_C(C_2)$ only if
$T \wedge \neg\mathcal{F}_C(C_2) \models \neg\mathcal{F}_C(C_1)$ only if
$T \wedge C_2 \models C_1$ (because $\neg\mathcal{F}_C(C) = C$ for all productions C). □

This lemma reduces to Lemma 8 when T is empty.
Again it is straightforward to show that

Theorem 15. $(C, \preceq_{C,T})$ *and* $(D, \preceq_{D,T})$ *are order-isomorphic for all theories* T.

And again this allows us to compute the $rlgg_C$, whose definition is analogous, using $rlgg_D$.

Corollary 16. *Let* C_1 *and* C_2 *be two productions and* T *a theory. Then*

$$rlgg_{C,T}(C_1, C_2) = \mathcal{F}_D(rlgg_{D,T}(\mathcal{F}_C(C_1), \mathcal{F}_C(C_2))).$$

This also means that the $rlgg_{C,T}$ inherits all the properties of the dual $rlgg_{D,T}$. Using this operation again solves many of the problems with the operations proposed by Vere [23, 24], Kodratoff and Ganascia [6] and Vrain [26], in particular, uniqueness, use of functors and also handling inequalities. To handle inequalities, it suffices to add the clauses $different(a, b)$ and $different(a, c)$, etc. for all different combinations of known constants to the theory.

To illustrate the use of background knowledge we take the following example of Kodratoff and Ganascia [6]. The example also illustrates that the use of functors is possible.

Example 2. Consider
$C_1 = red(a) \wedge red(b) \wedge shape(b, square)$, and
$C_2 = red(c) \wedge shape(d, square)$.

The background knowledge T contains the "color hierarchy":
$color(X, red) \vee \neg red(X)$.
$color(X, green) \vee \neg green(X)$.
$color(X, yellow) \vee \neg yellow(X)$.

Also known is the fact that each object has a color. Kodratoff and Ganascia express this as: $\forall X \exists Y : color(X, Y)$. In clausal form we can make use of a Skolem functor $col/1$, and express this as the clause $color(X, col(X))$ in T.

Finally T contains the above mentioned clauses that express that different constants represent different objects.

The production $red(X) \wedge red(Y) \wedge square(Z) \wedge different(X, Z)$ is an lgg_C of the two productions C_1 and C_2. The "reduced" form of this production is: $G_1 = red(X) \wedge square(Z) \wedge different(X, Z)$.

The production $red(X) \wedge red(Y) \wedge square(Z) \wedge different(X, Z) \wedge color(U, V) \wedge color(W, Z)$ is an $rlgg_{C,T}$ of C_1 and C_2 with respect to the given background knowledge. The "reduced" form of this production w.r.t. θ-subsumption is: $G_2 = red(X) \wedge square(Z) \wedge different(X, Z) \wedge color(W, Z)$.

Kodratoff and Ganascia obtain G_1 and G_2 by structurally matching C_1 and C_2 in two different ways. Whereas they call these two possible generalisations between which one cannot choose "because they have an equal number of variables", the relationship of structural matching with Plotkin's work reveals that G_1 *subsumes* G_2 w.r.t. θ-subsumption. This means that G_2 is a more specific generalisation, which could therefore be preferred over G_1.

Note that, unlike in structural matching, this has the advantage that no further heuristics (e.g., the counting of variables) is needed, since the relative least general generalisation is unique modulo reduction. Furthermore, whereas structural matching explicitly records all variable bindings and controls the introduction of new variables heuristically, Plotkin's algorithm deals with all these problems in a uniform way.

7 Conclusion

We have shown the order-isomorphisms between Plotkin's framework and the framework of structural matching. This isomorphism implies that the results obtained in one framework can be transferred to the other. This in turn leads to an improved structure on the space of productions for use in concept-learning.

Finally, we hope that this work will stimulate further cross-fertilization between structural matching and ILP. Some challenging remaining research issues include: can we adapt rlgg based ILP systems, such as Muggleton and Feng's Golem for use in structural matching?

Acknowledgements

Luc De Raedt is supported by the Belgian National Fund for Scientific Research. Peter Idestam-Almquist is supported by the Swedish Research Council for Engineering Sciences (TFR). Luc De Raedt and Peter Idestam-Almquist were also supported by the ESPRIT Basic Research Projects No. 6020 and 20.237 on Inductive Logic Programming I and II. The authors would like to thank Maarten Van Someren for suggestions for improving this paper.

References

1. G. Bisson. Learning in FOL with a Similarity Measure. In *Proceedings of AAAI*, 1992.
2. L. De Raedt. Interactive Theory Revision: an Inductive Logic Programming approach, Academic Press, 1992.
3. L. De Raedt and M. Bruynooghe. A theory of clausal discovery. In *Proceedings of the 13th International Joint Conference on Artificial Intelligence*, pages 1058–1063. Morgan Kaufmann, 1993.
4. L. De Raedt and S. Džeroski. First order jk-clausal theories are PAC-learnable. *Artificial Intelligence*, 70:375–392, 1994.
5. L. De Raedt. Induction in Logic. In *Proceedings of the 3rd Multistrategy Learning Workshop*, 1996.
6. J.G. Ganascia and Y. Kodratoff. Improving the generalization step in learning. In R.S Michalski, J.G. Carbonell, and T.M. Mitchell, editors, *Machine Learning: an artificial intelligence approach*, volume 2, pages 215–241. Morgan Kaufmann, 1986.
7. R. Gemello, F. Mana, and L. Saitta. Rigel: An inductive learning system. *Machine Learning*, 6:7–35, 1991.

8. F. Hayes-Roth and J. McDermott. An interference matching technique for inducing abstractions. *Communications of the ACM*, 21:401–410, 1978.

9. P. Idestam-Almquist. Generalisation under implication using or-introduction. In *Proceedings of the 6th European Conference on Machine Learning*, volume 667, pages 56–64. Lecture Notes in Artificial Intelligence, 1993.

10. P. Idestam-Almquist. Generalization of clauses relative to a theory *Machine Learning*, in press, 1997.

11. S. Lapointe and S. Matwin. Sub-unification: a tool for efficient induction of recursive programs. In *Proceedings of the 9th International Workshop on Machine Learning*. Morgan Kaufmann, 1992.

12. M.J. Maher. Equivalences of logic programs. In *Proceedings of Third International Conference on Logic Programming*, Berlin, 1986. Springer.

13. S. Muggleton and L. De Raedt. Inductive logic programming: theory and methods. *Journal of Logic Programming*, Vol. 19-20, 1994.

14. S. Muggleton. Inverting implication. *Artificial Intelligence*, 1994. To appear.

15. S. Muggleton. Inductive Logic Programming. *New Generation Computing*, 8:295–317, 1991.

16. S. Muggleton and C. Feng. Efficient induction of logic programs. In *Proceedings of the 1st conference on algorithmic learning theory*, pages 368–381. Ohmsma, Tokyo, Japan, 1990.

17. S. Muggleton and W. Buntine. Machine invention of first order predicates by inverting resolution. In *Proceedings of the 5th International Workshop on Machine Learning*, Morgan Kaufmann, 1988.

18. G. Plotkin. A note on inductive generalization. In *Machine Intelligence*, volume 5, pages 153–163. Edinburgh University Press, 1970.

19. G. Plotkin. *Automatic Methods of Inductive Inference*. PhD thesis, Edinburgh University, 1971.

20. G. Plotkin. A further note on inductive generalization. In *Machine Intelligence*, volume 6, pages 101–124. Edinburgh University Press, 1971.

21. J.R. Quinlan. Learning logical definitions from relations. *Machine Learning*, 5:239–266, 1990.

22. G. Sablon, L. De Raedt, and M. Bruynooghe. Iterative Versionspaces. *Artificial Intelligence*, 69:393-409, 1994.

23. S.A. Vere. Induction of concepts in the predicate calculus. In *Proceedings of the 4th International Joint Conference on Artificial Intelligence*, pages 282–287. Morgan Kaufmann, 1975.

24. S.A. Vere. Induction of relational productions in the presence of background information. In *Proceedings of the 5th International Joint Conference on Artificial Intelligence*, Morgan Kaufmann, 1977.

25. S.A. Vere. Multilevel counterfactuals for generalizations of relational concepts and productions. *Artificial Intelligence*, 14:139-164,1980.

26. C. Vrain. Ogust: A system that learns using domain properties expressed as theorems. In Y. Kodratoff and R.S. Michalski, editors, *Machine Learning: an artificial intelligence approach*, volume 3, pages 360–381. Morgan Kaufmann, 1990.

Classification by Voting Feature Intervals*

Gülşen Demiröz and H. Altay Güvenir

Department of Computer Engineering and Information Science
Bilkent University, 06533 Ankara, Turkey
email: {demiroz, guvenir}@cs.bilkent.edu.tr

Abstract. A new classification algorithm called VFI (for *Voting Feature Intervals*) is proposed. A concept is represented by a set of *feature intervals* on each feature dimension separately. Each feature participates in the classification by distributing real-valued votes among classes. The class receiving the highest vote is declared to be the predicted class. VFI is compared with the *Naive Bayesian Classifier*, which also considers each feature separately. Experiments on real-world datasets show that VFI achieves comparably and even better than NBC in terms of classification accuracy. Moreover, VFI is faster than NBC on all datasets.

1 Introduction

Learning to classify objects has been one of the primary problems in machine learning. Bayesian classifier originating from work in recognition is a probabilistic approach to inductive learning. Bayesian approach to classification estimates the posterior probability that an instance belongs to a class, given the observed feature values for the instance. The highest estimated probability determines the classification. Naive Bayesian Classifier (NBC) is a fast, classical Bayesian classifier assuming independence of features. NBC has been found successful in terms of classification accuracy in many domains, including medical diagnosis, compared with Assistant, which is an ID3-like [8] inductive learning system [5]. It has also been concluded that induction of decision trees is relatively slow as compared to NBC [5].

Considering each feature separately is common in both NBC, CFP (for *Classification by Feature Partitions*) [3], and k-NNFP [1] classification algorithms. Both CFP and k-NNFP represent the knowledge as sets of projections of the training dataset on each feature dimension. K-NNFP stores all instances as their projections on each feature dimension, while CFP constructs disjoint *segments* of feature values on each feature dimension. The classification in CFP and k-NNFP is based on a majority voting done among individual predictions of features. The encouraging results and the advantages of the representation and voting schemes such as speed and handling missing feature values motivated us to come up with a new classification algorithm called the VFI (for *Voting Feature Intervals*). The concept is still represented as projections on each feature dimension separately,

---

* This project is supported by TUBITAK (Scientific and Technical Research Council of Turkey) under Grant EEEAG-153.

but the basic unit of representation is a *feature interval* in VFI. Unlike segments in CFP, a feature interval can represent examples from a set of classes instead of a single class. The voting scheme, where a feature votes for one class, used both in CFP and k-NNFP, is also modified such that each feature distributes its vote among several classes.

The voting scheme in VFI is analogical with the probability estimation in NBC. In NBC, each feature participates in the classification by assigning probability values for each class and the final probability of a class is the product of individual probabilities measured on each feature. In VFI, each feature distributes its vote among classes and the final vote of a class is the sum of all individual votes given the features. The results of the experiments show that VFI achieve comparably and even better than NBC on some real-world datasets and usually better than CFP and k-NNFP in terms of classification accuracy. Moreover, VFI has been shown to be faster than all other three classifiers, which suffer more on datasets having large number of instances and/or features.

The next section will describe the VFI algorithm in detail. In Section 3, the complexity analysis and the empirical evaluation of VFI and NBC are presented. Finally, Section 4 concludes with some remarks and plans for future work.

2   The VFI Algorithm

This section describes the VFI classification algorithm in detail. First, a description of VFI is given. Then, the algorithm is explained on an example dataset.

2.1   Description of the Algorithm

The VFI algorithm is a non-incremental classification algorithm. Each training example is represented as a vector of feature values plus a label that represents the class of the example. From the training examples, VFI constructs feature intervals for each feature. The term *interval* is used for feature intervals throughout the paper. An interval represents a set of values of a given feature, where the same subset of class values are observed. Two neighboring intervals contain different sets of classes.

The training process in the VFI algorithm is given in Figure 1. The procedure *find_end_points(TrainingSet, f, c)* finds the lowest and the highest values for linear feature f from the examples of class c and each observed value for nominal feature f from the examples in *TrainingSet*. For each linear feature $2k$ values are found, where k is the number of classes. Then the list of $2k$ end-points is sorted and each consecutive pair of points constitutes a feature interval. For nominal features, each observed value found constitutes a *point interval* of a single value.

Each interval is represented by a vector of $< lower, count_1, \ldots, count_k >$ where *lower* is the lower bound of that interval, $count_i$ is the number of training instances of class i that fall into that interval. Thus, an interval may represent several classes. Only the lower bounds are kept, because for linear features the upper bound of an interval is the lower bound of the next interval and for

```
train(TrainingSet):
begin
        for each feature f
            for each class c
                EndPoints[f] = EndPoints[f] ∪ find_end_points(TrainingSet, f, c);
            sort(EndPoints[f]);
            /* each pair of consecutive points in EndPoints[f] form a feature interval */
            for each interval i /* on feature f */
                for each class c
                    /* count the number of instances of class c falling into interval i */
                    interval_class_count[f, i, c] = count_instances(f, i, c);
end.
```

Fig. 1. Training phase in the VFI Algorithm.

nominal features upper and lower bounds of every interval are equal. The $count_i$ values are computed by the $count\_instances(i, c)$ function in Figure 1. When a training instance of class i falls on the boundary of two consecutive intervals of linear feature f, then $count_i$ of both intervals are incremented by 0.5. In the training phase of the VFI algorithm the feature intervals for each feature dimension are constructed. Note that since each feature is processed separately, no normalization of feature values is required. The classification phase of the VFI algorithm is given in Figure 2. The process starts by initializing the votes of each class to zero. For each feature f, the interval on feature dimension f into which e_f falls is searched, where e_f is the f value of the test example e. If e_f is unknown (missing), that feature gives a vote zero for each class. Hence, the features containing missing values are simply ignored. Ignoring the feature about which nothing is known is a natural and plausible approach.

If e_f is known, the interval i into which e_f falls is found. For each class c, feature f gives a vote equal to

$$feature\_vote[f, c] = \frac{interval\_class\_count[f, i, c]}{class\_count[c]}$$

where $interval\_class\_count[f, i, c]$ is the number of examples of class c which fall into interval i of feature dimension f. If e_f falls on the boundary of two intervals i and $i + 1$ of a linear feature, then a vote equal to the average of the votes suggested by the intervals i and $i + 1$ is given. For nominal features, only point intervals are constructed and each value must fall in an interval. The individual vote of feature f for class c, $feature\_vote[f, c]$, is then normalized to have the sum of votes of feature f equal to 1. Hence, the vote of feature f is a real-valued vote less than or equal to 1. Each feature f collects its votes in an individual vote vector $< vote_{f,1}, \ldots, vote_{f,k} >$, where $vote_{f,c}$ is the individual vote of feature f

---

classify(e): /* e: example to be classified */
begin
      for each class c
        $vote[c] = 0$
      for each feature f
        for each class c
            $feature\_vote[f, c] = 0$ /*vote of feature f for class c*/
        if e_f value is known
           $i = \text{find\_interval}(f, e_f)$
           $feature\_vote[f, c] = \frac{interval\_class\_count[f, i, c]}{class\_count[c]}$
           $\text{normalize\_feature\_votes}(f)$; /* such that $\sum_c feature\_vote[f, c] = 1$ */
           for each class c
               $vote[c] = vote[c] + feature\_vote[f, c]$;
      return class c with highest $vote[c]$;
end.

Fig. 2. Classification in the VFI Algorithm.

for class c and k is the number of classes. Then the individual vote vectors are summed up to get a total vote vector $< vote_1, \ldots, vote_k >$. Finally, the class with the highest total vote is predicted to be the class of the test instance.

A class is predicted for the test instance in order to be able to measure the performance by percentage of correct classifications on unseen instances in the experiments. With this implementation, VFI is a *categorical classifier*, since it returns a unique class for a test instance [6]. Instead, $\frac{vote[c]}{\sum_k vote[k]}$ can be used as the probability of class c which makes VFI a more general classifier. In that case, VFI returns a probability distribution over all classes.

2.2 An Example

In order to describe the VFI algorithm, consider the sample training dataset on the left of Figure 3. In this dataset, we have two linear features f_0 and f_1, and there are 3 examples of class A and 4 examples of class B. The constructed concept description after the training phase is shown in Figure 3. There are 5 intervals for each feature. The lower bound of the leftmost intervals is -INFINITE and the upper bound of the rightmost intervals is INFINITE. The second interval on feature dimension of f_0 can be represented as $< 1, 1.5, 0 >$, where 1 is the lower bound of the interval, 1.5 is count of training instances of class A, and 0 is the count of training instances of class B that falls into that interval.

In order to describe the classification phase of the VFI algorithm, consider a test example $test = < 5, 3, ? >$. On feature f_0 dimension, the $test_0 = 5$ falls into the fourth interval as shown with an arrow in Figure 3. That interval has

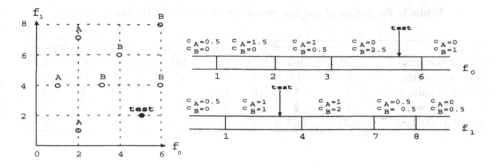

Fig. 3. A sample training dataset and the concept description learned by VFI.

a count $c_A = 0$ for class A and a count $c_B = 2.5$ for class B, so the vote vector of f_0 is $vote_0 =< 0/3, 2.5/4 >$. The normalized vote vector is $vote_0 =< 0, 1 >$. This means that feature f_0 votes 0 for class A and 1 for class B. On the other feature dimension, test example falls into the second interval. That interval has a count $c_A = 1$ for class A and a count $c_B = 1$ for class B, so the vote vector of f_1 is $vote_1 =< 1/3, 1/4 >$. The normalized vote vector is $vote_1 =< 0.57, 0.43 >$. Finally, the votes of the two features are summed up correspondingly and total vote vector is $vote =< 0.57, 1.43 >$. VFI votes 0.57 for class A and 1.43 for class B, so class B with the highest vote is predicted as the class of the test example.

3 Evaluation of the VFI Algorithm

This section presents the space and time complexity analyses and the empirical evaluation of VFI. The VFI algorithm is compared with CFP, k-NNFP, and NBC in terms of classification accuracy, and training and testing times.

3.1 Complexity Analysis

The VFI algorithm represents a concept description by feature intervals on each feature dimension. Each feature dimension has at most $2k + 1$ intervals where k is the number of classes. Each interval requires $k + 1$ memory units, one for the lower bound of the interval and k for the count of each class. So each feature dimension requires $(2k + 1)(k + 1)$ space and since there are d features, the total space requirement of the VFI algorithm is $d(2k + 1)(k + 1)$ which is $O(dk^2)$. On the other hand, the space requirement of NBC is $O(m)$ at worst case, where m is the number of training instances.

In the training phase of the VFI algorithm, for each training instance the corresponding intervals on each feature dimension is searched and the counts of corresponding classes are incremented. Since there are m training instances, d feature dimensions, and at most $2k + 1$ intervals on each feature dimension, this makes up $md(2k + 1)$ total, which is $O(mdk)$. Hence, the training time of VFI increases with the number of features and classes, and the size of the dataset.

Table 1. Properties of the real-world datasets used in the comparisons.

Data Set:	bcancerw	cleveland	glass	horse	hungarian	iris	musk	page	segment
No. of Instances	699	303	214	368	294	150	476	5473	2310
No. of Features	9	13	9	22	13	4	166	10	19
No. of Nomin. Feat.	0	8	0	15	8	0	0	0	0
No. of Classes	2	2	6	3	2	3	2	5	7
Missing Values (%)	0.25	0.15	0	30	20	0	0	0	0

On the other hand, the training time complexity of NBC is $O(vdm)$, where v is the average number of distinct values per feature. Hence, the training time of NBC increases with the number of features and distinct values per feature, and the size of the dataset. Since in real-world datasets $k << v$ especially for linear features, the training time for VFI is less than that of NBC.

In the classification phase of the VFI algorithm, for each feature, the interval that the corresponding feature value of the test example falls into, is searched and the individual votes of each feature is summed up to get the total votes. Since there are at most $2k + 1$ intervals on each feature dimension and there are d features, the classification phase takes at worst case $d(2k + 1)$ which is $O(dk)$. Hence, the testing time of VFI increases with the number of features and classes. The test time complexity of NBC is $O(dkv)$, which means that the testing time of NBC increases with the number of features, distinct values per feature, and classes. Since an extra factor of v does not exist in the complexity of VFI and in real-world datasets $k << v$ especially for linear features, the testing time for VFI is less than that of NBC.

3.2 Empirical Evaluation on Real-World Datasets

In this section we present an empirical evaluation of the VFI algorithm on real-world datasets provided by the machine learning group at the University of California at Irvine [7]. An overview of the datasets is shown in Table 1. The features V3, V25, V26, V27, and V28 are deleted from the original Horse-colic (called horse in the tables) dataset and feature V24 is used as the class. The dataset Page-blocks is also called as page in short. The classification accuracy of the algorithms is used as one measure of performance. The most commonly used classification accuracy metric is the percentage of correctly classified instances over all test instances. 5-fold cross-validation technique, which ensures that the training and test sets are disjoint, is used to measure the classification accuracy in the experiments. In addition to the accuracy comparisons, the average running time of the algorithms are also compared.

The classification accuracies of CFP, k-NNFP ($k = 1$), VFI, and NBC obtained by 5-fold cross-validation on nine real-world datasets are given in Table 2. VFI usually outperforms k-NNFP but sometimes CFP outperforms VFI where

Table 2. Classification accuracy (%) of VFI, NBC, CFP, and k-NNFP ($k = 1$) obtained by 5-fold cross-validation on nine real-world datasets.

Data Set:	bcancerw	cleveland	glass	horse	hungarian	iris	musk	page	segment
VFI	95.14	82.49	57.48	79.35	82.62	95.33	77.73	87.39	77.02
NBC	97.28	80.84	52.34	80.96	82.94	92.0	71.68	89.8	80.74
CFP	95.85	83.82	54.17	81.53	81.59	94.67	60.49	89.77	66.75
k-NNFP	94.0	67.62	57.0	66.84	70.04	90.0	69.54	90.52	75.1

Table 3. Average running times (msec.) of VFI, NBC, CFP, and k-NNFP ($k = 1$) on a SUN/Sparc 20/61 workstation. Training is done with 4/5 and Testing with 1/5 of the dataset. 0 means time is less than 1 msec.

Data Set:	bcancerw	cleveland	glass	horse	hungarian	iris	musk	page	segment
VFI (Train)	21.2	15	11.6	25.4	14.8	4	306.2	205.2	131.2
NBC (Train)	89	66	48.8	102.4	54	12	2071	4004	1586
CFP (Train)	149.4	102	71.4	151.4	79.4	17	3973	4400	10253
k-NNFP (Train)	121.6	67.4	17	277.6	157.6	5.4	738.8	978	713.8
VFI (Test)	5	2	2.2	4	2	0	67.6	72	79
NBC (Test)	9	11.2	17	12	8.6	1.8	896	2308	2541
CFP (Test)	8.4	5.6	6.2	6.8	4.6	2	439.6	550.4	1533
k-NNFP (Test)	3.6	3	3.6	4.8	2	0	197	170	145

CFP is given some parameters. In four of the datasets VFI outperforms NBC, in other four NBC performs better, and in Hungarian dataset they perform equally. The largest differences in accuracy are observed on the Glass and the Musk datasets on which VFI outperforms NBC.

The superiority of VFI over NBC is indeed in its speed. The average training and testing run times of all classifiers are given in Table 3. It is observed that VFI is always faster than NBC both in training and testing as expected due to the reasons discussed in Section 3.1. VFI is in fact the fastest classifier among four classifiers in terms of both training time and testing time on all datasets with the only exception of the Bcancerw dataset where k-NNFP is slightly faster only in testing. Table 3 also shows that both train and test time of all the classifiers on large datasets like Page-blocks and Segment are larger than that of smaller datasets. The larger run times of all classifiers on the Musk dataset than that of smaller ones shows the effect of the number of features on the run times.

4 Conclusions

The VFI classifier has similarities with the Naive Bayesian Classifier, in that they both consider each feature separately. Since each feature is processed separately, the missing feature values that may appear both in the training and test instances are simply ignored both in NBC and VFI. In other classification algorithms, such as decision tree inductive learning algorithms, the missing values cause problems [9]. This problem has been overcome by simply omitting the feature with the missing value in both NBC and VFI. Another advantage of both classifiers is that they can make a general classification returning a probability distribution over all classes instead of a *categorical classification* [6]. Also note that the VFI algorithm, in particular, is applicable to concepts where each feature can be used in the classification of the concept independently. One might think that this requirement may limit the applicability of the VFI, since in some domains the features might be dependent on each other. Holte has pointed out that the most datasets in the UCI repository are such that, for classification, their features can be considered independently of each other [4]. Also Kononenko claimed that in the data used by human experts there are no strong dependencies between features because features are properly defined [5].

The experimental results show that VFI performs comparably and even better than NBC and usually better than CFP and k-NNFP on real-world datasets. Moreover, VFI has a speed advantage over CFP, k-NNFP, as well as NBC, which is known to be a fast classifier.

For future work, we plan to integrate a feature weight learning algorithm to VFI, since both relevant and irrelevant features have equal voting power in this version of VFI. Genetic algorithms can be used to learn weights for VFI [2] as well as several other weight learning methods [10].

References

1. Akkuş, A., & Güvenir, H. A. (1995). K Nearest Neighbor Classification on Feature Projections. *Proceedings of ICML '96*, 12–19.
2. Demiröz, G., & Güvenir, H. A. (1996). Genetic Algorithms to Learn Feature Weights for the Nearest Neighbor Algorithm. *Proceedings of BENELEARN-96*, 117-126.
3. Güvenir, H. A., & Şirin, İ. (1996). Classification by Feature Partitioning. *Machine Learning*, Vol. 23, 47–67.
4. Holte, R. C. (1993). Very simple classification rules perform well on most commonly used datasets. *Machine Learning*, Vol. 11, 63–91.
5. Kononenko, I. (1993). Inductive and Bayesian Learning in Medical Diagnosis. *Applied Artificial Intelligence*, Vol. 7, 317-337.
6. Kononenko, I. & Bratko, I. (1991). Information-Based Evaluation Criterion for Classifier's Performance. *Machine Learning*, Vol. 6, 67–80.
7. Murphy, P. (1995). *UCI Repository of machine learning databases*, [Anonymous FTP from ics.uci.edu in the directory pub/machine-learning databases]. Department of Information and Computer Science, University of California, Irvine.
8. Quinlan, J. R. (1986). Induction of decision trees. *Machine Learning*, Vol.1, 81–106.
9. Quinlan, J. R. (1989). Unknown attribute values in induction. *Proceedings of 6th International Workshop on Machine Learning*, 164–168.
10. Wettschereck,D. & Aha, D. W. (1995). Weighting Features. *Proceedings of the First International Conference on Case-Based Reasoning (ICCBR-95)*.

Constructing Intermediate Concepts by Decomposition of Real Functions

Janez Demšar[1], Blaž Zupan[2], Marko Bohanec[2], Ivan Bratko[1,2]

[1] Faculty of Computer and Information Sciences, 1000 Ljubljana, Slovenia
{janez.demsar, ivan.bratko}@fri.uni-lj.si
[2] Jozef Stefan Institute, 1000 Ljubljana, Slovenia
{blaz.zupan, marko.bohanec}@ijs.si

Abstract. In learning from examples it is often useful to expand an attribute-vector representation by intermediate concepts. The usual advantage of such structuring of the learning problem is that it makes the learning easier and improves the comprehensibility of induced descriptions. In this paper, we develop a technique for discovering useful intermediate concepts when both the class and the attributes are real-valued. The technique is based on a decomposition method originally developed for the design of switching circuits and recently extended to handle incompletely specified multi-valued functions. It was also applied to machine learning tasks. In this paper, we introduce modifications, needed to decompose real functions and to present them in symbolic form. The method is evaluated on a number of test functions. The results show that the method correctly decomposes fairly complex functions. The decomposition hierarchy does not depend on a given repertoir of basic functions (background knowledge).

1 Introduction

A learning problem can often be formulated as the problem of reconstructing a function f of a number of arguments $\mathbf{x} = x_1, x_2, \ldots$ from a given set of example points $f(\mathbf{x}_j)$. In the usual machine learning terminology, $x_1, x_2, \ldots$ are called attributes, and f is called the class. The usual induction algorithms reconstruct f by considering all the attributes at the same time. However, often it is beneficial to find useful "intermediate" concepts which would allow a decomposition of the learning problem. Hopefully, f would be easier to express in terms of suitable intermediate concepts, and in turn, these would be easy to express in terms of the original attributes or further intermediate concepts. It is generally believed that such a structuring of the learning domain would also lead to more comprehensible description of the learned concepts.

In this paper, we develop a technique for discovering useful intermediate concepts when both the class and the attributes are real-valued. It is based on function decomposition that results in a hierarchy of intermediate functions which can be illustrated by a kind of dataflow diagram (Fig. 1). The technique works bottom-up by selecting a subset of the original attributes, say $\{x_2, x_3\}$, and constructing a function ϕ_1 so that it would succesfully replace the two attributes x_2, x_3. As a result of this step, a new attribute ϕ_1 is constructed and the process recursively combines the attribute set $\{x_1, \phi_1, x_4, x_5\}$.

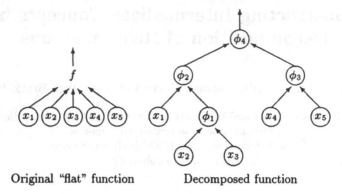

Original "flat" function   Decomposed function

Fig. 1. "Flat" and decomposed function

Functional decomposition is a method which, given a tabular representation of a function, discovers a hierarchy of appropriate subfunctions and variables. The output of the algorithm is a decomposition tree or, generally, a directed acyclic graph with input variables as leaves and subfunctions as internal nodes. A decomposition algorithm was originally developed in late 1940's and 1950's by Ashenhurst [1] and Curtis [2] to be used for decomposition of boolean functions in switching circuits design. However, the method was rarely used in practice, mostly because of its computational intractability. Much later, the interest in the algorithm has been renewed. Perkowski et al. [5] improved the original algorithm to handle incompletely specified functions, and Luba [4] proposed to decompose multi-valued functions by representing a multi-valued variable by a set of Boolean variables. Zupan and Bohanec [7] developed an algorithm that induces a hierarchy of multi-valued variables without the need to represent them as Boolean. Also, their work shows that the algorithm is applicable in fairly complex machine learning tasks.

Not much work has been done to extend the algorithm to decomposition of real-valued functions. Ross [6] discusses the possible use of the method for functions with real valued outputs and inputs but he does not propose any algorithm for general use.

In this paper, we extended the algorithm to handle continuous variables and functions. The proposed method not only discovers a suitable function hierarchy but enables symbolic representation of the discovered function, using a predefined set of basic functions, like $\sin, \cos, \exp$ or $\ln$.

The paper is organized as follows. Section 2 introduces the real function decomposition method, which is experimentally evaluated in Section 3. Section 4 concludes the paper and outlines possible directions of further work.

2 Method

This section first introduces the basic algorithm for functional decomposition of nominal functions. Then, it focuses on the changes of this algorithm that are needed to perform the decomposition of real function.

2.1 The Basic Decomposition Algorithm

The input for algorithms that are based on Curtis' function decomposition algorithm [2] is a function $f(X)$, "sampled" in a finite number of points, where X is an argument vector. The function is presented as a table of attribute-value vectors, each consisting of values of input variables $\mathbf{x}_k$ and a function value $z_k = f(\mathbf{x}_k)$. In the usual machine learning terminology, each row of this table corresponds to an example. The basic step of the decomposition consists of two substeps:

- find a suitable partition of the set of input variables (X) into "free" (A) and "bound" (B) sets, $A \cup B = X$,
- find appropriate functions F and ϕ such that $f(X) = F(A, \phi(B))$.

The basic step is then recursively repeated on functions F and ϕ.

The partition can be selected using heuristic methods [5]. Alternative approach is to investigate all possible partitions and choose the one that induces the best functions ϕ and F according to some criterion. Often, we speed up the partition selection by examining only disjunctive splits, $A \cap B = \emptyset$, and/or decompositions with only two bound variables, $|B| = 2$. However, there are cases when such restrictions prevent the algorithm from discovering an appropriate function hierarchy or even from discovering any hierarchy at all.

Function ϕ is not uniquely defined by the set of bound variables. The algorithm first determines which combinations of values of input variables from B must not yield the same value of ϕ. It does so by finding all pairs of examples $f(\mathbf{x}_j) = z_j$, $f(\mathbf{x}_k) = z_k$ with pairwise equal values of free variables, $\mathbf{a}_j = \mathbf{a}_k$, and different function value, $z_j \neq z_k$. The intermediate function ϕ must have different values for $\mathbf{b}_j$ and $\mathbf{b}_k$, otherwise there would not exist any function F such that $F(\mathbf{a}_j, \phi(\mathbf{b}_j)) = z_j$ and $F(\mathbf{a}_k, \phi(\mathbf{b}_k)) = z_k$. This fact can be easily proved by contradiction; if $\mathbf{a}_j = \mathbf{a}_k$ and we set $\phi(\mathbf{b}_j) = \phi(\mathbf{b}_k)$ then if F existed, it would obviously have the same value for both examples, $F(\mathbf{a}_j, \phi(\mathbf{b}_j)) = F(\mathbf{a}_k, \phi(\mathbf{b}_k))$, which leads to $z_j = z_k$.

Pairs $(\mathbf{b}_j, \mathbf{b}_k)$ that must not give the same value of ϕ are called incompatible. The incompatibility relation is presented in the form of the incompatibility graph. By coloring the graph (or by finding the maximum clique on its complement, the compatibility graph), possible inputs for ϕ, vectors $\mathbf{b_j}$, are divided into M subsets; members of the same subset M_i yield the same value $\phi(\mathbf{b}_j) = m_i$. The intermediate function ϕ therefore maps each $\mathbf{b}_j$ to the corresponding set M_i. The value of induced variable m_i is added to each rule to replace variables from $B \setminus A$.

For purposes of switching circuits design, the algorithm was first used on Boolean functions. An extension of this approach to handle nominal functions with more than two different output values is presented in [7].

2.2 Algorithm for Real-Function Decomposition

The basis of our method is the decomposition algorithm described in the previous section, limited to disjunctive splits, $A \cap B = \emptyset$, with two bound variables, $|B| = 2$. When adapting it for decomposition of real functions, several problems have to be dealt with.

First, since each variable generally has an infinite domain, it is practically impossible that the learning set contains any instances with pairwise equal values of free variables which are needed to show the incompatibilities of bound values.

The next problem is the interpretation of intermediate function ϕ: the original algorithm defines values of ϕ to serve as indices to sets M_i. The function ϕ is nominal rather than ordinal and since the algorithm was developed for the design of switching circuits where the interpretation is unnecessary, it does not intend to present the discovered function in the symbolic form, i.e. to recognize it as, for example, an **and** function. Instead, functions ϕ and F are left in tabular form. As shown in [7], the interpretation of a discrete function ϕ can be done manually provided that its input and output variables have only small number of possible values. When using the algorithm to *learn* the function of *real values*, rule tables that are constructed by the original algorithm are normally very large, and the search for a symbolical form of the intermediate functions cannot be left to the expert.

Interpretation of an intermediate function is also important because it ensures that the learned function is not defined only on points that appear in the rule table.

Discretization of examples. One possible way to generate incompatible pairs is to discretize the examples. After the discretization, some pairs of examples might have pairwise equal values of all the arguments. A straightforward discretization of function values may assign different discrete function values to such pairs. This way, the function would become ambiguous. To avoid this, the function value is "granulized": all pairs of examples with the same discretized values of variables $\mathbf{x}'_j = \mathbf{x}'_k$ are examined and the maximal difference of their function values $g = \max_{j,k} |f(\mathbf{x}_j) - f(\mathbf{x}_k)|$ is used for the size of the grain. Function values z_{j_1} and z_{j_2} are considered different if $|z_{j_1} - z_{j_2}| > g$. This approach works optimally for functions f with a constant gradient over the whole definition area. If this is not the case, the discretized learning examples accurately describe the areas with larger gradient, but underrepresents all other areas. The consequences and solutions of the problem shall be discussed later.

A crucial problem of discretization is determining the most suitable number of intervals. Coarse discretization can significantly lower the accuracy of constants in derived functions or even cause an incorrect decomposition. On the other hand, a finer discretization results in a sparser coverage of the domain of the function. As a consequence, the incompatibility graph has low connectivity and bears almost no information on intermediate function ϕ since there exist many different optimal colorings, yielding many different functions.

The interpretation of the intermediate function. The result of coloring the incompatibility graph is a division of the bound variables' space into the areas M_i with points which will yield the same value of ϕ, i.e. $M_i = \{(x_{i,j}, y_{i,j}) : \phi(x_{i,j}, y_{i,j}) = c_i\}$. In other words, the coloring proposes contour lines – or, because of discretization, contour strips – of the real function ϕ. Unfortunately, it provides neither the numerical values c_i nor the difference between function values on neighbouring contour strips (the gradient of ϕ). The symbolic form of ϕ has to be obtained from the shape of the strips.

First, consider a linear function ϕ. Its contour strips are straight lines. If we plot a colored graph of a discretized linear function in a coordinate system, contour strips are visible as strips of the same color. The function ϕ that we are looking for is of the form

$$\phi(x, y) = k_1(ax + y) + k_2 \tag{1}$$

Coefficients k_1 and k_2 cannot be determined at this stage since they do not have any impact on the shape of the strips. They should be determined in further steps of decomposition and incorporated in the intermediate function at the parent node.

The coefficient a is derived from the slope of the strips. Ideally, all the points $(x_{i,j}, y_{i,j}) \in M_i$ would lie on the same line $ax + y = c_i$. Because of discretization and, possibly, noise, the points are actually scattered around this line. As the measure of fit we choose the sum of squared Euclidean distances from the line,

$$E_i(a, c_i) = \sum_{j=1}^{n_i} \left[\frac{ax_{i,j} + y_{i,j} - c_i}{\sqrt{a^2 + 1}} \right]^2 \tag{2}$$

with $(x_{i,j}, y_{i,j}) \in M_i$ and $n_i = |M_i|$. To obtain the optimal a, the total sum of squared distances is minimized using the partial derivative

$$\frac{\partial E(a, \mathbf{c})}{\partial a} = \frac{\partial \sum_{i=1}^{M} E_i(a, c_i)}{\partial a} = 0 \tag{3}$$

Solution of this equation for a gives the optimal value of a. The quality of the approximation can be measured by Pearson's correlation coefficient r which, in its original form

$$r = \frac{\sum_j (x_j - \bar{x})(y_j - \bar{y})}{\sqrt{\sum_j (x_j - \bar{x})^2} \sqrt{\sum_j (y_j - \bar{y})^2}} \tag{4}$$

measures the linear correlation between variables x_j and y_j. Since we deal with more than one group of points, the Pearson's coefficient must be generalized to

$$r_g = \frac{\sum_{i,j}(x_{i,j} - \overline{x_i})(y_{i,j} - \overline{y_i})}{\sqrt{\sum_{i,j}(x_{i,j} - \overline{x_i})^2}\sqrt{\sum_{i,j}(y_{i,j} - \overline{y_i})^2}} \tag{5}$$

where $\overline{x_i} = \frac{1}{n_i}\sum_{j=1}^{n_i} x_{i,j}$ and $\overline{y_i} = \frac{1}{n_i}\sum_{j=1}^{n_i} y_{i,j}$. In this form, the coefficient is still normalized to be between -1 and 1, with $|r_g| = 1$ meaning the maximum linearity of the strips and $|r_g| = 0$ no linearity.

Other, non-linear functions are sought by transformation to a linear function. For example, contour strips of $\phi(x,y) = x^a y$ are same as those of $\phi(x,y) = a\ln(x) + \ln(y)$ or $\phi(x,y) = aX + Y$ where $X = \ln(x)$ and $Y = \ln(y)$. Our algorithm searches for all the functions of the form $\phi(x,y) = ag(x) + h(y)$ and $\phi(x,y) = [g(x)]^a h(y)$ by using transformations $x_{i,j} \to g(x_{i,j})$, $y_{i,j} \to h(y_{i,j})$ and $x_{i,j} \to a\ln g(x_{i,j})$, $y_{i,j} \to \ln h(y_{i,j})$, respectively. Functions g and h are from a predefined set of basic functions, for example $\{\mathrm{Id}, \sin, \exp, \ln\}$. All the possible functions are evaluated and the one with the greatest $|r_g|$ is chosen.

The root of the decomposition tree. The decomposition process stops when the free set of attributes is empty. The values of the decomposed function F are not necessarily equal to the values of the original function f. However, for an analyticaly expressible function f, if the algorithm finds the correct decomposition and there is no noise, the method guarantees that the value of $f(\mathbf{x})$ can be reconstructed from $F(\mathbf{x})$. Our program tries to find a function g and constants a and n, such that $f(\mathbf{x}) = ag(F(\mathbf{x})) + n$. The function g is from the same set of basic functions as mentioned above. For each function, a and n are found by the classical least-squares method and the difference between $f(\mathbf{x})$ and $ag(F(\mathbf{x})) + n$ is measured by corrected relative error [3]. The most accurate function is added to the decomposition tree as the root's parent.

Discarding invalid contour strips. Besides the noise in the data, the algorithm also encounters the noise caused by discretization of variables and granulation of function value. The noise of variables is partially reduced by robust statistic methods used for deriving ϕ. A more serious problem occurs as a consequence of the granulation of function value which affects the graph coloring, especially when function's gradient strongly changes across the definition area. Areas with small gradient are covered with much wider contour strips than areas with larger gradient; in some cases they also differ in shape.

A simple and effective method that can overcome this problem calculates Pearson's r for each strip and discards all the strips with $|r|$ significantly lower than the average $|r|$.

The problem of similar functions. Another problem that the algorithm has to cope with is the problem of distinguishing between similar functions. For example, when the width of discretization interval is 0.1 and $|x| < 0.75$, functions

x and $\sin(x)$ are indistinguishable. One of possible solutions of this problem is to use non-equidistant discretization, which is, however, difficult to perform. A different solution is to introduce the cost for each function used. This way, the program is given background knowledge of which functions are expected and which are less likely to occur. The cost of the function is subtracted from the absolute value of the correlation coefficient when comparing different candidates for function ϕ. Even more complex background knowledge can be given by forbidding or penalizing the function within certain contexts. For example, when observing some physical phenomena, we shall allow functions sin and ln but strongly penalize combinations $\sin + \ln$ and $\sin \cdot \ln$.

The third and the safest way to deal with similar functions is to involve an expert which intervenes when the algorithm has to decide between functions with a similar correlation coefficient.

2.3 Complexity of the Algorithm

A single step of decomposition consists of discretizing the attribute (time complexity is $O(N)$), sorting the rule table ($O(N \log N)$), deriving the incompatibility graph ($O(Nk)$), coloring it ($O(k^2)$) and interpreting the coloring ($O(Ns^2)$), where N is the number of examples. k is the number of combinations of discretized bound variables values, which is at most equal to the product of number of discretization intervals. s is the number of basic functions. To select a partition when decomposing a function of l variables, $l(l-1)/2$ possible partitions must be considered, which gives the complexity of

$$O\left(l^2(N + N \log N + Nk + k^2 + Ns^2)\right)$$

Since the decomposition algorithm induces a binary tree, the step above must be repeated $l - 1$ times, therefore the total complexity is

$$O\left(\sum_{i=2}^{i=l} i^2(N + N \log N + Nk + Ns^2 + k^2)\right)$$
$$= O\left(l^3(N + N \log N + Nk + Nk^2 + Ns^2)\right)$$

Empirical tests show that sorting is far slower than other operations even for relatively small number of examples, so we can estimate the time complexity as $O\left(l^3 N \log N\right)$.

This result shows the main advantage of this method in comparison with some existing methods of function discovery, such as GoldHorn [3], which performs an exhaustive search over the space of functions it can represent. We can note that GoldHorn's complexity increases exponentially with the depth of function and number of subfunctions but linearly in the number of examples, while our algorithm's complexity is practically independent of the number of basic functions.

3 Experimental Evaluation

The algorithm was tested on several functions specially chosen to explore its advantages and drawbacks. All the functions were within the program's search space, i.e. their hierarchical decomposition did not require any basic functions that were unknown to the program.

$f(x, y) = x + 2y + 3$. This simple linear function is used to roughly measure the number of examples that the algorithm needs to discover the correct form of the function and derive accurate coefficients. The program was run 10 times for each number of randomly chosen examples for the function ($x, y \in [0, 10]$). The results are shown in Table 1.

#examples	correct ϕ	$\bar{a}$	σa
20	2	2.041	0.164
25	3	1.862	0.160
30	6	1.980	0.132
40	7	2.024	0.064
50	10	2.032	0.044
100	10	2.049	0.032
500	10	2.053	0.016
1000	10	2.000	0.014

Table 1. Decomposing function $f(x, y) = x + 2y + 3$: Accuracy and correctness of the form of the discovered function

$f(x, y, z) = 2.5xy + 0.5z$. This function illustrates some difficulties due to equidistant discretization and granulation. The program is expected to decompose it as shown in Figure 2.

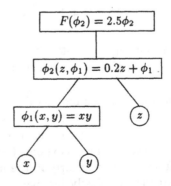

Fig. 2. Function $f(x, y, z) = 2.5xy + 0.5z$: The decomposition tree

If $x, y, z \in [0, 10]$, the gradient of $\phi_1 = xy$ is greater for larger than for smaller x and y. Since granulation is the same over the whole area, the area with the low function's gradient is colored as a wide strip (the left-bottom strip on the Figure 3). Its shape clearly differs from other areas. It cannot be used to determine the slope of the (linearized) functions so the program, after comparing its r with the average, chooses to ignore it.

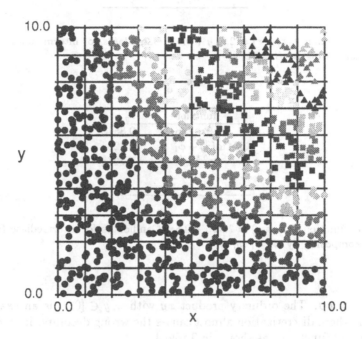

Fig. 3. Function $f(x, y, z) = 2.5xy + 0.5z$: Contour strips of the first step of the decomposition when decomposing by $B = \{x, y\}$.

On the other hand, other strips do not adequately represent the goal function and the Table 2 shows that there are other functions with almost equal r_g coefficient. The reason for high ranking of functions of type ln +Id and Id + Id is that the most representative contour strips are merged in a single strip and ignored, while the rest of strips are already close to linear without any transformation.

After the first step of the decomposition is made, ϕ_1 is introduced that directly depends on x and y and has values between 0 and 100, so $2.5\phi_1 \in [0, 250]$. The other remaining variable z is between 0 and 10, $0.5z \in [0, 5]$, hence it is negligible in comparison with ϕ_1. If both variables are discretized using the same number of intervals, the algorithm discovers functions like $0.001z + \phi_1$ and the measure of quality r_g is very low (< 0.07). If we (manually) increase the number of intervals for z, the algorithm detects its role in the function and chooses the correct type of intermediate function (see Table 3).

function	r_g
$x^{1.00}y$	0.9505
$5.09\ln(x)+y$	0.9368
$0.19x+\ln(y)$	0.9276
$1.00x+y$	0.8918
$\ln(x)^{5.92}e^y$	0.8348
$\vdots$	

Table 2. Function $f(x,y,z)=2.5xy+0.5z$: Candidates for intermediate function ϕ_1 when decomposing by $B=\{x,y\}$

function	r_g
$0.19z+\phi_1$	0.8513
$0.54\ln(z)+\phi_1$	0.7254
$z^{0.54}e^{\phi_1}$	0.7254
$\vdots$	

Table 3. Function $f(x,y,z)=2.5xy+0.5z$: Candidates for intermediate function ϕ_2 when decomposing by $B=\{xy,z\}$

$f(x,y)=xy$. The ordinary product xy with $x,y\in[0,1]$ is an example of a function where discretization almost causes the wrong decomposition due to the similarity of functions, as shown in Table 4.

function	r_g
xy	0.9712
$\sin^{1.08}(x)y$	0.9702
$x^{0.91}\sin(y)$	0.9701
$\sin(x)^{0.99}\sin(y)$	0.9688
$\vdots$	

Table 4. Function $f(x,y)=xy$: Candidates for intermediate function ϕ.

The quantitative error of wrong decision would be small since $\sin(x)\approx x$ but an expert may be unable to interpret the resulting decomposition.

$f(x, y, w, z) = x + \sin(y + \ln(wz))$. The program expresses the discovered function in a variety of different ways, which can presumably help an expert to interpret the meaning of derived functions.

Function $f(x, y, w, z) = x + \sin(y + \ln(wz))$ can be rewritten as $f(x, y, w, z) = x + \sin(y + \ln w + \ln z))$. In the first step, some of the best ranking candidates for ϕ_1 are as shown in Table 5. Besides functions $\phi_1(w, z) = wz$, $\phi_1(y, w) = y + \ln(w)$ and $\phi_1(y, z) = y + \ln(z)$, the program also proposes $\phi_1(y, z) = e^y z$ and $\phi_1(y, w) = e^y w$. These can be used later in $\phi_2(y, w, z) = \ln(\phi_1(y, z)) + \ln(w)$ or $\phi_2(y, w, z) = \ln(\phi_1(y, w)) + \ln(z)$, respectively, or even in $\phi_2(y, w, z) = w\phi_1(y, z)$ or $\phi_2(y, w, z) = z\phi_1(y, w)$ to write the function as $f(x, y, w, z) = x + \sin(\ln(wye^y))$. The last form is, however, not in algorithm's search space if the set of basic functions does not contain the composed function $\sin \circ \ln$.

function	r_g
$w^{0.97} z$	0.7901
$(0.99y + \ln(z))$	0.7630
$e^{0.99y} z$	0.7630
$0.99y + \ln(w)$	0.6640
$e^{0.99y} w$	0.6640
$\vdots$	

Table 5. Function $f(x, y, w, z) = x + \sin(y + \ln(wz))$: Candidates for an intermediate function ϕ when decomposing by $B = \{x, y\}$.

$f(x, y, w, z) = x + \ln(y + \ln(w + z))$. This experiment shows the algorithm's ability to decompose complex nested functions. It also proves that the number of graph's colors and r_g are not necessarily correlated and that the latter is much more accurate criterion for selecting the appropriate partition. Table 6 lists all possible partitions, number of colors, the best intermediate functions, and their r_g for the first step of decomposition.

Among three possible partitions for the next step, the algorithm again chooses the right one, $A = \{x\}$, $B = \{y, \phi_1\}$ and $\phi_2 = y + \ln(\phi_1)$, as shown in Table 7.

In the last step, the only possible partition is $A = \{\}$, $B = \{x, \phi_2\}$ and the program correctly interprets the colored graph as $\phi_3 = 0.98x + \ln(\phi_2)$. Thus, the discovered function is $0.98x + \ln(1.09y + \ln(1.02w + z))$.

$f(x, y) = \sin(x + y)$. For $x, y \in [0, 7]$, this function is non-injective and the program is unable to decompose it, as shown in Table 8. The reason is in repeating colors of contour strips, as already explained and shown on Figure 4.

bound variables	# colors	function	r_g
w, z	19	$1.02w + z$	0.8673
y, w	14	$2.27y + \ln(w)$	0.7924
y, z	13	$11.17y + z$	0.7794
x, z	19	$32.09x + z$	0.7127
x, w	11	$28.63x + w$	0.6935
x, y	6	$1.13e^x + \sin(y)$	0.5134

Table 6. Function $f(x, y, w, z) = x + \ln(y + \ln(w + z))$: Possible partitions, number of colors, the best intermediate function and its linearity for the first step of decomposition.

bound variables	# colors	function	r_g
y, ϕ_1	26	$1.09y + \ln(\phi_1)$	0.9317
x, ϕ_1	19	$2.72x + \ln(\phi_1)$	0.9030
x, y	17	$2.22x + \sin(y)$	0.8898

Table 7. Function $f(x, y, w, z) = x + \ln(y + \ln(w + z))$: The second step of decomposition with $\phi_1 = w + z$.

4 Conclusion

The experiments presented in this paper indicate that the proposed method is able to correctly decompose relatively complex functions and can be successfully used to discover a symbolic representation of a tabulated function. On the other hand, the accuracy of constants appearing in the symbolic representation is low due to the discrete nature of the method. However, as described in [3], the accuracy can be further improved by the simplex method. Since discretization and granulation also cause other difficulties, like indistinguishable similar functions and ignoring of variables with small impacts on the value of the function, future

function	r_g
$0.00e^x + \sin(y)$	0.2869
$0.26\ln(x) + \cos(y)$	0.2674
$-3.52\cos(x) + \ln(y)$	0.2656
$2139.49\sin(x) + e^y$	0.2455
$0.05x + \cos(y)$	0.2389
$\vdots$	

Table 8. Function $f(x, y) = \sin(x + y)$: Candidates for an intermediate function ϕ.

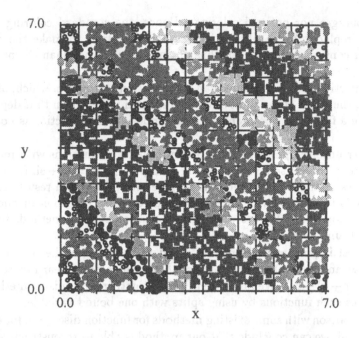

Fig. 4. Function $f(x, y, z) = f(x, y) = \sin(x + y)$: Contour strips.

research should address the design of method that avoids the use of discrete structures.

An interesting question is what happens if the algorithm misses the right intermediate function, for example, if it chooses $\phi(x, y) = x \sin(y)$ or $\phi(x, y) = x + y$ instead of $\phi(x, y) = xy$. If the wrong decision is made because of the similarity of functions in the definition area (like Id and sin), the mistake should not affect the upper layers of decomposition tree. When the wrong decision is a consequence of discarding some contour strips, our decomposition can go astray completely. The algorithm should therefore be improved not to rely on local decisions but to perform a beam search, where several candidate intermediate functions are chosen and later discarded if they show to be unusable.

Classical coloring algorithms are appropriate for graphs with vertices that correspond to nominal values. If they are used on ordinal values, they obviously ignore the information about the position of vertices in the space of bound attributes. In our case, ignoring the location of vertices may cause the discrepancy between coloring and the next phase of the process, the interpretation of colors. Classical graph coloring heuristics that try to minimize the number of colors used are suitable for the decomposition of nominal functions, where the number of colors influences the cardinality of the intermediate function and the criterion, used to choose the partition, normally chooses the partition with less colors. For decomposition of ordinal and real functions, the functions and partitions are evaluated using quite a different criterion, the r_g coefficient, which in some cases even encourages non-optimal colorings. Hence, the standard coloring method should be replaced by an alternative method that tries to make the areas of same color continuous and linear, thus optimizing r_g rather than the number of colors.

Non-injective functions produce an incompatibility graph in which, after it is linearized, the strips of the same color are repeated in a pattern that depends on the type of a function. The problem of decomposing such function is not solved yet.

Another unsolved problem is the decomposition of functions with more than one occurrence of the same variable, for example $f(x, y) = x + \sin(x + y)$. The method presented in this paper fails to give any meaningful result. However, the methods to support such decompositions do exist for Boolean and multi-valued functions [5, 7]. We are working on extension of these methods to handle real-valued functions as well.

The most important problem that is yet to be solved is the problem of coefficients k_1 and k_2 in (1) when they are to appear in non-linear functions such as $\sin(k_1(ax + y) + k_2)$. We are currently investigating a promising method that decomposes such functions by using splits with one bound variable.

In comparison with some existing methods for function discovery, for example GoldHorn [3], we can conclude that our method is able to reconstruct relatively complex functions but with low accuracy of coefficients, while GoldHorn offers high accuracy on functions of limited complexity. The time complexity of our method is low, since all the slow phases (like graph coloring) can be replaced by faster, yet efficient heuristic algorithms. GoldHorn performs an exhaustive search of all possible functions to a given depth. This grows exponentially with the depth and the number of basic functions (background knowledge). On the other hand, our functional decomposition uses a "divide and conquer" approach which significantly improves the efficiency. Also it should be noted that the complexity in our case is relatively low. The time complexity of the algorithm is cubic in the number of attributes, at most $O(N \ln N)$ in the number of examples, and practicallly independent of the number of basic functions (size of background knowledge).

References

1. R. L. Ashenhurst (1952): *The Decomposition of Switching Functions*, Technical report, Bell Laboratories BL-1(11), 541-602
2. H. A. Curtis (1962): *Design of Switching Circuits*, D. Van Nostrand Company
3. V. Križman (1993): *Noise handling in dynamic system modelling* Master thesis (in Slovene), University Ljubljana, Faculty of Computer and Information Science
4. T. Luba (1995): Decomposition of Multiple-valued Functions, *25th Intl. Symposium on Multiple-valued Logic*, 256-261, Bloomington, Indiana.
5. M. A. Perkowski *et al.* (1996): *Unified Approach to Functional Decomposition of Switching Functions*, Unpublished technical report, Wright Laboratory WL/AART-2, Ohio

6. T. D. Ross *et al.* (1994): On the Decomposition of Real-valued Functions, *3rd International Workshop of Post-Binary VLSI Systems*
7. B. Zupan, M. Bohanec (1996): *Learning Concept Hierarchies from Examples by Function Decomposition*, Technical Report, J. Stefan Institute, URL ftp://ftp-e8.ijs.si/pub/reports/IJSDP-7455.ps

Conditions for Occam's Razor Applicability and Noise Elimination

Dragan Gamberger[1] and Nada Lavrač[2]

[1] Rudjer Bošković Institute, Bijenička 54,10000 Zagreb, Croatia
E-mail: gambi@lelhp1.irb.hr
[2] Jožef Stefan Institute, Jamova 39, 1000 Ljubljana, Slovenia
E-mail: nada.lavrac@ijs.si

Abstract. The Occam's razor principle suggests that among all the correct hypotheses, the simplest hypothesis is the one which best captures the structure of the problem domain and has the highest prediction accuracy when classifying new instances. This principle is implicitly used also for dealing with noise, in order to avoid overfitting a noisy training set by rule truncation or by pruning of decision trees. This work gives a theoretical framework for the applicability of Occam's razor, developed into a procedure for eliminating noise from a training set. The results of empirical evaluation show the usefulness of the presented approach to noise elimination.

1 Introduction

The Occam's razor principle, commonly attributed to William of Occam (early 14th century), states: "Entities should not be multiplied beyond necessity." This principle is generally interpreted as: "Among the theories that are consistent with the observed phenomena, one should select the simplest theory" [9].

Occam's razor is the principle explicitly or implicitly used in many inductive learning systems. This principle suggests that among all the hypotheses that are correct for all (or for most of) the training examples one should select the simplest hypothesis; it can be expected that this hypothesis is most likely to capture the structure inherent in the problem and that its high prediction accuracy can be expected on objects outside the training set [14]. This principle is also used by noise handling and predicate invention algorithms because noise handling and predicate invention have the aim to simplify the generated rules or decision trees in order to avoid overfitting a noisy training set.

Despite the successful use of the Occam's razor principle as the basis for hypothesis construction (e.g., implemented in tree pruning and rule truncation mechanisms), several problems arise in practice. First is the problem of the definition of the most appropriate complexity measure that will be used to identify the simplest hypothesis. The problem is that different measures can select different simplest hypotheses for the same training set. This holds for any Kolmogorov complexity based measure [9], including the MDL (Minimal Description Length) [14, 16], that use approximations of an ideal complexity measure. Second, recent experimental work has undoubtly shown that applications of the Occam's razor may not always lead to the optimal prediction accuracy; a systematic way of improving the results generated by the application of the Occam's razor principle has even been suggested [17]. This is somewhat shocking for the inductive learning community because the principle is the basis of most practical and popular inductive learning systems (e.g., [12]). Additional disorientation is caused by the so-called "conservation law of generalization performance" [15].

Although it is rather clear [13] that real-word learning tasks are different from the set of all theoretically possible learning tasks as defined in [15], there remains the so-called "selective superiority problem" that each algorithm performs best in some but not all domains [1], which can be in a way explained by the bias-variance tradeoff [6]. Our work contributes to the understanding of the abovementioned phenomena by studying for which domains (real or theoretically possible) an inductive learning algorithm based on the Occam's razor principle has a theoretical chance for successful induction.

In this paper, we elaborate the conditions for Occam's razor applicability: for noiseless two class domains we define conditions that guarantee that a hypothesis, that is correct for all the training examples and is the simplest with respect to a selected complexity measure of predefined properties, is correct also for examples outside the training set. So the theorems theoretically solve the problems opened by the "conservation law" by showing that under given conditions effective hypothesis induction is possible. The theorems also theoretically solve the problems concerning the applicability of the Occam's razor principle by giving explicit conditions when the principle can help in induction. In reality, the presented theorems are much less useful because their conditions are so strict that they are rarely fulfilled in practice. For practical applications, the theorems are more interesting for indicating the properties that need to be satisfied for the effective induction using the Occam's razor principle. Moreover, they are the basis for the proposed algorithm for noise elimination.

The paper presents a theoretical framework for the applicability of the Occam's razor principle in Sections 2–7. Section 8 proposes an algorithm for eliminating noise from a training set, and Section 9 provides experimental evidence for the usefulness of the proposed approach to noise elimination.

2 Basic problem definition

We assume a propositional inductive task that starts from a set of training examples E that are part of some example domain D, $E \subset D$. Each of the examples is either positive or negative (a two class problem) and is described by a fixed set of attribute values. Some attribute values can be unknown. The aim of inductive learning systems is to construct a hypothesis (rule, decision tree) with the largest rate of correct class predictions over yet unseen examples in D.

Suppose that domain D is ideal in the sense that it contains no errors (noise) and no contradictions. In such a case, a target theory T that needs to be discovered is correct for all the examples in D (i.e., it is true for all the positive and false for all the negative examples in D). Every inductive learner uses some form

Intuitively, the notion of a saturated training set E means that E has (more than) enough training examples for inducing a correct target hypothesis H_T. A consequence of Definition 3 and Lemma 2 is that, under conditions of an unchanged language bias and complexity measure, any subset of a non-saturated training set is also non-saturated, and any superset of a saturated training set remains saturated. The fact $g(D) = c(H_T)$ implies that any non-saturated training set E can be transformed into a saturated set by adding training examples to E.

Suppose that the complexity $c(H_T)$ is finite. Under this condition, the ideal curve of $g(E)$ values for one of the many possible sequences of training sets with the following property:

$$\emptyset \subset E_1 \subset E_2 \subset ... \subset E_n ... \subset E_S \subset ... \subset D$$

is presented in Figure 1. In the rest of the paper, this curve is called a *complexity curve*. In reality, this function is insreasing in a stepwise manner, where the step magnitude depends on the sensitivity of the used complexity measure.

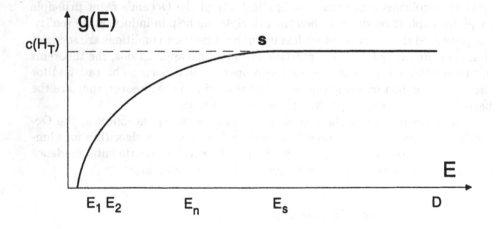

Fig. 1. An ideal curve of CLCH (Complexity of the Least Complex correct Hypothesis) values for a sequence of training domains E with the following property: $\emptyset \subset E_1 \subset E_2 \subset ... \subset E_n \subset ... \subset E_S \subset ... \subset D$.

As a consequence of Lemma 2, the curve is monotonically increasing, and $g(E) \leq c(H_T)$ for every E. The curve must have a saturation point (S in Figure 1) since the smallest subset of D, denoted by E_S, exists which completely determines the target hypothesis and for which it is true that $g(E_S) = c(H_T)$. The training sets E, $E_S \subset E$, with CLCH values in the saturation part of the of knowledge representation which defines the hypothesis space. In this work, the target hypothesis H_T denotes the simplest hypothesis from the hypothesis space that is correct for all the examples in D. It represents the target theory in the given hypothesis space. A necessary (but not a sufficient) condition for a hypothesis H to be the target hypothesis H_T is that it must be correct for all the examples in E. But as this condition may be true for many hypotheses, the inductive learning problem is to select the most appropriate one.

3 Complexity of the least complex hypothesis

Suppose that a hypothesis complexity measure $c(H)$ is defined and let $H_t = H_t(E)$ be a hypothesis that is correct for all the training examples in E. For every training set E it is theoretically possible to find many different hypotheses H_t and to determine their complexity $c(H_t)$. By selecting the hypothesis of a minimal complexity ($arg\ min_t\ c(H_t)$), the complexity of the least complex hypothesis from the hypotheses space that is correct for all the examples in E can be determined. In this work it is called the least complex correct hypothesis, and its complexity, denoted by $g(E) = min_t\ c(H_t)$, is the so-called CLCH value (Complexity of the Least Complex correct Hypothesis). If E is an empty set or a set consisting of examples of only one class then $g(E) = 0$ by definition. From the definition for the target hypothesis H_T it follows that $g(D) = c(H_T)$.

Definition 1. A complexity measure c is *reasonable* if for two hypotheses, H_1 and H_2, where H_2 is obtained by conjunctively or disjunctively adding conditions to H_1, the following relation holds: $c(H_1) \leq c(H_2)$.[3]

The paper assumes that the used complexity measure $c(H)$ is reasonable.

Lemma 2. *Let* $c(H)$ *be a complexity measure and* $g(E) = min_t\ c(H_t)$.

$$If\ E_1 \subset E_2\ then\ g(E_1) \leq g(E_2).$$

Proof: Every hypothesis that is correct for all the examples in E_2 is correct also for all the examples in E_1. So the correct hypothesis of a minimal complexity for E_2 is also correct for all the examples in E_1, and $g(E_2)$ can not be smaller than $g(E_1)$. □

4 Complexity curve

Definition 3. A training set E is called *saturated* if $g(E) = c(H_T)$. Otherwise it is called *non-saturated*.

---

[3] All complexity measures used in practical inductive systems are reasonable. But, for example, if $c(H)$ is a reasonable complexity measure then the complexity measure defined as $-c(H)$ or as $1/c(H)$ is not reasonable.

complexity curve (at the right of point S) are saturated training sets, whereas the training sets E, $E \subset E_S$, at the left of point S are non-saturated.

The saturation property has some interesting characteristics:

- The CLCH value $g(E)$ is defined with respect to the given hypothesis space. Changes in the language bias can change the hypothesis space and the set of hypotheses over which the CLCH value for E is computed. So the changes in the language bias can change the $g(E)$ values and the conditions for the saturation property of the training set. If by changes in the learning bias a non-saturated training set is converted into a saturated set, this is a reliable sign that a more appropriate bias was found.

- The CLCH value is defined with respect to a selected complexity measure. Although the properties of the complexity curve do not depend on the properties of the complexity measure (except that it must be reasonable), this does not mean that the properties of the complexity measure have no influence on the practical curve form for the given training set E. Namely, the same training set can be saturated for one complexity measure and non-saturated for another. The choice of an appropriate complexity measure is in this sense similar to the choice of an appropriate language bias and depends exclusively on the characteristics of domain D. In most cases, a consequence of the use of an inappropriate complexity measure and/or an inappropriate hypothesis space is that a training set E should contain a larger number of examples in order to be saturated.

- For an example domain D, many different sequences of training sets with the property $\emptyset \subset E_1 \subset E_2 \subset ... \subset E_n \subset ... \subset D$ can be constructed, resulting in different complexity curve forms. If the same E_n occurs in different set sequences, then, given a fixed language bias and complexity measure, it can not be saturated according to one complexity curve and non-saturated according to another. This follows from the fact that the saturation property is defined by the condition $g(E) = c(H_T)$ which does not depend on the properties of other elements in the sequence. All the complexity curves are still monotonically increasing because of the property that any subset of a non-saturated training set is non-saturated and that any superset of a saturated training set is saturated.

The most important implication of the properties of the saturated training sets is that the conditions for successful Occam's razor based induction can be formulated as theorems. On the other hand, the complexity curve has also interesting properties when noisy examples are included in the training set. On this basis, a novel noise handling approach can be defined (see Section 8).

5 Occam's razor theorems

Definition 4. Two hypotheses are *substantially different* if they predict a different class for at least one example in D.

Theorem 5. *A saturated training set E is a necessary condition for the applicability of Occam's razor.*

Proof: Suppose that E is a non-saturated training set, therefore $g(E) < c(H_T)$. The target hypothesis H_T is defined as the simplest hypothesis in the hypothesis space that is correct for all the examples in D, therefore $g(D) = c(H_T)$. Since $g(E) < g(D)$, a hypothesis H_t, which is correct for all the training examples in E and has the minimal complexity, has a smaller complexity than the complexity of the least complex hypothesis that is correct for all the examples in D. This means that H_t can not be correct for all the examples in D and that it is substantially different from H_T with a worse prediction accuracy in D. In the case of a non-saturated training set E, the application of Occam's razor will therefore *always* result in the selection of a wrong target hypothesis. The conclusion is that a saturated training set is a necessary condition for the applicability of Occam's razor. □

It must be noted that the consequences of Theorem 5 do not depend on the properties of the selected complexity measure. Non-optimal prediction results obtained by Occam's razor, reported in [17], can be interpreted as the consequence of non-saturated training sets used in the experiments. This follows from the fact that improved prediction accuracy was obtained by hypotheses modifications on the domain parts in which training sets did not have any training examples [17].

Definition 6. A complexity measure is *ideal* if it is so sensitive that no two substantially different hypotheses H_1 and H_2 in the hypothesis space have the same complexity, and that it can not hold that $c(H_1) = c(H_2) = g(E)$.

Theorem 7. *An ideal complexity measure is a necessary condition for the applicability of Occam's razor.*

Proof: Suppose that a non-ideal complexity measure is used and that there are two substantially different correct hypotheses H_1 and H_2 for which $c(H_1) = c(H_2) = g(E)$, where $g(E)$ is the complexity of the least complex hypothesis correct for all examples in E. In this case, the correct target hypothesis $H_T = H_1$ or $H_T = H_2$ can be selected only by chance. Consequently, an ideal complexity measure is a necessary condition for the applicability of Occam's razor. □

The sufficient condition for Occam's razor applicanbility can now be defined.

Theorem 8. *If $E \subset D$ is a saturated training set, and the hypothesis complexity measure c is ideal, then the simplest hypothesis that is correct for all the examples in E is correct also for all the examples in D.*

Proof: For a saturated training set E it is true that $g(E) = c(H_T)$. In the case of an ideal complexity measure no two substantially different hypotheses can have the same complexity value. This means that the simplest hypothesis for E is the same as, or non-substantially different from, the target hypothesis for D. The non-substantial difference means that the two hypotheses have the same class predictions over the whole domain D. Consequently, a saturated training set and an ideal complexity measure are a sufficient condition for the applicability of Occam's razor. □

The importance of Theorem 8 is that it theoretically proves that successful induction is possible. But the practical usefulness of the theorem is very restricted. The main problem is that the saturation property of the training set E can not be tested by verifying the condition $g(E) = c(H_T)$ because $c(H_T)$ could be determined only from D. Although a practical algorithm for the saturation test is suggested in the following section, this test (or any other test based only on the training set) regardless of its precision, can never guarantee that E is indeed saturated. Moreover, no practical application of the Occam's razor principle can guarantee that the induced hypothesis is correct for the whole D or that no other better hypothesis exists.

An additional problem regarding Theorems 7 and 8 is that it is difficult or even impossible to guarantee that a complexity measure is ideal for the given hypothesis space. So the second condition of Theorem 8 can not be fulfilled in practice either. A non-ideal complexity measure can also lead to an additional unreliability of the practical algorithm for the saturation test.

The conclusion is that in practice applying Occam's razor can never guarantee the optimality of the chosen hypothesis. But applications of very different practical complexity measures that are all known to be non-ideal have undoubtly shown that the selection of an appropriate complexity measure is not a critical problem and that effective induction is possible also using non-ideal complexity measures. Results presented in Section 9 show that even using a complexity measure of a rather low sensitivity (a large number of substantially different hypotheses having the same complexity) can enable induction with a high prediction accuracy. Theorem 7 shows that theoretically only a distinction between ideal and non-ideal complexity measures is important. In practice, when the user can choose among different non-ideal measures, the preference should be given to measures that are more sensitive.

6 Practical saturation test

The form of the complexity curve presented in Figure 1 suggests that the saturation property of E may be detected by checking whether in its subset or superset neighbourhood the CLCH values do not change. As in real learning situations only subsets of E can be formed, the practically implementable saturation test can be stated as follows:

"If for all the possible subsets E_x that can be formed by the exclusion of one (or few) examples from E it is true that $g(E_x) = g(E)$, then E is saturated".

The problem of this test is that it can not guarantee that E is saturated. Namely, in practice, the complexity curve does not always have such an ideal form as presented in Figure 1; non-saturated training sets E may also have small areas of subsets of constant CLCH values. This can especially occur in the case of unrepresentable training sets, e.g., when all the examples in E are from a small part of D. Generally, by increasing the number of E_x subsets in the test, the reliability of the test can be increased but the answer that a training set is saturated can never be completely reliable. An additional problem, arising due to a non-ideal complexity measure, is that the condition $g(E_x) = g(E)$ can be satisfied although in the ideal case it should not be.

Algorithm 1 tests whether a training set E, given as the input to the algorithm, is saturated or not. In addition, the output of the algorithm is the so-called *critical subset A*, containing examples whose elimination may lead to a saturated training set.

Algorithm 1 *SaturationTest(E)*
    Input: E (training set)
    Parameter: r (saturation test level)
    Output: $(true, \emptyset)$ or $(false, A)$, where A is the critical subset of E
        flag $f \leftarrow true$, critical set $A \leftarrow \emptyset$
        determine $g(E)$
        for $a = 1, \ldots, r$ **do**
            while a different subset A, $A \subset E$, $|A| = a$ can be selected **do**
                form $E_x = E \setminus A$
                determine $g(E_x)$
                if $g(E_x) < g(E)$ **then** flag $f = false$ and exit the for loop
            end while
        end for
        if flag $f = false$ **then** output $(false, A)$
        else output $(true, \emptyset)$

The practical number of E_x subsets is variable and depends on domain properties, the number of training examples, and the expected result reliability. In practice, the number of E_x subsets is limited by the number r of examples which may be excluded from E in order to obtain E_x subsets. In Algorithm 1, the range of r is set to $[1, 3]$.

7 Complexity curve for noisy training sets

The presented definitions of the CLCH value $g(E)$ and the complexity curve enable a novel systematic approach to noise handling by example elimination. This is currently the most interesting practical implication of the theory presented in the paper.

Let us define a noisy example as an example in D for which the target theory T and, consequently, the target hypothesis H_T are not correct. There can be different reasons for the occurrence of noisy examples in the training set E. Such examples make the inductive learning task much more complex because the basic assumption used in previous sections that H_T must be correct for all the training examples does not hold. The problem of noise handling has been approached in different ways: noise-handling mechanisms can be incorporated in search heuristics, in stopping criteria or in post-processing (e.g., [12]). Systems employing such procedures are called *noise-tolerant* systems since they try to avoid overfitting the possibly noisy training set.

Let us suppose that e_n is a noisy example for which the target hypothesis is not correct. If e_n is in contradiction with one or more training examples in E then it is easy to detect noise by detecting contradictions, i.e., examples that differ only in their class value. By eliminating a pair of examples that causes the contradiction, noise can be eliminated from the training set. This is a simple and straightforward noise elimination procedure, but consequently some non-noisy examples can be eliminated as well. But more frequently, e_n is not in contradiction with any of the training examples in E. Suppose that e_n is such a noisy example and that in the training set E there are no contradictions even when it includes noise. This condition is necessary because no hypothesis can be correct for all the training examples if it includes contradictions, and consequently the value $g(E)$ for such E can not be determined.

Theorem 9. *Assume an ideal complexity measure. If E is a saturated subset of D, e_n is a noisy example, and $E_n = E \cup \{e_n\}$, then $g(E) < g(E_n)$.*

Proof: Lemma 2 implies that $g(E) \leq g(E_n)$. The least complex hypothesis correct for all the examples in E is the target hypothesis (since E is a saturated training set) and for E_n the least complex hypothesis is not the target hypothesis (since the target hypothesis is not correct for e_n). As the used complexity measure is ideal, the complexity of two substantially different hypotheses must be different, hence $g(E) < g(E_n)$. □

The ideal curve of $g(E)$ values for a sequence of training sets with the property $\emptyset \subset E_1 \subset E_2 \subset ... \subset E_{n-1} \subset E_n \subset ...$ where E_{n-1} is a saturated non-noisy training set and E_n is obtained from E_{n-1} by adding of one (or more) noisy examples, is presented in Figure 2. The increase of the $g(E)$ value after the inclusion of noisy examples is a consequence of Theorem 9.

8 Noise handling by noise elimination

Suppose that E_n is obtained from a noiseless and saturated set E_{n-1} by adding of exactly one noisy example e_n. When applying the saturation test (Algorithm 1) on the set E_n, the result is that E_n is detected as non-saturated because there exists $E_x = E_{n-1} = E_n \setminus \{e_n\}$ such that $g(E_x) < g(E_n)$. This means that after adding a noisy example e_n the saturated training set is no longer saturated. This also means that Algorithm 1 can be used as a procedure to detect the presence of noise in the training set: it enables to identify a noisy example e_n as the difference between the starting training set E_n and its subset E_x which results in a lower $g(E_x)$ value, i.e., $\{e_n\} = E_n \setminus E_x$.

To generalize, more than one noisy training example can be added to a saturated training set, thus the approach can be modified by extending the range of

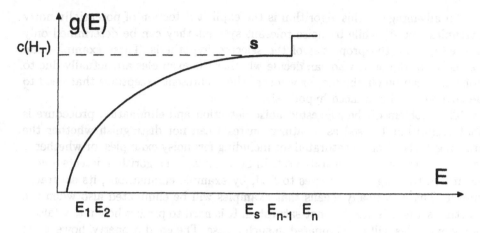

Fig. 2. An ideal curve of CLCH (Complexity of the Least Complex correct Hypothesis) values for a sequence of training domains E, where $E_n = E_{n-1} \cup \{e_n\}$, and e_n is a noisy example.

E_x subsets. Consequently, by again reversing the argument, Algorithm 1 can be used iteratively so that in each iteration one or a few detected noisy examples are excluded from the training set, and such a reduced training set is the input for the next iteration of noise elimination. This approach is general but it can not guarantee that the detection of noisy examples will be successful in all the situations. Namely, it is theoretically possible that noisy examples occur in such a combination that the elimination of any single noisy example does not enable to decrease the CLCH value. But even for very noisy practical applications this is actually not a serious problem, especially if the saturation test level used in the saturation test equals 2 or 3.

The iterative noise elimination algorithm that results in the reduced training set with eliminated noisy examples is presented in Algorithm 2.

Algorithm 2 *NoiseElimination(E)*
    Input: E (training set)
    Output: E (reduced training set), A (critical example set)
        $A \leftarrow \emptyset$
        repeat
            apply $SaturationTest(E) = (f, A')$
            if $(f, A') = (true, \emptyset)$ **then** exit the repeat loop
            else $E \leftarrow E \setminus A'$, $A \leftarrow A \cup A'$
        end repeat
        output (E, A)

An advantage of this algorithm is the explicit detection of potentially noisy examples (set A) while by noise tolerant systems they can be determined only indirectly from the properties of the selected hypothesis. These examples can be shown to the user, who can decide whether the examples are actually due to noise and can be eliminated, or whether they represent exceptions that need to be covered by the induced hypothesis.

The problem of the suggested noise detection and elimination procedure is that Algorithm 1 (used as a saturation test) can not distinguish whether the training set is indeed a saturated set including few noisy examples, or whether it is a non-noisy but non-saturated set. In both cases, the algorithm detects a non-saturated training set and tries to find, by example eliminations, its saturated subset. This practically means that examples will be eliminated also when the starting set is noiseless but not-saturated. It is hard to predict how many falsely noisy examples will be eliminated in such a case. The good property, however, is that even in such an unfavourable situation, after iterative elimination of quasi noisy examples the result will be a reduced saturated training set that correctly captures some subconcept of the target theory.

Compared with other noise handling procedures used in inductive learning, the described noise elimination approach has a worse time complexity. It is the consequence of its iterative nature where in every iteration only one or a few noisy examples can be detected and eliminated. And each iteration is time consuming because it includes many CLCH value computations for E_x subsets where the number of different E_x subsets must be large in order to guarantee the algorithm's noise sensitivity. For practical purposes, a substantially quicker heuristic algorithm for noise elimination has been developed [5] based on the above ideas. On the other hand, the main advantage of the algorithm is that noise handling is separated from the hypothesis construction process. Because of that, hypothesis construction is not influenced by noisy examples and therefore the employed learning techniques do not need to incorporate noise handling.

9 Experimental results with noise elimination

The presented saturation test and noise elimination algorithms are implemented in the ILLM (Inductive Learning by Logic Minimization) system [3], a propositional rule learner characterized by the systematic usage of the Occam's razor principle. The system constructs rules in the mixed DNF-CNF form from a set of (automatically or user defined) literals. The used hypothesis complexity measure in ILLM is defined as the number of different literals used to construct a rule. This complexity measure turns out to be well suited for the realization of the described algorithms because it enables that the CLCH value computations can be performed by relatively fast and simple covering algorithms over the set of all example pairs built of one positive and one negative training example. Although this property significantly improves the time complexity of the CLCH value computations, in ILLM a heuristic covering algorithm and a heuristic modification of the noise elimination algorithm had to be implemented in order to obtain a

Number of introduced class errors	LINUS-ILLM Reduced			LINUS-ILLM Original
	Total number of eliminated examples	Correctly eliminated ex.	Acc.	Acc.
0	3.6 (5,4,2,3,4)	0.0 (0,0,0,0,0)	99.8	99.5
10	13.3 (15,14,12,13,14)	10.0 (10,10,10,10,10)	99.8	97.7
20	24.0 (25,24,22,25,24)	20.0 (20,20,20,20,20)	99.8	95.1
30	36.2 (38,38,32,33,35)	30.0 (30,30,30,30,30)	99.8	93.6
40	41.4 (58,44,43,19,43)	35.0 (40,40,40,16,39)	98.4	92.2
50	39.2 (31,40,46,39,40)	33.0 (26,36,33,33,37)	95.9	90.2

Table 1. Averages and numbers of eliminated examples in 5 domains with 1000 training examples in datasets with 0–50 class errors, together with the average classification accuracy in the reduced datasets and the original datasets prior to noise elimination.

reasonable overall execution speed. See [3] for the details of the ILLM algorithm, whereas the descriptions of the heuristic CLCH value computation and heuristic noise elimination algorithms can be found in [4, 5].

9.1 KRK chess endgame

The results of the ILLM noise elimination algorithm are presented for the well-known inductive logic programing problem of learning illegal positions in a King-Rook-King chess endgame. Five domains with 1000 training examples were selected. A selected number of intentionally introduced class errors was introduced in the training dataset, resulting in datasets with 0, 10, 20, 30, 40 and 50 incorrect class assignments. Test sets consisted of 4000 examples. For other details of the experiment see [4], including the description of the LINUS transformation procedure [8] for solving this relational learning problem. LINUS using ILLM was used for hypothesis formation.

The results are given in Table 1. The obvious expectation that the training sets of 1000 training examples without intentionally introduced noise are saturated, was disproved by the experiments. The noise elimination algorithm resulted in the elimination of 2-5 'noisy' training examples per experiment. The accuracy of rules constructed from reduced training sets was 99.8% . The result seems surprising since the KRK domain is known to be noiseless. However, it is also known that in this domain there is a subconcept (white king blocks the check given by the white rook) with a small number of examples that describe this situation. Examples for this subconcept (although correct) are detected, because of their small number, by the described noise elimination algorithm as potentially noisy examples and are therefore eliminated from the training sets. Generated rules from the reduced training sets did not include the critical subconcept and the prediction accuracy resulted in the accuracy of 99.8%.

When a small amount of intentional classification noise was added to the training examples (between 10 and 30 examples per experiment), the noise elimination procedure successfully detected all the actual noise and additionally excluded examples representing the critical subconcept described above. The result is that the induced rules from the reduced training sets have the same accuracy of 99.8% as those obtained from the noiseless domain. With more than 3% of inserted noise (more than 30 corrupted examples), the noise elimination could not correctly detect all the noisy examples. It also sometimes detected as 'noisy' the examples that are neither noisy nor examples of the critical subconcept. The achieved accuracies are in this situation lower than those obtained for the noiseless domain, but they are still very high.

The right column in Table 1 (accuracy of LINUS-ILLM without noise elimination) is also very interesting. Let us first observe the results in the first row of Table 1. One would expect that in the case when it is in advance known that a domain is noiseless (a very rare practical situation) it might be better not to use the suggested noise elimination algorithm. In this case rule induction is done from the training set which includes a small number of examples of the critical subconcept. But in contrast with the expectations, the prediction accuracy of 99.5% is lower than the one obtained by eliminating examples for the critical subconcept. The reason is that the training sets including the examples of the critical subconcept are non-saturated (as detected also by the noise elimination algorithm) and learning from such domains can sometimes lead to unexpected results which mostly depend on the characteristics of the used complexity measure. On the other hand, exclusion of the examples of the critical subconcept has the drawback that some correct examples have been eliminated but it has enabled that the reduced training sets can be saturated and that all other subconcepts can be induced effectively. The advantage of the suggested noise elimination algorithm is even more obvious if training sets include noise which can be seen from other rows in the last column in Table 1.

9.2 Early diagnosis of rheumatic diseases

Another experimental domain is a real medical problem of early diagnosis of rheumatic diseases which is known to be a difficult machine learning problem due both to its nature and to the imperfection in the dataset. The domain includes 8 diagnostic classes. In order to enable noise elimination, each training set was transformed to 8 different two-class subproblems. Noise elimination, described in detail in [5], was performed on each two-class subproblem where an example was eliminated from the original training set if it was detected as noisy in any of the subproblems. In this way, the reduced training set was generated. The performance of the noise elimination algorithm was tested so that the well known CN2 algorithm [2] was used on both the original and reduced training sets. Experiments were performed on 10 different partitions of data into 70% training and 30% testing examples. For each partition, in total 3 experiments were done: CN2 with the significance test for noise handling applied to the original training set, CN2 without significance test applied to the original training set, and CN2

Partition	Accuracy			Relative information score		
	CN2-ST Original	CN2-NoST Reduced	CN2-NoST Original	CN2-ST Original	CN2-NoST Reduced	CN2-NoST Original
1	47.5	45.3	38.1	17.0	26.0	21.0
2	45.3	44.6	44.6	20.0	28.0	23.0
3	51.1	47.5	45.3	17.0	24.0	19.0
4	44.6	38.8	43.9	17.0	20.0	24.0
5	46.0	41.7	40.3	21.0	25.0	22.0
6	49.6	50.4	48.2	15.0	24.0	26.0
7	44.6	46.8	42.4	21.0	31.0	27.0
8	41.0	43.2	38.8	21.0	25.0	19.0
9	43.9	48.2	45.3	16.0	29.0	23.0
10	39.6	43.2	41.7	23.0	25.0	23.0
Average	45.3	45.0	42.9	18.8	25.7	22.7

Table 2. Accuracy and relative information score results on 10 partitions of the rheumatology training set.

without significance test applied to the reduced training set. Results for the classification accuracy and relative information score are given in Table 2 [5].

In order to compare the results of the proposed noise elimination algorithm to the CN2 significance test noise-handling mechanism, columns CN2-ST-Original and CN2-NoST-Reduced in Table 2 need to be be compared. This is actually the most interesting comparison since, in terms of the classification accuracy, CN2 with the significance test (CN2-ST) is known to perform well on noisy data. On the other hand, in order to observe the effect of noise elimination, the results in columns CN2-NoST-Original and CN2-NoST-Reduced need to be compared.

The effect of noise elimination (CN2-NoST-Reduced) is comparable to CN2 (CN2-ST-Original) in terms of the classification accuracy, but a significant improvement was achieved in terms of the relative information score [7].

10 Summary

This work discusses the conditions for the Occam's razor applicability. To do so, the notion of the complexity of the least complex hypothesis (CLCH value) that is correct for all training examples is introduced. On this basis, the complexity curve that reflects a dependency between a sequence of training sets and the corresponding CLCH values is presented. Conditions for the existence of the saturation part of the complexity curve are given. It is shown that a training set whose CLCH value is in the saturation part of the complexity curve, and the ideal sensitivity of the used complexity measure are the necessary and sufficient conditions for the application of the Occam's razor principle in hypothesis formation, guaranteeing the optimal prediction accuracy of the induced hypothesis. Based on the properties of the complexity curve for intentionally introduced noisy examples, the conditions for effective noise elimination are elaborated and an iterative noise elimination procedure is proposed. The results of empirical evaluation show the usefulness of the presented approach to noise elimination.

Acknowledgements

This research was financially supported by the Croatian Ministry of Science, the Slovenian Ministry of Science and Technology, and the ESPRIT Project 20237 Inductive Logic Programming 2. The authors are grateful to an anonymous reviewer for many valuable comments on the submitted version of the work, and to Sašo Džeroski for contributing to the evaluation of the noise elimination algorithm on the rheumatology dataset, collected by the specialists of the University Medical Center in Ljubljana. Our thanks goes also to Vladimir Pirnat, Aram Karalič and Igor Kononenko who prepared this data in a form appropriate for the experiments.

References

1. Brodley, M.: Recursive automatic bias selection for classifier construction. Machine Learning 20 (1995) 63–94
2. Clark, P., Niblett, T.: The CN2 Induction Algorithm. Machine Learning 3 (1989) 261–284
3. Gamberger, D.: A minimization approach to propositional inductive learning. In Proc. of the 8th European Conference on Machine Learning (1995) 151–160
4. Gamberger, D., Lavrač, N.: Noise detection and elimination applied to noise handling in a KRK chess endgame. In Proc. of the 5th International Workshop on Inductive Logic Programming (1996) 59–75
5. Gamberger, D., Lavrač, N., Džeroski, S.: Noise Elimination in Inductive Concept Learning: A case study in medical diagnosis. In Proc. of the 7th International Workshop on Algorithmic Learning Theory (1996) 199–212.
6. Kohavi, R., Wolpert, D.H.: Bias Plus Variance Decomposition for Zero-One Loss Functions. In Proc. of the 13th International Conference on Machine Learning (1996) 275–283
7. Kononenko, I., Bratko, I.: Information-based evaluation criterion for classifier performance. Machine Learning 6 (1991) 67–80
8. Lavrač, N., Džeroski, S.: Inductive Logic Programming: Techniques and Applications. Ellis Horwood (1994)
9. Li, M., Vitányi, P.: An Introduction to Kolmogorov Complexity and its Applications. Springer (1993)
10. Quinlan, J.R.: Induction of Decision Trees. Machine Learning 1 (1986) 81–106
11. Quinlan, J.R.: Learning Logical Definitions from Relations. Machine Learning 5 (1990) 239–266
12. Quinlan, J.R.: C4.5: Programs for Machine Learning. Morgan Kaufmann (1992)
13. Rao, R., Gordon, D., Spears, W.: For every generalization action, is there really an equal or opposite reaction? Analysis of conservation law. In Proc. of the 12th International Conference on Machine Learning (1995) 471–479

14. Rissanen, J.: Modeling by the shortest data description. Automatica **14** (1978) 465–471
15. Schaffer, C.: A conservation law for generalization performance. In Proc. of the 11th International Conference on Machine Learning (1994) 259–265
16. Stahl, I.: Compression Measures in ILP. In L. De Raedt (ed.): Advances in Inductive Logic Programming IOS Press (1996) 295–307
17. Webb, G.I.: Further Experimental Evidence against the Utility of Occam's razor. Journal of Artificial Intelligence Research **4** (1996) 397–417

Learning Different Types of New Attributes by Combining the Neural Network and Iterative Attribute Construction

Yuh-Jyh Hu

Information and Computer Science Department
University of California, Irvine

Abstract. Most of the current constructive induction algorithms degrade performance as the target concept becomes larger and more complex in terms of Boolean combinations. Most are only capable of constructing relatively smaller new attributes. Though it is impossible to build a learner to learn any arbitrarily large and complex concept, there are some large and complex concepts that could be represented in a simple relation such as prototypical concepts, e.g., m-of-n, majority, etc. In this paper, we propose a new approach that combines the neural net and iterative attribute construction to learn relatively short but complex Boolean combinations and prototypical structures. We also carried a series of systematic experiments to characterize our approach.

Keywords: classification, constructive induction, neural networks.

1 Introduction

Poor representation limits the performance of concept learners. One approach to mitigate the limitation is to construct new features. The need for useful new features has been suggested by many researchers (Matheus, 1991; Aha, 1991; Kadie, 1991; Ragavan *et. al.*, 1993). Constructing new features by hand is often difficult (Quinlan, 1983). The goal of constructive induction is to automatically transform the original representation space into a new one where the regularity is more apparent (Dietterich & Michalski, 1981; Mehra *et. al.*, 1989), thus yielding improved classification accuracy.

There are currently many constructive induction algorithms based on the strategy of constructing new attributes, including FRINGE (Pagallo, 1989), GREEDY3 (Pagallo & Haussler, 1990), DCFringe (Yang *et. al.*, 1991), CITRE (Matheus & Rendell, 1989), LFC (Ragavan & Rendell, 1993; Ragavan *et. al.*, 1993), MRP (Perez & Rendell, 1995), GALA (Hu & Kibler, 1996), etc. Unfortunately, most of the current constructive induction algorithms degrade performance as the target concept becomes larger and more complex in terms of Boolean combinations such as prototypical concepts (Perez & Rendell, 1996). Though MRP is demonstrated to learn several complex relations, the meaning of its extensional representation is implicit in the data, and usually difficult to interpret.

Most of the efforts of constructive induction have been directed to improved classification accuracy. However, in addition to accuracy the comprehensibility of new attributes could also be important, especially when the new attributes represent intermediate concepts, which may further understanding of the domain of interest. Without understandable new attributes, the contribution of constructive induction is limited. Because the new attributes that reflect the intermediate concepts are likely to be useful, we currently concentrate on two types of intermediate concepts, i.e., (1) complex but relatively short Boolean combinations and (2) prototypical structures. Combinations of these intermediate concepts into one target concept can easily produce DNF expressions with tens or hundreds of terms, which are difficult to learn. Our goal is to construct these two types of new attributes that represent the intermediate concepts, but unlike MRP's extensional representation, we describe our new attributes in a human-understandable form.

In this paper, we introduce a multi-strategy approach that combines the neural network with GALA. It successfully constructs Boolean combinations and prototypical structures. The Boolean combinations are explicitly represented, and the prototypical structures are clearly described by the weights and thresholds of the neural network. This combination approach, like GALA, is a preprocessor approach. It could be applied to other standard learning algorithms.

2 Combining Neural Network with Iterative Attribute Construction

2.1 Motivation

One important issue in constructive induction is the types of new attributes constructed (Hu & Kibler, 1996). If we represent the new attributes in disjunctive normal form, we could build a spectrum of the attributes based on the number of terms involved. At one end are the ones with relatively smaller numbers of terms; at the other, those with many terms. There is no uniform correlation between the number of terms and the capability of the algorithms, and there is no universal algorithm to cover the whole spectrum. One possible approach to covering more of the spectrum is to combine different construction strategies.

GALA, a preprocessor approach to constructive induction, which applies relative measures and iterative attribute combination techniques is capable of generating complex but relatively smaller Boolean combinations as new attributes (Hu & Kibler, 1996), thus it could be used to construct those new attributes that belong to one end of the spectrum. The general control flow of GALA is described in fig 1.

However, as any iterative attribute construction algorithm, it has an inherent drawback, i.e., as the concept becomes larger in the number of terms in disjunctive normal form, they fail to find useful new attributes. Larger numbers of attribute combinations incur more attribute interaction that hinders the performance of the algorithms (Hu & Kibler, 1996; Perez & Rendell, 1996). Therefore,

```
Given:  a set of attributes P, training examples E, threshold and
        new attributes NEW
        (NEW is empty when GALA invoked the first time)
Return: a set of new attributes NEW

Procedure GALA(P,E,threshold,NEW)
  If (size(E) > threshold) and (E is not all of same class)
    Then Set Bool to Boolean attributes from Booleanize(P,E)
         Set Pool to attributes from Generate(Bool,E)
         Set Best to attribute in Pool with highest gain ratio
             (if more than one, pick one of smallest size)
         Add Best to NEW
         Split on Best
         N = {}
         For each outcome, Si, of Split on Best
             Ei = examples with outcome Si on split
             NEWi = GALA(P,Ei,threshold,NEW)
             N = N + NEWi
         NEW = NEW + N
         Return NEW
    Else Return {}
```

Fig. 1. GALA

we need another construction strategy to cover the other end of the spectrum. Because it is impossible to build a learner to learn any arbitrarily long and complex concept, we currently concentrate on the prototypical structures, such as the m-of-n rules, majority, etc, which often exist in the real domains like medical diagnoses (Spackman, 1988).

Given a target concept containing prototypical structures and other complex but relatively shorter Boolean combinations, our strategy is to first extract the prototypical structure and represent it as a single new attribute. Second, with the new prototypical attributes added to the primitives, we then apply GALA to extract the remaining Boolean combinations in the target concept. Since the new attributes generated encapsulates the complexity of the prototypical structures, GALA is able to learn the remaining Boolean combinations. The question left is how we extract the prototypical structures.

The multilayer perceptron is probably the most studied neural network technique (Hertz et. al., 1991; Kung, 1993). Each hidden unit draws a simple decision surface in the input space, and then the output units combine these individual regions to form a final region corresponding to the target concept. As the decision region of each hidden unit is formulated in a linear function, some of the hidden units are likely to converge to meaningful linear threshold functions, and could be used as the basis of prototypical structures such as the m-of-n rules, majority, etc. The linear threshold functions could then be transformed into new attributes to represent prototypical structures. Therefore, the neural network is our answer to the question left above. The general framework of our approach is described in fig 2.

```
Given : a set of training examples E
        a set of primitive attributes P
Return: a set of new attributes NEW

Procedure ANN-GALA(E,P)
   H = hidden units from ANN(E)
   Transform H to a set of new attributes N
   Represent E in P+N as E'
   NEW={}
   NEW = N + GALA(P+N,E',threshold,NEW)
   Return (NEW)
```

Fig. 2. General Framework of Combining ANN with GALA

2.2 How to Apply Neural Network

Since GALA generates new attributes in terms of Boolean combinations, the new attributes generated are human-understandable. However, the new attributes directly derived from the hidden units of the neural network are difficult to interpret.

From the point of view as a prototypical structure, there are two causes of the incomprehensibility. The first is the irrelevant primitive attributes. In the feed-forward neural netwrok architecture, each hidden unit is fully connected to all the input units (i.e., primitive attributes). After the network converges, the links between the hidden units and the irrelevant input units may still carry non-zero weights. These irrelevant non-zero weights, though usually small, make the representation difficult to interpret. It would be more human-interpretable if all the irrelevant weights are zero. The other cause is the weights themselves. The weights are unlikely to be integers after the network converges. It is difficult to infer the prototypical structures from a set of non-integer weights. For example, a 3-of-5 rule is better represented by $X_1 + X_2 + X_3 + X_4 + X_5 \geq 3$ than $1.02X_1 + 0.98X_2 + 1.05X_3 + 0.97X_4 + 0.98X_5 \geq 2.93$.

To overcome the above problems, we propose a two-stage weight normalization method. The irrelevant weights are usually significantly smaller than others in magnitude and often with opposite sign. In the first stage, we use the mean of the weight magnitude as the criterion. The weights below the mean and of the opposite sign are set to zero. The reason why we consider the sign is that in case all input units are relevant and of the same sign, we will not discard any relevant weight simply because it is below the mean. Along with the change of weights, we use the difference between the hidden unit value before and after the weight change to adjust the threshold of the hidden unit. In the second stage, we normalize the weights with the mean of the remaining non-zero weights and apply the round-off function to suppress other insignificant weights to zero. More details could be found in fig 3.

```
Given : a set of weights and thresholds W,
        a set of training examples E
Return: a set of normalized weights and thresholds

Procedure normalize(W,E)
  Let W' be W
  Let m be the mean of the absolute values
      of the weights in W'
  Let s be the sign (i.e., + or -) of the weight with
      max absolute value
  For each weight w' in W'
    if (abs(w') < m) and (w' with opposite sign to s)
        w' = 0
  sumdiff = 0
  For each training example e in E
    sumdiff = sumdiff+(eW-eW')
  diff = sumdiff/|E|
  Let m be the mean of the absolute values
      of the non-zero weights in W'
  For each weight w' and threshold t' in W'
    w' = round(w/m);
    t' = round((t'+diff)/m);
  Return (W')
```

Fig. 3. Weights and Thresholds Normalization

The set of weights and thresholds are difficult to interpret, but after we *normalize* them the concept represented by these weights and thresholds is easier to understand. We use $(\sum_{i=1}^{8} x_i \geq 5) + x_1\bar{x}_3\bar{x}_5 x_7 + \bar{x}_2\bar{x}_4\bar{x}_6 x_8$, a Boolean function with total 12 attributes, as an example to illustrate the idea. Using 5% of the total 4096 examples as the traing set, we trained a neural net with the back-propagation algorithm. The neural net has 12 input units, 6 hidden units and one output unit.

The weights and thresholds before and after normalization are shown in fig. 4. In fig. 4, each hidden unit is described by 12 weights followed by a threshold. Before normalization, the weights and thresholds we learned are not understandable even though the fifth hidden unit approximately converged to $\sum_{i=1}^{8} x_i \geq 5$. However, after the normalization, the fifth hidden unit is easily interpreted as a 5-of-8 rule.

```
The weights of the hidden units before normalization :
Hidden Unit 1:   4.43948,-0.90867,-1.85273,-0.09461,-2.56182,
                 0.44131, 3.80673, 0.88315, 1.21998,-0.02205,
                 0.03032,-1.60084,      threshold = -7.18849

Hidden Unit 2: -3.00333, 2.49571, 3.30566, 1.22784, 3.31664,
                 1.30544,-2.78767, 0.28106,-0.92781, 0.50652,
                 0.62082, 1.21651,      threshold =  2.36028

Hidden Unit 3:   1.49163,-0.95159,-0.32819,-0.27491, 1.43506,
                -0.56259, 1.37591, 0.87493, 0.52599,-0.69051,
                 1.22448, 2.60315,      threshold = -2.63325

Hidden Unit 4: -1.09608,-3.30526,-1.54907,-2.02781, 0.96142,
                -1.87570,-0.97085, 1.95589,-2.10087, 0.95469,
                 0.62773, 1.00338,      threshold = -2.89914

Hidden Unit 5:   3.13984, 3.82628, 3.94562, 3.75279, 3.37203,
                 3.75229, 3.07394, 3.34460,-0.24504, 0.06971,
                -0.26181,-0.70992,      threshold = -15.6727

Hidden Unit 6:   0.48870, 1.04775, 0.81234, 0.72570,-0.11177,
                 0.78070, 0.52246,-0.42331, 0.66164,-0.36449,
                -0.41729,-0.08977,      threshold =  0.41798

The weights of the hidden units after normalization :
Hidden Unit 1:   2, 0,-1, 0,-1, 0, 1, 0, 0, 0, 0,-1, threshold = -2
Hidden Unit 2: -1, 1, 1, 1, 1, 1,-1, 0, 0, 0, 0, 1, threshold =  1
Hidden Unit 3:   1, 0, 0, 0, 1, 0, 1, 0, 0, 0, 1, 2, threshold = -3
Hidden Unit 4: -1,-2,-1,-1, 0,-1, 0, 1,-1, 0, 0, 0, threshold =  0
Hidden Unit 5:   1, 1, 1, 1, 1, 1, 1, 1, 0, 0, 0, 0, threshold = -5
Hidden Unit 6:   0, 1, 1, 1, 0, 1, 0, 0, 1, 0, 0, 0, threshold =  0
```

Fig. 4. Results of Normalization

3 Experimental Results

There are three purposes of our experiments. One is to demonstrate that the new attributes generated could improve the predictive accuracy of the standard learning algorithms. Another is to verify that combining the neural network and GALA covers more of the attribute spectrum that we introduced earlier. The third is the characterization of the conditions under which our approach is likely to perform better.

We examined our approach across a variety of Boolean functions. This allows us full control of the experiments, and we could exactly verify whether our approach could extract all the intermediate concepts. For example, given a target concept $(\sum_{i=1}^{8} x_i \geq 5) + x_1 \bar{x}_3 \bar{x}_5 x_7 + \bar{x}_2 \bar{x}_4 \bar{x}_6 x_8$, to determine whether the Boolean combination attributes generated are correct we compare them with the Boolean combinations (i.e., $x_1 \bar{x}_3 \bar{x}_5 x_7 + \bar{x}_2 \bar{x}_4 \bar{x}_6 x_8$) in the target concept. As for prototypical structures, the weights and thresholds of the hidden units are compared to the prototypical structure (i.e., $\sum_{i=1}^{8} x_i \geq 5$) in the target concept, and checked if they are exactly presented as the following. Note that irrelevant weights are set to zero.

```
Hidden Unit : 1, 1, 1, 1, 1, 1, 1, 1, 0, 0, 0, 0, threshold = -5
```

Each function is defined on 12 Boolean attributes that produce total 4096 examples. We used 5% and 10% of the total 4096 examples as the training set respectively, and the rest as the testing set.

3.1 Pure Prototypical Concepts

The first part of the experiments is to verify if our neural network strategy is able to extract the prototypical structures when they are the only intermediate concepts in the target concept. We tested several prototypical concepts, including m-of-n, majority (a special case of m-of-n), exact-m-of-n, etc. The summary of the functions are described in table 1. The results are averaged over 20 runs, and reported in table 2.

The second (and sixth) column of table 2 denotes the percentage averaged over 20 runs that the neural network successfully extracted the prototypical structures. The third and fourth (also seventh and eighth) columns denote the accuracy of the neural net and C4.5 (Quinlan 1993) respectively. The new accuracy of C4.5 after adding the new attributes derived from the hidden units is presented in column 5 and 9. Significant difference between the C4.5's accuracy before and after adding the new attributes is marked with "*".

3.2 Concepts composed of prototypical structures and Boolean Combinations

Besides the concepts which contain prototypical structures only, there exist other concepts that are composed of prototypical structures and Boolean combinations

Table 1. Summary of Pure Prototypical Concepts

Concept	Description
P1	$\sum_{i=1}^{12} x_i \geq 5$
P2	$(\sum_{i=1}^{6} x_i \geq 4) + (\sum_{i=7}^{12} x_i \geq 4)$
P3	$(\sum_{i=1}^{6} x_i \geq 4) + (\sum_{i=5}^{10} x_i \geq 4)$
P4	$\sum_{i=1}^{10} x_i = 3$
P5	$\sum_{i=2}^{10} x_i \geq 5$
P6	$\sum_{i=5}^{6} x_i = \sum_{i=7}^{8} x_i$
P7	$\sum_{i=3}^{6} x_i = \sum_{i=7}^{10} x_i$
P8	$\sum_{i=3}^{6} x_i > \sum_{i=7}^{10} x_i$

Table 2. Results of Pure Prototypical Concepts

	5%				10%			
Concept	%	NN	C4.5	+NN	%	NN	C4.5	+NN
P1	100	99.9	82.2	100.0*	100	100.0	82.7	100.0*
P2	95	98.8	73.4	98.9*	100	99.9	77.5	100.0*
P3	65	97.5	79.2	96.1*	95	99.9	84.7	99.7*
P4	15	93.4	83.2	94.3*	85	98.6	83.9	99.2*
P5	100	100.0	76.4	100.0*	100	100.0	79.9	100.0*
P6	100	99.4	72.1	100.0*	100	100.0	77.3	100.0*
P7	100	99.5	63.8	100.0*	100	99.9	64.9	100.0*
P8	100	100.0	79.9	100.0*	100	100.0	84.3	100.0*

together, e.g., $(\sum_{i=1}^{8} x_i \geq 5) + x_1\bar{x}_3\bar{x}_5x_7 + \bar{x}_2\bar{x}_4\bar{x}_6x_8$, where $\sum_{i=1}^{8} x_i \geq 5$ is the prototypical structure, and $x_1\bar{x}_3\bar{x}_5x_7 + \bar{x}_2\bar{x}_4\bar{x}_6x_8$ is the Boolean combinations.

The second part of the experiments is to verify if the multi-strategy approach could extract the prototypical structures and Boolean combinations respectively, given a target concept that is composed of prototypical structures and Boolean combinations. Thus, in addition to the percentage that the neural network successfully extracted the prototypical structures, we also examined how many terms in the Boolean combinations GALA successfully generated.

These concepts are further categorized into two categories by comparing the example space covered, i.e., whether the prototypical structure significantly covers more example space than any term in the Boolean combinations. If this condition is true, we call this category of concepts "dominant prototypical concepts"; otherwise, "nondominant prototypical concepts".

Dominant Prototypical Concepts In this category, we tested 9 Boolean concepts summarized in table 3. The literals in the Boolean combinations could be included in, separated from, or overlapped with the prototypical structure.

Table 3. Summary of Dominant Prototypical Concepts

Concept	Description
D1	$(\sum_{i=1}^{8} x_i \geq 5) + x_1\bar{x}_3\bar{x}_5x_7 + \bar{x}_2\bar{x}_4\bar{x}_6x_8$
D2	$(\sum_{i=1}^{8} x_i \geq 5) + x_9\bar{x}_{11}\bar{x}_1x_3 + \bar{x}_{10}x_{12}x_2\bar{x}_4 + x_{11}\bar{x}_1x_3x_5$
D3	$(\sum_{i=1}^{8} x_i \geq 5) + x_9\bar{x}_{10}\bar{x}_{11}x_{12} + \bar{x}_9x_{10}\bar{x}_{11}\bar{x}_{12} + x_9\bar{x}_{10}x_{11}\bar{x}_{12}$
D4	$(\sum_{i=1}^{6} x_i \geq 3) + x_1\bar{x}_2\bar{x}_3x_4 + \bar{x}_2x_3\bar{x}_4\bar{x}_5 + x_3\bar{x}_4x_5\bar{x}_6$
D5	$(\sum_{i=1}^{6} x_i \geq 3) + x_1\bar{x}_3\bar{x}_7x_8 + \bar{x}_3x_4\bar{x}_8x_9 + x_2\bar{x}_5x_9x_{10}$
D6	$(\sum_{i=1}^{6} x_i \geq 3) + x_7\bar{x}_8\bar{x}_9x_{10} + \bar{x}_9x_{10}\bar{x}_{11}\bar{x}_{12} + x_7\bar{x}_9x_{10}\bar{x}_{11}$
D7	$(\sum_{i=1}^{8} x_i \geq 5) + x_1\bar{x}_2\bar{x}_3 + \bar{x}_3x_5\bar{x}_8 + \bar{x}_4x_6\bar{x}_7 + x_7x_8\bar{x}_4$
D8	$(\sum_{i=1}^{8} x_i \geq 5) + x_1\bar{x}_9\bar{x}_{10} + \bar{x}_3x_{11}\bar{x}_{12} + \bar{x}_5x_7\bar{x}_9 + x_6\bar{x}_{10}x_{11}$
D9	$(\sum_{i=1}^{8} x_i \geq 5) + x_9\bar{x}_{10}x_{11} + x_9x_{11}\bar{x}_{12} + x_{10}\bar{x}_{11}\bar{x}_{12} + x_9\bar{x}_{11}x_{12}$

Table 4. Results of Dominant Prototypical Concepts (5%)

	5%				
Concept	%	DNF	NN	C4.5	+NN	+NN+GALA
D1	85	1.1,0.0	94.4	78.4	94.7*	95.5#
D2	55	0.8,0.3	90.5	77.7	87.3*	91.0#
D3	50	1.0,0.3	92.7	68.6	86.2*	91.8#
D4	50	0.0,1.1	96.9	91.5	97.2*	97.4#
D5	70	0.1,0.6	94.5	85.1	93.1*	93.8#
D6	100	0.0,1.0	97.1	84.3	96.1*	97.3#
D7	15	0.4,0.1	88.8	82.2	86.1*	89.3#
D8	15	0.3,0.3	85.1	75.1	82.2*	84.0#
D9	80	0.1,0.8	95.5	78.8	95.9*	97.5#

The results are reported in table 4 and 5. The second column has the same meaning as column 2 (and column 6) in table 2. The first number in the third column presents the average number of terms constructed by GALA that exactly correspond to those in the Boolean combinations in the target concept, and the second number denotes the average number of terms that approximate. By approximate we mean that the term is part of the Boolean conjuncts (i.e., overly general). For example, given a target concept $(\sum_{i=1}^{8} x_i \geq 5) + x_1 x_2 x_3 + x_3 x_4 x_5 + x_1 x_5 x_7$, we may have the following terms such as $x_1 x_2$ and $x_3 x_4$ that approximate $x_1 x_2 x_3$ and $x_3 x_4 x_5$ respectively.

The fourth and fifth columns denotes the accuracy of the neural net and C4.5 respectively. The new accuracy of C4.5 after adding the new attributes generated by the neural net alone is presented in column 6. Column 7 denotes the new accuracy of C4.5 after adding all the new attributes constructed by the neural net and GALA together. Significant difference between the C4.5's accuracy before and after adding the new attributes is marked with "*" and "#" respectively.

Table 5. Results of Dominant Prototypical Concepts (10%)

Concept	%	DNF	NN	C4.5	+NN	+NN+GALA
				10%		
D1	100	1.2,0.2	99.3	82.2	99.5*	99.7#
D2	90	2.0,0.4	96.3	80.7	96.1*	98.2#
D3	85	1.0,0.8	99.7	72.7	97.3*	97.9#
D4	40	0.0,1.0	99.6	97.1	99.1*	99.2#
D5	85	0.7,0.6	96.5	91.5	95.8*	97.8#
D6	100	0.0,1.7	98.5	89.7	98.1*	99.2#
D7	35	0.9,0.1	95.7	88.6	93.8*	94.2#
D8	70	1.8,0.2	92.9	81.1	93.4*	95.5#
D9	100	0.4,0.7	99.8	82.2	99.9*	99.9#

Nondominant Prototypical Concepts For the second category, we tested 3 concepts. These concepts are summarized in table 6, and table 7 and 8 present these results. Note that in the first test concept (i.e., ND1), the percentage (i.e., column 2) is 0, and the average number of terms generated by GALA that correspond to the Boolean combinations is also low (i.e., column 3). The reason is that the neural net strategy failed to extract the prototypical structure, and the literals of the Boolean combinations (i.e., $x_1..x_5$) are included in the prototypical structure; therefore, most of the new attributes generated by GALA are part of the prototypical structure instead of the Boolean combinations.

3.3 Analysis

In the first part of the experiments, all the Boolean functions are either the combination of linearly separable concepts or simply linearly separable concepts themselves. As expected, the neural network strategy successfully extracted the prototypical structures in almost every Boolean function. This demonstrates

Table 6. Summary of Nondominant Prototypical Concepts

Concept	Description
ND1	$(\sum_{i=1}^{5} x_i \geq 4) + x_1 x_3 \bar{x}_4 + x_2 \bar{x}_3 x_5 + x_1 \bar{x}_2 \bar{x}_4 + x_2 x_4 \bar{x}_5$
ND2	$(\sum_{i=1}^{5} x_i \geq 4) + x_1 \bar{x}_9 \bar{x}_{10} + \bar{x}_3 x_{11} \bar{x}_{12} + \bar{x}_5 x_7 \bar{x}_9 + x_6 \bar{x}_{10} x_{11}$
ND3	$(\sum_{i=1}^{5} x_i \geq 4) + x_6 \bar{x}_8 \bar{x}_9 + x_8 \bar{x}_{10} x_{11} + x_7 \bar{x}_9 x_{12} + x_7 x_{11} \bar{x}_{12}$

Table 7. Results of Nondominant Prototypical Concepts (5%)

5%						
Concept	%	DNF	NN	C4.5	+NN	+NN+GALA
ND1	0	0.3,1.2	97.3	98.4	97.8	99.1
ND2	15	2.1,0.2	84.3	80.2	82.6*	90.5#
ND3	0	2.8,0.0	82.3	82.5	81.1	92.7#

that when the target concept is a pure prototypical concept, the hidden units
are likely to converge to the prototypical structures. After the normalization of
the weights and thresholds, the prototypical structures are explicitly represented
by the hidden units. By adding the prototypical structures as new attributes,
we significantly improve the accuracy of C4.5.

When the target concept is composed of prototypical structures and Boolean
combinations, our multi-strategy approach performed differently on the two categories of the concepts (i.e., dominant and nondominant). If the prototypical
structures in the target concept significantly cover more example space (i.e., the
dominant prototypical concepts as defined earlier), the neural net strategy is
able to separate the prototypical structures from the Boolean combinations, and
consequently the hidden units could converge to the prototypical structures as
in the pure prototypical concepts. After we transform the prototypical structures into new attributes, GALA could avoid the complexity of the prototypical
structures that has been encapsulated in the new prototypical attributes, and
thus extract the remaining Boolean combinations.

Table 8. Results of Nondominant Prototypical Concepts (10%)

10%						
Concept	%	DNF	NN	C4.5	+NN	+NN+GALA
ND1	0	0.0,0.1	99.7	99.5	99.8	100.0
ND2	45	2.5,0.1	94.2	86.6	94.8*	98.5#
ND3	25	2.0,0.5	92.5	88.5	93.2*	96.1#

As for the nondominant prototypical concepts, the neural network has difficulties distinguishing the prototypical structures from the Boolean combinations. Therefore, the hidden units are unable to converge to any meaningful prototypical structure. GALA, in this case, treats the whole target concept as a *big* Boolean combination concept, and extracts as many terms as possible. These terms may be either part of the prototypical structures or of the Boolean combinations.

4   Conclusion

When describing constructed attributes in disjunctive normal form, we have an attribute spectrum based on the number of terms involved. Unfortunately, there is no universal learning algorithm that could learn the whole spectrum.

We currently concentrate on relatively short but complex Boolean combinations and prototypical structures. The objective of this paper is to learn these two types of attributes and represent the new attributes in a human-understandable form, unlike other systems that adopt extensional representation. We proposed a new approach that combines the neural network and iterative attribute construction. With different characteristics and advantages, the neural network strategy is used to learn the prototypical structures; the iterative attribute construction algorithm, to learn the complex Boolean combinations. The new attributes generated are either explicitly represented in terms of Boolean combinations or human-understandably described by the weights and thresholds of the hidden units (Section 2.2).

Besides introducing the new approach, we also carried a series of systematic experiments to characterize our approach. We tested and analyzed our multistrategy approach on different categories of concepts, and conclude that example space coverage plays an important role in the characterization (Section 3.3).

Though there exist more complex concepts than those we studied in this paper, we argue that our test concepts are inspired by the real domains such as medical diagnoses. Those simplifications do not prevent us from analyzing the essential information. Our results illustrate other directions for future research in multi-strategy learning and constructive induction.

References

Aha, D. "Incremental Constructive Induction: An Instanced-Based Approach", in Proceeding of the 8th Machine Learning Workshop, p117-121, 1991.

Dietterich, T. G. & Michalski, R. S. "Inductive Learning of Structural Description : Evaluation Criteria and Comparative Review of Selected Methods", Artificial Intelligence 16 (3), p257-294, 1981.

Hertz, J., Krogh, A. and Palmer, R. G. "Introduction to the Theory of Neural Computation", Addison-Wesley, 1991.

Hu, Y. & Kibler, D. "Generation of Attributes for Learning Algorithms", in Proceeding of the 13th National Conference on Artificial Intelligence, p806-811, 1996.

Kadie, C. M. "Quantifying the Value of Constructive Induction, Knowledge, and Noise Filtering on Inductive Learning", in Proceeding of the 8th Machine Learning Workshop, p153-157, 1991.

Kung, S. Y. "Digital Neural Networks", Prentice Hall, 1993.

Matheus, C. J. & Rendell, L. A. "Constructive Induction on Decision Trees", in Proceeding of the 11th International Joint Conference on Artificial Intelligence, p645-650, 1989.

Matheus, C. J. "The Need for Constructive Induction", in Proceeding of the 8th Machine Learning Workshop, p173-177, 1991.

Mehra, P., Rendell, L. A., Wah, B. W. "Principled Constructive Induction", in Proceeding of the 11th International Joint Conference on Artificial Intelligence, p651-656, 1989.

Pagallo, G. "Learning DNF by Decision Trees", in Proceeding of the 11th International Joint Conference on Artificial Intelligence.

Pagallo, G. & Haussler, D. "Boolean Feature Discovery in Empirical Learning", Machine Learning 5, p71-99, 1990.

Perez, E. & Rendell, L. "Using Multidimensional Projection to Find Relations", in Proceeding of the 12th Machine Learning Conference, p447-455, 1995.

Perez, E. & Rendell, L. "Learning Despite Concept Variation by Finding Structure in Attribute-based Date", in Proceeding of the 13th Machine Learning Conference, p391-399, 1996.

Quinlan, J. R. "Learning efficient classification procedures and their application to chess end games" , in Michalski et. al.'s Machine Learning : An artificial intelligence approach. (Eds.) 1983.

Quinlan, J. R. C4.5 : Programs for Machine Learning, Morgan Kaufmann, San Mateo, CA, 1993.

Ragavan, H., Rendell, L., Shaw, M., Tessmer, A. "Complex Concept Acquisition through Directed Search and Feature Caching", in Proceeding of the 13th International Joint Conference on Artificial Intelligence, p946-958, 1993.

Ragavan, H. & Rendell, L. "Lookahead Feature Construction for Learning Hard Concepts", in Proceeding of the 10th Machine Learning Conference, p252-259, 1993.

Rendell L. A. & Ragavan, H. "Improving the Design of Induction Methods by Analyzing Algorithm Functionality and Data-Based Concept Complexity", in Proceeding of the 13th International Joint Conference on Artificial Intelligence, p952-958, 1993.

Spackman, K. "Learning Categorical Decision Criteria in Biomedical Domains", in Proceeding of the 5th International Workshop on Machine Learning, p36-46, 1988.

Yang, D-S., Rendell, L. A., Blix, G. "A Scheme for Feature Construction and a Comparison of Empirical Methods", in Proceedingof the 12th International Joint Conference on Artificial Intelligence, p699-704, 1991.

Metrics on Terms and Clauses

Alan Hutchinson

Department of Computer Science, King's College London

Abstract. In the subject of machine learning, a "concept" is a description of a cluster of the concept's instances. In order to invent a new concept, one has to discover such a cluster. The necessary tool for clustering is a metric, or pseudo-metric. Here are presented families of pseudo-metrics which seem well suited to such tasks. On terms and literals, we construct a new kind of metric from the substitutions which arise through subsumption. From these, it is easy to form metrics on clauses, by a technique due to F.Hausdorff. They will be applicable to generalization from sets of ground clauses, to discovery of heuristic guidance for theorem proving, and to inductive logic programming.

We start by describing some pseudo-metrics on terms. They are constructed by means of Plotkin's *least general generalisation* (*lgg*) of two terms (see [6]). A term u is *subsumed* by another, w, if there is a substitution ϑ for which $w\vartheta = u$. The *lgg* of two terms u and v is a term w which subsumes them both, and which is itself subsumed by any other such w' subsuming u and v. If $w\vartheta = u$ and $w\varphi = v$ then the metric is a measure of the complexities of the substitutions ϑ and φ .

Example 1. The *lgg* of the two terms

$$play(Mary, Ann, James, skipping)$$

$$play(Mary, Ann, Ann, skipping)$$

is

$$play(Mary, Ann, x, skipping).$$

The second family contains pseudo-metrics on disjunctive clauses. A clause can be regarded as the finite set of its literal disjuncts. Syntactically, a literal is like a term, so the first metrics can be applied to literals. For each metric on literals, there is an associated *Hausdorff metric* on finite sets of literals. We present a few kinds of situations where these metrics may help.

1 Metrics on Terms

Suppose that S is a real-valued function on substitutions satisfying the following five conditions:

1. for any substitution ϑ, $S\vartheta \geq 0$;

2. $S\varepsilon = 0$ where ε is the identity substitution;
3. for any three terms u, v and w, if

$$\rho : u \longrightarrow v \quad \text{and} \quad \sigma : v \longrightarrow w \quad \text{and} \quad \tau : u \longrightarrow w$$

are all most general, then

$$S\tau \le S\rho + S\sigma$$

4. under the same assumptions as for 3/,

$$S\sigma \le S\tau$$

5. if u_1 and u_2 are any two terms which can be unified, and u is formed by unifying them with any substitutions

$$\varphi_1 : u_1 \longrightarrow u \quad \text{and} \quad \varphi_2 : u_2 \longrightarrow u$$

and v is a *lgg* of u_1 and u_2, and

$$\rho_1 : v \longrightarrow u_1 \quad \text{and} \quad \rho_2 : v \longrightarrow u_2 \quad \text{are most general,}$$

then

$$S\rho_1 + S\rho_2 \le S\varphi_1 + S\varphi_2.$$

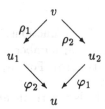

(Note that u and φ_1 and φ_2 need not be most general.)

Definition 1. In that case, say S is a *size* on substitutions.

We shall examine a family of examples of sizes when we have seen why they are interesting.

If S is a size on substitutions, and t_1 and t_2 are any two terms, and u is their *lgg*, and $\vartheta_1 : u \longrightarrow t_1$ and $\vartheta_2 : u \longrightarrow t_2$ are most general, then say

$$d_S(t_1, t_2) = S\vartheta_1 + S\vartheta_2.$$

Proposition 2. *The function d_S is a pseudo-metric on the set of terms.*

Proof.
d_S is non-negative, by 1/.
d_S is symmetric, by the form of its definition.
$d_S(t,t) = 0$ for any term t, by 2/.
We show that $d_S(t_1,t_2) \leq d_S(t_1,t_3) + d_S(t_3,t_2)$.
Say u is the *lgg* of t_1 and t_2
  v_1 is the *lgg* of t_1 and t_3
  v_2 is the *lgg* of t_2 and t_3
  w is the *lgg* of v_1 and v_2.

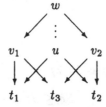

For convenience, write $S(ab)$ for $S\vartheta$ whenever $a\vartheta = b$ and ϑ is most general. By the conditions on the size function S,

$$S(ut_1) \leq S(wt_1) \qquad\qquad \text{by 4/}$$
$$\leq S(v_1t_1) + S(wv_1) \qquad \text{by 3/}$$
$$S(wv_1) + S(wv_2) \leq S(v_1t_3) + S(v_2t_3) \qquad \text{by 5/}$$

so

$$S(ut_1) + S(ut_2) \leq S(v_1t_1) + S(v_1t_3) + S(v_2t_2) + S(v_2t_3)$$

$\square$

2 Examples of Sizes

It remains to discover a family of size functions. Suppose that each function symbol f is assigned a non-negative real number wt_f called it *weight*. (A constant is just a function symbol of arity zero). For any subsitution ϑ, let

$$S\vartheta = \sum \{wt_f \mid \exists x(x \text{ is a variable and } f \text{ occurs in } x\vartheta)\}.$$

Note that each weight wt_f only occurs at most once in the sum, however often the symbol f may occur in values of ϑ.

Example 2. Suppose that

$$\vartheta = [f(g(a), f(a,b))/x,\ b/y,\ x/z]$$

$$wt_f = 2; \quad wt_g = 0; \quad wt_a = 4; \quad wt_b = 1; \quad wt_c = 6.$$

Then

$$S\vartheta = 2 + 0 + 4 + 1 = 7$$

Proposition 3. *Any such function S is a size.*

Proof.

1. Since wt_f is non-negative for each f, so is $S\vartheta$.
2. $S\varepsilon$ is the empty sum, which is 0.
3. τ is the restriction of $\rho\sigma$ to the free variables of u. Hence every function symbol occurring in values of τ also occurs in values of ρ or σ, so

$$S\tau \leq S\rho + S\sigma.$$

4. Suppose that, for some variable x, a function symbol f occurs in $x\sigma$. Since σ is most general, two cases may arise: either x occurs in u and $x\rho$ is x, or for some variable y occurring in u, x occurs in $y\rho$. If x occurs in u and $x\rho$ is x then $x\tau$ must be $x\sigma$. If x occurs in $y\rho$ where y occurs in u then $y\tau$ must be $y\rho\sigma$. In either event, f occurs in some value of τ. Hence

$$S\sigma \leq S\tau.$$

5. Suppose that f occurs in $x\rho_1$; then, since ρ_1 is most general, x must occur at some place p in v, and since v is least general, the terms $x\rho_1$ and $x\rho_2$ do not begin with the same symbol. If $x\rho_2$ were not a variable then u_1 and u_2 could not be unified; so $x\rho_2$ is some variable, say y. Since $v\rho_1\varphi_2 = v\rho_2\varphi_1 = u$,

$$x\rho_1\varphi_2 = x\rho_2\varphi_1 = y\varphi_1$$

and f occurs in $x\rho_1\varphi_2$ so f occurs in $y\varphi_1$, so $S\rho_1 \leq S\varphi_1$. Similarly, $S\rho_2 \leq S\varphi_2$ and so

$$S\rho_1 + S\rho_2 \leq S\varphi_1 + S\varphi_2.$$

$\square$

3   Metrics on Clauses

As in reference [6], a clause can be regarded as the finite set of its disjuncts, which are atomic formulas and negated atomic formulas.

Example 3. The clause

$$likes(Mary, John) \ \wedge \ likes(John, Ann) \ \wedge \ \neg proud(John) \ \Rightarrow$$
$$play(Mary, Ann, John, skipping)$$

is equivalent to

$$\neg likes(Mary, John) \ \vee \ \neg likes(John, Ann) \ \vee \ proud(John) \ \vee$$
$$play(Mary, Ann, John, skipping)$$

so it can be depicted as the set of literals

$$\{\neg likes(Mary, John), \ \neg likes(John, Ann), \ proud(John),$$
$$play(Mary, Ann, John, skipping)\}.$$

We use the

Lemma (see [5] page 131, problem D). *If (X, d) is any metric space, then the function*

$$d'(A, B) = \max \begin{cases} \max_{x \in A} \min_{y \in B} d(x, y) \\ \max_{y \in B} \min_{x \in A} d(x, y) \end{cases}$$

is a metric on the set of nonempty finite subsets of X. If d is a pseudo-metric then so is d'.

This metric d' is often called the *Hausdorff metric* for d.

Proof. For any nonempty finite subsets A and B of X, $d'(A, B)$ is clearly well defined; non-negative; symmetric; zero if $A = B$; and, if d is a metric, nonzero if $A \neq B$. If $Y \subseteq X$ and $r > 0$ then say $V_r Y = \{x \in X \mid \exists y \in Y \; d(x, y) \leq r\}$. Observe that

$$d'(A, B) = \min\{r \mid A \subseteq V_r B \; \wedge \; B \subseteq V_r A\}.$$

If C is any other nonempty subset of X, and if

$$C \subseteq V_r A \; \wedge \; A \subseteq V_r C \; \wedge \; C \subseteq V_s B \; \wedge \; B \subseteq V_s C$$

then $\forall x \in A \; \exists z \in C \; (d(x, z) \leq r \; \wedge \; \exists y \in B \; d(z, y) \leq s)$ so $A \subseteq V_{r+s} B$. Similarly, $B \subseteq V_{r+s} A$. Hence if $d'(A, C) \leq r$ and $d'(B, C) \leq s$ then $d'(A, B) \leq r + s$. Hence $d'(A, B) \leq d'(A, C) + d'(B, C)$. □

Example 4. Suppose that (X, d) is the set of integers with the usual distance function, and

$$A = \{2, 4, 5\} \quad \text{and} \quad B = \{1, 2, 5, 8\}$$

then

$d(x, y)$	$y \in B$:	1	2	5	8	$\min_{y \in B} d(x, y)$
$x \in A$:	2	1	0	3	6	0
	4	3	2	1	4	1
	5	4	3	0	3	0
$\min_{x \in A} d(x, y)$		1	0	0	3	

so

$$\max_{x \in A} \min_{y \in B} d(x, y) = 1$$

$$\max_{y \in B} \min_{x \in A} d(x, y) = 3$$

so

$$d'(A, B) = 3.$$

Hausdorff's construction has become popular in the study of fractals.

Syntactically, the only difference between terms and literals is that a term may begin with a function symbol whereas a literal starts with a predicate symbol or a negated predicate symbol. If we treat predicate symbols and negated predicate symbols like function symbols, as in [6], then the metrics d_S on terms can be extended to literals. A clause is a finite set of literals, so the metrics we want on clauses are the Hausdorff metrics of the metrics d_S.

4 Terms and Clauses Containing Variables

These pseudometrics were originally devised for clustering of ground terms and clauses. A referee pointed out that they behave oddly when applied to terms containing variables; for instance, if x and y are variables then

$$d_S(p(x,x), p(x,y)) = 0$$

for *every* size function S. It appears that they may have limited value if one attempts to cluster non-ground clauses. However, there is a solution: one can assign weights to variables, just as one does to constants. Formally, this can be justified, without rewriting all the propositions and proofs, by the following trick.

> Say L is the language in which the clauses are expressed. There is an associated *meta-language* $\mathcal{ML}$ in which x and y, variables of L, are *constants*. (The construction of $\mathcal{ML}$ is too elaborate to describe here, although it is straightforward: see [4].) $\mathcal{ML}$ is another first order language, so all the above constructions can be performed in it.

Thus, if one assigns weights to variables of L, then the functions d_S are still metrics, and they detect the difference between $p(x,x)$ and $p(x,y)$.

Inductive logic programming (ILP) constructs non-ground clauses in which the names of variables are chosen arbitrarily, as long as they are distinct within any one clause. Unless one takes care, this could disrupt the clustering process.

Example 5. The two clauses

$$p(x,y,z) \Rightarrow q(x,y)$$
$$p(x,z,y) \Rightarrow q(x,z)$$

are logically equivalent, but there could be a strictly positive distance between them (in the Hausdorff metric of a suitable meta-level d_S); and they might have different distances from a third clause, such as

$$p(x,y,z) \Rightarrow r(x,y).$$

There is a simple solution to this phenomenon. If C and D are any two terms (or clauses), say

$$A_C = \{C\vartheta \mid \vartheta \text{ is an } invertable \text{ substitution}\}$$

so, for instance, when C is $p(x,y,z) \Rightarrow q(x,y)$ then A_C contains

$$p(x,y,z) \Rightarrow q(x,y) \quad \text{and} \quad p(x,z,y) \Rightarrow q(x,z) \quad \text{and} \quad p(z,x,y) \Rightarrow q(z,x).$$

Define A_D similarly; and then let the distance $d(C,D)$ be

$$\max \begin{cases} \max_{x \in A_C} \min_{y \in A_D} d_S(x,y) \\ \max_{y \in A_D} \min_{x \in A_C} d_S(x,y) \end{cases}$$

If all variables have the same weight then, although the sets A_C and A_D are infinite, this is well defined and calculable, and it is a pseudometric, and it is invariant under renaming of variables, and it assigns a strictly positive distance between $p(x,x)$ and $p(x,y)$.

5 Applications and Discussion

The metric most commonly used in machine learning is the Hamming distance. This serves well when data are described by attributes with disjoint discrete sets of possible values. It fails to reveal all detail when two different attributes can have the same value. It is also not so useful when each datum is described by an elaborate term in which a subterm can occur twice in different positions.

Example 6. Vere [7] showed how one may construe ground clauses from an instance of apparent causes and their effect. Plotkin [6] showed how one can generalise from a set of similar ground clauses. (See [3] for details.) It is essential to Vere's method that subterms are repeated.

One problem with this process in real situations is that often there is a plethora of possible ground clauses which could be construed and generalised from. In any one case, Vere's method is likely to form ground clauses with irrelevant features. Each example situation will contribute one clause including precisely the relevant features, and several more with irrelevant ones too. If a learner forms clusters in the set of all such ground clauses, using the metrics described here, then those clauses with only attributes common to all situations will form a largest cluster. (There may be several clusters with the maximal number of members, but among them, just one cluster will contain longest clauses.) This is the cluster from which one should generalise.

Example 7. Suppose that a learner should discover heuristic rules to guide theorem proving by natural deduction. A proof is usually found by working back from the target theorem. The hard step is application of the $\Rightarrow E$ rule:

$$\frac{S : p \Rightarrow q \quad S : p}{S : q}$$

When this is used, the root sequent $S : q$ is given and one must choose a suitable p. The key is to choose p so that both p and $p \Rightarrow q$ are provable. This involves finding a p which matches two or more suitable sub-formulas in S.

For a task like this, a Hamming distance would not find suitable clusters of examples from which one could generalise and form useful heuristic rules. A metric based on subsumption, like the ones described above, might serve better.

When extended with weights for variables, the metrics d_S also have potential application to ILP. In the present state of the art, as represented for instance by RIBL [1], an ILP system must overcome noise and redundant features by forming clusters of training instances. Each training instance is a set of literals. The particular similarity measure used for clustering in RIBL depends on a data base in which it finds sets of literals with common terms, rather like those which Vere assembles into clauses.

The similarity measures currently used show scope for improvement. Ideally, similarity (or difference) should be measured by some function which has a simple general definition and convenient properties, such as a metric. The particular measure encoded into RIBL depends not just on the two examples being compared but also on the data base, which adds complication. If it were replaced with a metric such as some d_S then the resulting program might be more amenable to theoretical analysis and comparisons. It could also incorporate a clustering algorithm such as one of those discussed by Allan Gordon in [2]. RIBL extrapolates by a weighted voting system, based on k nearest neighbours. If instead it extrapolated from a cluster, found by standard methods, then there would be no need for a choice of k. Clustering is still to some extent a black art, because nobody has yet come up with an acceptable formal definition of what is a cluster, but some good work has been done and we may as well take advantage of it.

The metrics d_S are not suitable for all the requirements of RIBL because they are not designed to handle continuous attributes. If two constants a and b are real numbers, then we would prefer $d_S(a, b)$ to be dependent on the difference between a and b, rather than $wt_a + wt_b$. More generally, if terms and clauses are constructed from constants a and b in some metric space (X, δ), then one would like the d_S-distance to depend on $\delta(a, b)$. I hope that the metrics d_S can be so extended.

References

1. W. Emde and D. Wettschereck. Relational instance-based learning. In L.Saitta, editor, *ICML-96*, pages 122–130, Bari, Italy, 1996. Morgan Kaufmann.
2. A. D. Gordon. Hierarchical classification. In P.Arabie, L.J.Hubert, and G. De Soete, editors, *Clustering and Classification*, pages 65–121. World Scientific, 1996.
3. A. Hutchinson. *Algorithmic Learning*. Oxford University Press, 1994, 1995.
4. A. Hutchinson. First order meta theories. *Logic Journal of the IGPL*, 5(1):96–144, 1997.
5. J. L. Kelley. *General Topology*. Springer-Verlag, 1955.
6. G. D. Plotkin. A note on inductive generalization. In B.Meltzer and D.Michie, editors, *Machine Intelligence 5*, pages 153–163. Edinburgh University Press, 1969.
7. S. A. Vere. Induction of relational productions in the presence of background information. In *IJCAI*, volume 1, pages 349–355, 1977. Cambridge, MA.

Learning When Negative Examples Abound

Miroslav Kubat, Robert Holte, and Stan Matwin

Department of Computer Science, University of Ottawa
150 Louis Pasteur, Ottawa, Ontario, K1N 6N5 Canada
{mkubat,holte,stan}@csi.uottawa.ca

Abstract. Existing concept learning systems can fail when the negative examples heavily outnumber the positive examples. The paper discusses one essential trouble brought about by imbalanced training sets and presents a learning algorithm addressing this issue. The experiments (with synthetic and real-world data) focus on 2-class problems with examples described with binary and continuous attributes.

1 Introduction

The specific problem addressed here is learning from *imbalanced training sets* where examples from one class heavily outnumber examples from the other class. Highly imbalanced training sets occur in applications where the classifier is to detect an infrequent, albeit important, event: a fraudulent telephone call (Fawcett and Provost, 1996), an unreliable telecommunications customer (Ezawa, Singh, and Norton, 1996), or a rare diagnosis such as the thyroid diseases in the UCI repository. Extremely imbalanced classes also arise in information retrieval (Lewis and Catlett, 1994).

Performace of concept learning is customarily assessed with *accuracy:* the percentage of testing examples correctly classified by the induced classifier. In the case of imbalanced training sets, though, this is inappropriate. For instance, Kononenko and Bratko (1991) report a domain where a medical specialist achieved 64% accuracy, while 80% examples represented the majority class. Should he decide to always predict only the majority class, the expert would improve accuracy but probably lose his patients in the process.

Other performance indicators are needed. The information retrieval community uses *precision* and *recall* and combines them into the so-called F-measure (Lewis and Gale, 1994). Another good idea is the information-based criterion suggested by Kononenko and Bratko (1991). Swets (1988) measures the area under the curve that depicts the relation between the error rate observed on negative examples and the accuracy observed on positive examples. In our research on the detection of oil spills, we wanted to maximize the geometric mean (*g-mean*) $g = \sqrt{acc+ \cdot acc-}$, where $acc+$ is the percentage of positive examples correctly recognized and $acc-$ is the percentage of negative examples correctly recognized. Geometric mean is high when both $acc+$ and $acc-$ are high *and* when the difference between $acc+$ and $acc-$ is small. This criterion was chosen because it was consistent with the requirements of our customer; however, most of the ideas presented below will be valid with other criteria as well.

What do such criteria betray about the behavior of learning algorithms in applications with imbalanced training sets? This is best illustrated with a ficticious experiment. Choose randomly n positive and n negative examples, and run C4.5 on them. Then increase the number of negatives in increments of n (with the same n positives) and repeat the learning. In many applications, g-mean measured on an independent testing set (with the same distribution of positives and negatives) sooner or later significantly drops.

This problem has been noted in the neural-network community, where suggested solutions duplicate examples, create new examples, or increase the learning rate for examples of the underrepresented class (DeRouin et al. 1991). In the symbolic learning community, the problem has been addressed by weighing training examples (Pazzani et al., 1994), by windowing (Catlett, 1991), and by sampling (Lewis and Catlett, 1994). A natural approach exploits distinct costs assigned to false positives and false negatives (Pazzani et al., 1994).

In Section 2, we offer a hypothesis why abundant negatives hurt: the reason is that the positive and negative classes in real-world domains often overlap. The hypothesis underlies the simple learning algorithm SHRINK described in Section 3. Experiments illustrating its behavior are reported in Section 4.

2 Why Abundant Negatives Hurt

We assume a scenario where the agent is provided with a set of pairs $[(\mathbf{x}, c(\mathbf{x}))]$ where $\mathbf{x}$ is a vector of attribute values (binary or continuous) and $c(\mathbf{x})$ is the corresponding concept label. To keep the work focussed, we consider only two-class problems.

Our point can be illustrated by the case of two *overlapping* classes. As the number of negative examples grows, so does the likelihood that the nearest neighbor of *any* example in the region of overlap will be negative. The *k-nearest-neighbor* rule will thus correctly recognize most examples of the majority class while failing on the minority class.

A *decision-tree* generator partitions the instance space into regions labeled with the class that has majority in the region. With imbalanced classes, the regions with mixed positives and negatives will tend to be labeled with the preponderant class. By another perpective, each positive example is eventually separated from other positives by a "wall" of negatives and the tree generator either stops splitting, in which case negatives are a majority, or it keeps splitting until it forms a tiny region around each positive.

Consider an experimental testbed where random examples are generated according to normal distribution with $\mu_+ = [0, 0]$ and $\sigma_+ = [1, 1]$ for the positives, and with $\mu_- = [2, 0]$ and $\sigma_- = [2, 2]$ for the negatives. In all runs, the same 50 training positives are used, while the number of negatives grows from 50 to 800 in increments of 50. Performance is measured on an independent testing set with the same proportion of positive and negative examples as the training set. The results of C4.5 (Quinlan, 1993) and 1-NN are shown in Figure 1: with

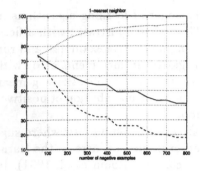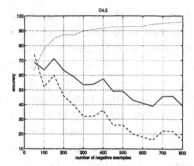

Fig. 1. Running the 1-NN rule (left) and of C4.5 (right) on the gauss data. Horizontal axis: the number of negatives. Dashed: accuracy on positives; dotted: accuracy on negatives; solid: g-mean.

abundant negatives, the performance on the majority class exceeds 90% and the performance on the minority class collapses.

(In C4.5, we used the default parameter setting while being aware that better results might be achieved by their more careful adjustment. The graphs show performances of unpruned trees: in the given domain, existing pruning techniques often degenerate the tree to a single leaf labeled with the majority class—the very event that we wanted to avoid.)

3 The System SHRINK

To cope with the domination of negative examples in mixed regions, our system SHRINK *insists* that a mixed region be labeled as positive, whether positive examples prevail in the region or not. That changes the learner's focus: search for the *best positive region,* one with the maximum ratio of positives to negatives.

The system is restricted to search for a *single* region to be labeled as positive, and is thus ill-suited for disjunctive concepts. The justification is that partitioning rare positives into two or more subsets leaves virtually nothing to be reliably reasoned about, considering the presence of freak outliers which, with such small numbers, could well be mistaken for additional disjuncts.

The concept will be represented by the *network of tests* depicted in Figure 2. The tests on numeric attributes have the form $x_i \in [\min a_i; \max a_i]$ where i indexes the attributes. For boolean attribues the tests will have the form of $x_i = 0$ or $x_i = 1$. Denote by h_i the output of the i-th test and let $h_i = 1$ if the test suggests a positive label and $h_i = -1$ otherwise. The example is classified as positive if $\sum_i h_i \cdot w_i > 0$, where w_i is the weight of the i-th test.

The *weights* are determined by an algorithm by Freund and Schapire (1995): Denote by **p** a vector assigning to each example its "importance." The vector is fixed during learning. In the simplest case, $p_j = 1$ for any j. Alternatively, p_j can be set to a higher value for a positive example, and to a lower value for a

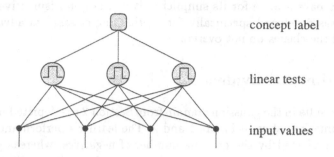

concept label

linear tests

input values

Fig. 2. A classifier in the form of a network of tests.

negative example. Define the loss vector $\mathbf{l_i} = [l_{1i}, \dots, l_{ji}, \dots]$ so that $l_{ji} = 0$ if the j-th example is classified correctly by the i-th test, and $l_{ji} = 1$ otherwise. The overall error of the i-th test is calculated as $e_i = \mathbf{l_i} \cdot \mathbf{p}^T$ and the corresponding weight is obtained as $w_i = \log(e_i/(1 - e_i))$. The intuition behind this expression is to assign higher weights to tests with less errors on the training set.

In the search for the tests, SHRINK begins by establishing the "best" interval along each attribute. To find it, the program begins with the smallest interval containing all positive examples and on every iteration shrinks the interval by eliminating either the left or right endpoint, whichever results in the better g-mean score. This produces a set of nested intervals that are scanned for the one with the maximum score. The intervals thus shrink from one attribute value to the next, hence the program's name.

When the intervals have been found, SHRINK discards tests with $g > 0.5$ (so as to get rid of less relevant attributes), and then calculates the weights of each of the remaining tests using the formula mentioned above. The procedure is summarized in Table 1.

Table 1. Control structure of SHRINK

---

1) For each attribute:
  • Sort the examples by the attribute's value;
  • The initial interval is $[\min a_i, \max a_i]$ where $\min a_i$ and $\max a_i$ are the min and max values observed for the i-th attribute in positive examples;
  • Remove either $\min a_i$ or $\max a_i$, whichever reduces more radically the number of negative examples in the interval; record the value of g-mean (g) for the new interval;
  • Repeat the previous step as long as there is at least one positive example in the interval, and then return the interval with maximum g.
5) Discard tests with $g < 0.5$.
6) Calculate the weight of each test.

SHRINK pays a price for its simplicity: it will fail on disjunctive concepts, and, as it was developed specifically for overlapping classes, its advantage will disappear if the classes do not overlap.

4 Experimental Evidence

SHRINK's results in the gaussian domain from Section 2 are depicted in Figure 3, using the same format as in Figure 1 and 2. The learner's performance does not appear to be affected by the growing number of negatives: whereas g-mean for C4.5 dropped with the growing number of negatives from about 70% to less than 40%, SHRINK kept a steady performance slightly above 75%.

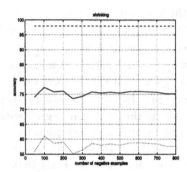

Fig. 3. Performance of SHRINK on the 2-dim data

The claim that SHRINK overcomes the problems with imbalanced classes is corroborated by experiments with the following real-world domains.

Oil-slick data. (our current research) Oil slicks I: 21 positives, 350 negatives; 39 numeric attributes; 7-fold cross-validation. Oil slicks II: 24 positives, 400 negatives; 44 numeric attributes; 8-fold cross-validation.

Sleep data. (An earlier project of one of the authors, see Kubat, Pfurtscheller, and Flotzinger, 1994). The original task was modified to recognize the occurence of class REM. Two files, slightly adapted from the original, were used: KR2 with 150 positives and 750 negatives; BR2 with 140 positives and 700 negatives. 15 numeric attributes; 5-fold cross-validation.

Euthyroid and Hypothyroid from the UCI repository (Murphy and Aha, 1994). We deleted all examples **age** and **sex** had missing values and we removed attribute **TBG_measured** because its values were frequently missing. From Euthyroid, we randomly selected 240 positives and 2400 negatives. From Hypothyroid, we selected 120 positives and 2400 negatives. 18 boolean and 6 numeric attributes; 5-fold cross-validation.

In the oil-slick domains, the ratio between the positive and negative examples is very high. For this reason, the importance vector **p** was set so that p_i for a positive example was r times higher than in the case of a negative example. The value of r is determined as $r = n_n/n_p$ where n_n is the number of negative examples and n_p is the number of positive examples. In the other domains (sleep and thyroid), $p_i = 1$ for all i. Auxiliary experiments (not reported here) have shown that SHRINK'S performance was not very sensitive to precise values in the importance vector.

Table 2. g-means in oil-slicks I

# neg.	C4.5	1-NN	SHRINK
140	66.5	40.0	66.9
210	51.0	43.5	68.2
280	52.6	29.8	68.0
350	48.2	27.6	67.5

Table 3. g-means in oil-slicks II

# neg.	C4.5	1-NN	SHRINK
160	83.9	55.9	75.8
240	82.3	59.8	74.9
320	83.2	49.1	72.6
400	80.5	44.8	73.8

Table 4. g-means in sleep data: KR

# neg.	C4.5	1-NN	SHRINK
150	81.0	76.3	68.6
300	79.4	75.1	71.7
450	76.9	73.0	74.7
600	72.3	70.3	73.8
750	72.0	67.8	75.9

Table 5. g-means in sleep data: BR

# neg.	C4.5	1-NN	SHRINK
140	84.5	84.5	69.7
280	83.9	86.0	71.0
420	83.2	85.7	70.2
560	78.7	83.5	72.2
700	78.4	78.9	73.1

Table 6. g-means in euthyroid data

# neg.	C4.5	1-NN	SHRINK
480	94.3	71.5	71.7
960	94.3	67.0	78.1
1440	94.7	63.2	74.6
1920	91.1	62.2	73.7
2400	88.2	60.8	74.0

Table 7. g-means in hypothyroid

# neg.	C4.5	1-NN	SHRINK
360	95.7	93.1	93.5
840	96.3	93.0	94.8
1320	95.4	91.0	94.4
1800	95.6	89.2	94.7
2280	93.6	88.9	95.0

The results are summarized in Tables 2 through 7 for growing numbers of negatives. For reference, the tables give also results achieved by C4.5 and 1-NN. (The poor results of 1-NN in some domains, such as oil-slick II, are caused by a high number of irrelevant attributes.) In all domains, the performance of 1-NN decreases with the growing number of negatives. The performance of C4.5 drops in all domains save for the hypothyroid data file, where it remains virtually unchanged regardless of the number of negatives.

SHRINK's performance steadily increases with the growing number of negatives in oil slicks I, and in both sleep-data domains. In the hypothyroid domain, the improvement is marginal. Only in the euthyroid domain did SHRINK's performance drop with increasing number of negatives. When presented with *all* available examples, SHRINK outperformed C4.5 in three (out of 6) domains and outperformed 1-NN in five domains. In some domains, the limits of SHRINK's representation language were reached even with small numbers of negatives and could not be improved by providing more negatives. As an aside, our algorithm tended to yield better results on positive examples than on negative examples. A more detailed study would exceed the scope of this brief contribution and will appear in a full-length paper currently under preparation.

To obtain evidence that the performance of SHRINK can be attributed to the chosen evaluation criterion, we have run the program on the same data, this time using mean accuracy. Expectedly, SHRINK now turned out to be useless, invariably relapsing to 100% on negatives and 0% on positives whenever the ratio between the positives and negatives exceeded 3, in some domains even earlier.

The approach should not be viewed as a panacea. In some domains, such as the glass data from the UCI repository, the performance of C45 and 1-NN does not degrade with increasing numbers of negatives. SHRINK will also lose its edge if the concept is disjunctive.

5 Conclusion

The poor behavior of existing learners in domains with imbalanced training sets can be caused by the fact that examples of the majority class can "infest" the region of the minority class. This can be due to class-label noise or to the overlap between the two classes. In this paper, we described a novel technique that is robust against this phenomenon.

In *future research,* analytical and practical studies of essential learning algorithms should be addressed. One should also study decision-tree generators using (e.g. in attribute-value splitting) criteria maximizing g-mean or other criteria of this kind. Whereas our experiments focussed on two-class problems, multiclass domains present new challenges: $n - 1$ underrepresented classes and one dominating class can be different case than $n - 1$ balanced classes with a single underrepresented class. Techniques for sampling the examples from the majority class should be investigated.

Acknowledgements

The research was partially supported by Precarn Inc. and NSERC. The sleep data belong to the Department of Medical Informatics, Technical University Graz, and have been recorded and classified under a grant from the 'Fonds zur Förderung der wissenschaftlichen Forschung' (S49/03). Thanks are due to Gert Pfurtscheller for his kind permission to use these data.

References

Ambrosino, R., Buchanan, R., Cooper, G.F., and Fine, M. (1995). The Use of Misclassification Costs to Learn Rule-Based Decision Support Models for Cost-Effective Hospital Admission Strategies. *Proceedings of the 19th Annual Symposium on Computer Applications in Medical Care (SCAMC'95)* pp. 304–308

Bloedorn, E., Mani, I., and MacMillan, T.R. (1996). Machine Learning of User Profiles: Representational Issues. *Proceeding of the National Conference on Artificial Intelligence, AAAI'96* pp. 433–437

Catlett, J. (1991). Megainduction: A Test Flight. *Proceedings of the 8th International Workshop on ML* (pp.596–599), San Mateo, CA: Morgan Kaufmann

DeRouin, E., Brown, J., Beck, H., Fausett, L, and Schneider, M. (1991). Neural Network Training on Unequally Represented Classes. In Dagli, C.H., Kumara, S.R.T. and Shin, Y.C. (eds.): *Intelligent Engineering Systems Through Artificial Neural Networks*, ASME Press, New York, 135–145

Ezawa, K.J., Singh, M. and Norton, S.W. (1996). Learning Goal Oriented Bayesian Networks for Telecommunications Management. *Proceedings of the International Conference on Machine Learning, ICML'96* (pp. 139–147), Bari, Italy, Morgan Kaufmann

Fawcett, T and Provost, F. (1996). Combining Data Mining and Machine Learning for Effective User Profile. *Proceedings of the 2nd International Conference on Knowledge Discovery and Data Mining* (pp. 8–13), Portland OR, AAAI Press

Freund, Y. and Schapire, R.E. (1995). A Decision-Theoretic Generalization of On-Line Learning and an Application to Boosting. *Proceedings of the 2nd Annual European Conference on Computational Learning Theory* (pp.23–37)

Kononenko, I. and Bratko, I. (1991). Information-Based Evaluation Criterion for Classifier's Performance. *Machine Learning*, 6, 67–80

Kubat, M., Pfurtscheller, G., and Flotzinger D. (1994). AI-Based Approach to Automatic Sleep Classification. *Biological Cybernetics*, 79, 443–448

Lang, K. (1995). Newsreader: Learning to Filter News. *Proceedings of the 12th International Conference on Machine Learning, ICML'95* (pp. 331–339), Tahoe Lake, CA, Morgan Kaufmann

Lewis, D. and Catlett, J. (1994). Heterogeneous Uncertainty Sampling for Supervized Learning. *Proceedings of the 11th International Conference on Machine Learning, ICML'94* (pp. 148–156), New Brunswick, New Jersey, Morgan Kaufmann

Lewis, D. and Gale, W. (1994). Training Text Classifiers by Uncertainty Sampling. *Proceedings of the 17th Annual International ACM SIGIR Conference on Research and Development in Information Retrieval*

Murphy, P. and Aha, D. (1994). UCI Repository of Machine Learning Databases [machine-readable data repository]. Technical Report, University of California, Irvine

Murthy, S., Kasif, S., & Salzberg, S. (1994). A System for Induction of Oblique Decision Trees. *Journal of Artificial Intelligence Research*, 2, 1–32

Pazzani, M, Merz, C., Murphy, P., Ali, K., Hume, T., and Brunk, C. (1994). Reducing Misclassification Costs. *Proceedings of the 11th International Conference on ML, ICML'94* (pp. 217–225), New Brunswick, New Jersey, Morgan Kaufmann

Quinlan J.R. (1993). *C4.5: Programs for Machine Learning*. Morgan Kaufmann, San Mateo

Swets, J.A. (1988). Measuring the Accuracy of Diagnostic Systems. *Science*, 240, 1285–1293

A Model for Generalization Based on Confirmatory Induction

Nicolas Lachiche[1] and Pierre Marquis[2]

[1] CRIN/CNRS - INRIA Lorraine, Bâtiment LORIA, Campus scientifique B.P. 239, 54506 Vandœuvre-lès-Nancy Cedex, France - e-mail: lachiche@loria.fr
[2] CRIL/Université d'Artois, Rue de l'Université, S.P. 16, 62307 Lens Cedex, France - e-mail: marquis@lens.lifl.fr

Abstract. Confirmatory induction is based on the assumption that unknown individuals are similar to known ones, i.e. they satisfy the properties shared by known individuals. This assumption can be represented inside a non-monotonic logical framework. Accordingly, existing approaches to confirmatory induction take advantage of the machinery developed so far for non-monotonic inference. However, they are based on completion policies that are unnecessary strong for the induction purpose. The contribution of this paper is twofold: some basic requirements that any model for generalization based on confirmatory induction should satisfy are proposed. Then, a model for generalization based on Hempel's notion of confirmation is introduced. This model is rational in the sense that it satisfies the rationality postulates we exhibit; moreover, the completion principle on which this model is based captures exactly the similarity assumption, hence the model can be considered minimal as well.

1 Introduction

Inductive generalization is inference of general laws from examples. It is a central concern of Machine Learning and the Philosophy of Sciences; accordingly, many researches have been devoted to it for several decades. Despite a huge amount of work on this topic, both from philosophers, logicians and AI researchers, *there is no consensus on what induction precisely is*. Indeed, different kinds of induction can easily be envisioned, and they cannot be reduced to some common ground. This diversity has been recently acknowledged by the AI community. Particularly, Flach [5] clearly points out two forms of induction, so-called explanatory induction and confirmatory induction.

Given some background knowledge Th, *explanatory induction* aims at generating generalizations G which deductively explain the observation report E, in the sense that in every world where Th and G are true, E is also true. Formally, we have: $G \wedge Th \models E$.

Contrastingly, *confirmatory induction* is based on the evidence that an inductive hypothesis does not necessarily need to explain some observations, but to be confirmed by them in some sense. For instance, if all what I know is that Tweety is a bird, Tweety flies, Superman flies, Garfield is a cat and every cat is not a bird, then provided that every unknown individual behaves like the known ones (i.e. every individual possesses every property shared by both Tweety, Superman and Garfield), Woodstock can be assumed flying whenever it is known to be a bird. Similar conclusions can be drawn with every bird. More formally,

$$G =_{def} \forall X (bird(X) \Rightarrow flies(X))$$

can be considered as a generalization of

$$E =_{def} \{bird(Tweety), \ flies(Tweety), \ flies(Superman),$$
$$cat(Garfield), \ \forall X(cat(X) \Rightarrow \neg bird(X))\}.$$

Though G is not a logical consequence of evidence E, it is satisfied (we also say "confirmed") by every known individual.

Within confirmatory induction, there is no need to keep separate some background knowledge with the observation report; every piece of knowledge is viewed as evidence and incorporated into E. Clearly enough, E is not a logical consequence of G, hence G cannot be viewed as an explanation of E (at least, with a deductive meaning): assuming that every bird flies does not explain at all why Tweety is a bird.

While explanatory induction is commonly viewed as reversed deduction, confirmatory induction can be considered as deduction from a completed theory [14,9]. The implicit completion of E which is performed must capture the assumption that *every unknown individual is similar to the known ones, i.e. it exhibits the same properties.* This "induction principle" is often referred to as *the similarity assumption.*

Viewing induction as deduction w.r.t. a completed theory allows one to put forward interesting connections with several non-monotonic inference formalisms, including the closed-world assumption [17] and its generalizations [13], Clark's completion [2] [19] and some forms of circumscription [11] [12]. Indeed, non-monotonic inference can often be considered as deduction from a completed theory. However, inductive inference is non-monotonic inference of a special kind, and it does not come down to any standard form of non-monotonic inference. Such a confusion exists in the models for confirmatory induction by [6,10,15,16,14]. All these approaches take advantage of the machinery developed for non-monotonic inference but they do not make a precise separation between the knowledge level of induction (i.e. what is a generalization?) and the inference level of induction (i.e. how to compute generalizations?). In particular, the notions of confirmation on which such approaches are based are not clearly pointed out. In our opinion, a clear separation between confirmation and generalization is necessary for a good understanding of confirmatory generalization. Moreover, the rationality issue is not addressed. Thus, some features of existing approaches are motivated by the intended notion of generalization (at the knowledge level) whereas some other ones, e.g. restrictions of the representation language, are required by the machinery used to derive generalizations (at the inference level).

The contribution of this paper is twofold. First, some basic requirements that any model for generalization based on confirmatory induction should satisfy are pointed out. Second, a model for generalization based on Hempel's proposal for confirmation is presented. Both the language of evidence and the language of generalizations used in this model are more expressive than the languages used in existing approaches. Consequently, this model allows one to derive generalizations that cannot be built up using previous models for generalization; it also prevents from generating unexpected generalizations.

2 Rationality Postulates for Generalization

The purpose of this section is to point out some requirements that every model for generalization should satisfy. Particularly, we focus on generalization at the knowledge level.

Let us define *a model for generalization based on confirmatory induction* as a 5-uple $\langle L_E, L_H, L_G, \hspace{2pt}\vdash\hspace{-6pt}\sim, \hspace{2pt}\approx\hspace{-8pt}\mid\rangle$. L_E (resp. L_H, L_G) is a representation language of observation reports including eventually some background knowledge (resp. of confirmed statements, of generalizations). $\vdash\hspace{-6pt}\sim$ is a confirmation relation between L_E and L_H, and $\approx\hspace{-8pt}\mid$ a generalization relation between L_E and L_G.

In such models, the notion of confirmed statement and the notion of generalization are kept separate. While confirmatory induction aims at deriving statements supported by some evidence, inductive generalization aims at pointing out general laws supported by some evidence. Thus confirmatory generalization must satisfy:

- *Confirmatory foundation:* if $E \approx\hspace{-8pt}\mid G$, then $E \hspace{2pt}\vdash\hspace{-6pt}\sim G$.
- *Ampliative reasoning:* if $E \models G$, then $E \hspace{2pt}\not\approx\hspace{-8pt}\mid G$.
- *Generality condition:* if $E \approx\hspace{-8pt}\mid G_1$, $E \approx\hspace{-8pt}\mid G_2$ and $G_1 \models G_2$, then $G_1 \equiv G_2$.

The first postulate characterizes generalizations based on confirmatory induction. The ampliative reasoning postulate and the generality condition postulate allow one to discriminate generalizations among all confirmed statements: generalizations must convey new information, and as much information as possible.

Since inferring generalizations from evidence consists in selecting some statements among those confirmed by evidence, generalization benefits of some rationality postulates for confirmation given by Hempel [7,8] and Flach [5], namely:

- *Verification principle:* if $E \approx\hspace{-8pt}\mid H$ and $E \wedge H \models F$, then $E \wedge F \approx\hspace{-8pt}\mid H$.
- *Falsification principle:* if $E \approx\hspace{-8pt}\mid H$ and $E \wedge H \models F$, then $E \wedge \neg F \not\approx\hspace{-8pt}\mid H$.
- *Consistency condition:* if E is consistent, then E is consistent with the whole set of the hypotheses it confirms.
- *Right equivalence:* if H_1 and H_2 are equivalent and $E \approx\hspace{-8pt}\mid H_1$, then $E \approx\hspace{-8pt}\mid H_2$.
- *Left equivalence:* if E_1 and E_2 are equivalent and $E_1 \approx\hspace{-8pt}\mid H$, then $E_2 \approx\hspace{-8pt}\mid H$.
- *Cautious monotonicity:* if $E \approx\hspace{-8pt}\mid H$ and $E \approx\hspace{-8pt}\mid F$, then $E \wedge F \approx\hspace{-8pt}\mid H$.

The other rationality postulates for confirmation proposed by Hempel and Flach cannot be kept for generalization. Ampliative reasoning requires the entailment condition and reflexivity to be given up. Generality condition is not compatible with right weakening, cumulative right weakening and right AND introduction. Left OR introduction must also be rejected because it is not compatible with the similarity assumption itself; for instance, $\forall X, flies(X)$ is confirmed by $flies(Superman)$ and by $flies(Tweety)$, but we are not ready to consider it as confirmed by $flies(Superman) \lor flies(Tweety)$ (just because $\forall X, flies(x)$ could not be derived from $flies(Superman) \lor flies(Tweety)$ if the universe were reduced to $\{Superman, Tweety\}$).

All the requirements above do not define a unique model for generalization. They aim only at characterizing some properties that a rational model for generalization should satisfy. We call *minimal models for generalization* those relying on completion policies allowing one to capture the similarity assumption and nothing else. The completeness issue of these postulates is not addressed in this paper; while we consider that every reasonable model for generalization should satisfy these postulates, we do not claim that the converse is also the case.

3 Existing Approaches to Generalization are not Minimal ones

In this section, we show that existing approaches to generalization based on confirmation [6,10,15,16,14] use completion principles unnecessary strong for the induction purpose. Indeed, the similarity assumption cannot be accurately represented by the completion policies used in these approaches, even if it is embodied in them. Intuitively, the similarity assumption requires the universe to be circumscribed to known *individuals*, only, while completion principles used in non-monotonic inferences aim mainly at circumscribing *properties* of such individuals. As a consequence, these approaches can easily produce unexpected generalizations and miss interesting ones.

Let us recall that Helft's model for generalization is based on subimplication [1], Marquis', Muggleton and De Raedt's, De Raedt and Dzeroski's models on inference w.r.t. minimal Herbrand model and De Raedt and Bruynooghe's on Clark's completion. These three forms of non-monotonic inference circumscribe some properties that individuals satisfy; particularly, they give to positive information a special status w.r.t. negative information: every positive ground fact which cannot be deduced from the evidence database is assumed false. Because such a completion is not always desired, unexpected generalizations can be generated. For instance, $E =_{def} \{orange(Garfield), bird(Tweety)\}$ does not confirm $G =_{def} \forall X, \neg orange(X) \lor \neg bird(X)$ unless E is explicitly completed with $\{\neg orange(Tweety), \neg bird(Garfield)\}$, thanks to the closed-world assumption. Clearly enough, such a completion formula has nothing to do with induction.

A second problem with existing approaches is that the completion of a consistent database may easily result in an inconsistent database, whatever minimal models [6,10,16,14] or Clark's completion [15] are used. In order to deal with this problem, the representation languages of evidence and generalizations are restricted in the approaches mentioned above. Once again, such restrictions are not required by the similarity assumption. They may lead one to miss some interesting generalizations. For instance, none of the approaches above allows one to consider $\forall X, orange(X) \lor bird(X)$ as a generalization of $orange(Garfield) \lor bird(Tweety)$.

4 A Model for Generalization based on Hempel's Notion of Confirmation

In this section, a model for generalization $\langle L_E, L_H, L_G, \vDash, \approx \rangle$ is pointed out. It satisfies the requirements stated in Section 2 and is minimal as well. Interestingly, it does not suffer from the impediments described above.

4.1 Confirmation

The notion of confirmation on which our model is based is close to those proposed by Hempel [7]. Intuitively, E confirms H if and only if E would entail H if the universe were reduced to the set of individuals appearing in E. In other words, E confirms H whenever H is a logical consequence of E under the similarity assumption. Because no additional assumptions are taken into account, the models for generalization based on such a notion of confirmation can be considered as minimal ones.

Definitions. In order to figure out what the universe would be when restricted to known individuals, Hempel introduced the concept of *development of a formula for a finite class of individual constants*:

Definition 1. The development of a first-order formula H for a finite class of individual constants C, noted $D_C(H)$, is inductively defined as follows:

$$D_C(\neg H) =_{def} \neg D_C(H) \qquad D_C(H \Rightarrow G) =_{def} D_C(H) \Rightarrow D_C(G)$$
$$D_C(H \wedge G) =_{def} D_C(H) \wedge D_C(G) \qquad D_C(H \vee G) =_{def} D_C(H) \vee D_C(G)$$
$$D_C(\forall x H) =_{def} \bigwedge_{c \in C} D_C(H[x \leftarrow c]) \qquad D_C(\exists x H) =_{def} \bigvee_{c \in C} D_C(H[x \leftarrow c])$$
$$D_C(H) =_{def} H, \text{ if H is ground}$$

where $H[x \leftarrow c]$ is the formula which results from replacing in H every free occurrence of x by c.

In our approach, we consider the *Herbrand domain* of E, i.e. the set C_E of all constant symbols occurring in E as the set of known individuals. For instance, the development of the formula $H =_{def} \forall X (bird(X) \Rightarrow flies(X))$ for the Herbrand domain of

$$E =_{def} \{bird(Tweety), flies(Tweety), flies(Superman),$$
$$cat(Garfield), \forall X (cat(X) \Rightarrow \neg bird(X))\}$$

is the ground formula

$$(bird(Tweety) \Rightarrow flies(Tweety))$$
$$\wedge (bird(Superman) \Rightarrow flies(Superman)$$
$$\wedge (bird(Garfield) \Rightarrow flies(Garfield)).$$

This ground formula represents the same information than H provided that the universe is reduced to $\{Tweety, Superman, Garfield\}$.

Definition 2. $- L_E$ is the language of universal formulas of function-free first-order logic without equality such that at least one constant symbol occurs in the representation of any observation report, i.e. the Herbrand domain of any E is finite and non-empty.

– We also impose that $L_H = L_E$.

Definition 3. Let $E \in L_E$ and $H \in L_H$ s.t. $C_H \subseteq C_E$. $E \mathrel{\vert\!\sim} H$ if and only if $E \models D_{C_E}(H)$.

In our approach, hypothesis H is confirmed by evidence E whenever H can be deduced from E under the similarity assumption. Accordingly, this notion of confirmation can be considered as a refinement of Flach's consistency-based confirmation [3,4], where E and H are only required to be consistent alltogether.

The various restrictions put on L_E and L_H are motivated as follows. First, if empty Herbrand domains were allowed (e.g. $\forall X, flies(X)$ is considered as an admissible evidence), then confirmed statements which are inconsistent with the corresponding evidence could be easily derived (e.g. $\forall X, \neg flies(X)$ is confirmed by $\forall X, flies(X)$ since the development of $\forall X, \neg flies(X)$ for the empty Herbrand domain is true). This would violate the consistency condition. The absence of equality in the language allows one to reject evidence like $E =_{def} \forall X, (X \neq Superman)$. Indeed, since the development of $H =_{def} \forall X, (X = Superman)$ for $\{Superman\}$ is $Superman = Superman$, which must be considered true in every first-order language with equality, H would be confirmed by E. Once again, the consistency condition would be violated. A similar problem would occur with $E =_{def} \exists X, \neg flies(X) \wedge flies(Superman)$ and $H =_{def} \forall X, flies(X)$ if existential formulas were accepted in the language of evidence. This is why this is not the case. Finally, the Herbrand domain of confirmed statements H is required to be included in the Herbrand domain of the corresponding evidence E, so as to avoid the happening of "miraculously generated" individuals in confirmed statements.

Hempel's Confirmation. Though the confirmation relation above is close to Hempel's proposal [8], it differs from it in several ways. First, our notion of confirmation corresponds to Hempel's *direct confirmation*. We do not consider confirmation defined by extending direct confirmation with logical consequence, as Hempel did to satisfy the entailment condition, because this postulate is not compatible with the ampliative reasoning postulate (cf. Section 2).

Additionally, we do not impose H to be valid whenever $D_{C_E}(H)$ is valid; for instance, given $E =_{def} flies(Tweety)$ and $H =_{def} \forall X, flies(X) \vee \forall X, \neg flies(X)$, we consider that the fact that $D_{C_E}(H) = flies(Tweety) \vee \neg flies(Tweety)$ is valid, while H is not, does not prevent E from confirming H.

Finally, assimilating known individuals with the Herbrand domain of evidence imposes to consider $E_1 =_{def} flies(Superman) \wedge (flies(Superman) \vee flies(Tweety))$ and $E_2 =_{def} flies(Superman)$ as two different evidences. Indeed, while these two formulas are logically equivalent, they do not convey the same information w.r.t. individuals of the domain: from the first one, we want to conclude that two individuals belong to the domain. Such a distinction has a significant influence on the confirmatory relation: in our model, $H = \forall X, flies(X)$ is considered as confirmed by E_2 but not by E_1; as a consequence, left logical equivalence is satisfied by $\mathrel{\vert\!\sim}$ if we consider that two formulas are equivalent if and only if they are logically equivalent and share the same Herbrand domain, i.e they are logically equivalent under the domain-closure axiom and the unique name axiom. Hempel addressed this problem differently by considering only the *essential constants* of E, i.e. constants of E that must occur in every formula logically equivalent to E [8].

4.2 Generalization

Definition 4. As a representation language L_G for generalizations, we consider the language of confirmed statements L_H, restricted to universal clauses.

This last restriction could be easily given up but we take it because clausal theories are easy to understand. Moreover, it is helpful at the inference level. Excluding the equality symbol from the language of generalizations is necessary to avoid considering as a generalization the domain-closure axiom which is always confirmed since it is implicit in the logic.

Definition 5. Let $E \in L_E$ and $G \in L_G$. $E \approx\!\!\!| \ G$ if and only if

- $E \mathrel{|\!\sim} G$, and
- $E \not\models G$, and
- If G' is a clause such that $E \mathrel{|\!\sim} G'$, $E \not\models G'$ and $G' \models G$, then $G \models G'$.

The rationality postulates for confirmatory generalization given in Section 2 are satisfied by $\approx\!\!\!|$. Obviously, $\approx\!\!\!|$ satisfies the first three postulates (confirmatory foundation, ampliative reasoning and generality condition). Verification and falsification principles and cautious monotonicity also hold. The consistency condition is satisfied as well (the proof is similar to the one proposed by Hempel in [7]). Right equivalence is a consequence of properties of the development of a universal formula for a finite class of individual constants also proved by Hempel [7]. Finally, left equivalence holds provided that logical equivalence over the same Herbrand domain is considered.

Generalizations G are derived thanks to a generate-and-test search strategy. Especially, a candidate formula for generalization is first generated, then checked for generalization. Such a generate-and-test approach is also used in all existing techniques. So as to promote the production of most general clauses first, the language of generalizations is searched w.r.t. subsumption ordering. The search can be realised through iterative deepening or a variant of SE-tree search [18] for a first-order logic language without functional symbols. The search can also be constrained by focusing on clauses built up exclusively from a user-defined set of predicates, or by limiting the number of literals in generalizations.

Given the database
$\{bird(Tweety),\ cartoon(Tweety),\ flies(Superman), cartoon(Superman)\}$,
Claudien, the system described in [15], produces the set of generalizations:
$$\{\forall X, \neg bird(X) \lor \neg flies(X);\ \forall X, \neg bird(X) \lor cartoon(X);$$
$$\forall X, \neg flies(X) \lor cartoon(X);\ \forall X, \neg cartoon(X) \lor bird(X) \lor flies(X)\}.$$
Contrastingly, our model gives the set:$\{\forall X, cartoon(X); \forall X, bird(X) \lor flies(X)\}$.

Clearly enough, the clauses generated thanks to our model are more general ones; moreover, the unexpected generalization $\forall X, \neg bird(X) \vee \neg flies(X)$ is avoided in our approach.

References

1. Geneviève Bossu and Pierre Siegel. Saturation, nonmonotonic reasoning and the closed-world assumption. *Artificial Intelligence*, 25:13–63, 1985.
2. Keith L. Clark. Negation as failure. In Hervé Gallaire and Jack Minker, editors, *Proceedings of the Symposium on Logic and Databases*, pages 293–322, New York, 1978. Plenum Press.
3. Peter Flach. *Inductive Logic Programming*, chapter A framework for Inductive Logic Programming, pages 193–210. S. Muggleton, academic press edition, 1992.
4. Peter Flach. *Conjectures: an inquiry concerning the logic of induction*. PhD thesis, Tilburg University, 1995.
5. Peter Flach. Rationality postulates for induction. In *Proc. TARK'1996*, pages 267–281, De Zeeuwse Stromen, The Netherlands, 1996.
6. Nicolas Helft. Induction as nonmonotonic inference. In *Proc. KR'89*, pages 149–156, Toronto, Canada, 1989. Morgan Kaufmann.
7. C. G. Hempel. A purely syntactical definition of confirmation. *Journal of Symbolic Logic*, 8(4):122–143, 1943.
8. C. G. Hempel. Studies in the logic of confirmation. *Mind*, 54(213 & 214):1–26 & 97–121, 1945.
9. Nicolas Lachiche and Pierre Marquis. Abduction, induction and completion policies. In Peter Flach, editor, *ECAI'96 Workshop on Abductive and Inductive Reasoning*, pages 43–46, Budapest, Hungary, 1996.
10. Pierre Marquis. Building up inductive generalizations from facts. In *Proc. ECAI'92*, pages 446–450, Vienna, Austria, 1992. Wiley & Sons.
11. John McCarthy. Circumscription: a form of non-monotonic reasoning. *Artificial Intelligence*, 13:27–39, 1980.
12. John McCarthy. Applications of circumscription to formalizing common-sense knowledge. *Artificial Intelligence*, 28:89–116, 1986.
13. Jack Minker. On indefinite databases and the closed world assumption. In *Proc. CADE'82*, pages 292–308, Berlin, Germany, 1982. Lecture Notes in Computer Science 138, Springer-Verlag.
14. Stephen Muggleton and Luc De Raedt. Inductive logic programming: Theory and methods. *Journal of Logic Programming*, 19:629–679, 1994.
15. Luc De Raedt and Maurice Bruynooghe. A theory of clausal discovery. In *Proc. IJCAI'93*, pages 1058–1063, Chambéry, France, 1993.
16. Luc De Raedt and Saso Dzeroski. First-order jk-clausal theories are pac-learnable. *Artificial Intelligence*, 70:375–392, 1994.
17. Raymond Reiter. On closed-world data base. In Hervé Gallaire and Jack Minker, editors, *Proceedings of the symposium on logic and data bases*, pages 55–76, New York, 1978. Plenum Press.
18. Ron Rymon. Search through systematic set enumeration. In *Proc. KR'92*, pages 539–550, Cambridge, Massachusetts, USA, 1992. Morgan Kaufmann.
19. John C. Shepherdson. Negation in logic programming. In Jack Minker, editor, *Foundations of deductive databases and logic programming*, pages 19–89, 1988.

Learning Linear Constraints
in Inductive Logic Programming

Lionel Martin and Christel Vrain

LIFO - Université d'Orléans - BP 6759
45067 Orléans Cedex 2 - France
email: {martin,cv}@lifo.univ-orleans.fr

Abstract. In this paper, we present a system, called ICC, that learns constrained logic programs containing function symbols. The particularity of our approach is to consider, as in the field of Constraint Logic Programming, a specific computation domain and to handle terms by taking into account their values in this domain. Nevertheless, an earlier version of our system was only able to learn constraints $X_i = t$, where X_i is a variable and t is a term. We propose here a method for learning linear constraints. It has already been a lot studied in the field of Statistical Learning Theory and for learning Oblic Decision Trees. As far as we know, the originality of our approach is to rely on a Linear Programming solver. Moreover, integrating it in ICC enables to learn non linear constraints.

1 Introduction

This paper is mainly devoted to the problem of handling numeric data in Inductive Logic Programming. This involves several points: defining a formal framework for studying this problem, learning numeric relations, introducing functional terms. From the semantic point of view, a consensus has emerged about the semantics of definite logic programs in terms of Herbrand interpretations, whereas several semantics have been defined for normal logic programs that can be based either upon the classical two-valued logics or upon multi-valued logics. Nevertheless, pure logic programs do not enable to express numeric expressions. In Prolog, meta-predicates, as for instance the primitive *is a*, have been defined to deal with numeric values, but the semantics of such programs can no longer be studied in terms of Herbrand interpretations. To deal with this problem, a new field, called Constraint Logic Programming, has rapidly grown: it enables to express constraints that are interpreted in a specific domain of computation, as for instance, the set of integers, or the reals.

In this paper, we propose a new approach for learning logic programs containing function symbols. Instead of relying on the syntactic form of terms, we propose to consider a domain of computation and to build new terms based on their values in this domain and on the interest of these values for discriminating positive and negative examples. In an earlier version [6], the prototype, called ICC, that we have developed in the framework of Constraint Logic Programming, was limited to constraints $X_i = t$, where X_i is a variable and t is a term in which X_i does not occur. The main contribution of this paper is to propose a method, based on Linear Programming techniques, to learn relevant linear constraints and to integrate it in the system ICC, in order to learn non linear constraints.

This paper is organized as follows. Section 2 recalls basic definitions about Constraint Logic Programming. In Section 3, the system ICC is described. In Section 4, a method to learn linear inequalities is proposed as well as the way it is integrated in ICC.

2 Basic definitions

2.1 Syntax

We briefly recall some basic notions about constraint logic programming, that can be found in [5, 2]. We consider:

- an infinite set of variables $\mathcal{V}$,
- a set, denoted by Σ, of function symbols,
- a set, denoted by Π_C, of constraint predicate symbols, containing at least the predicate $=$,
- a set, denoted by Π_P, of predicate symbols definable by a program.

A *term* over $\mathcal{V}$ and Σ is inductively defined as follows: a variable v of $\mathcal{V}$ is a term and, if f is a function symbol of Σ, if n is the arity of f, $n \geq 0$ and if $t_1, \ldots, t_n$ are terms then $f(t_1, \ldots, t_n)$ is a term.

A *primitive constraint* has the form $p(t_1, \ldots, t_n)$, where p is a predicate symbol of Π_C and $t_1, \ldots, t_n$ are terms.

A *constraint* is a first-order formula built with primitive constraints. In the remaining of the paper, we consider only the class $\mathcal{L}_\Sigma$ of constraints defined as the smallest set of constraints that contains all primitive constraints and is closed under variable renaming, conjunction and existential quantification.

An *atom* has the form $p(t_1, \ldots, t_n)$, where p is a predicate symbol of Π_P and $t_1, \ldots, t_n$ are terms.

A *constrained atom* is a pair (c, p), where c is a constraint and p is an atom.

A *constrained clause* is an expression $a \leftarrow c \,\square\, b_1, \ldots, b_n$, where c is a constraint and $b_1, \ldots b_n$ are atoms.

A *CLP program*, also called a *constrained program*, is a collection of constrained clauses.

Example 1. The following CLP program:

$\quad facto(X, Y) \leftarrow X = 0, Y = s(0).$
$\quad facto(X, Y) \leftarrow X = s(Z), Y = T * X \,\square\, facto(Z, T).$

defines *factorial* ($\Sigma = \{0, s, *\}$, $\Pi_C = \{=\}$ and $\Pi_P = \{facto\}$).

The variable X is *linked* in the constrained clause $A_0 \leftarrow c_1, \ldots, c_m \,\square\, A_1, \ldots, A_n$, if X occurs in A_0 or, if there is a primitive constraint c_i or an atom A_j that contains the variables X and Y such that Y is linked in C. A constrained clause C is *linked* if all its variables are linked.

2.2 The constraint domain and its semantics

In the field of Constraint Logic Programming, we usually consider a specific constraint domain over which computation is performed. A (Σ, Π_C)-*structure* $\mathcal{D}$ is composed of a non-empty set D, an assignment of a function $f_D : D^n \to D$, for each $f \in \Sigma$, and an assignment of a function $p_D : D^n \to \{True, False\}$, for each $p \in \Pi_C$.

Example 2. In Example 1, a (Σ, Π_C)-structure can be defined on the domain D of positive integers. It interprets the function 0 by the positive integer 0, the function s as the usual function *successor* on the set of positive integers, the function $*$ as the usual multiplication on the set of positive integers.

If $\mathcal{D}$ is a (Σ, Π_C)-structure, a $\mathcal{D}$-*atom* has the form $p(d_1, \ldots, d_n)$, where $p \in \Pi_P$ and $d_i \in D$, $1 \leq 1 \leq n$. The set of all $\mathcal{D}$-atoms is called the $\mathcal{D}$-*base*.

Let $\mathcal{D}$ be a (Σ, Π_C)-structure and let t be a ground term. The interpretation of the ground term t, w.r.t. $\mathcal{D}$, denoted by $I_D(t)$, is defined as follows: if $f \in \Sigma$ and if $t_1, \ldots, t_n$ are terms, then $I_D(f(t_1, \ldots, t_n)) = f_D(I_D(t_1), \ldots, I_D(t_n))$,

In the following, $Const(F)$ denotes the set of constants of D appearing in the expression F and $Term_\Sigma(D')$ (where D' is a set of constants of D) denotes the set of terms built with constants of D' and function symbols of Σ.

If $\mathcal{D}$ is a (Σ, Π_C)-structure, a *valuation* v is a function: $V \to D$.
Let v be a valuation, $v = \{X_1/d_1, \ldots, X_n/d_n\}$ where $d_1, \ldots, d_n \in D$. The *set of inverse valuations* of v, denoted by $V^{-1}(v)$, is defined by: $v^{-1} \in V^{-1}(v)$ iff $v^{-1} = \{d_1/X_{i_1}, \ldots, d_n/X_{i_n}\}$ with $v(X_{i_j}) = d_j$.
Let $A = p(d_1, \ldots, d_n)$ be a $\mathcal{D}$-atom and let v be the valuation $\{X_1/d_1, \ldots, X_n/d_n\}$. If $v^{-1} \in V^{-1}(v)$, $v^{-1} = \{d_1/X_{i_1}, \ldots, d_n/X_{i_n}\}$, then $v^{-1}(A)$ denotes the atoms $p(X_{i_1}, \ldots, X_{i_n})$.
Let $\mathcal{D}$ be a (Σ, Π_C)-structure and let T be a set of terms. An *inverse interpretation* of a constant d w.r.t T is the subset of T composed of the terms t that satisfy $I_D(t) = d$. This set is denoted by $I_T^{-1}(d)$.

3 The system ICC

The learning task of ICC is specified by:

1. a set Σ of function symbols and a set Π_C of constraint predicates,
2. a (Σ, Π_C)-structure $\mathcal{D}$,
3. a set BASE of basic predicates defined by a set, denoted by BK$^+$, of $\mathcal{D}$-atoms,
4. a set TARG of target predicates, specified by two sets of $\mathcal{D}$-atoms: E$^+$ and E$^-$ with E$^+ \cap$ E$^- = \emptyset$. The set E $=$ E$^+ \cup \neg$E$^-$ represents the intended interpretation and in the following, Π_P denotes the set BASE $\cup$ TARG.

A $\mathcal{D}$-atom e is $\mathcal{D}$-covered with respect to $\mathrm{E}^+ \cup \mathrm{BK}^+$ by a constrained clause C $= A_0 \leftarrow c \,\square\, A_1, \ldots, A_n$ iff there exists a valuation v which satisfies c and such that $v(A_0) = e$ and $v(A_i) \in \mathrm{E}^+ \cup \mathrm{BK}^+$ for $i = 1 \ldots n$. Such a valuation is called a *covering valuation for* e.

The aim of ICC is to find a constrained program, built over Σ, Π_C, and Π_P which $\mathcal{D}$-covers the positive examples and which $\mathcal{D}$-covers no negative ones.

The method used to build linked constrained clauses is a classical one, that consists in iteratively adding to the body of the clause, either a constrained atom or a constraint until no negative example is $\mathcal{D}$-covered. We recall here the way relevant constraints are built. A similar method has been developed for building relevant constrained atoms. For more details, see [6].

Since a clause must $\mathcal{D}$-covers at least a $\mathcal{D}$-uncovered positive example, the first step of the algorithm is to choose (randomly) a $\mathcal{D}$-uncovered positive example $e \in \mathrm{E}^+$ and to build a clause which $\mathcal{D}$-covers e and as many $\mathcal{D}$-uncovered positive examples as possible. The positive example e enables us to build a set of relevant constraints and a set of relevant constrained atoms, and then a classical entropy measure [10] enables to choose the best constraint or the best constrained atoms. Therefore, let $e \in \mathrm{E}^+$ be a $\mathcal{D}$-uncovered positive example, let C be a clause that $\mathcal{D}$-covers e and some negative examples, and let v be a covering valuation for e. The set of primitive constraints, denoted by $Constr$, that can be added to C in order to refine it, is computed as follows:

Algorithm 1. Main Algorithm of ICC.

1- Compute the set $T = Term_\Sigma(Const(v))$.
2- Compute $D' = \{I_{\mathcal{D}}(t) \mid t \in T\}$.
3- Build $PC = \{p_i(d_{i_1}, \ldots, d_{i_n})\} \mid p_i \in \Pi_C, d_{i_j} \in D', p_i(d_{i_1}, \ldots, d_{i_n})$ true in $\mathcal{D}\}$.
4- Compute $I_T^{-1}(PC) = \{I_T^{-1}(cc) \mid cc \in PC\}$
5- Remove trivial constraints from $I_T^{-1}(PC)$
6- Compute $Constr = \bigcup_{v^{-1} \in V^{-1}(v)} v^{-1}(I_T^{-1}(PC))$

Example 3. Biases are introduced in ICC to reduce the set T, which have enabled ICC to learn the following constrained logic programs, respectively defining *factorial* and *member*.

Learned program	$\|\mathrm{E}^+\|$	$\|\mathrm{E}^-\|$
$facto(X, Y) \leftarrow X = 0, Y = succ(0)$.	7	6
$facto(X, Y) \leftarrow Z = pred(X), T = div(Y, X) \,\square\, facto(Z, T)$.		
$member(X, Y) \leftarrow X = head(Y)$.	12	6
$member(X, Y) \leftarrow Z = X, T = body(Y) \,\square\, member(Z, T)$.		

As has been mentioned in the introductory section, the constraints learned by ICC have been limited to expressions $X_i = t$, where X_i denotes a variable and t a term. In Section 4, we present a method for learning linear inequalities and in Section 5, we explain how it is integrated in ICC.

4 Learning linear constraints

Let us suppose that we have built the clause $b_0 \leftarrow c \,\square\, b_1, \ldots b_n$ and let us call $X_1, \ldots, X_n$ the numeric variables that have been introduced in this clause. Our goal is to find a linear constraint:
$$c' : a_0 + a_1 * X_1 + \ldots + a_n * X_n \leq 0$$
such that the clause $b_0 \leftarrow c, c' \,\square\, b_1, \ldots b_n$ $\mathcal{D}$-covers a maximum of positive examples and a minimum of negative examples. The problem $\mathcal{P}$ that must be solved can be, more generally, stated as follows:

Let $X_1, \ldots, X_n$ be n numeric variables. Let $[v_i, lab_i]_{1 \leq i \leq m}$ be m examples where v_i denotes a valuation: $\{X_1, \ldots, X_n\} \to D$ and $lab_i \in \{+, -\}$, depending whether v_i represents a positive example or a negative one.
Find $a_0, \ldots, a_n$ such that:

- the number of valuations v_i that satisfy $lab_i = +$ and $a_0 + a_1 * v_i(X_1) + \ldots + a_n * v_i(X_n) \leq 0$ is maximal, and
- the number of valuations v_i that satisfy $lab_i = -$ and $a_0 + a_1 * v_i(X_1) + \ldots + a_n * v_i(X_n) > 0$ is maximal.

In the following, $\mathcal{I}n_i^+$ denotes the inequality $a_0 + \Sigma_{j=1}^n a_j * v_i(X_j) \leq 0$, whereas $\mathcal{I}n_i^-$ denotes the inequality $a_0 + \Sigma_{j=1}^n a_j * v_i(X_j) > 0$. In these inequalities, $v_i(X_j)$ are numeric values whereas $a_0, \ldots, a_n$ become variables.

Example 4. Let us suppose that we have two variables: X_1 represents the radius of a circle and X_2 represents the length of a square. Let us consider the target concept, expressing the following relation between a circle and a square: *"the square can be drawn inside the circle"*. The set of examples is defined by:
$\{[1, 3, 3, +], [2, 3, 3, +], [3, 3, 3, +], [4, 3, 3, +], [5, 3, 3, +], [6, 3, 3, +],$
$[7, 3, 3, -], [8, 3, 3, -], [9, 3, 3, -], [10, 3, 3, -], [11, 3, 3, -], [12, 3, 3, -]\}$
where a tuple $[i, c_1, c_2, l]$ represents the i-th example (v_i, lab_i) with $v_i = \{X_1/c_1, X_2/c_2\}$ and $lab_i = l$.

In the best case, we would like to find a_0, a_1, a_2 such that for each $i = 1..6$, $\mathcal{I}n_i^+$ is satisfied (for example $\mathcal{I}n_1^+ = a_0 + a_1 * 3 + a_2 * 3 \leq 0$) and for each $j = 7..12$, $\mathcal{I}n_j^-$ is satisfied (for example $\mathcal{I}n_7^- = a_0 + a_1 * 5 + a_2 * 2 > 0$).

A solution to $\mathcal{I}n_i^+ \cup \mathcal{I}n_i^-$ would give the equation of an hyperplane that separates the positive examples from the negative ones. Nevertheless, in many cases, this set has no solutions and we only aim at maximizing the number of inequalities that are satisfied. We solve this problem by using linear programming techniques, that can be expressed as follows:

$$
\begin{cases}
LP_g : maximize \ \Sigma_{j=1}^n c_j x_j \\
\quad subject \ to \\
\quad\quad \Sigma_{j=1}^n a_{ij} x_j \leq b_i, \ for \ i = 1, 2, \ldots, m \\
\quad\quad l_j \leq x_j \leq u_j, \ for \ j = 1, \ldots, n \\
\quad where \ x_j \ is \ a \ real \ or \ an \ integer.
\end{cases}
$$

The problem $\mathcal{P}$ differs from the general LP_g problem for two reasons: first, our objective function is only to maximize the number of satisfied inequalities; secondly, strict inequalities appear in $\mathcal{I}n_j^-$.

Therefore, we replace the set $[\mathcal{I}n_i^+]_{\{i|lab_i=+\}}$ by the following set $[\mathcal{I}n_i''^+]_{\{i|lab_i=+\}}$:
$$\mathcal{I}n_i''^+: a_0 + \Sigma_{j=1}^n a_j * v_i(X_j) \leq \sigma_i * C,$$
where C denotes a fixed constant the value of which will be very high and where σ_i takes either the value 0 or 1. The underlying idea is that if the value of C is high enough, the inequality $a_0 + \Sigma_{j=1}^n a_j * v_i(X_j) \leq \sigma_i * C$ will be satisfied with $\sigma_i = 1$.

In the same way we built the set $[\mathcal{I}n_i'']_{\{i|lab_i=-\}}$ containing the following inequalities:
$$\mathcal{I}n_i''^-: a_0 + \Sigma_{j=1}^n a_j * v_i(X_j) \geq \epsilon - \sigma_i * C$$
where ϵ is a sufficiently low value which allows to remove the strict inequalities.

The set of inequalities $[\mathcal{I}n_i''^+]_{\{i|lab_i=+\}} \cup [\mathcal{I}n_i''^-]_{\{i|lab_i=-\}}$ contains $(n+1) + m$ variables, $a_0, \ldots, a_n, \sigma_1, \ldots, \sigma_m$. Let us recall that the number n is the number of numeric variables that have been introduced in the clause, whereas m is the number of positive and negative instances.

Minimizing $\Sigma_{i=1}^m \sigma_i$ enables to maximize the number of inequalities that are satisfied among $[\mathcal{I}n_i^+]_{\{i|lab_i=+\}} \cup [\mathcal{I}n_i'^-]_{\{i|lab_i=-\}}$.

The linear problem that is solved can thus be stated as follows:

$$
\left\{
\begin{array}{l}
minimize\ \Sigma_{i=1}^m \sigma_i \\
subject\ to \\
\quad a_0 + \Sigma_{j=1}^n a_j * v_i(X_j) \leq \sigma_i * C,\ i = 1, \ldots, m\ and\ lab_i = +, \\
\quad a_0 + \Sigma_{j=1}^n a_j * v_i(X_j) \geq \epsilon - \sigma_i * C,\ i = 1, \ldots, m\ and\ lab_i = - \\
\quad a_j \in D,\ for\ all\ j = 0, \ldots, n, \\
\quad \sigma_i \in \{0, 1\},\ for\ all\ i = 1, \ldots, m.
\end{array}
\right.
$$

5 Integration in ICC

As has already been mentioned, ICC is based on a top-down strategy: while negative examples are extensionally covered, the current clause is refined by adding a literal to its body. Let us suppose that the variables $X_1, \ldots, X_n$ have already been introduced in the clause. Each time a new numeric variable is introduced, the system ICC calls the system lp_solve, developed by M.R.C.M. Berkelaar[1]. When lp_solve succeeds in solving the associated linear problem, the values of σ_i enables to compute the number of positive instances and the number of negative instances that are $\mathcal{D}$-covered by the learned inequality which in turn, enable to compute the gain of this linear constraint. The literal that is introduced in the body of the clause is chosen, according to an entropy measure, among:

- the set of relevant constraints built by ICC,

---

[1] Eindhoven University of Technology, Eindhoven, The Netherlands

- the set of relevant constrained atoms built by ICC,
- if possible, the inequality $a_0 + a_1 * X_{j_1} + \ldots + a_p * X_{j_p} \leq 0$, which expresses a relation between the numeric variables $X_{j_1}, \ldots, X_{j_p}$ which have already been introduced in the clause.

In the system ICC, it is possible to introduce function symbols, as for instance the function $square : \mathbf{N} \rightarrow \mathbf{N}$. In this case, ICC searches for constraints c' : $a_0 + \Sigma_{i=1}^{m} a_i * X_i \leq 0$, where the variables X_i are either numeric variables which appear in the clause, or terms built with variables appearing in the clause.

Example 5. Let us consider, for instance, the concept $contains(O, R)$ meaning that *the object O can be drawn inside a circle of radius R* and let us consider the basic predicate $square(O, N)$ expressing that O is a square and that its length is N. If the function sqr (that computes the square of a number) is given, then ICC learns the following program:

$contains(a, b) \leftarrow square(a, b).$
$contains(a, b) \leftarrow square(a, d), 0.92.sqr(b) -0.40.sqr(d) -5b + 1.91.d +5.82 > 0.$

6 Conclusion

The system ICC is a system that builds, if possible, a constrained logic program, that $\mathcal{D}$-covers the positive examples and $\mathcal{D}$-covers no negative examples. It has been implemented in Sicstus Prolog on a Sun 4.

The experiments that we have made have already given positive results. Nevertheless, even if the system *lp_solve* that we use is efficient, so that searching for linear inequalities does not seem very expensive, the search space in ICC is, in general, very large due to the introduction of new terms. Biases have been introduced, as for instance the limitation of the depths of terms. Nevertheless, they are fixed before the learning process and we would like to study more dynamic biases linked to the learning problem and specifying terms or atoms that seem relevant.

Comparison with other works: Some systems already deal with the problem of learning constrained logic programs, as for instance, [11, 8]. In [11], the system combines a version space strategy with a divide-and-conquer strategy and the constraints that are learned mainly express bounds for variables. The strategy developed in [8] is an extension of Golem [7] to handle numeric constraints.

The problem of learning linear inequalities has already been a lot studied in the literature. It has been studied from a theoretical point of view, in [12]. There are two main differences with the Support Vector machines, defined in [12]: first, we intend to minimize the number of misclassified examples whereas their aim is to minimize the empirical risk; secondly, our method relies on Linear Programming techniques which is, as far as we know, original. This has also been studied in the field of learning decision trees, as for instance [1, 9]: generally, the underlying systems start from an initial inequation and perturb the coefficients until

169

the impurity measure reaches a local minimum; in OC1 [9], a non deterministic step enables to get out the local minimum.

Finally, the idea of changing the feature space in order to learn non linear constraints has already been introduced in [12] and in [4]. Nevertheless, in our framework the functions that can be introduced in the equations depends on the underlying Constraint Logic Programming language, whereas in [4], the set of functions is reduced to the product between variables and to the square of a variable.

References

1. Breiman, Friedman, Olshem, Stone, 1993. Classification of Regression Trees. Chapman & Hall.
2. Bergère M., Ferrand G., Le Berre F., Malfon B., Tessier A., 1995. La programmation logique avec contraintes revisitée en termes d'arbres de preuve et de squelettes. Rapport de recherche 95-06, LIFO, université d'Orléans.
3. Chvátal V., 1983. Linear Programming. Freeman.
4. Ittner A., Schlosser M., 1996. Non-Linear Decision Trees - NDT. Proceedings of the 13th International Conference on Machine Learning (ICML 96), L. Saitta (Ed.), Bari, Italy.
5. Jaffar J., Maher M.J., 1994. Constraint Logic Programming: A Survey. Jal of Logic Programming, vol. 19/20, may/july 1994, pp. 503-581, Elsevier Science Publishing.
6. Martin L., Vrain Ch., 1996. Induction of contraint logic programs. Proceedings of the Algorithmic Learning Theory workshop, ALT 96, Sidney, Australia.
7. Muggleton S., Feng C., 1992. Efficient Induction of Logic Programs. Inductive Logic programming. The A.P.I.C. Series N° 38, S. Muggleton (Ed.), Academic Press. pp. 281-298.
8. Mizoguchi F., Ohwada H., 1995. An Inductive Logic Programming Approach to Constraint Acquisition for Constraint-based Problem Solving. Proc. of the 5th Intl Workshop on Inductive Logic Programming, L. De Raedt (Ed.), pp. 297-323.
9. Murthy S., Kaisf S., Salzberg S., Beigel R., 1993. OC1: Randomized Induction of Oblique Decision Trees. Proceedings of the 11th National Conference on AI, AAAI-93, Cambridge, MIT Press, pp. 323-327
10. Quinlan J.R., 1990. Learning Logical Definitions from Relations. *Machine Learning Journal*, Vol. 5, Kluwer Academic Publishers, pp. 239-266.
11. Rouveirol C., Sebag M., 1995. Constraint Inductive Logic Programming. Proc. of the Fifth International Workshop on Inductive Logic Programming, L. De Raedt (Ed.), Leuven, September 1995, pp. 181-198.
12. Vapnik V.N., 1995. *The Nature of Statistical Learning Theory*. Springer.

Finite-Element Methods with Local Triangulation Refinement for Continuous Reinforcement Learning Problems

Rémi Munos

DASSAULT-AVIATION, DGT-DTN-EL-Et.Avances,
78 quai Marcel Dassault, 92214 Saint-Cloud, FRANCE
and
CEMAGREF, LISC, Parc de Tourvoie,
BP 121, 92185 Antony Cedex, FRANCE
Tel : (0)1 40 96 61 79. Fax : (0)1 40 96 60 80
E-mail: Remi.Munos@cemagref.fr

Abstract. This paper presents a reinforcement learning algorithm designed for solving optimal control problems for which the state space and the time are continuous variables. Like Dynamic Programming methods, reinforcement learning techniques generate an optimal feed-back policy by the mean of the value function which estimates the best expectation of cumulative reward as a function of initial state. The algorithm proposed here uses finite-elements methods for approximating this function. It is composed of two dynamics : the *learning dynamics*, called *Finite-Element Reinforcement Learning*, which estimates the values at the vertices of a triangulation defined upon the state space, and the *structural dynamics*, which refines the triangulation inside regions where the value function is irregular. This mesh refinement algorithm intends to solve the problem of the combinatorial explosion of the number of values to be estimated. A formalism for reinforcement learning in the continuous case is proposed, the Hamilton-Jacobi-Bellman equation is stated, then the algorithm is presented and applied to a simple two-dimensional target problem.

1 Introduction

In this paper, we are concerned with adaptive non-linear control problems, like target or obstacle problems, viability problems or optimization problems, for which the state space and the time are continuous variables. In order to define an optimal control, reinforcement learning (RL) builds the *value function* which estimates the best expectation of future reinforcement for all possible controls as a function of initial state.

In the continuous case, the value function has to be represented by a general approximation system using a finite set of parameters. Several techniques have been proposed, for example by using neural networks (see [Bar90], [Gul92], [Lin93] and many others), fuzzy controllers (see [Now95]) or other approximation systems (see the sparse-coarse-coded CMACs of [Sut96]). However, as it has been pointed out in [Bai95] and [BM95], in general, the combination of reinforcement learning algorithms with such function approximators does not converge. The *Residual-gradient advantage updating* proposed in [HBK96] is a convergent algorithm in the sense of the convergence of gradient descent methods. But the problem with these methods is how to find a suitable architecture for the network, i.e. which permits to approximate the value function. Besides, gradient descent methods only insure local optimum.

Here, we present a direct reinforcement learning algorithm that uses finite-element methods with a local mesh refinement process for approximating the value function. The algorithm consists of the combination of these two dynamics:

- **The learning dynamics**: for a given triangulation of the state space, the *Finite-Element Reinforcement Learning* (FERL) modifies the values of the vertices according to the reinforcement obtained during the running of trajectories, so the value function is approximated with a piecewise linear function. The FERL algorithm used here is a convergent RL algorithm (see [Mun96]).
- **The structural dynamics** that locally refines the mesh of the triangulation in order to build an relevant triangulation whose precision depends on the regularities of the value function. Its starts with a rough triangulation composed of a small number of large simplexes (knowledge of a novice) and builds an accurate triangulation (knowledge of an expert) according to the learning dynamics. This structural dynamics can be seen as a categorization process via reinforcement from the environment.

Section 2 introduces a formalism for the study of reinforcement learning in the continuous case. *Section 3* describes the FERL algorithm for a given triangulation of the state space (i.e. the learning dynamics). *Section 4* presents the structural dynamics. *Section 5* illustrates this algorithm with an example of target problem in a two dimensional space.

2 Reinforcement Learning, the Continuous Case

In order to estimate the performances of a reinforcement learning algorithm, we need to compare the function computed by the algorithm to the value function of the continuous process.

In the following, we consider *deterministic systems* with *infinite time horizon* and *discounted reinforcement*. Let $x(t) \in \bar{O}$ be the state of the system with the state space O bounded, open subset of $\mathbb{R}^d$. The evolution of the system depends on the current state $x(t)$ and control $u(t)$; it is defined by a differential equation :

$$\frac{d}{dt}x(t) = f(x(t), u(t))$$

where the control $u(t)$ is a bounded, Lebesgue measurable function with values in a compact U. From any initial state x, the choice of the control $u(t)$ leads to a unique trajectory $x(t)$. Let τ be the exit time of $x(t)$ from $\bar{O}$ (with the convention that if $x(t)$ always stays in $\bar{O}$, then $\tau = \infty$). Then, we define the discounted reinforcement functional of state x, control $u(.)$:

$$J(x; u(.)) = \int_0^\tau \gamma^t r(x(t), u(t))dt + \gamma^\tau R(x(\tau))$$

where $r(x, u)$ is the *running reinforcement* and $R(x)$ the *terminal reinforcement*. γ is the *discount factor* $(0 \leq \gamma < 1)$.

The **objective of the control problem** is to find the optimal feed-back control $u^*(x)$ that optimizes the reinforcement functional for initial state x.

RL techniques belongs to the class of DP methods which compute the optimal control by the means of the **value function**:

$$V(x) = \sup_{u(.)} J(x; u(.)) \tag{1}$$

which is the maximum value of the functional as a function of initial state x.

In the RL approach, the system tries to approximate this function without knowing the state dynamics f nor the reinforcement functions r, R. Thus, RL appears as a constructive and iterative process, based on experience, that estimates the value function by successive approximations.

Following the dynamic programming principle, the value function satisfies a first-order nonlinear partial differential equation called the *Hamilton-Jacobi-Bellman* equation (see [FS93] for a survey).

Theorem 1 (Hamilton-Jacobi-Bellman). *If V is differentiable at $x \in O$, let $DV(x)$ be the gradient of V at x, then the following HJB equation holds at x.*

$$V(x) \ln \gamma + \sup_{u \in U}[DV(x).f(x, u) + r(x, u)] = 0$$

Besides, V satisfies the following boundary condition:

$$V(x) \geq R(x) \text{ for } x \in \partial O$$

The challenge of learning the value function is motivated by the fact that from V, we can deduce the following optimal feed-back control policy:

$$u^*(x) = \arg \sup_{u \in U}[DV(x).f(x, u) + r(x, u)]$$

In the following, we intend to approximate the value function with piecewise linear functions defined by their values at the vertices of a triangulation of the state space.

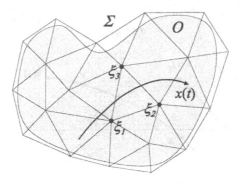

Fig. 1. Triangulation Σ of the state space O. A trajectory $x(t)$ crosses the simplex (ξ_1, ξ_2, ξ_3).

3 The Learning Dynamics

Let us consider a triangulation Σ such that the set of simplexes covers O (see figure 1). By using a finite-element convergent approximation scheme (derived from [Kus90]), the continuous control problem may be approximated by a Markovian Decision Process whose state space is the set of vertices $\{\xi\}$.

The value function V is approximated by a piecewise linear function V^Σ defined by its values at the vertices $\{\xi\}$. The value of V^Σ at any point x inside some simplex $(\xi_0, ..., \xi_d)$ is a linear combination of V^Σ at the vertices $\xi_0, ..., \xi_d$:

$$V^\Sigma(x) = \sum_{i=0}^{d} \lambda_{\xi_i}(x) V^\Sigma(\xi_i) \text{ for all } x \in \text{simplex } (\xi_0, ..., \xi_d)$$

with $\lambda_{\xi_i}(x)$ the *barycentric coordinates* of x inside the simplex $(\xi_0, ..., \xi_d) \ni x$. (We recall that the definition of the barycentric coordinates $\lambda_{\xi_i}(x)$ is such that: $\sum_{i=0}^{d} \lambda_{\xi_i}(x).(\xi_i - x) = 0$ and: $\sum_{i=0}^{d} \lambda_{\xi_i}(x) = 1$).

We approximate the Hamilton-Jacobi-Bellman equation with the Finite-Element scheme:

$$V^\Sigma(\xi) = \sup_{u \in U} \left[\gamma^{\tau(\xi,u)}.V^\Sigma(\eta(\xi,u)) + \tau(\xi,u)r(\xi,u) \right] \qquad (2)$$

where $\eta(\xi, u)$ is the projection of ξ in a direction parallel to $f(\xi, u)$ onto the opposite side of the simplex (see figure 2) and $\tau(\xi, u)$ is such that :

$$\eta(\xi, u) = \xi + \tau(\xi, u)f(\xi, u)$$

From the linearity of V^Σ upon the simplexes, (2) is equivalent to :

$$V^\Sigma(\xi) = \sup_{u \in U} \left[\gamma^{\tau(\xi,u)}.\sum_{j=1}^{d} \lambda_{\xi_j}(\eta(\xi,u)).V^\Sigma(\xi_j) + \tau(\xi,u)r(\xi,u) \right]$$

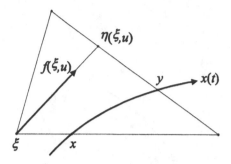

Fig. 2. A trajectory going through a simplex. $\eta(\xi, u)$ is the projection of ξ in a direction parallel to $f(\xi, u)$ onto the opposite side of the simplex. $\frac{y-x}{\lambda_\xi(x)}$ is a good approximation of $\eta(\xi, u) - \xi$.

which is a Dynamic Pogramming equation for a finite Markov Decision Process whose state space is the set of vertices $\{\xi\}$, and the probabilities of transition from state ξ to the adjacent states $\{\xi_j\}_{j=1..d}$ with control u are the barycentric coordinates $\lambda_{\xi_j}(\eta(\xi, u))$.

By introducing the Q-values $Q^\Sigma(\xi, u)$ such that $V^\Sigma(\xi) = \sup_{u \in U} Q^\Sigma(\xi, u)$ and thanks to a contraction property due to the discount factor γ, Dynamic Programming theory (see [Ber87]) insures that there is a unique solution, called V^Σ, that satisfies equations:

$$Q^\Sigma(\xi, u) = \gamma^{\tau(\xi, u)} . V^\Sigma(\eta(\xi, u)) + \tau(\xi, u) r(\xi, u) \text{ for } \xi \in O \qquad (3)$$
$$Q^\Sigma(\xi, u) = R(\xi) \text{ for } \xi \notin O$$

Here, it is not possible to use directly a Real Time Dynamic Programming algorithm (see [BBS91]) for solving iteratively equation (3) because the dynamics f (thus $\eta(\xi, u)$ and $\tau(\xi, u)$) is unknown. The model-based approach should be to build in a first time a model of the dynamics f and then to use DP methods with this model. In this paper, we are interested in the model-free approach which consists in an on-line and direct learning, that is which does not build any model of the dynamics. The Finite-Element Reinforcement Learning (introduced in [Mun96]) is a model-free RL algorithm that uses approximation of $\eta(\xi, u)$ and $\tau(\xi, u)$ thanks to the available on-line knowledge.

3.1 Presentation

Suppose that a trajectory $x(t)$ enters inside simplex T at point $x = x(t_1)$. At time t_1 suppose that a control u is chosen and kept until the trajectory leaves T at $y = x(t_2)$ (see figure 2). Let $\tau_x = t_2 - t_1$. Let $T_{in} \ni x$ be the $(d-1)$-input-simplex and $T_{out} \ni y$ the $(d-1)$-output-simplex.

The algorithm presented in the next section is the iterated version of equation (3) which uses:

$$\frac{V^{\Sigma}(y) - V^{\Sigma}(x)}{\lambda_{\xi}(x)} + V^{\Sigma}(\xi) \text{ as an approximation of } V^{\Sigma}(\eta(\xi, u))$$

$$\frac{\tau_x}{\lambda_{\xi}(x)} \text{ as an approximation of } \tau(\xi, u).$$

These approximations come from the linearity of V^{Σ} inside T and that from Thales' theorem, $\frac{y-x}{\lambda_{\xi}(x)}$ is an approximation of $\eta(\xi, u) - \xi$.

3.2 The Finite-Element Reinforcement Learning

In the following, we assume that the action space U is finite. Let $Q_n^{\Sigma}(\xi, u)$ and $V_n^{\Sigma}(\xi)$ be the iterated values of $Q^{\Sigma}(\xi, u)$ and $V^{\Sigma}(\xi)$. Let us choose a constant $\lambda \in (0, 1]$ close to zero. Initial values $Q_0^{\Sigma}(\xi, u)$ are initialized to any value.

Consider a trajectory $x(.)$ going through a simplex T with a control u. When the trajectory leaves T at y, if the following conditions:

* $\lambda_{\xi}(x) \geq \lambda$ (this relation eliminates cases for which $\lambda_{\xi}(x)$ is too small)
* $\forall \xi_i \in T_{in} \cap T_{out}, \lambda_{\xi_i}(y) \geq \lambda_{\xi_i}(x) + \lambda$ (these relations imply that $y - x$ strictly belongs to the cone of vertex ξ and base T_{out} and insure that for small simplexes, $\eta(\xi, u) \in T_{out}$).

are satisfied, then update the Q-value of vertex ξ opposite to the exit side T_{out} for control u with:

$$Q_{n+1}^{\Sigma}(\xi, u) = \gamma^{\frac{\tau_x}{\lambda_{\xi}(x)}} \left(\frac{V_n^{\Sigma}(y) - V_n^{\Sigma}(x)}{\lambda_{\xi}(x)} + V_n^{\Sigma}(\xi) \right) + \frac{\tau_x}{\lambda_{\xi}(x)} r(x, u) \qquad (4)$$

When the trajectory reaches the border of the state space, at time τ, the closest vertex $\xi_j \notin O$ from the exit point $x(\tau)$ is updated with:

$$V_{n+1}^{\Sigma}(\xi_j) = R(x(\tau))$$

Remark. With some additional hypotheses on the dynamics f and the regularities of r, R and ∂O, this algorithm converges to the value function of the continuous problem as n tends to infinity and the size of the simplexes tends to zero (see [Mun96]).

Meanwhile, for a given triangulation, the V_n^{Σ}-values do not converge as n tends to infinity. In order to insure the convergence, we need to combine the learning dynamics with a triangulation refinement process, called structural dynamics.

4　The Structural Dynamics

The structural dynamics intends to build a triangulation such that the simplexes enclose states whose value function is almost linear. Here, we choose the "general towards specialized" approach : the initial triangulation is composed of a small number of large simplexes ; then the structural dynamics refines the triangulation at places where the value function is irregular (the simplexes of low reinforcement discriminant skill).

4.1　The Delaunay Triangulation

In this paper, we chose the Delaunay triangulation, which is a very used triangulation technique for finite-elements methods when the state space is of low dimensionality. Delaunay triangulation is built from the basis of a set of vertices and is close related to the Voronoi diagram (there is a dual relationship). The study of Delaunay triangulations and their properties are beyond the scope of this paper (see for example some recent work : [Mid93], [Rup94]). We will only give a definition in the 2-dimensional case :

Given a finite set of points, 3 points contribute a triangle to the Delaunay triangulation if the circumscribing circle through those points contains no other points in its interior.

4.2　The Delaunay Refinement Process

The refinement process consist of adding new vertices and compute the Delaunay triangulation associated to the new set of vertices (we use the incremental Watson' algorithm [Wat81], see figure 3).

The choice of adding a new vertex inside a given simplex depends on a criterion based on the expected reinforcement average variation : the *Q-deviation*. For each vertex ξ and control u, the Q-deviation $E_n^\Sigma(\xi, u)$ is incrementally updated at the same time as the Q-value is by :

$$E_{n+1}^\Sigma(\xi, u) = \frac{1}{n+1} \left(n.E_n^\Sigma(\xi, u) + \left[Q_{n+1}^\Sigma(\xi, u) - Q_n^\Sigma(\xi, u) \right]^2 \right)$$

and the Q-deviation $E_n^\Sigma(T)$ of a simplex T is the sum of the Q-deviations of its vertices ξ for controls u such that the dynamics $f(\xi, u)$ "goes inside" T.

The refinement rule is the following :

If the Q-deviation of a simplex T is superior to some value, add to the set of vertices the barycenter of T (for example, in figure 3, the barycenter of the gray simplex is added to the list of vertices).

Remark. The refinement of boundary simplexes (those whose all vertices except one are outside O) consists in adding the barycenter of the vertices that are outside O (see an illustration in section 5).

Remark. During the triangulation refinement process, some initial averaged Q-values (for the next learning dynamics) are attributed to the points added to the list of vertices. This insures a continuous learning through successive structural dynamics processes.

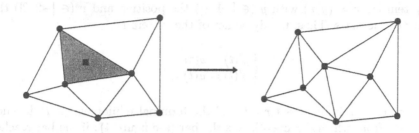

Fig. 3. Addition of a new point (the square dot) to the set of vertices and the resulting Delaunay triangulation

For a given triangulation, we have to distinguish two phases during the learning dynamics :

- The *transitional phase* during which reinforcements are propagated upon the whole state space according to the dynamics.
- The *almost stationary phase* during which the Q-values oscillate around an average value.

Either a Q-value converges, so its Q-deviation tends to 0, or it does not and the Q-deviation does not tend to 0. So the Q-deviations are a measure of the irregularity of the expected reinforcement (thus indirectly of the value function).

The structural dynamics consists in refining the triangulation at places where the Q-deviation of the simplexes are high. Then the new triangulation becomes more precise at the irregularities of the value function.

A succession of learning and structural dynamics is executed until the Q-deviations of all simplexes are small enough.

Remark. The refinement criterion used here, based on the Q-deviations, is very simple and may be improved by taking into account other factors like the existence of a change in the optimal control inside a simplex, or the coherence of the values at the vertices of a simplex depending on the local optimal control. The Q-deviation criterion is only an illustration of a possible local measure for triangulation refinement process, and it is used in the following simulation.

5 Illustration with a Simple Target Problem

5.1 Description

Let us consider a mass moving on a bar (segment $[-1, 1]$) which has to stop at one of its extremities. The control consists in pushing the mass with a constant strength either on the left or on the right (the control is $u = \pm 1$). The state of the system is: $x = (y, v)$ with y ($\in [-1, 1]$) the position and v ($\in [-2, 2]$) the velocity of the mass. Thus, the dynamics of the system is :

$$\begin{cases} y'(t) = v(t) \\ v'(t) = u(t) \end{cases}$$

Let the running reinforcement $r = 0$ and the terminal reinforcement R depends on the side from which the mass leaves the bar (see figure 4) : if the bar reaches the left extremity with a null velocity (left target) then it receives $R = +1$, if it reaches the right extremity with a null velocity (right target), it receives $R = +2$. If it reaches an extremity with a positive velocity, the terminal reinforcement will decrease with the velocity (until $R = -1$ for the maximal velocity).

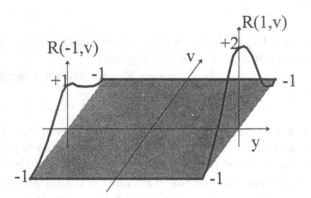

Fig. 4. The terminal reinforcement $R(y, v)$. $R = +1$ (resp. $R = +2$) at the left (resp. right) extremity of the bar for a null velocity. R decreases until -1 for the maximal velocity.

Thus, the objective of the learning is twice: first, the system has to learn to reach, as fast as possible, each extremity of the bar with a low velocity, as much as possible. Then, it has to learn to choose which extremity (the right one with a possible reinforcement of $+2$ or the left one with $+1$) is the best depending on its position and velocity (thus on the time required for reaching the target).

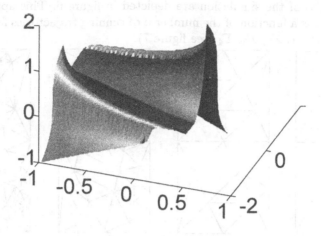

Fig. 5. The (exact) value function $V(x)$.

5.2 The Optimal Solution

In this example, it is easy to compute exactly the value function (see figure 5) and the optimal control. Thus we can estimate the difference between the computed V_n-values and the optimal value function. A measure of this approximation error is the error sup:

$$\text{Error sup} = \sup_{x \in O} \left| V_n^\Sigma(x) - V(x) \right|$$

5.3 Numerical Results

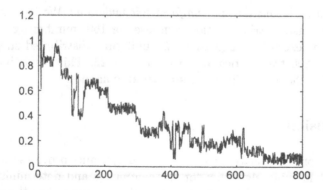

Fig. 6. The error sup as a function of the number of running trajectories.

The results of the simulation are depicted in figure 6. This approximation error is given as a function of the number n of running trajectories for successive triangulations Σ_1, Σ_2, Σ_3, Σ_4 (see figure 7).

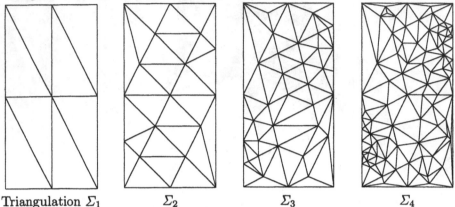

Triangulation Σ_1 Σ_2 Σ_3 Σ_4

Figure 7: Successive triangulations during the simulation.

Initial triangulation (Σ_1) corresponds to $1 \le n \le 100$. For $n = 100$, the simplexes whose Q-deviation is higher than 0.001 are refined, which leads to triangulation Σ_2. In a same way, triangulation Σ_3 occurs at $n = 200$, and triangulation Σ_4 occurs at $n = 400$ and is kept until the end of the simulation.

5.4   Analyze of the Results

Globally, the error sup tends to 0 as successive learning and structural dynamics are executed. At the end of the simulation, the error sup is lower than 0.1 and continues to oscillate around 0.05.

By comparison to the (exact) value function of figure 5, we observe that the refinement process occurs at places where V is the most irregular.

Comparison with a constant and uniform triangulation: We have run a simulation with a constant triangulation composed of 160 (number lightly superior to the 153 simplexes of triangulation Σ_4) uniformly distributed simplexes and obtained with 800 trajectories an error sup of 0.22. This result indicates the benefit of using the local refinement structural dynamics.

6   Conclusion

The combination of the learning and structural dynamics provides an interesting reinforcement learning algorithm for the continuous and deterministic case. A first improvement should be to study the stochastic case (when the evolution of the system is governed by a stochastic differential equation) for which we could use the Q-learning (see [Wat89]) version of FERL rule:

$$\Delta Q_n^\Sigma(\xi, u) = \alpha_n \left[\gamma^{\frac{\tau_x}{\lambda_\xi(x)}} \left(\frac{V_n^\Sigma(y) - V_n^\Sigma(x)}{\lambda_\xi(x)} + V_n^\Sigma(\xi) \right) - Q_n^\Sigma(\xi, u) + \frac{\tau_x}{\lambda_\xi(x)} r(x, u) \right]$$

with some decreasing learning rate α.

The local refinement criterion based on the Q-deviations generates a triangulation that adapts to the regularities of the value function. Meanwhile, the refinement process used here is very simple and sometimes generates more simplexes than necessary. A possible improvement should be to consider a structural dynamics including both "bottom-up" and "top-down" processes, for example by suppressing some points at places where locally, the computed Q-values are regular, or by moving some vertices according to the dynamics f. Another approach should consist on a triangulation initialized around terminal reinforcements and progressively increasing inside the state space during the running of trajectories.

References

[Bai95] Leemon Baird. Residual algorithms : Reinforcement learning with function approximation. *Machine Learning : proceedings of the Twelfth International Conference*, 1995.

[Bar90] Andrew G. Barto. *Neural networks for control.* W.T. Miller, R.S.Sutton, P.J. Werbos editors. MIT press, Cambridge, Massachussetts, 1990.

[BBS91] Andrew G. Barto, Steven J. Bradtke, and Satinder P. Singh. Real-time learning and control using asynchronous dynamic programming. Technical Report 91-57, Computer Science Department, University of Massachusetts, 1991.

[Ber87] Dimitri P. Bertsekas. *Dynamic Programming : Deterministic and Stochastic Models.* Prentice Hall, 1987.

[BM95] J.A. Boyan and A.W. Moore. Generalization in reinforcement learning : Safely approximating the value function. *Advances in Neural Information Processing Systems*, 7, 1995.

[FS93] Wendell H. Fleming and H. Mete Soner. *Controlled Markov Processes and Viscosity Solutions.* Applications of Mathematics. Springer-Verlag, 1993.

[Gul92] Vijay Gullapalli. *Reinforcement Learning and its application to control.* PhD thesis, University of Massachussetts, Amherst., 1992.

[HBK96] Mance E. Harmon, Leemon C. Baird, and A. Harry Klopf. Reinforcement learning applied to a differential game. *Adaptive Behavior*, 4:3–28, 1996.

[Kus90] Harold J. Kushner. Numerical methods for stochastic control problems in continuous time. *SIAM J. Control and Optimization*, 28:999–1048, 1990.

[Lin93] Long-Ji Lin. *Reinforcement Learning for Robots using Neural Networks.* PhD thesis, Carnegie Mellon University, Pittsburg, Pennsylvania, 1993.

[Mid93] Terje Midtbo. *Spatial Modelling by Delaunay Networks of Two and Three Dimensions.* PhD thesis, Norwegian Institute of Technology, 1993.

[Mun96] R. Munos. A convergent reinforcement learning algorithm in the continuous case : the finite-element reinforcement learning. *International Conference on Machine Learning*, 1996.

[Now95] Ann Now. Fuzzy reinforcement learning. an overview. *Advances in Fuzzy Theory and Technology*, 1995.

[Rup94] Jim Ruppert. A delaunay refinement algorithm for quality 2-dimensional mesh generation. *Journal of Algorithms*, 1994.

[Sut96] Richard S. Sutton. Generalization in reinforcement learning : Successful examples using sparse coarse coding. *Advances in Neural Information Processing Systems*, 8, 1996.

[Wat81] D.F. Watson. Computing the n-dimensional delaunay tessellation with application to voronoi polytopes. *The Computer Journal*, 24:167–172, 1981.

[Wat89] Christopher J.C.H. Watkins. *Learning from delayed reward*. PhD thesis, Cambridge University, 1989.

Inductive Genetic Programming
with Decision Trees

Nikolay I. Nikolaev[1]and Vanio Slavov[2]

[1] Department of Computer Science, American University in Bulgaria,
Blagoevgrad 2700, Bulgaria, e-mail: nikolaev@nws.aubg.bg

[2] Information Technologies Lab, New Bulgarian University,
Sofia 1113, Bulgaria, e-mail: vslavov@inf.nbu.acad.bg

Abstract. This paper proposes an empirical study of inductive Genetic Programming with Decision Trees. An approach to development of fitness functions for efficient navigation of the search process is presented. It relies on analysis of the fitness landscape structure and suggests measuring its characteristics with statistical correlations. We demonstrate that this approach increases the global landscape correlation, and thus leads to mitigation of the search difficulties. Another claim is that the elaborated fitness functions help to produce decision trees with low syntactic complexity and high predictive accuracy.

1 Introduction

Inductive concept learning is considered search for concept descriptions that model accurately given data. The inductive learning has to construct concept descriptions which: first, cover most of the data; second, feature by high extrapolation power; and, third, have reasonable length. Nowadays, stochastic complexity (minimum description length) measures [6],[7],[8] are used for achieving these qualities. The stochastic complexity measures keep a balance between the syntactic complexity and predictive accuracy of the inferred descriptions.

Evolutionary algorithms [1],[5] are random search methodology that could be employed for inductive learning. They build concept descriptions with reproduction, recombination and mutation operators. The evolutionary search could be viewed as navigation by the genetic operators on their landscapes determined by a fitness function. The fitness landscape structure is the only information for search navigation. The evolutionary algorithms perform well on fitness landscapes that contain relevant information about the search goal [4]. On such landscapes they can find global, or nearly-global solutions, reliably and quickly.

This research was motivated by the fact that the navigation difficulties are influenced by the fitness function, as they obviously depend on how the landscape has been created. An approach to developing fitness functions for efficient search upon a global fitness landscape analysis is presented. The approach helps to make fitness functions that provide enough information for locating the global optima on the landscape. The fitness distance correlation [4] measure is used for estimating the correspondence between the fitness of a point and its distance to a global optimum in the search space of the task.

The approach is illustrated with elaboration of a fitness function for efficient concept learning by inductive Genetic Programming with Decision Trees (GPDT) [9]. The claim is that a careful design of a stochastic complexity fitness function helps to achieve: first, mitigating the navigation difficulties by increasing the global landscape correlatation, and, second, keeping a balance between the parsimony and accuracy of the decision trees. The experiments show that the inductive GPDT is really useful when it continuously promotes genotypes with low syntactic complexity and high predictive accuracy.

This paper presents GPDT in section two. It includes the genetic decision tree-like programs, the reproduction, recombination and mutation operators, and the fitness function. The study of GPDT with a special statistical measure is given in section three. Finally, conclusions are derived.

2   Genetic Programming with Decision Trees

2.1   Genetic Decision Tree-like Programs

The Genetic Programming (GP) paradigm can be used for solving inductive concept learning tasks [3],[5] by manipulating a population of decision trees [7]. The search could be organized by modifying the size and shape of decision trees with recombination and mutation operators. The GP is appropriate for inductive learning as it allows the size of the trees to be discovered automatically.

The presented GPDT evolves genetic programs in the form of decision trees [7]. In context of the learning task and in terms of the chosen description language, the nodes of the decision tree are attributes of the concept features, and the leaves denote the class of the concept. Since a decision tree can be viewed as a representation of a composition of functions, it is easy to determine how the tree components serve as genetic material: the concept attributes could naturally be functional nodes, and the concept classes could be terminal leaves.

2.2   Reproduction, Recombination and Mutation Operators

GPDT breeds a population of decision trees with three genetic operators: reproduction, recombination and mutation. Currently, steady state reproduction is employed with fitness proportionate selection [1].

The recombination operator for GPDT performs crossover [5] by cutting and splicing two parent trees in randomly chosen nodes. The crossover operator maintains the closure property [5] and derives only syntactically correct decision trees. That is why the cross points in the parent trees are selected so that only offsprings having nonrepeating attributes on each branch can result.

An uniform replacement mutation operator has been developed especially for GPDT. The operator traverses a decision tree in depth-first manner and changes each visited node or leaf with a probability $Pm = x/length(DT)$, where: x is a parameter. When a functional node is encountered, it is replaced with equal probability by another randomly chosen functional or terminal node. A terminal is replaced again with equal probability by a randomly chosen functional or terminal. This uniform mutation also preserves the closure property [6]. When a functional node is to be replaced with a functional node, the new one is chosen so that it does not appear in the above and below contexts.

2.3 The Stochastic Complexity Fitness Function

The purpose of inductive learners is to identify concepts that best model given examples. The stochastic complexity measures [6],[7],[8] provide sound criteria for data modeling. In terms of decision trees, these are criteria for isolation of parsimonious trees, with minimal syntactic complexity, and accurate trees, which model well the examples. A balance between accuracy and parsimony is very important for efficient evolutionary search [3]. We clarify this revelation is sense that the use of ready formulae does not necessarily lead to better results.

Experiments into inductive GPDT were carried out with the recent measure of Quinlan [8]. This measure [8] was originally prepared for pruning decision trees, but it is reasonable to employ it for growing decision trees also:

$$F(DT) = min\{I(DT) + I(e|DT)\}$$

$$I(DT) = n_f + n_l + n_f \times log_2(f) + n_l \times log_2(l)$$
$$I(e|DT) = tp \times (-log_2(P(e|tp))) + fp \times (-log_2(1 - P(e|tp))) +$$
$$tn \times (-log_2(P(e|tn))) + fn \times (-log_2(1 - P(e|tn)))$$

It has been found, however, that during evolutionary learning distinct decision trees have been assigned equal stochastic complexity values. That is why, we modify the measure so that the relative frequencies of the examples are computed with the following conditional probabilities [9]:

$$P(e|tp) = P(e|tp_1 + tp_2 + ... + tp_{N_p}) = \sum_{i=1}^{N_p} P(tp_i) \times P(e|tp_i)$$
$$P(e|tn) = P(e|tn_1 + tn_2 + ... + tn_{N_n}) = \sum_{i=1}^{N_n} P(tn_i) \times P(e|tn_i)$$

where: n_f-functional nodes in DT; n_l-leaves in DT; f-possible functions; l- leaf classes; N_p- positive leaves; N_n- negative leaves; tp-true positive examples; fp-false positive examples; tn-true negative examples; fn-false negative examples.

This calculation of the relative frequencies of the examples with conditional probabilities has the advantage that it accurately evaluates a decision tree as a disjoint combination of conjunctive components formed along the branches.

3 Studies of Inductive GPDT

This research investigates the different fitness landscape structures that arise from different fitness functions employed in inductive GPDT. Such analysis is valuable as the navigation difficulties are monitored by the global structure of the fitness landscape, which is a global search characteristics of the task.

3.1 Fitness Distance Correlation

The fitness distance correlation (FDC) measure [5] provides evidences for the global correlation character of the fitness landscape:

$$FDC(F,D) = \frac{\sum_{i=0}^{M}(F_i - \bar{F}) \times (D_i - \bar{D})}{\sqrt{\sum_{i=0}^{M}(F_i - \bar{F})^2} \times \sqrt{\sum_{i=0}^{M}(D_i - \bar{D})^2}}$$

where: M - is the number of the steps considered, and $M > 0$; F_i- is the fitness at step i ; D_i - is the distance at step i ; $\bar{F} = (1/(M+1)) \times \sum_{0}^{M} F_i$, and $\bar{D} = (1/(M+1)) \times \sum_{0}^{M} D_i$ are weighted means.

The FDC is calculated with pairs (F, D) recorded during random walks on the landscape. The distance $D = Dist(DT, O)$ is defined as the number of one-point mutations needed to produce the optimal decision tree O from a particular decision tree DT. Since the stochastic complexity fitness function has a minimizing effect, FDC is 1 when the correlation is maximal.

3.2 The Fitness Landscape

The fitness landscape here is a methaphore that relates decision tree-like genotypes with their fitnesses, calculated with the stochastic complexity function. Such a view has the advantage that the fitness landscape could be reliably examined as special statistical measures for estimation of its characteristics exist. The landscape consists of points with fitnesses. The differences between the fitnesses of these points form the correlation structure of the landscape. The differences between the decision trees could be precisely identified as their fitnesses are points on different hills, valleys, and slopes of the correlation structure.

The FDC measure summarizes whether the global optima is accessible from a given point on the landscape. The distance to the global optimum should decrease with improving the fitness. Abstractly, this means that the global optima is visible and therefore the landscape is mountable.

3.3 Experimental Results

The elaborated stochastic complexity formula was built in GPDT as a fitness function. Two kinds of experiments were conducted: first, with groups of uniformly generated examples, and, second, with benchmark datasets.

The landscape analysis with FDC started with the measure of Quinlan [8]. Two groups each of 5 sets of examples for different decision trees with up to 6 attributes have been generated. The domains for the attributes consisted of 2 to 4 discrete values. The sampling decision trees were symmetric and anisymmetric. The first group included 5 symmetric trees, which left subtree mirrors the right subtree. The second group included 5 anti-symmetric trees with different depths: shallow, medium, and deep. The parameter x of the probability Pm was: $x = 0.05$. Walks on 1500 landscape points have been carried out.

Symmetric Decision Trees The results from the tests on each of the 5 sets are visualized by scatter plots and abbreviated *FDC* summaries. Figure 1 presents the scatter plot for the fitness/distance relationship derived from the 5th symmetric set (the remaining four scatter plots almost coincid with it). It reveals that the fitnesses and the distances produced with the measure of Quinlan are uncorrelated. The fitness values vary within a small range nevertheless the distances to the globally optimal tree increase or decrease. Moreover, this has been noted for inductive tasks which are not very difficult. For all the 5 tasks the averaged *FDC* values from the measure of Quinlan are in $[-0.2 \div -0.025]$.

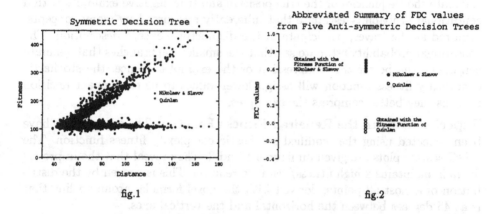

fig.1   fig.2

Anti-symmetric Decision Trees The global landscape is obviously uncorrelated as the *FDC* values were near 0. Another series of tests with anti-symmetric decision trees have been conducted using the same parameters. Figure 3, with the scatter plots of *FDC* derived from the 10th example set, shows that there is no clear correlation between the fitnesses and their distances to the optima. When evaluated with the formula of Quinlan, the points on the landscape are within a tight band parallel to the horizontal axis. The formula failed to evaluate differently trees, which are at different distances to the global optima.

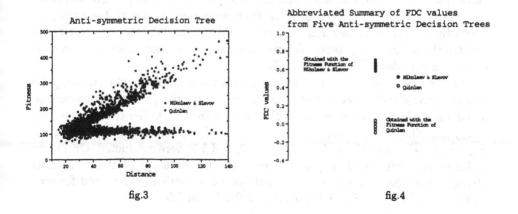

fig.3   fig.4

The abbreviated summary of averaged FDC from 10 trials with the sets for anti-symmetric trees is given on Figure 4. The FDC values were near 0, this time higher within the interval $[0.035 \div -0.125]$, which says that there is virtually no correlation between the fitness and the distance to the global optima. In other words, the problems were difficult for the measure of Quinlan, which is against the common sense as they have been deliberately generated as easy. After a careful examination it was found that when evaluated with this fitness function some offspring decision trees have the same fitness as their parents.

Improving the Fitness Function Our objective was to make the formula to account for the number of the branches in a decision tree. The idea is to calculate the frequencies of the true positive and true negative examples with a conditional probability estimate that inherently measures how many concepts, acquired at the leaves, participate in the disjunctive concept description. The conditional probability estimate say that the smaller the branches that generate conjuncts, the better the compression of the examples. Hence, the stochastic complexity fitness function will assign lower values to more compact decision trees as they better compress the examples.

Experiments with the Repaired Fitness Function The experiments have been repeated using the modified stochastic complexity fitness function. The FDC scatter plots are given on figures 1 and 3. They reveal that the improved formula maintains a high fitness/distance relation. This is proven by the distribution of almost all points, derived with the novel formula, around a line that is at 45 degrees between the horizontal and the vertical axes.

The abbreviated summaries with average FDC values from 10 trials are given on figures 2 and 4. While the FDC values derived with the formula of Quinlan are within the range $[-0.2 \div 0.035]$, those derived with the improved formula are in the interval $[0.57 \div 0.845]$. That is why, the FDC values from Figure 2 and Figure 4 allow to conclude that the landscape has been tuned from misleading to straightforward, according to the original definitions [5]. Thus, the repair of the formula made the global fitness landscape more correlated.

Experiments with Classical Benchmark Datasets The improved stochastic complexity function was tested also by running GPDT on two classical benchmark datasets : the Iris data [7]; and the Multiplexor-11 data [7]. The accuracy and complexity of the evolved decision trees were compared with the ones produced by C4.5 [7] after learning from exactly the same data sets and testing on exactly the same testing sets. We used the pruned decision trees produced by C4.5 with confidence level $CF = 25\%$.

The Iris data set consists of 150 examples from 3 classes. For training 100 examples were used. They include 4 continuous attributes, which we discretized in advance. The parameters were: $PopulationSize = 50$, $Generations = 100$, $P_{Crossover} = 0.8$, and $P_{Mutation} = 0.2$. Tests with the formula of Quinlan and the improved one, using values of x: $0.5, 1, 1.5, 2$, and 2.5, were conducted. On Figure 5 the average fitnesses from 10 runs with the Iris data are plotted. The best fitnesses, visualized on Figure 6, are obtained only with the improved formula and values of x: $0.5, 0.8, 1, 1.2, 1.5, 2, 2.5, 2.95, 3$, and 3.5.

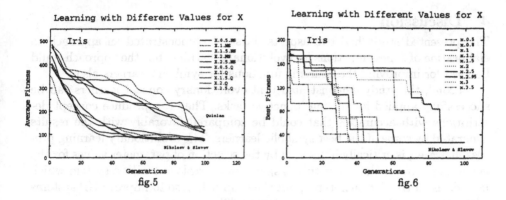

fig.5 fig.6

The plots on Figure 5 reveal that the evolutionary learner with the improved formula solves the Iris task more accurately. As evidences the more stable curves serve. With the Quinlan's formula the evolution was periodically misleaded. Figure 6 shows that all of the runs with the improved fitness formula converged to the same decision tree. The size of the tree, to which all the runs of GPDT converged, was 4, exactly the same as the decision tree generated by C4.5. The classification accuracy on unseen test data was also the same 98.7%. Note that this is an indication for a slightly overpruned decision tree, but this is because of the simplistic manual discretization of the continuous attributes.

Figures 7 and 8 represent results derived when learning concepts from the Multiplexor-11 [7] data set. They describe an 11-bit multiplexor with 3 attributes for the address bits, and 8 for the data bits. There were randomly generated 100 examples for training and 1000 for testing. The decision tree produced by C4.5 for the training set was with length 39, and the decision tree produced by GPDT with length 7. The accuracy of the tree of C4.5 on unseen data was 71.63% and the accuracy of the GPDT tree was 81.54%. The difficulty of this inductive task can be understood from the small band in which the curves on Figure 7 appear. The band of curves produced with the formula of Quinlan is more rugged and implies unstable evolutionary search.

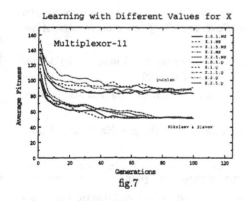

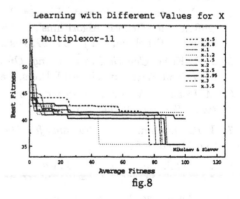

fig.7 fig.8

4 Discussion

The presented study had two aspects. First, it demonstrated an approach to elaboration of fitness functions for evolutionary learning, but the approach could be used for improving the heuristic functions for symbolic learners also.

Second, the study demonstrated that evolutionary concept learners can be successfully applied for solving inductive tasks. They can produce concept descriptions with accuracies that could be compared favorably with the results generated by some of the best symbolic learners. The evolutionary learning process, however, is critically influenced by the selection of parameter values for the genetic operators. Note that these aspects were exploited with a system which uses decision tree-like genotypes, but they can help also to improve GP systems with other genetic program representations [3].

5 Conclusion

This paper continues the study of the navigation and the structure of the search carried out by inductive learners. Statistical correlations were used to measure the quality of the solutions in order to make the search more efficient. The contribution of the paper is twofold: first, it developed a general stochastic complexity formula for eastimating decision trees appropriate for incremental and batch learners; and, second, a relationship between the performance and the representation in inductive evolutionary learners has been found.

References

1. J. Holland, *Adaptation in Natural and Artificial Systems*, A Bradford Book, The MIT Press, Cambridge, MA, 1992.
2. J. Horn and D.E. Goldberg, 'Genetic Algorithm Difficulty and the Modality of Fitness Landscapes', in *Foundations of Genetic Algorithms*, L.D.Whitley and M.D.Vose (eds.), Morgan Kaufmann Publ., San Mateo, CA, 243-269, 1995.
3. H. Iba, H. de Garis and T. Sato, 'Genetic Programming using a Minimum Description Length Principle', in *Advances in Genetic Programming*, K.Kinnear (ed.), The MIT Press, 265-284, 1994.
4. T. C. Jones and S. Forrest, 'Fitness Distance Correlation as a Measure of Search Difficulty for Genetic Algorithms', in *Proc. Sixth Int. Conference on Genetic Algorithms*, L.Eshelman (ed.), 184-192, 1995.
5. J. R. Koza, *Genetic Programming: On the Programming of Computers by Means of Natural Selection*, The MIT Press, Cambridge, MA, 1992.
6. M. Li and P. Vitanyi, *An Introduction to Kolmogorov Complexity and Its Applications, Springer-Verlag*, NY, 1993.
7. J. R. Quinlan, *C4.5: Programs for Machine Learning*, Morgan Kaufmann Publ., San Mateo, CA, 1993.
8. J. R. Quinlan, 'MDL and Categorical Theories (Continued) ', in *Proc. Int. Conference on Machine Learning, ICML-95*, Tahoe City, CA, 1995.
9. V. Slavov and N. Nikolaev, 'Fitness Landscapes and Inductive Genetic Programming', in *Proc. Third Int. Conf. on Artificial Neural Networks and Genetic Algorithms, ICANNGA'97*, Springer, Vienna, 1997.

Parallel and Distributed Search for Structure in Multivariate Time Series

Tim Oates, Matthew D. Schmill and Paul R. Cohen

Computer Science Department, LGRC
University of Massachusetts
Box 34610
Amherst, MA 01003-4610
{oates,schmill,cohen}@cs.umass.edu

Abstract. Efficient data mining algorithms are crucial for effective knowledge discovery. We present the Multi-Stream Dependency Detection (MSDD) data mining algorithm that performs a systematic search for structure in multivariate time series of categorical data. The systematicity of MSDD's search makes implementation of both parallel and distributed versions straightforward. Distributing the search for structure over multiple processors or networked machines makes mining of large numbers of databases or very large databases feasible. We present results showing that MSDD efficiently finds complex structure in multivariate time series, and that the distributed version finds the same structure in approximately $1/n$ of the time required by MSDD, where n is the number of machines across which the search is distributed.

1 Introduction

Knowledge discovery in databases (KDD) is an iterative process in which data is repeatedly transformed and analyzed to reveal hidden structure. The analysis portion of KDD, the actual search for structure in data, is called data mining. Efficient data mining algorithms are necessary when the number of databases to be mined is large, when the amount of data in a given database is large, or when many iterations of the transform/analyze cycle are required. The ease with which vast quantities of electronically available information can be generated and stored gives rise to the former two conditions. Parallel and distributed data mining algorithms can quickly mine large amounts of data by taking full advantage of existing hardware, both multiple processors on one machine and multiple machines on a network. Multi-Stream Dependency Detection (MSDD) is an easily parallelized data mining algorithm that performs an efficient systematic search for complex structure in multivariate time series of categorical data.

MSDD finds *dependencies* between patterns of values that occur in multivariate time series of categorical data. We call each univariate time series a *stream* of data. Dependencies are unexpectedly frequent or infrequent co-occurrences of patterns in the streams. MSDD finds the k strongest dependencies in a set of streams by performing a *systematic* search over the space of all possible dependencies. Systematic search expands the children of search nodes in a manner that ensures that no node can ever be generated more than once [9–12, 14]. Because non-redundant expansion is achieved without access to large, rapidly changing data structures, such as lists of open and closed nodes, the search space can be divided between multiple processes on multiple machines. Only a small amount of inter-process communication is required to keep the list of the k strongest dependencies globally consistent.

Because MSDD returns a list of the k strongest dependencies, rather than all of the dependencies that it encounters during the search, it is possible to use upper bounds on the values of a node's descendants to prune. The expressiveness of MSDD's rule representation allows the algorithm to find complex structure in data, but also leads to an exponential search space, making effective pruning essential. We use the G statistic as a measure of dependency strength, and develop optimistic bounds on the value of G for the descendants of a node to prune.

The remainder of the paper is organized as follows: Section 2 discusses systematic search in detail. Section 3 presents the MSDD algorithm, defines the space of dependencies that the algorithm explores, and develops domain independent pruning techniques. Section 4 shows how the systematicity of MSDD's search can be exploited to develop parallel and distributed versions of the algorithm. Section 5 explores the ability of the core algorithm to find interesting and complex structure in multivariate time series, and compares the speed of the centralized (MSDD) and distributed (D-MSDD) versions of the algorithm. Section 6 reviews related work, and Section 7 concludes.

2 Systematic Search

MSDD's search for the k strongest dependencies in a set of streams is *systematic*, leading to search efficiency and parallelizability. Systematic search non-redundantly enumerates the elements of search spaces for which the value or semantics of any given node are independent of the path from the root to that node. Webb calls such search spaces *unordered* [14]. Consider the space of disjunctive concepts over the set of literals $\{A, B, C\}$. Given a root node containing the empty disjunct, *false*, and a set of search operators that add a single literal to a node's concept, a *non*-systematic elaboration of the search space contains (among other redundancies) six variants of a single concept – $A \vee B \vee C$, $A \vee C \vee B$, $B \vee A \vee C$, $B \vee C \vee A$, $C \vee A \vee B$ and $C \vee B \vee A$. Each variant is semantically the same as the other five, yet syntactically distinct. In the space of disjunctive concepts, the semantics of any node's concept is unaffected by the path taken from the root to that node. For example, the two paths below yield semantically identical leaf nodes:

$$\textit{false} \to A \to A \vee B \to A \vee B \vee C$$
$$\textit{false} \to C \to C \vee B \to C \vee B \vee A$$

Clearly, naive expansion of nodes in unordered search spaces leads to redundant generation and wasted computation.

Systematic search of unordered spaces generates no more than one syntactic form of each semantically distinct concept. That is accomplished by imposing an order on the search operators used to generate the children of a node, and applying only those operators at a node that are higher in the ordering than all other operators already applied along the path to the node. Let op_A, op_B and op_C be the operators that add the literals A, B and C respectively to a node's concept. If we order those operators so that $op_A < op_B < op_C$, then the corresponding space of disjunctive concepts can be enumerated systematically so that each semantically distinct concept appears exactly once. For example, the concept A is obtained by applying operator op_A to the root node. Because $op_B > op_A$ and $op_C > op_A$, both op_B and op_C can be applied to the concept A, generating the child concepts $A \vee B$ and $A \vee C$. In contrast, the concept C, which is obtained by applying op_C to the root node, has no children. Because all other operators (op_A and op_B) are lower in the ordering than op_C, none will be applied and no children will be generated.

The fact that unordered search spaces can be explored without redundant node generation through systematic search is the key to parallelizing MSDD. Given any search node in the tree, the only information required to simultaneously generate that node's children and avoid redundant node generation is the operator ordering (e.g. $op_A < op_B < op_C$). For example, each of the subtrees rooted at the three children of the root node, A, B and C, could be expanded by systematic search algorithms running on different machines. The machine expanding node B would generate its children by applying all operators higher in the ordering than op_B, yielding the single child $B \vee C$ through the application of operator op_C. Because no operators are higher in the ordering than op_C, the node $B \vee C$ has no children, and the subtree rooted at B has been completely explored. Not only was no communication with the search algorithms running on the other machines required to expand that subtree, there was no need to know that they even existed or that other portions of the search space were being explored.

3 The MSDD Algorithm

MSDD accepts as input a set of streams that are used to define the space of dependencies the algorithm will search and to evaluate the strength of dependencies. The set of m input streams is denoted $S = \{s_1, \ldots, s_m\}$, and the ith stream is composed of categorical values, called *tokens*, taken from the set $\mathcal{V}_i$. All of the streams in S must have the same length, and we assume that all of the tokens occurring at a given position in the streams were recorded synchronously.

MSDD searches for dependencies expressed as rules of the following form: "If an instance of pattern x begins in the streams at time t, then an instance of pattern y will begin at time $t + \delta$ with probability p." Such rules are denoted $x \stackrel{\delta}{\Rightarrow} y$. We call x the *precursor* and y the *successor*. p is computed by counting the number of time steps on which an occurrence of the precursor is followed δ time steps later by an occurrence of the successor, and dividing by the total number of occurrences of the precursor. To keep the space of patterns and the space of dependencies finite, we consider patterns that span no more than a constant number of adjacent time steps. Precursors can span at most w_p time steps, and successors can span at most w_s time steps. Both w_p and w_s are parameters of the MSDD algorithm.

Patterns of tokens (precursors and successors) are represented as sets of 3-tuples of the form $\tau = (v, s, d)$. Each 3-tuple specifies a stream, s, a token value for that stream, v, and a temporal offset, d, relative to an arbitrary time t. Because such patterns can specify token values for multiple streams over multiple time steps, they are called *multitokens*.[1] Tuples that appear in precursors are drawn from the set $T_p = \{(v, s, d) | 1 \leq s \leq m, v \in \mathcal{V}_s, 0 \leq d < w_p\}$. Likewise, tuples that appear in successors are drawn from the set $T_s = \{(v, s, d) | 1 \leq s \leq m, v \in \mathcal{V}_s, 0 \leq d < w_s\}$.

MSDD performs a general-to-specific search over the space of possible dependencies, starting with a root node that specifies no token values for either the precursor or the successor ($\{\} \Rightarrow \{\}$). Search operators either add a term from T_p to a node's precursor or add a term from T_s to a node's successor. To perform a systematic search over the space of possible dependencies between multitokens, we impose the following order on the terms in T_p and T_s: All of the terms in T_p are lower than all of the terms in T_s. For any $\tau_i, \tau_j \in T_p$, τ_i is lower than τ_j if $d_i < d_j$ or if $d_i = d_j$ and $s_i < s_j$. That is, terms in T_p are ordered first by their temporal offset, and then by their stream index. Likewise for terms in T_s.

Because MSDD returns a list of the k strongest dependencies, if we can derive an upper bound on the value of the evaluation function f for all of the descendants of a given node, then we can use that bound to prune the search. Suppose the function $fmax(N)$ returns a value such that no descendant of N can have an f value greater than $fmax(N)$. If at some point during the search we remove a node N from the open list for expansion, and $fmax(N)$ is less than the f value of all k nodes in the current list of best nodes, then we can prune N. There is no need to generate N's children because none of the descendants of N can have an f value higher than any of the current best nodes; none of N's descendants can be one of the k best nodes that will be returned by the search. The use of an optimistic bounding function is similar to the idea behind the h function in A* search. That is, if a goal node is found whose cost is less than underestimates of the cost-to-goal of all other nodes currently under consideration, then that goal node must be optimal. Pruning based on optimistic estimates of the value of the descendants of a node has been used infrequently in rule induction algorithms, with ITRULE [13], OPUS [14] and PROGOL [7] being notable exceptions.

In practice, we use the G statistic computed for 2x2 contingency tables to measure dependency strength, and we have derived bounds on the value of G for the descendants of a node, making it an ideal candidate for f. The interested reader is referred to [8] for more details.

---

[1] The definition of a multitoken given here is an extension of the one given in previous descriptions of the algorithm [9].

4 Parallel and Distributed MSDD

In the same way MSDD guarantees non-redundant generation of search nodes, MSDD guarantees that distinct nodes at the same depth in the search tree are parent to completely disjoint sets of children. The result is a search space that can be trivially partitioned into computationally independent subsets, and consequently MSDD is an algorithm well suited for parallel and distributed implemetation. We begin by discussing a parallel implementation of MSDD

The easy partitioning of MSDD's search space allows us to treat any intermediate search node as a root of a new search tree. Consider the goal of "basic" MSDD; search for elaborations on the completely general rule $\{\} \rightarrow \{\}$ that maximize the evaluation function f. A more general, parallelized approach is to search for elaborations on *an arbitrary rule* that maximize f. In this way, we treat each node as an "island", independent of anything else MSDD has learned, spawning a new thread to perform the search as if the node were the root.

An efficient parallel implementation of MSDD is possible because the search at any given node does not require access to previously elaborated search tree. The threads of P-MSDD need only non-exclusive read access to the time series and exclusive write access for insertions into the queue of k best nodes. Using a semaphore to provide exclusive writes to the k best list, the computation of MSDD can be effectively balanced over many processing elements.

4.1 Distributed MSDD

The implementation of parallel MSDD can be translated easily to an efficient distributed algorithm. This algorithm, D-MSDD, makes use of a client-server TCP tools to perform D-MSDD's search over a network of cooperating systems.

The D-MSDD algorithm begins with the *server*. The server is responsible for initiating the search, mediating communication, and declaring the search finished. Any number of *client* machines may contact the server to declare themselves as eligible for aiding in the search. This declaration process is called *registration*, where the server takes note of each client machine, issuing it a unique identifier for future communication. Once a desirable number of clients have registered, the server is ready to initiate the search process.

The distributed search proceeds on each participant machine according to a local *agenda*. Each machine's agenda is an independent partition of the unexplored MSDD search space. As with P-MSDD, the only shared strucutres are the list of k best dependencies and the dataset itself. Each machine participating in a D-MSDD search maintains local copies of these structures, keeping them synchronized through network message passing. We simulate the accessing of shared data by sending *best* messages to describe a candidate node for the k best list. We emulate the load balancing that goes on on a parallel machine by passing *node* messages that transfer nodes from an overloaded machine's agenda to a machine with a lighter agenda.

5 Empirical Results

In this section we compare the performance of MSDD and D-MSDD. For each of three datasets, the two algorithms found the $k = 20$ strongest dependencies. We ran D-MSDD on both two and three machines connected via a local area network. The datasets, which were all taken from the UC Irvine repository, included chess end-games, solar flares, and congressional voting records. The results are summarized below in Table 1. The table shows the number of nodes expanded, CPU cycles consumed, and the number of messages sent to keep the list of the k best dependencies consistent. When D-MSDD ran on two and three machines (the D-MSDD – 2 and D-MSDD – 3 cases respectively), the table contains the sum of the value over all machines participating in the search. Note that relatively few search nodes were required to find the 20 strongest dependencies in exponential spaces; pruning based on optimistic estimates of G is effective. Because the distributed search may be at different depths on different machines, the total number of nodes expanded may vary depending on when strong dependencies are found and used for subsequent pruning. However, in each case the total number of CPU cycles required to complete the search remains fairly constant, independent of the number of participating machines. Because load-balancing between the machines is fine grained, n machines can complete the search for structure roughly n times faster than one machine.

Dataset	Algorithm	Search Nodes	CPU Cycles	Messages
vote	MSDD	107,858	6,911,826	0
	D-MSDD – 2	124,234	7,915,858	7024
	D-MSDD – 3	115,375	7,963,435	6697
chess	MSDD	22,346	1,507,160	0
	D-MSDD – 2	27,073	1,573,309	1321
	D-MSDD – 3	31,955	1,793,743	2964
solar	MSDD	12,199	805,920	0
	D-MSDD – 2	13,544	906,188	457
	D-MSDD – 3	17,941	1,095,695	1,706

Table 1. Comparison of MSDD and D-MSDD on three dataset.

6 Related Work

Several systematic search algorithms have appeared in the literature [9–12, 14], all of them variations on the basic idea of imposing an order on search operators, and applying only those operators at a node that are higher in the order than all other operators that have been applied on the path from the root to the node.

Our use of optimistic bounds on the value of the node evaluation function for pruning systematic search spaces is similar to the OPUS algorithm [14], which in turn is a generalization of the same idea as applied to non-systematic search in the ITRULE induction algorithm [13]. MSDD and ITRULE return the k best rules, whereas OPUS returns a single goal node or the single node with the highest value.

Both parallel algorithms and consideration of data with a temporal component are rare in the KDD and data mining literature. Holsheimer and Kersten describe a system for inducing rules from large relational databases that performs a parallelized beam search over the space of possible rules and accesses the data through a parallel DBMS [5]. However, their system is limited to classification rules (a conjunct of literals predicting a single literal), and it can miss high quality rules due to the use of beam search. Aronis and Provost developed a parallel algorithm that builds new features from existing features in relational databases [2]. The newly constructed features are then passed to a standard (serial) inductive learning algorithm. While parallelism speeds the search for new features, it does not affect the speed with which rules using those features can be learned. Agrawal and Shafer [1] explore several parallel algorithms for mining association rules from very large databases, and Dehaspe and De Raedt [4] present a parallel implementation of the CLAUDIEN clausal discovery system. Berndt and Clifford describe a dynamic programming algorithm for finding recurring patterns in univariate time series [3], and Mannila et al. [6] developed an algorithm that finds frequently occurring episodes in event-based data (e.g. event logs generated by telecommunications networks).

7 Conclusion

In this paper we presented the MSDD data mining algorithm which performs a systematic search for structure in multivariate time series. MSDD discovers the k strongest dependencies between pairs of multitokens, arbitrary patterns of values that can span multiple streams and multiple time steps. MSDD prunes the search space with an upper bound on the value of the descendant of a given node, and we derived such a bound on the value of G. We recognized that systematic search over unordered spaces is easily parallelized, and developed D-MSDD, a distributed version of MSDD. MSDD is a powerful tool for discovering complex structure in very large databases due to the efficiency and expressiveness of the core algorithm and the ease with which the search for structure can be distributed over multiple machines on a network via D-MSDD.

Acknowledgements

This research was supported by ARPA/Rome Laboratory under contract numbers F30602-91-C-0076 and F30602-93-0100, and by a National Defense Science and Engineering Graduate Fellowship. The U.S. Government is authorized to reproduce and distribute reprints for governmental purposes not withstanding any copyright notation hereon. The views and conclusions contained herein are those of the authors and should not be interpreted as necessarily representing the official policies or endorsements either expressed or implied, of the Advanced Research Projects Agency, Rome Laboratory or the U.S. Government. We thank the anonymous reviews for helpful suggestions.

References

1. R. Agrawal and J. C. Shafer. Parallel mining of association rules: Design, implementation and experience. Technical Report RJ 10004, IBM, 1996.
2. John M. Aronis and Foster J. Provost. Efficiently constructing relational features from background knowledge for inductive machine learning. In *Working Notes of the Knowledge Discovery in Databases Workshop*, pages 347–358, 1994.
3. Donald J. Berndt and James Clifford. Using dynamic time warping to find patterns in time series. In *Working Notes of the Knowledge Discovery in Databases Workshop*, pages 359–370, 1994.
4. Luc Dehaspe and Luc De Raedt. Parallel inductive logic programming. In *Proceedings of the MLnet Familiarization Workshop on Statistics, Machine Learning and Knowledge Discovery in Databases*, 1995.
5. Marcel Holsheimer and Martin L. Kersten. Architectural support for data mining. In *Working Notes of the Knowledge Discovery in Databases Workshop*, pages 217–228, 1994.
6. Heikki Mannila, Hannu Toivonen, and A. Inkeri Verkamo. Discovering frequent episodes in sequences. In *Proceedings of the First International Conference on Knowledge Discovery and Data Mining*, pages 210–215, 1995.
7. S. Muggleton. Inverse entailment and progol. *New Generation Computing*, 13:245–286, 1995.
8. Tim Oates and Paul R. Cohen. Searching for structure in multiple streams of data. In *Proceedings of the Thirteenth International Conference on Machine Learning*, pages 346 – 354, 1996.
9. Tim Oates, Dawn E. Gregory, and Paul R. Cohen. Detecting complex dependencies in categorical data. In *Preliminary Papers of the Fifth International Workshop on Artificial Intelligence and Statistics*, pages 417–423, 1994.
10. Patricia Riddle, Richard Segal, and Oren Etzioni. Representation design and brute-force induction in a boeing manufacturing domain. *Applied Artificial Intelligence*, 8:125–147, 1994.
11. Ron Rymon. Search through systematic set enumeration. In *Proceedings of the Third International Conference on Principles of Knowledge Representation and Reasoning*, 1992.
12. Jeffrey C. Schlimmer. Efficiently inducing determinations: A complete and systematic search algorithm that uses optimal pruning. In *Proceedings of the Tenth International Conference on Machine Learning*, pages 284–290, 1993.
13. Padhraic Smyth and Rodney M. Goodman. An information theoretic approach to rule induction from databases. *IEEE Transactions on Knowledge and Data Engineering*, 4(4):301–316, 1992.
14. Geoffrey I. Webb. OPUS: An efficient admissible algorithm for unordered search. *Journal of Artificial Intelligence Research*, 3:45–83, 1996.

Compression-Based Pruning of Decision Lists

Bernhard Pfahringer

Department of Computer Science, University of Waikato, New Zealand
email: bernhard@cs.waikato.ac.nz

Abstract. We define a formula for estimating the coding costs of decision lists for propositional domains. This formula allows for multiple classes and both categorical and numerical attributes. For artificial domains the formula performs quite satisfactory, whereas results are rather mixed and inconclusive for natural domains. Further experiments lead to a principled simplification of the original formula which is robust in both artificial and natural domains. Simple hill-climbing search for the most compressive decision list significantly reduces the complexity of a given decision list while not impeding and sometimes even improving its predictive accuracy.

1 Introduction

The *Minimum Description Length (MDL) Principle* (Rissanen 86), also called the *Minimum Message Length (MML) Principle* (Georgeff & Wallace 84), has been successfully applied in Machine Learning for a broad variety of problems (for a just a few selected papers see Quinlan & Rivest 89, Quinlan 93a, Forsyth et al. 94, Pfahringer 95a, Muggleton et al. 92). But recently also some problems with the MDL principle have been discovered (Quinlan 94, Quinlan 95). The problematic formula described in these papers is used by the C4.5RULES system for pruning the rule-sets of each class separately. Despite these theoretical concerns, in our own experimental experience (see e.g. results reported in Pfahringer 95a) we have found C4.5RULES to be a rather robust and reliable learner. The predictive accuracy of the induced ordered rule-sets (i.e. decision lists) is usually quite good, yet the rule-sets appear to be overly complex.

In this paper we introduce an alternative MDL-based formula for decision lists based on the ideas of Kononenko 95. This formula will be described in section 2. Section 3 will describe the algorithmic usage of the new formula and the experimental setup. In section 4 we first report on good results in artificial domains. But for some of the natural domains results using this original formula are just unacceptable. A hypothesis and a few experiments to explain these unpleasant findings then lead to a simplified version of the original formula which is broadly successful. Section 5 summarizes conclusions and discusses open problems and further research directions.

2 Estimating coding lengths of decision lists

Empirical induction is always faced with the problem of *overfitting* the data, especially in the presence of noise or irrelevant attributes. The MDL principle is a possible solution as it simultaneously judges both the simplicity and the accuracy of a particular induced theory. This is done by summing up both the estimated coding length of the theory and the estimated coding length of the training data given the theory:

```
Total coding length = Coding length to describe the model +
                      Coding length to describe the data,
                      given the model.
```

A theory is called *compressive*, if and only if its coding length is smaller than the coding length of the original training data (using the *null* theory). In Pfahringer 95b we have tried to pinpoint the origin of the problems described in Quinlan 94 and we have defined an alternative formula yielding some improvement. The main idea was to replace the global exception coding mechanism with a local one based on the sets of examples covered by each rule. In the following we will introduce an improved version of this formula using both better (i.e. smaller) coding length estimates in general and extending its applicability to multi-class problems and to both symbolic and numerical attributes.

In Pfahringer 95b we used the entropy of the distribution of symbols in a string to estimate its coding cost, which is valid in a information-theoretic sense, but inefficient for finite-length strings, as is exemplified in Kononenko 95. That paper defines the following formula for estimating the coding length of strings of finite length N constructed from k different possible symbols with respective absolute frequencies $c_1..c_k$:

$$cl(string) = log_2 \binom{N+k-1}{k-1} + log_2 \binom{N}{c_1..c_k} \tag{1}$$

The first part encodes the frequencies of the different symbols, which is sufficient information for constructing the decoder for the compressed string. The size of the compressed string itself is estimated by the second part of the formula.

Using this formula we can now define an MDL-based coding length estimate for decision lists. We assume that both the sender and the receiver know all examples and therefore all possible attributes, their types and values, and also the different possible classes. The sender only wants to transmit the correct classification of each example to the receiver. Furthermore we assume that the last rule of the decision-list has an empty set of conditions, therefore it acts as a kind of default rule, assigning some sensible classification to examples not covered by any previous rule. We use the majority class of all training examples not covered by any rule. Alternatively one could use the global majority class, especially in situations where the number of uncovered examples is very small thus leading to an unreliable class estimate.

Let us now define the total coding length of a decision-list as being just the sum of the coding lengths of its rules:

$$cl(dl) = \Sigma_i cl(rule_i) \tag{2}$$

The coding length estimate of a single rule is the sum of the estimate for encoding the conditions of this rule and the estimate for the class-label string of the examples covered by this rule (using formula 1). Note that we do not explicitly encode the class being predicted by this rule, we just assume that the majority class of the covered examples will be assigned:

$$cl(rule) = cl(tests) + cl(class\_label\_string) \tag{3}$$

The coding length estimate for all tests of a rule is a bit complicated due to the different possible kinds of tests. Categorical attributes involve testing for membership in some subset of all possible values, numerical attributes are tested for being either greater-equal or less-than some threshold. Therefore the coding length estimate for all tests of a single rule is the sum of these three different possible kinds of tests:

$$cl(tests) = cl(subset\_tests) + cl(greaterequal\_tests) + cl(lessthan\_tests) \tag{4}$$

Subset tests are estimated by first selecting those attributes actually involved in subset tests out of all categorical attributes, and then encoding the respective subsets:

$$cl(subsettests) = cl(choose(involved, all\_cat)) + \Sigma cl(subset) \tag{5}$$

The coding length of binary choices such as which attributes are actually used, or which subset of all possible values is tested, is always computed using formula 1. Additionally, it should be noted that this encoding schema assigns equal cost to both testing a categorical attribute for a specific single value (`attrX = valueY`, encoded as a subset-test for just this value) and to testing whether a categorical attribute is different from a specific single value (`attrX <> valueY`, encoded as a subset-test for all other possible values). This is due to the symmetry properties of formula 1.

Numerical tests are encoded in a similar fashion by first selecting the relevant subset of numerical attributes to be tested and than by encoding the respective thresholds. These thresholds are simply chosen from the set of all different values of the respective attribute actually occurring in training data passed down to this rule. This means we ignore possible values occurring only in examples already covered by earlier rules of the decision list. If there are n possible values, we can choose between $n - 1$ possible thresholds and therefore need $log_2(n - 1)$ bits for encoding a single threshold:

$$cl(lessthan\_tests) = cl(choose(involved, all\_num)) + \Sigma cl(threshold) \tag{6}$$

$$cl(greaterequal\_tests) = cl(choose(involved, all\_num)) + \Sigma cl(threshold) \tag{7}$$

$$cl(threshold) = log_2(n - 1) \tag{8}$$

This concludes the specification of the new formula (MDL0). To reiterate, its improvements are a better estimate based on the finite-length property of all encoded strings (as proposed in Kononenko 95), and its extended applicability. Now multiple classes as well as both categorical and numerical attributes are allowed in a domain.

3 Algorithmic usage

For evaluating the formula introduced in the previous section, we have implemented the following simple greedy hill-climbing search for pruning a given decision list (figure 1. The initial search starting point is the decision list returned by C4.5RULES having set all options of both C4.5 and C4.5RULES to their default values, except for enabling *subsetting* of categorical attributes. This results in a decision list being of exactly the syntax expected by our previously defined formula (see section 2). This initial decision list will also be used for comparison purposes later on.

```
mdl_prune(decision_list,training_examples)
{
  find best_basic_step
  if cl(pruned(decision_list,best_basic_step),training_examples) ≤
     cl(decision_list,training_examples)
     then mdl_prune(pruned(decision_list,best_basic_step),training_examples)
     else return decision_list
}
cl(decision_list,training_examples)
{ see section 2
}
```

Fig. 1. Pseudo-code for the pruning of decision lists.

Two basic operations are used for pruning a decision list: deleting a single test from the conditions of one rule or deleting a complete rule by itself. As long as the the total coding length does not increase, always the most compressive basic pruning step is chosen. Even though one might think that pruning complete rules is logically redundant as a basic step (a rule could be pruned by iteratively pruning all its tests), it can still make a big difference in greedy hill-climbing search. Pruning a single test effectively generalizes a rule thereby possibly increasing its coverage. This causes *fewer* examples to be passed on to rules further down the list. Quite contrary, deleting a complete rule causes *more* examples to be passed on, namely all those that used to be covered by the now deleted rule.

Additionally, as we allow for subset tests, one might even add a third pruning operator, namely deleting values from subsets. This would result in even more fine-grained pruning possibilities. We plan to implement such a pruning operator for further experiments.

4 Experimental Results

Ten complete 10-fold stratified cross-validation runs were carried out in each experiment reported below. We always list the mean predictive accuracies and the mean decision list sizes (simply measured as the total number of tests used) for both C4.5RULES and MDL_PRUNE.

4.1 Artificial Domains

Our initial experiments were carried out using two artificial data-sets: the parity of 5 boolean attributes in the presence of an additional 5 irrelevant boolean attributes and the 2-4 multiplexor in the presence of an additional 4 irrelevant attributes. Experiments involved different levels of class noise, where class noise is simulated by flipping the class bit of $N\%$ of the examples drawn at random. In all experiments all possible 1024 (2^{10}) examples were used.

Domain	Noise	Error		Size	
		C4	MDL0	C4	MDL0
Parity5-5	0%	0.00	0.00	160.0	80.0
	5%	8.59	7.96	222.3	148.4
	10%	18.70	22.38	305.6	262.6
	20%	33.29	43.58	259.4	154.6
Mux2-4-4	0%	0.00	0.00	46.4	22.4
	5%	6.39	5.66	70.7	59.6
	10%	11.53	11.39	80.5	52.3
	20%	25.39	24.31	97.9	16.6

Table 1. PARITY5-5 and MUX2-4-4: Average predictive error rates and average rule-set sizes for C4.5RULES and MDL_PRUNE at various levels of class noise.

Table 1 shows the average predictive errors and the average rule-set sizes for both C4.5RULES and MDL_PRUNE. We see that MDL_PRUNE performs quite satisfactorily. Rule-sets are always significantly smaller, sometimes even producing a five-fold reduction in size. And except for Parity5-5 at the 20% class noise level error rates are never dramatically worse, usually their difference is not statistically significant (as judged by a paired t-test).

4.2 Natural Domains

For experiments involving more natural domains we have chosen a few standard databases available from the UCI repository (Merz & Murphy 96). These selected databases range from small to mid-size with regard to number of examples. Some databases comprise solely categorical attributes, whereas others comprise solely numerical attributes, and finally there are a few comprising both categorical and numerical attributes. The selected databases also show a good mix of two-class and multi-class problems.

Domain	Cases	Classes	Cat	Num	Error		Size	
					C4	MDL0	C4	MDL0
Audiology	226	24	70	0	84.82	53.49	8.3	4.1
Breast-w	699	2	0	9	4.56	5.43	21.4	11.1
Credit-a	690	2	9	6	15.59	14.56	35.1	27.2
Diabetes	768	2	0	8	27.15	29.97	50.0	30.3
Glass	214	6	0	9	32.76	55.14	44.3	34.7
Hypo	3163	2	18	7	0.86	0.89	18.5	13.1
Labor	57	2	8	8	14.91	33.33	7.5	1.52
Lymph	148	4	18	0	21.62	32.29	20.5	9.4
Mush	8124	2	22	0	0.00	0.00	19.3	16.8
Sick	3772	2	22	7	1.71	1.76	49.5	29.6
Sonar	208	2	0	60	29.66	35.91	20.6	10.1
Soybean	683	19	35	0	7.80	27.75	63.7	35.5
Vote	435	2	16	0	4.71	4.89	16.7	13.1

Table 2. Properties, average predictive error rates and average rule-set sizes for C4.5RULES and MDL_PRUNE for various natural domains.

The properties of and the experimental results in these natural domains are listed in table 2. Even though we see the expected reduction in rule-set sizes just as we have experienced in artificial domains, the predictive error rates are less satisfactory. Rule-set size reduction is accompanied by a major degradation of predictive performance in some of the domains (see e.g. soybean, labor, lymph, or glass).

What is the reason of this at times abysmal performance? The first hypothesis was the suspicion that our coding schema for numerical tests (cf. equations 6 to 8) was indeed overly simplistic and too inefficient, thus leading to overly general rule-sets. But mediocre performance in solely categorical domains (e.g. soybean and lymph) ruled out this hypothesis as a single cause.

4.3 Modifying the coding length estimator

Inspecting the well-performing data-sets we see that these include all data-sets with more than 1000 training examples overall. Therefore we may conclude that a small number of available training examples might be one of the culprits. To clarify the impact of a small training set samples we devised the following experiment: can we increase the number of available examples in a sensible way? Simple-minded duplication of examples might seriously distort experimental results, because identical examples could be present in both the training and the test set, thus leading to a measure of rote learning capability only. More sophisticated, one could just duplicate the examples once after they have been assigned to the different cross-validation folds. Instead of actually duplicating examples, the same effect can easily be simulated inside the compression formula by modifying equation 3 in the following way:

$$cl(rule) = cl(tests) + f_{dup} * cl(class\_label\_string) \qquad (9)$$

By simply multiplying the original class-label string with a duplication factor f_{dup} we can easily simulate even vast artificial training sets. It is interesting to note that most practical systems using some MDL-based formula either internally weigh the two summands differently (Quinlan 93a) or even allow the user to specify weights explicitly (Cohen 95, Oliveira & Sangiovanni-Vincentelli 95).

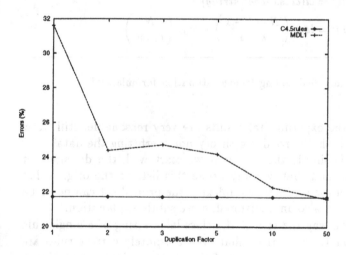

Fig. 2. Lymphgraphy: average error rates for various duplication factors.

Figures 2 and 3 depict the average predictive error rates and decision lists sizes respectively for various settings of f_{dup} in the lymph domain in comparison to the base error rates and sizes achieved by C4.5rules. We can clearly see that the predictive error steadily decreases until it is statistically insignificant for f_{dup} being 10. And even a much larger setting for f_{dup} still results in a significant almost two-fold reduction of the original rule-set's size.

How can this behaviour be explained? Certainly, for a duplication factor equal to 50, the explicit theory coding cost as computed by equations 4 to 8 is

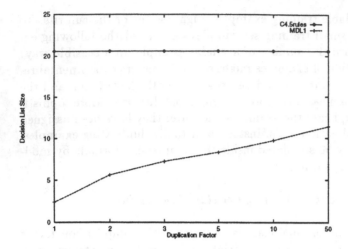

Fig. 3. Lymphgraphy: average rule-set sizes for various duplication factors.

$$cl(dl) = \Sigma_i cl(rule_i)$$
$$cl(rule) = cl(class\_label\_string)$$
$$cl(string) = log_2 \binom{N+k-1}{k-1} + log_2 \binom{N}{c_1..c_k}$$

Fig. 4. The final simplified coding length estimation formula (MDL1).

neglectably small. But the experimental results are very reasonable, still. How can this be the case? Why is the resulting theory not overfitting the data?

One of the reasons is simply the fact that we start with the decision list produced by C4.5rules, and that we only prune this list. So the original list forms an upper bound on the syntactic complexity, the pruned list can never be more complex. But there is also an additional, more subtle explanation.

If one investigates the way the size of the class-label string of a single rule is estimated by equation 1, one notices that even absolutely correct rules are assigned some non-zero cost. If all but one of the absolute class frequencies c_i are zero, equation 1 can be simplified to:

$$cl(string) = log_2 \binom{N+k-1}{k-1} \tag{10}$$

Therefore, even in the optimal case of absolutely correct rules we get some reasonable implicit accounting for the size an induced theory.

This immediately suggests the following simplification of our rule-set compression estimation. We can replace the original coding length estimation of single rules (equation 3) by simply:

$$cl(rule) = cl(class\_label\_string) \tag{11}$$

Domain	Error		Size	
	C4	MDL1	C4	MDL1
(Mu0) Mux24 0%	0.00	0.00	46.4	24.0
(Mu1) Mux24 10%	10.74	10.85	92.0	59.0
(Mu2) Mux24 20%	22.87	23.39	98.4	80.8
(Pa0) Par5 0%	0.00	0.00	160.0	80.0
(Pa1) Par5 10%	17.99	16.85	295.7	167.1
(Pa2) Par5 20%	29.72	27.21	298.7	202.2
(AU) Audiology	84.69	73.19	8.1	6.0
(BW) Breast-w	4.55	4.69	20.8	12.3
(CR) Credit-a	15.26	15.24	37.0	24.7
(DI) Diabetes	26.80	27.15	49.0	39.8
(GL) Glass	33.83	33.08	44.6	28.1
(HY) Hypo	0.88	0.89	18.2	10.1
(LA) Labor	14.91	14.56	7.7	3.9
(LY) Lymph	21.62	21.96	20.2	11.2
(MU) Mush	0.00	0.00	19.2	8.8
(SI) Sick	1.69	1.24	49.5	31.4
(SO) Sonar	29.18	29.51	21.5	16.4
(SY) Soybean	7.54	7.26	64.3	39.2
(VO) Vote	4.80	4.69	16.1	9.0

Table 3. Average predictive error rates and average rule-set sizes for C4.5RULES and the modified MDL1_PRUNE for various domains.

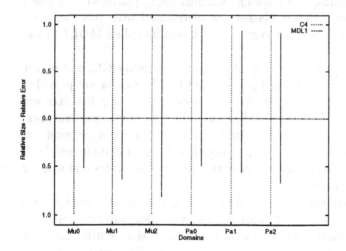

Fig. 5. Error rates and rule-set sizes for artificial domains.

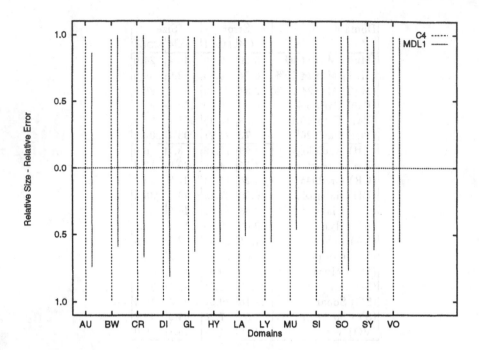

Fig. 6. Error rates and rule-set sizes for natural domains.

This means that we do not compute theory costs explicitly anymore! Therefore equations 4 to 8 are superfluous now, too. All the cost estimates are now just based on the number of subsets of training examples being produced by a given decision list and on how different classes are distributed over these subsets. Figure 4 summarizes this simplified version which will be called MDL1 in the following.

We have rerun all experiments using this simplified formula **MDL1** and report the final results in both table 3 and figures 5 and 6. The figures are provided for simplified relative comparisons. Both error rates and decision list sizes are mapped into the range of $[0, 1]$ by dividing all values by the respective maximal value. Error rates are depicted upwards from zero, whereas decision list sizes printed downwards. Both are grouped together for each domain and both **C4.5rules** and **MDL1**. Smaller impulses indicate smaller error rates and smaller decision list sizes respectively.

The simplified formula **MDL1** seems to do pretty well across all domains. Predictive accuracy is *never* significantly worse and in a few domains even improves somewhat. More importantly, the reduction in terms of size is still quite satisfactory, the pruned decision lists are approximately half as complex in most domains. Only for the two artificial domains there is some indication of overfitting in the presence of noise, as the sizes of the pruned decision lists tend to converge to the upper bound provided by C4.5RULES.

To give an idea for the improved intelligibility of induction results due to the

```
IF pension = none
THEN outcome = bad

IF longterm-disability-assistance = no
THEN outcome = bad

IF contribution-to-health-plan = none
THEN outcome = bad

IF wage-increase-first-year > 2.3
AND wage-increase-first-year < 2.65
THEN outcome = bad

IF pension <> none
AND longterm-disability-assistance <> no
AND contribution-to-health-plan <> none
THEN outcome = good

IF default
THEN outcome = bad
```

Fig. 7. An initial decision list for `labor` negotiation settlements as returned by C4.5RULES.

```
IF pension <> none
AND longterm-disability-assistance <> no
AND contribution-to-health-plan <> none
THEN outcome = good

IF default
THEN outcome = bad
```

Fig. 8. The pruned decision list for `labor` negotiation settlements as returned by the modified MDL1_PRUNE.

additional compression achievable over C4.5RULES when using the new formula, we list an example rule-set from the `labor` negotiation domain. This is a rather small database of final settlements in labor negotiations in Canadian industry. The initial decision-list induced by C4.5RULES is depicted in figure 7.

The new formula allows to considerably prune and simplify this rule-set to a much smaller rule-set of comparable predictive accuracy being depicted in figure 8. It is interesting to note that part of the simplification could have been achieved by simply removing logical redundancies. In the `labor` example the first three rules of the original set taken together are just the negation of the single rule predicting the opposite class. The supplied default rule would have predicted correctly anyway in these cases. On the other hand, pruning of the remaining fourth original rule for class **bad** is certainly not simply a removal of some logical redundancy.

So one might speculate that part of the additional amount of simplification gained is due to the global view on decision list simplification inherent in our approach. Whereas **C4.5rules** only optimizes sets of rules predicting the same class, we simplify decision lists as a whole. Thereby the interactions between the different subsets of rules and the default rule are taken into account in an implicit manner.

5   Conclusions

We have successfully engineered a new coding lengths formula for decision-lists, which allows for significant simplification of decision lists without impeding their predictive performance. Simpler decision lists are usually more intelligible as exemplified by an example given in the previous section. The final, simplified formula (figure 4) does not take into account theory cost explicitly, but it does so implicitly to a limited degree. This is one of the probable reasons impeding its original formulation. It also sets limits to the applicability of such a scheme to problems different from propositional rule-set pruning. When inducing and pruning a propositional decision-list in C4.5, a set of rather strong biases is involved in the search for an accurate decision list. Every single rule is of limited complexity, because its number of test-conditions is bounded by the total number of attributes. Additionally, the only disjunctions being induced are so-called internal value disjunctions. This prevents from having the complete theory complexity being shifted into a single rule of high explicit, but low implicit cost. However in the context of constructive induction, such a shift is possible. Therefore one would have to extend the formula to cope with arbitrarily complex attributes possibly derived by constructive induction. Application of the new formula in an ILP context might also be problematic. Although the number of possible conditions in a rule is usually bounded in an ILP system, too, these bounds tend to be much looser in general. More directly applicable scenarios being on our list for further research include variations on the search process itself like:

- Starting directly from a (pruned or unpruned) decision tree.
- Inducing a decision list from scratch using the new formula as its search heuristic.

Another promising direction should be the construction of a similar formula applicable to the prediction of continuous class values. This seems to be a prevalent problem in practise and has therefore got some attention in the Machine Learning community recently (Kramer 96, Quinlan 93b, Weiss & Indurkhya 95).

Instead of relying on the probably overly simple MDL1 formula of figure 4, one could try to estimate the appropriate value for f_{dup} of equation 9 for a given domain. Cross validation in a kind of wrapper approach (Kohavi 95) should be the right tool for this task.

Comparison to other pruning methods which are not based on a variation of the MDL principle are also necessary. A good starting point for this endeavour should be the work described in Fürnkranz 96.

Acknowledgements I would like to thank the ML group at Waikato University for providing an inspiring working environment. This research was sponsored by the Austrian Fonds zur Förderung der Wissenschaftlichen Forschung (FWF) by means of the following grant: Schrödingerstipendium Nr.J01269-MAT.

References

Cohen W.W.: Fast Effective Rule Induction, in Prieditis A. and Russell S.(eds.), *Proceedings of the 12th International Conference on Machine Learning (ML95)*, Morgan Kaufmann, San Francisco, 115-123, 1995.

Forsyth R.S., Clarke D.D., Wright R.L.: Overfitting Revisited: An Information-Theoretic Approach to Simplifying Discrimination Trees, *JETAI Journal of Experimental and Theoretical Artificial Intelligence*, 6,3, 1994.

Fürnkranz J.: Pruning Algorithms for Rule Learning, Österreichisches Forschungsinstitut für Artificial Intelligence, Wien, TR-96-07, 1996.

Georgeff M.P., Wallace C.S.: A General Selection Criterion for Inductive Inference, in O'Shea T.(ed.), *Proceedings of the Sixth European Conference on Artificial Intelligence (ECAI-84)*, Elsevier, Amsterdam, 1984.

Kohavi R.: Wrappers for Performance Enhancement and Oblivious Decision Graphs, Computer Science Dept., Stanford University, Stanford, CA 94305, USA, PhD Dissertation, 1995.

Kononenko I.: On Biases in Estimating the Multi-Valued Attributes, in Mellish C.S.(ed.), *Proceedings of the 14th International Joint Conference on Artificial Intelligence*, Morgan Kaufmann, San Mateo, CA, pp.1034-1040, 1995.

Kramer S.: Structural Regression Trees, in *Proceedings of the Thirteenth National Conference on Artificial Intelligence*, AAAI Press/MIT Press, Cambridge, MA, pp.812-819, 1996.

Merz C.J., Murphy P.M.: UCI Repository of machine learning databases, University of California, Department of Information and Computer Science, Irvine, CA, 1996. [http://www.ics.uci.edu/ mlearn/MLRepository.html]

Muggleton S., Srinivasan A., Bain M.: Compression, Significance, and Accuracy, in Sleeman D. and Edwards P.(eds.), *Machine Learning: Proceedings of the Ninth International Workshop (ML92)*, Morgan Kaufmann, San Mateo, CA, pp.338-347, 1992.

Oliveira A., Sangiovanni-Vincentelli A.: Inferring Reduced Ordered Decision Graphs of Minimal Description Length, in Prieditis A. and Russell S.(eds.), *Proceedings of the 12th International Conference on Machine Learning (ML95)*, Morgan Kaufmann, San Francisco, 1995.

Pfahringer B.: Practical Uses of the Minimum Description Length Principle in Inductive Learning, Institut für Med.Kybernetik u. AI, Technische Universität Wien, Dissertation, 1995.

Pfahringer B.: A New MDL Measure for Robust Rule Induction (Extended Abstract), in Lavrac N. and Wrobel S.(eds.), *Machine Learning: ECML-95*, Springer, Berlin Heidelberg New York, pp.331-334, 1995.

Quinlan, J.R.: Simplifying decision trees. Proc Workshop on Knowledge Acquisition for Knowledge-based Systems, Banff, Canada.(1986)

Quinlan J.R., Rivest R.L.: Inferring Decision Trees Using the Minimum Description Length Principle, *Information and Computation*, 80:227-248, 1989.

Quinlan, J.R.: C4.5: Programs for Machine Learning. Morgan Kaufmann Publishers, 1993.

Quinlan J.R.: Combining Instance-Based and Model-Based Learning, in *Proceedings of the Tenth International Conference on Machine Learning*, Morgan Kaufmann, San Mateo, CA, pp.236-243, 1993.

Quinlan J.R.: The Minimum Description Length Principle and Categorical Theories, in Cohen W.W. and Hirsh H.(eds.), *Machine Learning*, Rutgers University, New Brunswick, NJ, pp.233-241, 1994.

Quinlan J.R.: MDL and Categorical Theories (Continued), in Prieditis A. and Russell S.(eds.), *Proceedings of the 12th International Conference on Machine Learning (ML95)*, Morgan Kaufmann, San Francisco, 1995.

Rissanen J.: Stochastic Complexity and Modeling, in *The Annals of Statistics*, 14(3),p.1080-1100, 1986.

Weiss S.M., Indurkhya N.: Rule-based Machine Learning Methods for Functional Prediction, *Journal of Artificial Intelligence Research 3 (1995)*, 1995.

Probabilistic Incremental Program Evolution: Stochastic Search Through Program Space

Rafał Sałustowicz and Jürgen Schmidhuber

IDSIA, Corso Elvezia 36, 6900 Lugano, Switzerland
e-mail: {rafal, juergen}@idsia.ch
tel.: +41-91-9919838 fax: +41-91-9919839

Abstract. Probabilistic Incremental Program Evolution (PIPE) is a novel technique for automatic program synthesis. We combine probability vector coding of program instructions [Schmidhuber, 1997], Population-Based Incremental Learning (PBIL) [Baluja and Caruana, 1995] and tree-coding of programs used in variants of Genetic Programming (GP) [Cramer, 1985; Koza, 1992]. PIPE uses a stochastic selection method for successively generating better and better programs according to an adaptive "probabilistic prototype tree". No crossover operator is used. We compare PIPE to Koza's GP variant on a function regression problem and the 6-bit parity problem.

1 Introduction

Probabilistic Incremental Program Evolution (PIPE) synthesizes programs which compute solutions to a given problem. PIPE is inspired by recent work on learning with probabilistic programming languages [Schmidhuber, 1997] and by Population-Based Incremental Learning (PBIL) [Baluja and Caruana, 1995]. PIPE evolves tree-coded programs such as those used in Koza's variant of Genetic Programming [Koza, 1992], from now on simply referred to as GP. For earlier work on Genetic Programming see [Cramer, 1985; Dickmanns, 1987].

PIPE can be applied to any problem that GP can be applied to. PIPE's learning algorithm, however, is like PBIL's and very different from GP's. PIPE does not use the crossover operator. Instead, it uses a "probabilistic prototype tree" to combine experiences of different programs and to generate better and better programs.

Outline. Section 2 describes the basic data structures and procedures used by PIPE. Section 3 introduces the new learning algorithm. Section 4 compares the performance of PIPE and GP on function regression and 6-bit parity. Section 5 concludes.

2 Basic Data Structures and Procedures

Overview. PIPE generates programs according to an underlying *probabilistic prototype tree*.

Program Instructions. Programs contain instructions from a function set $F = \{f_1, f_2, \ldots, f_k\}$ with k functions and a terminal set $T = \{t_1, t_2, \ldots, t_l\}$ with

l terminals. For instance, to solve a one dimensional function approximation task one might use $F = \{+, -, *, \%, sin, cos, exp, rlog\}$ and $T = \{x, R\}$, where $\%$ denotes protected division ($\forall y, z \in \mathbb{R}, z \neq 0$: $y\%z = y/z$ and $y\%0 = 1$), $rlog$ denotes protected logarithm ($\forall y \in \mathbb{R}, y \neq 0$: $rlog(y)=\log(\text{abs}(y))$ and $rlog(0) = 0$), x is an input variable and R represents a generic random constant $\in [0;1)$ (see also "ephemeral random constant" [Koza, 1992]).

Program Representation. Programs are encoded in n-ary trees, with n being the maximal number of function arguments. Each argument is calculated by a subtree. The trees are parsed depth first from left to right. Sample program trees for a function approximation task are shown in Figure 1.

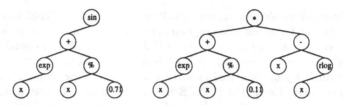

Fig. 1. *Sample program trees for function approximation. Left: $f(x)=sin(exp(x)+(x\%-0.71))$. Right: $f(x)=((exp(x)+(x\%0.11))*(x-rlog(x))$.*

Probabilistic Prototype Tree. The probabilistic prototype tree (PPT) is generally a *complete* n-ary tree. At each node $N_{d,w}$ it contains a random constant $R_{d,w}$ and a variable probability vector $\mathbf{P}_{d,w}$, where $d \geq 0$ denotes the node's depth (root node has $d = 0$) and w defines the node's horizontal position when tree nodes with equal depth are read from left to right ($0 \leq w < n^d$). The probability vectors $\mathbf{P}_{d,w}$ have $l + k$ components. Each component $P_{d,w}(I)$ denotes the probability of choosing instruction $I \in F \cup T$ at $N_{d,w}$. We maintain: $\sum_{I \in F \cup T} P_{d,w}(I) = 1$.

Program Generation. To generate a program PROG from PPT, an instruction $I \in F \cup T$ is selected with probability $P_{d,w}(I)$ for each accessed node $N_{d,w}$ of PPT. This instruction is denoted $I_{d,w}$. Nodes are accessed in a depth first way, starting at the root node $N_{0,0}$, and traversing PPT from left to right. Once $I_{d,w} \in F$ is selected, a subtree is created for each argument of $I_{d,w}$. If $I_{d,w} = R$, then an instance of R, called $V_{d,w}(R)$, replaces R in PROG. If $P_{d,w}(R)$ exceeds a threshold T_R, then $V_{d,w}(R) = R_{d,w}$. Otherwise $V_{d,w}(R)$ is randomly generated. Figure 2 illustrates the relation between the prototype tree and a possible program tree. We denote the result of applying PROG to data x PROG(x).

Tree Shaping. To reduce memory requirements we incrementally grow and prune the prototype tree.

Growing. Initially the PPT contains only the root node. Nodes are created "on demand" whenever $I_{d,w} \in F$ is selected and the subtree for an argument of $I_{d,w}$ is missing. Figure 3 shows a prototype tree after extraction of two programs.

Pruning. We prune subtrees of the PPT attached to nodes which contain at least one probability vector component above a threshold T_P. In case of functions we prune only subtrees that are *not* required as function arguments (see Figure 4). Pruning tends to discard old probability distributions that are irrelevant by now.

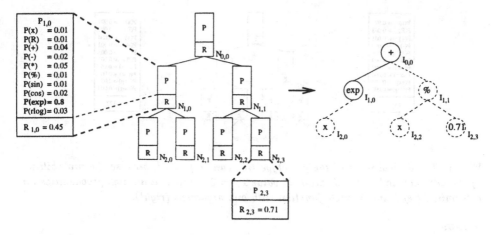

Fig. 2. *Left: example of node $N_{1,0}$'s instruction probability vector **P** and random constant R. Middle: probabilistic prototype tree PPT with details of node $N_{2,3}$. Right: possible extracted program PROG. At the time of creation of instruction $I_{1,0}$ the dashed part of PROG did not exist yet. $I_{2,3} = R$ is instantiated to $V_{d,w}(R) = R_{2,3} = 0.71$, because probability $P_{2,3}(R)$ (not shown) exceeds the random constant threshold T_R.*

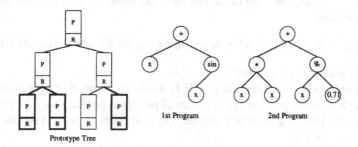

Fig. 3. *Left: prototype tree. Right: two generated programs. The highlighted parts of the prototype tree were created during construction of the second program.*

3 Learning

Overview. PIPE attempts to find better and better programs, program quality being measured by a scalar, real-valued "fitness value". PIPE guides its search to promising search space areas by incrementally building on previous solutions. It generates successive program populations according to the underlying probabilistic prototype tree *PPT* and stores in this tree the knowledge gained from evaluating the programs.

PPT Initialization. Each *PPT* node $N_{d,w}$ requires an initial random constant $R_{d,w}$ and an initial probability $P_{d,w}(I)$ for each instruction $I \in F \cup T$. We pick $R_{d,w}$ uniformly random from the interval $[0;1)$. To initialize instruction probabilities we use a constant probability P_T for selecting an instruction from T and $(1 - P_T)$ for selecting an instruction from F. $\mathbf{P}_{d,w}$ is then initialized as

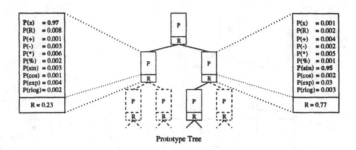

Prototype Tree

Fig. 4. *The dashed parts of the prototype tree can be pruned, because the probabilities of the adjacent nodes exceed threshold value $T_P = 0.9$ and contain high probabilities for a terminal (left) and a single function with one argument (right).*

follows:

$$P_{d,w}(I) := \frac{P_T}{l}, \forall I : I \in T \quad \text{and} \quad P_{d,w}(I) := \frac{1-P_T}{k}, \forall I : I \in F \quad (1)$$

Learning Framework. We combine two forms of learning: Generation-Based Learning (GBL) and Elitist Learning (EL). GBL is PIPE's main learning algorithm. EL's purpose is to make the the best program found so far an attractor. We execute:

1. GBL;   2. REPEAT { with probability P_{el} DO EL otherwise DO GBL }

Here P_{el} is a user-defined constant in $[0;1]$.

Generation-Based Learning. PIPE learns in successive generations, each comprising 5 distinct phases: (1) creation of program population, (2) population evaluation, (3) learning from population, (4) mutation of prototype tree and (5) prototype tree pruning.

(1) Creation of Program Population. A population of programs PROG_j ($0 < j \leq PS$; PS is population size) is generated using the prototype tree PPT as described in Section 2. The PPT is grown "on demand".

(2) Population Evaluation. Each program PROG_j of the current population is evaluated and assigned a non-negative "fitness value" $FIT(\text{PROG}_j)$. If $FIT(\text{PROG}_j) < FIT(\text{PROG}_i)$, then program PROG_j is said to embody a better solution than program PROG_i. Among programs with equal fitness we prefer shorter ones (Occam's razor), as measured by number of nodes. We define b to be the index of the *best* program of the current generation, and preserve the best program found so far in PROG^{el} (elitist).

(3) Learning from Population. Prototype tree probabilities are modified such that the probability $P(\text{PROG}_b)$ of creating PROG_b increases. We call this procedure `adapt_PPT_towards`(PROG_b). Our experiments indicate that it is beneficial to increase $P(\text{PROG}_b)$ *regardless* of PROG_b's length. To compute $P(\text{PROG}_b)$ we look at all PPT nodes $N_{d,w}$ used to generate PROG_b:

$$P(\text{PROG}_b) = \prod_{d,w:N_{d,w} \text{ used to generate } \text{PROG}_b} P_{d,w}(I_{d,w}(\text{PROG}_b)), \quad (2)$$

where $I_{d,w}(\text{Prog}_b)$ denotes the instruction of program Prog_b at node position d, w. Then we calculate a target probability P_{TARGET} for Prog_b:

$$P_{TARGET} = P(\text{Prog}_b) + (1 - P(\text{Prog}_b)) \cdot lr \cdot \frac{\varepsilon + FIT(\text{Prog}^{el})}{\varepsilon + FIT(\text{Prog}_b)}. \quad (3)$$

Here lr is a constant learning rate and ε a user defined constant. The fraction $\frac{\varepsilon + FIT(\text{Prog}^{el})}{\varepsilon + FIT(\text{Prog}_b)}$ implements *fitness dependent learning (fdl)*. We learn more from programs with higher quality (lower fitness) than from programs with lower quality (higher fitness). Constant ε determines the degree of *fdl*'s influence. If $\forall$ $FIT(\text{Prog}^{el})$: $\varepsilon \ll FIT(\text{Prog}^{el})$, then PIPE can use small population sizes, as generations containing only low-quality individuals do not affect the *PPT* much. Even learning with *only one* program per generation is then possible.

Given P_{TARGET}, *all* single node probabilities $P_{d,w}(I_{d,w}(\text{Prog}_b))$ are increased iteratively (in parallel):

REPEAT UNTIL $P(\text{Prog}_b) \geq P_{TARGET}$:
$P_{d,w}(I_{d,w}(\text{Prog}_b)) := P_{d,w}(I_{d,w}(\text{Prog}_b)) + c^{lr} \cdot lr \cdot (1 - P_{d,w}(I_{d,w}(\text{Prog}_b)))$

Here c^{lr} is a constant influencing the number of iterations. We use $c^{lr} = 0.1$, which turned out to be a good compromise between precision and speed.

Finally each random constant in Prog_b is copied to the appropriate node in *PPT*: if $I_{d,w}(\text{Prog}_b) = R$ then $R_{d,w} := V_{d,w}(R)$.

(4) Mutation of Prototype Tree. Mutation is PIPE's major exploration mechanism. Mutation of *PPT* probabilities is guided by the current best solution Prog_b. We want to explore the area "around" Prog_b. Probabilities $P_{d,w}(I)$ stored in all nodes $N_{d,w}$ that were accessed to generate program Prog_b are mutated with a probability P_{M_p}, defined as:

$$P_{M_p} = \frac{P_M}{(l + k) \cdot \sqrt{|\text{Prog}_b|}}, \quad (4)$$

where P_M is a free parameter setting the overall mutation probability and $|\text{Prog}_b|$ denotes the number of nodes in program Prog_b. The justification of the square root is empirical: we found that larger programs improve faster with a higher mutation rate. Selected probability vector components are mutated as follows:

$$P_{d,w}(I) := P_{d,w}(I) + mr \cdot (1 - P_{d,w}(I)), \quad (5)$$

where mr is the mutation rate, another free parameter. All mutated vectors $\mathbf{P}_{d,w}$ are then renormalized.

We see from assignment (5) that small probabilities (close to 0) are subject to stronger mutations than high probabilities. Otherwise mutations would tend to have little effect on the next generation.

(5) Prototype Tree Pruning. At the end of each generation we prune the prototype tree as described in section 2.

Elitist Learning. During elitist learning (EL) we adapt PPT towards the elitist program PROG^{el} by calling `adapt_PPT_towards(PROG`^{el}`)`, then we prune PPT. However, we neither mutate the probabilities of PPT nor create and evaluate a population, making EL computationally cheap. It focuses search on previously discovered promising parts of the search space. EL is particularly useful with small population sizes. It works efficiently in case of noise-free problems.

Termination Criterion. PIPE is run either for a fixed number of program evaluations PE (time constraint) or until a solution with fitness better than FIT_s is found (quality constraint).

4 Experimental Comparison with GP

In this section we compare our PIPE method to Koza's Genetic Programming variant (GP) on two problems. First, we investigate a continuous function regression problem. We use a non-trivial function to prevent either algorithm from simply guessing it. We then compare both algorithms on the 6-bit parity problem, a discrete task which allows for only 65 distinct fitness values. The limited number of fitness values permits us to test PIPE's built-in Occam's razor.

For both algorithms and problems we set $F = \{+, -, *, \%, sin, cos, exp, rlog\}$ and $T = \{x, R\}$ (see Section 2). For GP R denotes a set of constants from $[0;1)$ ("ephemeral random constant", see [Koza, 1992] for details).

4.1 Function Regression

The function to be approximated is:

$$f(x) = x^3 \cdot e^{-x} \cdot cos(x) \cdot sin(x) \cdot (sin^2(x) \cdot cos(x) - 1)$$

See Figure 5. The training (testing) data set D_{tr} (D_{te}) samples f at 101 equidistant points from the interval $[0;10]$ ($[0.05;10.05]$). D_{tr} is used for learning, D_{te} to test generalization. The fitness value for each program PROG is $FIT(\text{PROG}) = \sum_{\forall x \in D_{tr}} |f(x) - \text{PROG}(x)|$, its generalization performance $GEN(\text{PROG}) = \sum_{\forall x \in D_{te}} |f(x) - \text{PROG}(x)|$. We set $PE = 100000$ for both algorithms and tried many parameter settings for both PIPE and GP. Good parameters for PIPE are: P_T=0.8, $\varepsilon = 1$, P_{el}=0.2, PS=10, lr=0.2, P_M=0.2, mr=0.4, T_R=0.3, T_P=0.999999, $FIT_s = 0$. Good parameters for GP are: population size = 2000, crossover rate = 0.9, maximal tree depth = 10, initial depth = 2–6 with "half and half population initialization" and "over-selection" – see [Koza, 1992].

Results. 21 independent test runs were conducted for each algorithm. To obtain an idea how generalization performance relates to function approximation quality, consider Figure 6. Note that generalization performance $GEN(\text{PROG}) \approx 20$ can be obtained using a constant function.

PIPE's and GP's generalization performances are summarized in Figure 7. Generalization performances w are plotted against numbers of programs with $GEN(\text{PROG}) \leq w$.

The top 24% of all PIPE runs led to better results than all GP runs. On the other hand, the worst 33% of all PIPE runs led to worse results than all GP runs. PIPE's best solutions are better than GP's, but variance is higher, too.

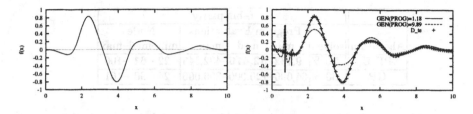

Fig. 5. $f(x) = x^3 \cdot e^{-x} \cdot cos(x) \cdot sin(x)$ $\cdot (sin^2(x) \cdot cos(x) - 1)$ **Fig. 6.** *Test data set D_{te} and approximations with $GEN(\text{Prog}) = 1.18$ and 9.89.*

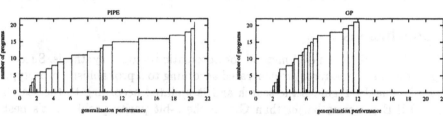

Fig. 7. *Cumulative histograms of PIPE's (left) and GP's (right) generalization performance on the function regression problem. Each box indicates how often PIPE's (left) and GP's (right) generalization performance was at least as good as the corresponding one.*

4.2 6-Bit Parity Problem

For this problem, Boolean values are represented by integers: 1 for true and 0 for false. The 6-bit parity function has 6 Boolean arguments; it returns 1 if the number of non-zero arguments is odd and 0 otherwise.

The fitness of a program is the number of patterns it classifies incorrectly. Best (worst) fitness for classifying all (no) patterns correctly is 0 (64). To fit the Boolean nature of the problem the real-valued output of a program is mapped to 0 if negative and to 1 otherwise. We set $PE = 500000$ for both algorithms. After a coarse parameter search we found the following good parameter settings. For PIPE: $P_T=0.6$, $\varepsilon = 1$, $P_{el}=0.05$, $PS=12$, $lr=0.01$, $P_M=0.4$, $mr=0.4$, $T_R=0.3$, $T_P=0.999999$, $FIT_s = 0$. For GP: population size = 2000, crossover rate = 0.9, maximal tree depth = 10, initial depth = 2–6 with *"half and half* population initialization" and "over-selection" – see [Koza, 1992]. The best GP parameters we found turned out to be the same as for the function approximation task, although we tried many combinations. PIPE was less robust with respect to parameter settings.

Results. 50 independent test runs were conducted for each algorithm. The shortest PIPE-program embodying a perfect solution was found after 5829 program evaluations. It has 22 nodes and computes:

```
(x2-((rlog(rlog(cos(0.530687)))%x2)%cos(((((x5-x3)-(x0+(x1-x4)))
                %rlog(0.699001)))))
```

Table 1 summarizes all results.

On this task, PIPE performed better than GP. It solved the problem more reliably (more often) and faster in the median (with fewer program evaluations).

Algorithm	solved	6-bit parity	
		Program Evaluations min– med –max	Nodes min–med–max
PIPE	70 %	9,432–**52,476**–482,545	22– **61** –100
GP	60 %	64,000–120,000–396,000	24– 90 –161

Table 1. *Summary of 6-bit parity results.*

PIPE also found less complex solutions (containing fewer nodes).

5 Conclusions

We introduced PIPE, a novel method for automatic program synthesis. Successive generations of programs are generated according to a probabilistic prototype tree *PPT*. The *PPT* guides the search and is updated according to the search results. PIPE performs better than GP on the 6-bit parity problem. It's best solutions to a function regression problem are better than GP's best solutions. GP's results have lower variance though.

References

[Baluja and Caruana, 1995] Baluja, S. and Caruana, R. (1995). Removing the genetics from the standard genetic algorithm. In Prieditis, A. and Russell, S., editors, *Machine Learning: Proceedings of the Twelfth International Conference*, pages 38–46. Morgan Kaufmann Publishers, San Francisco, CA.

[Cramer, 1985] Cramer, N. L. (1985). A representation for the adaptive generation of simple sequential programs. In Grefenstette, J., editor, *Proceedings of an International Conference on Genetic Algorithms and Their Applications*, Hillsdale NJ. Lawrence Erlbaum Associates.

[Dickmanns et al., 1987] Dickmanns, D., Schmidhuber, J., and Winklhofer, A. (1987). Der genetische Algorithmus: Eine Implementierung in Prolog. Fortgeschrittenenpraktikum, Institut für Informatik, Lehrstuhl Prof. Radig, Technische Universität München.

[Koza, 1992] Koza, J. R. (1992). *Genetic Programming – On the Programming of Computers by Means of Natural Selection.* MIT Press.

[Schmidhuber, 1997] Schmidhuber, J. (1997). A general method for incremental self-improvement and multi-agent learning in unrestricted environments. In Yao, X., editor, *Evolutionary Computation: Theory and Applications.* Scientific Publ. Co., Singapore. In press.

NeuroLinear: A System for Extracting Oblique Decision Rules from Neural Networks

Rudy Setiono and Huan Liu

Department of Information Systems and Computer Science
National University of Singapore
Singapore 116290

Abstract. We present NeuroLinear, a system for extracting oblique decision rules from neural networks that have been trained for classification of patterns. Each condition of an oblique decision rule corresponds to a partition of the attribute space by a hyperplane that is not necessarily axis-parallel. Allowing a set of such hyperplanes to form the boundaries of the decision regions leads to a significant reduction in the number of rules generated while maintaining the accuracy rates of the networks. We describe the components of NeuroLinear in detail using a heart disease diagnosis problem. Our experimental results on real-world datasets show that the system is effective in extracting compact and comprehensible rules with high predictive accuracy from neural networks.

1 Introduction

Neural networks have been widely used to solve classification problems. Comparisons between neural networks and decision trees algorithms for these problems have shown that in general neural networks can produce better accuracy rates [1, 2, 3, 4]. Recent developments in algorithms that extract rules from neural networks have made neural network techniques even more attractive. The extracted rules allow one to explain the decision process of a neural network. It is not surprising that in the past few years great efforts have been devoted to finding efficient and effective algorithms for extracting rules from a trained neural network

Gallant's connectionist expert systems [5] and Saito and Nakano's RN method [6] are two early works that attempt to generate rules from neural networks. These systems, however, do not actually extract rules from the networks; instead, they try to generate an explanation for each particular outcome of the networks.

The KT algorithm developed by Fu [7] is an algorithm that extracts rules from a trained network. It searches for subsets of connections to a network's unit with summed weight exceeding the bias of that unit. It is assumed that the unit's activation value is close to either 0 or 1. By searching for the proper subsets of the input connections, sets of rules are generated to describe under what conditions the unit's activation will take one of the two values.

The MofN algorithm of Towell and Shavlik [8] clusters the weights of the trained network into equivalence classes. Clusters that do not significantly affect the unit's activation are eliminated. The complexity of the network is further reduced by replacing the weights in all remaining clusters by the average weight of the individual cluster. The rules are generated in a similar way as by Fu's KT algorithm. However, because of the creation of clusters with averaged weights and the removal of unneeded clusters, it can be expected that the rules extracted will be simpler than those of KT algorithm.

An algorithm that extracts rules from networks that have been trained via the backpropagation method with penalty is proposed by Blassig [9]. A penalty term is added to the network's error function with the hope that a large number of the weights will have zero values after training and thus can be removed. In order to force the activation value of a unit to take on the value of either 0 or 1, the network's weights are restricted to be -6, 0, or 6, and the unit's bias to be either -3 or 3.

A simple rule extraction algorithm is presented by Setiono and Liu [10]. It is claimed that the rules extracted from neural networks are comparable to those generated by decision trees [11] in terms of accuracy and comprehensibility. The basic idea behind the algorithm is the fact that it is generally possible to replace the continuous activations of the hidden units by a small number of discrete ones. Rule extraction is realized in two steps. First, rules that describe the network outputs in terms of the discretized activation values of the hidden units are generated. Second, rules that describe each discretized hidden unit activation values in terms of the network inputs are constructed. By merging the rules obtained in these two steps, a set of rules that relates the inputs and outputs of the network is obtained.

While the algorithm can generate symbolic rules that mimic the predicted outcome of the original network, it works only for data with binary inputs (the implicit assumption, that the various hidden unit activation values are determined by only a small number of input values, excludes problems with continuous attributes where there can be infinitely many possible values taken by these attributes). Data with some continuous attributes need to be preprocessed before training the network. The preprocessing of the data entails dividing the values of the continuous attributes into intervals. This is achieved by the ChiMerge algorithm [12]. ChiMerge employs the χ^2 statistic to determine the division of the original intervals into their respective subintervals. All continuous attribute values that fall in the same subinterval are then represented by a unique discrete value for use as inputs to the neural network. Rules involving the discrete representations of the inputs are generated from the network. Given the boundaries of the subintervals furnished by ChiMerge, getting the rules in terms of the original continuous attributes is trivial.

An inherent problem introduced by the preprocessing of the data by ChiMerge is that each condition of a rule involving a continuous attribute determines an axis-parallel decision boundary. For many classification problems, it is often more natural to allow oblique hyperplanes to form the boundaries of the decision regions. In other words, instead of imposing the axis-parallel constraint, being able to generate oblique decision hyperplanes makes it possible to let the learning algorithm determine what kind of hyperplanes is more suitable for the data in hand. Oblique hyperplanes are more general and they may substantially reduce the number of rule conditions needed to describe the decision region. As a result, a more compact and comprehensible set of rules can be obtained.

In this paper, we describe how a set of rules, where each rule condition is given in the form of the linear inequality

$$\sum_i c_i x_i < \eta \tag{1}$$

where c_i is a real coefficient, x_i is the value of the attribute i, and η is a threshold, can be extracted from a neural network. The neural network that we use is the standard feedforward neural network with a single hidden layer. In contrast to the tree growing algorithms which generate the rules in a level-by-level and top-down fashion, rules are extracted from a network in two steps: from the hidden layer to the output layer and from the input layer to the hidden layer. Classification rules are obtained by merging the rules from these two steps. Unlike the decision tree algorithms [13, 11] which consider smaller and smaller subsets of the data to improve the accuracy of the rules, the neural network approach for rule generation considers the entire training set as a whole. Our experimental results show that more compact sets of rules with high accuracy rates can be obtained by the network approach.

The organization of the paper is as follows. Section 2 describes NeuroLinear, a system that we develop for extracting oblique decision rules from a neural network. The steps are described in detail by way of an example using a real-world dataset. Section 3 analyzes the merits of generating a set of classification rules with NeuroLinear. It also highlights the differences between the rules generated from a network and those from the decision-tree method C4.5 ([11]). Section 4 presents our experimental results on several real-word problems. Section 5 gives a brief conclusion of the paper.

2 Rule extraction with NeuroLinear

The process of extracting oblique decision rules from a neural network can be summarized in the following steps:

1. Select and train a network to meet a prespecified accuracy requirement. Remove the redundant connections in the network by pruning while maintaining the accuracy.
2. Discretize the hidden unit activation values of the network.
3. Extract rules that describe the network outputs in terms of the discretized network activation values.
   For each discretized hidden unit activation value, generate a rule in terms of the network's inputs.
   Merge the two sets of rules obtained above.

We shall use the Cleveland heart disease dataset to show the workings of NeuroLinear in detail.

2.1 Neural network training and pruning

The Cleveland heart disease data set can be obtained via anonymous ftp from the repository at the University of California, Irvine [16]. It consists of 303 patterns. Because we have not implemented a way to handle patterns with missing attribute values, we discard such patterns and use only the remaining 297 patterns. Each pattern is described by 13 attributes, 5 of which are continuous and the remaining 8 discrete. The attributes are summarized in Table 1. Each of the pattern is labeled either positive (presence of heart disease) or negative (absence of heart disease).

Table 1. The attributes of the Cleveland heart disease data set and network input units assigned to them.

Attribute	Type	Possible values/Range	Network inputs
C_1	Continuous	[29, 77]	I_1
D_2	Discrete	0 or 1	I_2
D_3	Discrete	1,2,3 or 4	I_3, I_4, I_5, I_6
C_4	Continuous	[94, 200]	I_7
C_5	Continuous	[126, 564]	I_8
D_6	Discrete	0 or 1	I_9
D_7	Discrete	0,1 or 2	I_{10}, I_{11}, I_{12}
C_8	Continuous	[71, 202]	I_{13}
D_9	Discrete	0 or 1	I_{14}
C_{10}	Continuous	[0, 6.2]	I_{15}
D_{11}	Discrete	1,2 or 3	I_{16}, I_{17}, I_{18}
D_{12}	Discrete	0,1,2 or 3	$I_{19}, I_{20}, I_{21}, I_{22}$
D_{13}	Discrete	3,6 or 7	I_{23}, I_{24}, I_{25}

Since the problem is a binary classification problem, one output unit is sufficient for the network. Positive patterns are given the target 1 and negative patterns 0. A hidden layer of 4 units is found to be sufficient to give the network a comparable accuracy rate to those reported in the literature. One input unit is assigned to each continuous attribute. Values of the continuous attributes are normalized such that their range is [0, 1]. Each value of a discrete attribute with n possible values is represented by an n-bit binary string, except when $n = 2$, only 1 bit is used (see the last column of Table 1). With an additional input unit to represent the hidden unit bias values, the total number of the network's input units is 26.

Given an n-dimensional input pattern x_i, the predicted output of the network at output unit p is computed as

$$S_{pi} = \sigma \left(\sum_{j=1}^{h} \delta \left((x_i)^T w_j \right) v_{pj} \right) \tag{2}$$

where

- h is the number of hidden units in the network.
- w_j is an n-dimensional vector of weights for the arcs connecting the input layer and the j-th hidden unit, $j = 1, 2, \ldots, h$. The weight of the connection from the ℓ-th input unit to the j-th hidden unit is denoted by $w_{j\ell}$.
- v_j is a C-dimensional vector of weights for the arcs connecting the j-th hidden unit and the output layer. The weight of the connection from the j-th hidden unit to the p-th output unit is denoted by v_{pj}.
- C is the number of output units.

The activation function of the hidden units is the hyperbolic tangent function

$$\delta(y) = (e^y - e^{-y})/(e^y + e^{-y}), \tag{3}$$

while the activation function of the output units is the sigmoid function

$$\sigma(y) = 1/(1 + e^{-y}). \tag{4}$$

The hyperbolic tangent function allows the activation values of the hidden units to be in the interval $[-1, 1]$, while the range of the sigmoid function used at the output units is $[0, 1]$.

The network is trained by minimizing the cross-entropy error function with weight decay [14]:

$$\theta(w, v) = -\sum_{i=1}^{k} \sum_{p=1}^{C} (t_{pi} \log S_{pi} + (1 - t_{pi}) \log(1 - S_{pi})) + P(w, v), \tag{5}$$

where k is the number of patterns in the training dataset, t_{pi} is the binary-valued target output for pattern x_i at output unit p, and $P(w, v)$ is the penalty term:

$$P(w, v) = \epsilon_1 \sum_{j=1}^{h} \left(\sum_{\ell=1}^{n} \frac{\beta w_{j\ell}^2}{1 + \beta w_{j\ell}^2} + \sum_{p=1}^{C} \frac{\beta v_{pj}^2}{1 + \beta v_{pj}^2} \right) + \epsilon_2 \sum_{j=1}^{h} \left(\sum_{\ell=1}^{n} w_{j\ell}^2 + \sum_{p=1}^{C} v_{pj}^2 \right), \tag{6}$$

(ϵ_1 and ϵ_2 are two positive penalty parameters and $\beta > 0$).

The penalty term $P(w, v)$ is added to the cross-entropy error function so that relevant connections can be distinguished from those irrelevant ones by the their magnitude. After training, it can be expected that the irrelevant connections will have small magnitude and therefore, they can be removed from the network with little or no effect on the accuracy of the network. Pruning is achieved by removing those connections with small magnitude. We train and prune the network such that it achieves an accuracy rate of at least 85 % on the training set.

Figure 1 depicts a pruned network for the Cleveland heart disease problem. The network has been trained with 90% of the patterns randomly picked from the dataset. The remaining 10% of the patterns are used to test the network's generalization capability. The pruned network has only 2 hidden unit and 10 connections left. Only one input, $\mathcal{I}_2$, is connected to the first hidden unit. A total of seven inputs are connected to the second hidden unit. The accuracy rates of this network are 86.14 % on the training data and 80.00 % on the testing data.

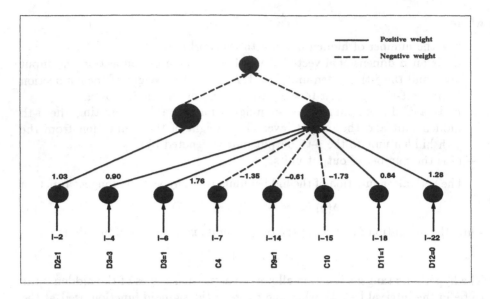

Fig. 1. A network with 10 connections and only 2 hidden units for the Cleveland heart disease dataset. The accuracy rates on the training set and the testing set are 86.14 and 80.00 %, respectively. The discrete input of the network is 0 or 1 depending on the original value of the corresponding nominal attributes (labeled with $\mathcal{D}$). For example, the second input $\mathcal{I}_4$ is equal to 1 if and only if the value of the attribute $\mathcal{D}_3$ is 3. The two inputs $\mathcal{I}_7$ and $\mathcal{I}_{15}$ correspond to the continuous attributes $\mathcal{C}_4$ and $\mathcal{C}_{10}$, respectively (see Table 1).

2.2 Chi2: Discretization of hidden unit activation values

The range of the activation values of the network's hidden units is the interval $[-1, 1]$, since they have been computed as the hyperbolic tangent of the weighted inputs (cf. Function 3). In order to extract rules from the network, it is better that these activation values be grouped into a small number clusters while at the same time preserving the accuracy of the network. We can expect to have a more concise set of rules if the number of clusters required is smaller. Chi2, an improved and automated version of ChiMerge, is the algorithm used for this purpose.

Given a dataset where each pattern is described by the values of the continuous attributes $\mathcal{A}_1, \mathcal{A}_2, \ldots$ and the class label of each pattern is known, Chi2 finds discrete representations of the patterns. Using the χ^2 statistic, Chi2 divides the range of the attributes into subintervals and assigns all values that fall in a subinterval a unique discrete value. The merging of adjoining subintervals takes place one at a time and attribute by attribute in a round robin fashion. This is intended to eliminate the ordering bias of attributes. The output of Chi2 is discretized data that preserve the discriminating power of the original data. Irrelevant attributes can be detected by their single intervals at the end of discretization and they can be removed. The outline of the algorithm is as follows:

The Chi2 algorithm

1. Let Chi-0 be an initial critical value.
2. For each attribute $\mathcal{A}_i$:
   (a) Sort the data according to the the input values of attribute i.
   (b) Form an initial set of intervals such that each interval contains only one unique value.
3. Initialize all attributes as "unmarked".
4. For each unmarked attribute $\mathcal{A}_i$:
   (a) For each adjoining pair of subintervals, compute the χ^2 values:

$$\chi^2 = \sum_{i=1}^{2} \sum_{j=1}^{k} \frac{(A_{ij} - E_{ij})^2}{E_{ij}} \tag{7}$$

   where:
      k: the number of classes,
      A_{ij}: the number of samples in the ith interval, jth class,
      R_i: the number of samples in the ith interval $= \sum_{j=1}^{k} A_{ij}$.
      C_j: the number of samples in the jth class $= \sum_{i=1}^{2} A_{ij}$.
      E_{ij} : expected frequency of A_{ij}, $E_{ij} = R_i \times C_j/N$. If R_i or $C_j = 0$, E_{ij} is set to 0.05,
      N: the total number of samples.
   (b) Find two subintervals with the lowest χ^2 value. If this value is less than Chi-0 and if merging the subintervals does not introduce conflicting data[1], then merge these subintervals, and repeat from Step 4(a). Else if merging the subintervals will introduce conflicting data, mark attribute i.
5. If there is still an unmarked attribute, then increase Chi-0 and repeat Step 4.

Only one parameter is required for Chi2. This parameter is the initial critical value Chi-0. This value is used to determine if the null hypothesis that the subintervals and the class labels are independent can be rejected. If the test statistic (Eqn. 7) exceeds the critical value Chi-0, the null hypothesis is rejected. Otherwise, the null hypothesis is not rejected and the subintervals are merged. The critical value Chi-0 is determined by α, the significance level of the test. For example, if $\alpha = 0.50$ and the number of classes in the data is 3, the critical value is 1.386. If no inconsistency in the data is introduced after merging of the subintervals with the initial value of Chi-0, the critical value Chi-0 is increased, i.e., the significance level is reduced to check the possibility of further merging of subintervals.

For the activation values of the two hidden units of network depicted in Figure 1, the subintervals found by Chi2 are:

---

[1] Conflicting data occur when there are two or more patterns from different classes with the same discretized attribute values.

- Hidden unit 1: 2 subintervals $[0.0, 0.77), [0.77, 1]$.
- Hidden unit 2: 3 subintervals $[-1.0, 0.05), [0.05, 0.47), [0.47, 1]$.

A pattern can thus be represented by a pair of integers (i, j) where i and j denote the subintervals into which its first and second hidden unit activation values fall, respectively. If no conflicting data is allowed in Chi2, it is possible to obtain rules that preserve the accuracy rate of the network for the original dataset using their discrete representations.

2.3   Rule extraction

Rules are first generated to describe the network outputs in terms of the discretized hidden unit activation values. Since there are only 2 intervals in the first hidden unit and 3 intervals in the second hidden unit found by Chi2, a maximum of only 6 combinations are possible. A set of simple rules will be able to distinguish the positive patterns from the negative ones. The rules are obtained by X2R [15], an algorithm that generates a set of rules with 100 % accuracy (provided that there are no conflicting patterns) from data with discrete inputs. Using the notations i and j to denote the activation values at the hidden units, the rules are:

- Rule 1: If $j = 3$, then Negative.
- Rule 2: If $i = 1$ and $j = 2$, then Negative.
- Default rule: Positive.

Rules in terms of the inputs that describe each possible values of i and j can be obtained using the weights of the network (see Figure 1). For the first hidden unit, we have that

$$1.03 \, \mathcal{I}_2 < \delta^{-1}(0.77) = 1.02 \Leftrightarrow i = 1$$
$$1.03 \, \mathcal{I}_2 \geq \delta^{-1}(0.77) = 1.02 \Leftrightarrow i = 2$$

($\delta^{-1}(.)$ is the inverse of the hyperbolic tangent function (3)). Since $\mathcal{I}_2$ is binary-valued, the above two rules can be simplified as: $\mathcal{I}_2 = 0$ if and only if $i = 1$. For the second hidden unit, the conditions are:

$$0.90 \, \mathcal{I}_4 + 1.76 \, \mathcal{I}_6 - 1.35 \, \mathcal{I}_7 - 0.61 \, \mathcal{I}_{14} - 1.73 \, \mathcal{I}_{15} + 0.84 \, \mathcal{I}_{18} + 1.28 \, \mathcal{I}_{22} < 0.05 \Leftrightarrow j = 1$$
$$0.05 \leq$$
$$0.90 \, \mathcal{I}_4 + 1.76 \, \mathcal{I}_6 - 1.35 \, \mathcal{I}_7 - 0.61 \, \mathcal{I}_{14} - 1.73 \, \mathcal{I}_{15} + 0.84 \, \mathcal{I}_{18} + 1.28 \, \mathcal{I}_{22} < 0.51 \Leftrightarrow j = 2$$
$$0.90 \, \mathcal{I}_4 + 1.76 \, \mathcal{I}_6 - 1.35 \, \mathcal{I}_7 - 0.61 \, \mathcal{I}_{14} - 1.73 \, \mathcal{I}_{15} + 0.84 \, \mathcal{I}_{18} + 1.28 \, \mathcal{I}_{22} \geq 0.51 \Leftrightarrow j = 3$$

The 2 continuous inputs $\mathcal{I}_7$ and $\mathcal{I}_{15}$ are the normalized values of the attributes $\mathcal{C}_4$ and $\mathcal{C}_{10}$, respectively (see Table 1). The equations that relate the normalized and the original attributes are

$$I_7 = \frac{C_4 - 94}{106}$$

$$I_{15} = \frac{C_{10}}{6.2}$$

Substituting these relations for the conditions of Rules 1 and 2, we have

- Rule 1: If $71.02\,I_4 + 138.20\,I_6 - C_4 - 47.83\,I_{14} - 21.87\,C_{10} + 65.93\,I_{18} + 100.36\,I_{22} \geq -53.95$, then Negative.
- Rule 2. If $I_2 = 0$ and $-90.07 \leq 71.02\,I_4 + 138.20\,I_6 - C_4 - 47.83\,I_{14} - 21.87\,C_{10} + 65.93\,I_{18} + 100.36\,I_{22} < -53.95$, then Negative.
- Default rule: Positive.

The accuracy of these rules on the training dataset is the same as that of the pruned network, i.e. 86.14 %. Although it cannot be guaranteed that the accuracy rate on the testing set will always be the same as the network's accuracy, for the set used in the experiment, the accuracy rates of the rules and the pruned network are identical.

3 Analysis

The result presented in the previous section indicates that NeuroLinear is effective in extracting oblique classification rules from a pruned neural network. When desired, it is possible to analyze the extracted rules further. For each possible combination of the discrete attribute values, a set of rules involving only the continuous attributes can be generated. The discrete inputs I_2, I_{14} and I_{18} each can have an input value of 0 or 1. The inputs I_4 and I_6 can have the paired-values of $(0,0), (0,1)$, or $(1,0)$. Hence, the various combinations of the discrete inputs could produce a total of 24 rule sets involving only the continuous attributes. Let us consider some of these rule sets:

1. The case when $I_2 = I_4 = I_6 = I_{14} = I_{18} = I_{22} = 0$ (or equivalently, $D_2 = 0, D_3 = 2$ or $4, D_9 = 0, D_{11} = 2$ or $3, D_{12} = 1, 2$ or 3):
   - Rule 1-2: If $C_4 + 21.87\,C_{10} \leq 90.07$, then Negative.
   - Default rule: Positive.
   (Rule 1-2 above is the disjunction of Rules 1 and 2).
2. The case when $I_2 = 1, I_4 = I_6 = I_{14} = I_{18} = I_{22} = 0$ (or equivalently, $D_2 = 1, D_3 = 2$ or $4, D_9 = 0, D_{11} = 2$ or $3, D_{12} = 1, 2$ or 3):
   - Rule 1: If $C_4 + 21.87\,C_{10} \leq 53.95$, then Negative.
   - Default rule: Positive.
3. The case when $I_2 = I_4 = 1, I_6 = I_{14} = I_{18} = I_{22} = 0$ (or equivalently, $D_2 = 1, D_3 = 3, D_9 = 0, D_{11} = 2$ or $3, D_{12} = 1, 2$ or 3):
   - Rule 1: If $C_4 + 21.87\,C_{10} \leq 124.97$, then Negative.
   - Default rule: Positive.

4. The case when $I_2 = I_6 = 1, I_4 = I_{14} = I_{18} = I_{22} = 0$ (or equivalently, $D_2 = 1, D_3 = 1, D_9 = 0, D_{11} = 2$ or $3, D_{12} = 1, 2$ or 3):
   - Rule 1: If $C_4 + 21.87\,C_{10} \leq 192.15$, then Negative.
   - Default rule: Positive.

The above rules clearly show that positive patterns and negative patterns are separated by the oblique line $C_4 + 21.87\,C_{10}$. For the different values of the discrete attributes, the threshold value is determined by the boundaries of the subintervals found by Chi2 and by the weights of the network between the discrete inputs and the hidden layer. Let us consider a pattern having its relevant discrete inputs all equal to 0 and label it the "base" case. According to the first set of rules above, such a pattern will be classified as negative if its continuous attributes satisfy the condition $C_4 + 21.87\,C_{10} \leq 90.07$. Let us now consider another pattern where the values of the relevant inputs are the same as the base pattern, expect for $I_2 = 1$. The pattern actually corresponds to a female patient if $I_2 = 0$, male otherwise. The second set of rules indicates that for a male patient having identical values for the other relevant discrete attributes, once the value of $C_4 + 21.87\,C_{10}$ exceeds 53.95, he will be diagnosed as positive. C4.5 rules obtained from a decision tree, where a discrete or a continuous attribute may be used as the branching attribute at any node in the tree, does not allow this kind of analysis.

4 Experimental results

We report our experiments with NeuroLinear in this section. Five datasets from the machine learning data repository at the University of California, Irvine are used to compare the performance of NeuroLinear to that of C4.5rules [11]. C4.5rules is chosen because the code is widely available and it has been commonly used by researchers in the machine learning community. It has been reported that C4.5rules performs well on many datasets. The datasets and the characteristics of their attributes are given in Table 2.

Table 2. Datasets used in the experiments.

Dataset	Size	Attributes	
		Discrete	Continuous
Australian Credit Approval	690	8	6
Boston Housing Data	506	1	12
Cleveland Heart Disease	297	5	8
Wisconsin Breast Cancer	699	0	9
Sonar Target	208	0	60

Following Towell and Shavlik [8], for each dataset, ten repetitions of ten-fold cross validation were performed using NeuroLinear. Each neural network was given a set of initial weights randomly generated in the interval $[-1, 1]$. For all networks, the following values were fixed: the number of hidden units was 4, the number of output unit was 1. The penalty parameters ϵ_1 and ϵ_2 were set at 0.1 and 10^{-3}, respectively. The value of β was 10. We list the average predictive accuracy rates of 100 neural networks for the 5 test datasets in Table 3.

Table 3. Average predictive accuracy rates (%) and its standard deviation. Each average has been computed from 100 pruned neural networks.

Dataset	Accuracy (Std. Dev.)
Australian Credit Approval	83.84 (5.96)
Boston Housing Data	81.52 (8.82)
Cleveland Heart Disease	78.92 (5.79)
Wisconsin Breast Cancer	94.57 (4.84)
Sonar Target	88.63 (11.56)

C4.5rules was run to perform ten-fold cross validation with its default parameter values. The results from C4.5rules and NeuroLinear are summarized in Tables 4 and 5 below.

Table 4. Accuracy rates (%) of C4.5rules and NeuroLinear.

Dataset	C4.5rules	NeuroLinear	P-value
Australian Credit Approval	84.22 (2.93)	83.64 (5.74)	0.60
Boston Housing Data	83.81 (5.90)	80.60 (9.12)	0.28
Cleveland Heart Disease	75.45 (7.17)	78.15 (6.86)	0.24
Wisconsin Breast Cancer	95.28 (2.51)	95.73 (3.75)	0.71
Sonar Target	85.61 (8.64)	85.39 (12.77)	0.96

In the two tables, the average accuracy rates and the average number of rules obtained by C4.5rules and NeuroLinear are given. The figures in parentheses are the standard deviations. The P-values are computed for testing the null hypothesis that the means of two groups of observations are equal. The P-values for the accuracy rates in Table 4 show that there is no significant difference in the mean accuracy rates of C4.5rules and NeuroLinear. On the other hand, the large differences in the numbers of rules of C4.5rules and NeuroLinear in Table 5 clearly demonstrate the effect of using oblique hyperplanes as the rule conditions. Their corresponding small P-values verify the significance of these differences.

Table 5. Number of rules of C4.5rules and NeuroLinear.

Dataset	C4.5rules	NeuroLinear	P-value
Australian Credit Approval	14.60 (2.88)	6.60 (4.40)	0.0001
Boston Housing Data	15.20 (3.01)	3.05 (3.23)	0.0001
Cleveland Heart Disease	12.90 (2.85)	5.69 (4.25)	0.0001
Wisconsin Breast Cancer	8.90 (1.20)	2.89 (2.52)	0.0001
Sonar Target	9.70 (1.57)	7.03 (3.73)	0.0003

Comparing the predictive accuracy rates of NeuroLinear to those of the pruned networks from which they are extracted, we note that they are not identical. This is not unexpected, while the decision surface of the networks can be highly nonlinear, the decision boundaries produced by NeuroLinear are piece-wise linear. The *fidelity* of the extracted rules, however, is high. Towell and Shavlik [8] define fidelity as the ability of the extracted rules to mimic the behavior of the network from which they are extracted.

5 Conclusion

We have presented NeuroLinear, a system for generating classification rules using neural networks. The three components of NeuroLinear make it possible to generate oblique decision rules, these are

1. An efficient neural network training and pruning algorithm.
2. Chi2 algorithm for discretization of hidden unit activation values.
3. X2R algorithm for generating perfect rules from a small dataset with discrete attributes values.

Comparisons of experimental results using real-world datasets reveal that NeuroLinear can achieve similar accuracy rates as C4.5rules with far fewer rules. It can be expected that the smaller rule-set will enable one to explain the classification process in a more meaningful and comprehensible way.

We may refer to patterns having all relevant discrete attribute values equal to zero as the base level. Hence, a set of base-level rules that involves only the continuous attributes can be obtained. Similar sets of rules for other patterns with one or more of nonzero discrete attributes are generated by NeuroLinear. These rules differ from those of the base-level rules only in the threshold values. The different thresholds for the various combinations of the discrete attributes values provide potentially valuable information regarding the patterns in the dataset. This interesting feature of the rules extracted by NeuroLinear is not possessed by those of C4.5rules.

Acknowledgment

We wish to thank the reviewers for their valuable comments and suggestions and S. Murthy of Siemens Corporate Research for pointing out an error in an earlier version of this paper.

References

1. T.G. Dietterich, H. Hild, and G. Bakiri, "A comparative study of ID3 and back-propagation for English text-to-speech mapping," in *Machine Learning: Proceedings of the Seventh International Conference*, Austin, Texas, 1990.
2. D.H. Fisher and K.B. McKusick. "An empirical comparison of ID3 and back-propagation," in *Proceedings of 11th Int. Joint Conf. on AI*, pp. 788–793, 1989.
3. J.R. Quinlan. "Comparing connectionist and symbolic learning methods," in S.J. Hanson, G.A. Drastall, and R.L. Rivest, eds., *Computational Learning Theory and Natural Learning Systems*, Vol 1 (A Bradford Book, The MIT Press, 1994) pp. 445–456.
4. J.W. Shavlik, R.J. Mooney, and G.G. Towell, "Symbolic and neural learning algorithms: An experimental comparison", *Machine Learning*, vol. 6, no. 2, 111–143, 1991.
5. S. Gallant, "Connectionist expert systems," *Comm. of the ACM*, vol. 31, no. 2, pp. 152–169, Feb. 1988.
6. K. Saito and R. Nakano, "Medical diagnosis expert system based on PDP model," in *Proc. IEEE Intl. Conf. on Neural Networks*, IEEE Press, New York, pp. I255-I266, 1988.
7. L. Fu, "Rule learning by searching on adapted nets," in *Proc. of the Ninth National Conference on Artificial Intelligence*, (1991) pp. 590–595.
8. G.G. Towell and J.W. Shavlik, "Extracting refined rules from knowledge-based neural networks," *Machine Learning*, vol. 13, no. 1, pp. 71-101, 1993.
9. R. Blassig. "GDS: Gradient descent generation of symbolic classification rules," in *Advances in Neural Information Processing*, Vol. 6, (Morgan Kaufmann, Los Angeles CA, 1994) pp. 1093–1100.
10. R. Setiono and H. Liu, "Symbolic representation of neural networks," *IEEE Computer*, March 1996, pp. 71–77.
11. J.R. Quinlan. *C4.5: Programs for Machine Learning*, San Mateo, CA: Morgan Kaufmann, 1993.
12. R. Kerber, "ChiMerge: Discretization of numeric attributes," in *The Proc. of the Ninth National Conference on AI*, AAAI Press/The MIT Press, 1992, pp. 123–128.
13. L. Breiman, J.H. Friedman, R.A. Olshen, and C.J. Stone, *Classification and Regression Trees*, Wadsworth & Brooks/Cole Advanced Books & Software, 1984.
14. J. Hertz, A. Krogh, and R.G. Palmer, "Introduction to the theory of neural computation," Redwood City, CA: Addison Wesley, 1991.
15. H. Liu and S.T. Tan, "X2R: A fast rule generator," in *Proceedings of IEEE International Conference on Systems, Man and Cybernetics*, IEEE Press, 1995.
16. P.M. Murphy and D.W. Aha, *UCI repository of machine learning databases [machine-readable data repository]*, Department of Information and Computer Science, University of California, Irvine, 1992.

Inducing and Using Decision Rules in the GRG Knowledge Discovery System

Ning Shan,[1,2] Howard J. Hamilton,[2], and Nick Cercone[2]

[1] Macro International Inc., 11785 Beltsville Drive, Calverton, MD, USA 20705,
E-Mail: ning@cs.uregina.ca
[2] Department of Computer Science, University of Regina, Regina, SK, Canada S4S
0A2, E-Mail: {hamilton,nick}@cs.uregina.ca

Abstract. We are developing the GRG knowledge discovery system for learning decision rules from relational databases. The GRG system generalizes data, reduces the number of attributes, and generates decision rules. A subsystem of this software learns decision rules using familiar and novel rule induction techniques and uses these rules to make decisions. This paper provides an overview of GRG, describes those aspects of the system most relevant to creating and using decision rules, and compares it to other machine learning approaches.

1 Introduction

The GRG software system is being designed for knowledge discovery from large relational databases (Shan et al. 1996). *Knowledge discovery* in databases (KDD) is "the nontrivial extraction of implicit, previously unknown, and potentially useful information from data" (Piatetsky-Shapiro et al. 1991). Knowledge discovery integrates techniques from statistics, machine learning, logic, and rough sets (Fayyad et al. 1996a; Fayyad et al. 1996b; Ziarko 1994). The central question in knowledge discovery research is how to turn information, expressed in terms of stored data, into knowledge expressed in terms of generalized statements about characteristics of the data. Including a machine learning technique in a knowledge discovery system requires addressing the issues of computational efficiency (to deal with the large amounts of data in databases) and robustness (to cope with missing or "noisy" data). In GRG, efficiency is obtained by generalizing the data to reduce its size and robustness is obtained as described in this paper.

Each of the three steps in the GRG system, *information generalization, information reduction*, and *rule generation*, transforms the data from the database to a higher level of abstraction. By integrating three approaches, we significantly reduce the computational complexity of analyzing large databases. In the first step, an *attribute-oriented concept tree ascension technique* (Cai et al. 1991) generalizes the data (either a complete relational database or a relation extracted by a query from a database). An $O(n)$ generalization algorithm is used for efficiency (Carter and Hamilton 1997). This generalization loses some information but substantially improves the efficiency of the following steps.

Feature selection (or *attribute reduction*) is the problem of choosing a small subset of attributes that ideally is necessary and sufficient to describe the concept. Feature selection accelerates learning and improves learning quality. We need a reliable and practically efficient method to eliminate irrelevant attributes. In the second step of GRG, a *reduction technique* (Pawlak 1991; Shan et al. 1995) generates a minimalized version of the data, called a *reduct*, which contains a minimal subset of the generalized attributes and a minimum number of distinct rows (tuples) for that subset. Details are given by Shan et al. (1996).

In the third step of GRG (see Section 3), a set of decision rules is derived from the reduct. Many approaches are based on "divide-and-conquer" (Quinlan 1986) or "separate-and-conquer" (Clark and Niblett 1989; Michalski 1983). The former recursively partitions the instance space until each remaining, small instance space belongs to a roughly uniform concept. The latter induces one rule at a time and removes the instances covered by this rule until no more rules can be generated. Such methods suffer from the *splintering problem*, where decisions are made with decreasing statistical support as the size of the sample dwindles. Statistical anomalies become harder to weed out, and noise sensitivity increases. Overfitting occurs, incorrect rules may be generated, and prediction accuracy is decreased (Domingos 1995; Holte et al. 1989). The "conquer-without-separating" strategy used in GRG and other systems (Domingos 1995; Ziarko and Shan 1995) can alleviate the splintering problem. It uses statistical measures to combat noise, because each rule is generated while taking into consideration the entire data set. Missing values are handled without being replaced by artificial values, since each equivalence class is accounted for as a specific rule being generated.

The decision rules embody the general patterns within the database, and can be used to interpret and understand the active mechanisms underlying the database. The technique for making decisions with these rules is described in Section 4. An empirical comparison between GRG and C4.5 on well-known machine learning problems is given in Section 5, and conclusions are drawn in Section 6.

2 Preliminary Stages

The GRG system investigates the relationship between two, user-defined groups of attributes, referred to as *condition attributes* C and *decision attributes* D. Given a set I of input instances (rows), the following preliminary steps are performed: (1) generalize all values according to user-defined concept hierarchies (Ning et al. 1996) and discretization functions (Ning et al. 1997); (2) convert all multivalued attributes in I into binary attributes (let m be the number of condition attributes in the result); (3) create separate decision tables $DT_1, \ldots, DT_d$ for each of d decision attributes; (4) delete all duplicate instances (rows) from $DT_1, \ldots, DT_d$; (5) delete redundant condition attributes from each decision table using the attribute reduction procedure described by Ning et al. (1996). The result of these five preliminary steps is to decomposes the original problem, with d possible values for the decision attribute (or combination of decision attributes), into d subproblems, each with a binary decision attribute.

3 Rule Generation

Rule generation is a key step in GRG. Each instance (row) in a decision table D_i can considered as a specific rule that matches only one equivalence class. When taking this view, we refer to the decision table D_i as a set R of rules. Such a rule can be generalized by removing conditions from the condition part of the rule. GRG's rule generation first checks whether a rule can be made more general by eliminating irrelevant attribute values. An attribute value in a rule is *irrelevant* if it can be removed from the rule without decreasing its expected classification accuracy, as computed from D_i. The resulting rules are called *maximally general rules* (or *minimal rules*) because each rule has the minimum number of conditions required to preserve the classification accuracy of the rule.

More technically, if r_i and r_j are valid rules where $cond(r_i) = cond(r_j)$ and $dec(r_i) = dec(r_j)$, then r_i and r_j are *logically equivalent rules*, where *cond* and *dec* give the values of the condition and decision attributes, respectively. If r_i and r_j are valid rules where $cond(r_i) \subset cond(r_j)$ and $dec(r_i) = dec(r_j)$, then r_j is *logically included* in r_i. If r_i and r_j are valid rules where $cond(r_i) \subseteq cond(r_j)$ and $dec(r_i) \neq dec(r_j)$, then r_i and r_j are *decision inconsistent*.

To obtain a set of maximally general rules R', each rule $r \in R$ is considered for dropping conditions. The algorithm initializes R' to empty and copies one rule $r_i \in R$ to rule r. One by one, each condition is dropped from rule r to create a new rule, and then this rule is checked for decision consistency with every other rule $r_j \in R$. If rule r is inconsistent, then the dropped condition is restored. After all conditions have been examined, the resulting rule r is a maximally generalized rule. Before rule r is added to R', it is checked for redundancy. After all rules have been processed, R' contains a set of maximally general rules that are as general as possible but retain the same classification accuracy as R.

A specific rule $r \in R$ may correspond to more than one maximally general rule. The maximally general rule derived depends on the order in which the attributes are processed. Thus, the maximally general rule obtained may not be best with respect to the conciseness or the coverage of the rule. Rather than evaluate all $2^m - 1$ possible subsets of conditions for a rule with m conditions, we use a heuristic solution based on significance values assigned by an evaluation function to every condition, before starting the process of dropping conditions. The significance value for a condition represents the relevance of the condition for the particular class. Higher significance values indicate greater relevance. In *post-pruning* (Quinlan 1993), conditions with *lower* significance values are dropped *first*. One evaluation function for a condition c_i of a rule is: $SIG(c_i) = P(c_i)(P(D|c_i) - P(D))$, where $P(c_i)$ is the probability of occurrence of the condition c_i; $P(D|c_i)$ is the conditional probability of the occurrence of the concept D conditioned on the occurrence of the condition c_i; $P(D)$ is the proportion of the concept D in the database (Ziarko and Shan 1995).

An alternative evaluation function, introduced here, is: $SIG'(c_i) = P(cond - \{c_i\})(P(D|cond - \{c_i\}) - P(D))$. Conditions with *higher* significance values are tested for dropping *first*. If a condition is dropped, the significance values of the remaining conditions are updated.

Algorithm GENRULES: Computes a set of maximally generalized rules.
Input: A set R of specific decision rules
Output: A set R' of maximally general rules

$R' \leftarrow \emptyset$
$n \leftarrow |R|$ /* n is the number of rules in R */
for $i = 0$ **to** $n - 1$ **do**
    $r \leftarrow r_i$
    $m \leftarrow |r|$ /* m is the number of attributes in rule r */
    Compute the significance value SIG' for each condition of rule r
    Sort the set of conditions of rule r based on the significance values
    for $j = 0$ **to** $m - 1$ **do**
        Remove the jth condition attribute C_j in rule r
        if r inconsistent with any rule in $R - r_i$ **then**
            Restore the dropped condition C_j to rule r
        endif
    endfor
    Remove any rule $r' \in R'$ that is logically included in rule r
    if rule r is not logically equivalent to or included in any rule $r' \in R'$ **then**
        $R' \leftarrow R' \bigcup r$
    endif
endfor

Suppose there are n decision rules (i.e., n rows) with m attributes in the set of rules R. The computation of the significance value, SIG', for one rule requires $O(mn)$ and the process of dropping conditions of one rule requires $O(mn)$. Thus, finding a maximally general rule for one decision rule requires $O(mn)$ time and finding maximally general rules for n decision rules requires $O(mn^2)$ time. Eliminating redundant rules is $O(n^2)$. The time complexity of our algorithm is $O(mn^2 + n^2) = O(mn^2)$.

4 Decision Making

Given a set of objects described by several attributes, the decision making problem consists of assigning to each object an appropriate decision value, i.e., classifying each object to an appropriate concept. This classification problem has been studied extensively and the approach described in the previous section is but one of many induction techniques suggested for creating decision rules. The general question of *how to use such decision rules* in the process of decision support has received less attention. A simple approach is adopted by many systems. Given an input object, a rule whose conditions are satisfied by this object, is selected. Typically, the first such rule is selected, although some approaches examine the support of the relevant rules, and choose the best supported rule. These systems use a single rule to suggest a decision and tend to minimize the number of rules used. In general, these approaches ignore the fact that the rules produced from data are inherently uncertain and the associated decision probabilities (if computed at all) are only crude estimates, rather weakly supported by available data.

On the other hand, the approach implemented in GRG and described below treats each rule as a piece of uncertain evidence, which by itself is of little value with respect to decision making, but which jointly with other rules can provide valuable input to the decision process. GRG uses as much evidence as possible in its decision making and tends to maximize the number of rules used. Such evidence can be combined in many ways, and our method is but one possibility.

We first define the criterion $Q(r)$ for rule quality. Let $[D = 1]$ denote the set of rows where the value of the decision attribute is 1, and let $[r]$ denote the set of rows where the values of the condition attributes are consistent with the condition part of rule r. $Q(r)$ is based on estimates of the following conditional probabilities:

(1) $P(r_C|D = 1)$, the probability that the values of the condition attributes for an input object are consistent with the condition part of rule r, if the value of the decision attribute is 1;
(2) $P(D = 1|r_C)$, the probability that the value of the decision attribute D is 1 for an input object, if the values of the condition attributes for the input object are consistent with the condition part of rule r;
(3) $P(r_C|D = 0)$, defined analogously.
(4) $P(D = 0|r_C)$, defined analogously.

Intuitively, if the random events r_C and $(D = 1)$ are related, then measures (1) and (2) should yield high values and measures (3) and (4) should yield low values. Based on this intuition, the quality criterion is defined as:

$$Q(r) = (P(r|D = 1) + P(D = 1|r) - P(r|D = 0) - P(D = 0|r))/2$$

Clearly, $-1 \leq Q(r) \leq 1$. $Q(r)$ can be seen as a measure of the bias of the set $[r]$ towards the set $[D = 1]$. This measure has two extremes: (1) $Q(r) = 1$ if $[r] = [D = 1]$, and (2) $Q(r) = -1$ if $[r] = [D = 0]$.

During rule generation, a collection of d rule sets corresponding to d possible decisions is created. Each set is used in turn as the current set, L_k ($k = 1, 2, \ldots, d$). To handle objects which do not match any rule, we add a default rule, which predicts the concept that appears most frequently in the database. Let X denote the input vector of condition attribute values, and let $L_k(X) \subseteq L_k$ be a subset of the current set L_k consisting of those rules whose conditions are satisfied by values of the input vector X. To select one of m possible decisions for X, a promising approach is to compute a decision score $S_k(X)$, for every $k = 1, 2, \ldots, d$, as follows:

$$S_k(X) = \sum_{r \in L_k(X)} Q_k(r).$$

This approach sums the rule quality measures $Q_k(r)$ computed for each rule. Then, the decision with the highest score is selected.

As given, this approach is sensitive to the number of rules in each set L_k ($k = 1, 2, \ldots, d$). To eliminate this sensitivity, we use the normalized decision score, defined as:

$$NS_k(X) = \begin{cases} -\frac{S_k(X)}{N_k} & \text{if } S_k(X) \leq 0 \\[2mm] \frac{S_k(X)}{M_k} & \text{if } S_k(X) > 0 \end{cases}$$

where

$$M_k = \sum_{r \in L_k^+} Q_k(r) \quad \text{and} \quad N_k = \sum_{r \in L_k^-} Q_k(r)$$

and

$$L_k^+ = \{r \in L_k : Q_k(r) > 0\},$$
$$L_k^- = \{r \in L_k : Q_k(r) \leq 0\}.$$

With the normalized definition we have $-1 \leq NS_k(X) \leq 1$.

During decision making, the decision with the normalized decision score closest to 1 is selected. That is, in extreme cases:

$NS_k(X) = 1$ indicates a strong "yes" for the decision k;

$NS_k(X) = -1$ indicates a strong "no" for the decision k; and

$NS_k(X) = 0$ indicates insufficient evidence for decision k.

5 Experimental Results

To evaluate the machine learning subsystem of GRG, we measured the prediction accuracy of the learned rules on test examples. We also compared this accuracy to that for C4.5RULE, the "rule" portion of the output generated by C4.5 run with default settings (Quinlan 1993). We chose 20 databases from the UC Irvine repository. Each database is stored and processed as a single relation table.

For our experiments, we used leave-one-out cross validation for each method on each database. Given a data set containing n objects, *leave-one-out testing* removes one object, generates rules using the remaining $n-1$ objects as a training sample, and tests these rules using the removed object as a test object. This procedure is repeated n times, using each object in turn. The prediction accuracy is calculated as the number of correctly classified objects divided by n. Leave-one-out testing is computationally expensive, but it gives a more reliable estimate of prediction accuracy than other approaches. Given the same algorithm and data set, leave-one-out testing always reports the same prediction accuracy. On the other hand, the more commonly used *ten-fold testing* strategy randomly partitions the data set into ten subsets and uses each in turn as a training sample. When applied repeatedly to the same algorithm, this method yields varying results because different random subsets are chosen.

Table 1 shows the results from the experiments described above; details are given by Shan et al. (1997). In each case, the better result is shown in bold face. For each database and algorithm, we report the prediction accuracy as determined by leave-one-out testing. On some databases, the behavior of the

Data Set	Size	#classes	GRG	C4.5
append	106	2	**93.40**	84.91
australian	690	2	82.03	**82.75**
balance-scale	625	3	**79.36**	77.28
breast-cancer(wisconsin)	699	2	**96.28**	96.00
credit-screening	690	2	**84.93**	84.49
german	1000	2	72.30	**72.50**
glass	214	7	**92.06**	71.50
heart	270	2	**77.04**	74.44
housing	506	2	**85.38**	83.20
ionosphere	351	2	93.16	**94.87**
iris	150	3	**96.00**	95.33
lenses	24	3	79.17	**83.33**
lung-cancer	32	3	**59.38**	50.00
pima	768	2	69.53	**74.87**
segment	2310	7	95.76	**96.10**
shuttle	15	2	**66.67**	40.00
soybean-small	47	4	95.74	**97.87**
tictac	958	2	98.75	**99.48**
wine	178	3	**97.19**	92.70
zoo	101	7	**94.06**	93.06

Table 1. Experimental Results

GRG system and C4.5RULE is similar. On 4 out of 20 databases, the GRG system has a considerably higher prediction accuracy than C4.5RULE. Overall, the prediction accuracy is higher for GRG than for C4.5RULE.

6 Conclusions

We have described the techniques used to create and use decision rules in the GRG knowledge discovery system. Experiments show that, when tested on 20 databases, GRG has generally higher prediction accuracy than C4.5RULE. We do not conclude that GRG is better for all applications than C4.5RULE. Different systems will be suitable for different real-world domains. With the growth of applications of knowledge discovery from databases, a variety of approaches are needed, and the techniques presented here provide a useful addition.

In future work, we will study a variety of measurements for attribute selection. Rule generation may be improved by allowing the generation of more general rules. As well, better results may be obtained by relaxing the current requirement that a general rule have the same classification accuracy as a specific rule. Finally, using partial matching instead of full matching might improve the prediction accuracy.

We have presented an initial description of the theoretical properties and empirical performance of the GRG system considered as a machine learning system. Further investigation is warranted to identify situations in which the system should perform well and appropriate settings for parameter values. Additional experiments on large data sets are required to determine how well the GRG system scales up.

References

Cai, Y., Cercone, N., Han, J.: "Attribute-Oriented Induction in Relational Databases," in Piatetsky-Shapiro, G. and Frawley, W.J. (eds.), *Knowledge Discovery in Databases*, AAAI/MIT Press (1991) 213–228

Carter, C.L., Hamilton, H.J.: "Efficient Algorithms for Attribute-Oriented Induction," *IEEE Trans. on Knowledge and Data Engineering* (1997) in press

Clark, P., Niblett, T.: "The CN2 Induction Algorithm," *Machine Learning* **3** (1989) 261–283

Domingos, P.: "Rule Induction and Instance-Based Learning: A Unified Approach," *Proc. IJCAI-95* (1995) 1226–1232

Fayyad, U.M., Piatetsky-Shapiro, G., Smyth, P., Uthurusamy, R. (eds.): *Advances in Knowledge Discovery and Data Mining*, AAAI/MIT Press (1996)

Fayyad, U., Piatetsky-Shapiro, G., Smyth, P.: "The KDD Process for Extracting Useful Knowledge from Volumes of Data," *CACM* **39**(11) (1996) 27–34

Michalski, R.S.: "A Theory and Methodology of Inductive Learning," in Michalski, R.S., Carbonell, J.G., and Mitchell, T.M., *Machine Learning: An Artificial Intelligence Approach*, Vol. 1 (1983) 83–134

Pawlak, Z.: *Rough Sets: Theoretical Aspects of Reasoning About Data*, Kluwer Academic (1991)

Piatetsky-Shapiro, G., Frawley, W.J., Matheus, C.J.: "Knowledge Discovery in Databases: An Overview," in Piatetsky-Shapiro, G. and Frawley, W.J. (eds.), *Knowledge Discovery in Databases*, AAAI/MIT Press (1991) 1–27

Quinlan, J.R.: *C4.5: Programs for Machine Learning*, Morgan Kaufmann, San Mateo, CA (1983)

Quinlan, J.R.: "Induction of Decision Tress," *Machine Learning* **1** (1986) 81–106

Shan, N., Ziarko, W., Hamilton, H.J., Cercone, N.: "Using Rough Sets as Tools for Knowledge Discovery", in *Proceedings of the 1st International Conference on Knowledge Discovery & Data Mining (KDD-95)*, Montreal, Canada, August (1995) 263–268

Shan, N., Hamilton, H.J., Cercone, N.: "GRG: Knowledge Discovery Using Information Generalization, Information Reduction, and Rule Generation", *International Journal on Artificial Intelligence Tools*, **5**(1 & 2) (1996) 99–112

Shan, N., Hamilton, H.J., Cercone, N.: "Inducing and Using Decision Rules in the GRG Knowledge Discovery System: Extended Report," Technical Report, Department of Computer Science, University of Regina, Regina, Canada (1997)

Ziarko, W.: *Rough Sets, Fuzzy Sets and Knowledge Discovery*, Springer-Verlag (1994)

Ziarko, W., Shan, N.: "Knowledge Discovery as a Search for Classification," in *Proc. of 23rd Annual Computer Science Conference Workshop on Rough Sets and Database Mining (CSC'95)* (1995)

Learning and Exploitation Do Not Conflict Under Minimax Optimality*

Csaba Szepesvári

Research Group on Artificial Intelligence, "József Attila" University, Szeged, Aradi vrt. tere 1, Hungary, H-6720

Abstract. We show that adaptive real time dynamic programming extended with the action selection strategy which chooses the best action according to the latest estimate of the cost function yields asymptotically optimal policies within finite time under the minimax optimality criterion. From this it follows that learning and exploitation do not conflict under this special optimality criterion. We relate this result to learning optimal strategies in repeated two-player zero-sum deterministic games.

Keywords. *reinforcement learning, self-optimizing systems, dynamic games*

1 Introduction

Reinforcement learning (RL) concerns practical problems related to learning of optimal behaviour in sequential decision tasks. The most popular theoretical framework adopted by RL researchers is that of Markovian Decision Problems (MDPs). One of the main questions in RL is what extent of exploration is needed for a learner so that the price of exploration does not become too demanding. Usually some exploration (e.g. the execution of explorative actions that seem sub-optimal for the learner) is needed otherwise the learner may not gather some relevant information and this may eventually prevent convergence to optimality, i.e., the need for exploration and exploitation conflict.

In this paper we show that it is possible to obtain asymptotically optimal behaviour for MDPs *under the minimax discounted total cost criterion* with an algorithm that uses an *asynchronous, on-line* dynamic programming (DP)[1] iteration while executing *actions that seem optimal according to the actual state of the learner's knowledge*. Minimax sequential decision problems arise for example in repeated (or dynamic) games which are of great popularity in the machine learning community. Asynchronous on-line DP is a variant of value iteration which is advantageous when the state and action sets are so large that it is impractical to run a DP algorithm off-line, or when one is satisfied with obtaining an asymptotically optimal behaviour on some "relevant" part of the state space.

---

* This research was supported by OTKA Grant No. F20132. I would like to thank András Krámli for numerous helpful discussions which helped me to clarify the presentation of this paper substantially.

The paper is organized as follows: In Section 2 we provide the necessary background. In Section 3 we present important preliminary results concerning self-optimizing policies, the convergence of real-time DP and the main theorem. In Section 4 we discuss the results, and relate them to the context of learning to play repeated, two-player, zero-sum deterministic games. Due to space limits we can not present the proofs. The complete proofs and also the proofs of the unattributed statements can be found in [11, 10].

2 Background

We use the terminology of optimal sequential decisions. A 5-tuple $P = (X, A, \mathcal{A}, p, c)$ is called a finite Markovian Decision Process (homogeneous controlled Markov chain in the control terminology) if

1. both X and A are finite sets called the *state* space and the *action* space of the model, respectively
2. $\mathcal{A}$ maps the states into the power-set of A ($\mathcal{A} : X \to 2^A$). Elements of the set $\mathcal{A}(x) \subseteq A$ are called the *addmissible actions* for state x – for convenience we introduce the set $U = \{ (x, a) \in X \times A \mid a \in \mathcal{A}(x) \}$
3. $p : U \times X \to [0, 1]$ is the transition probability function which satisfies $\sum_{y \in X} p(x, a, y) = 1$ for all $(x, a) \in U^2$ and
4. $c : U \times X \to \mathbb{R}$ is the immediate cost function

At every stage of the decision process the decision maker observes one of the states of X (called the state of the decision maker) and is allowed to choose an action from $\mathcal{A}(x)$, which is then applied as an input to the system. As a result, if the state of the decision maker was $x \in X$ and action a was chosen then the next state of the decision maker becomes $y \in X$ with probability $p(x, a, y)$. Further, the application of action a in state x incurs an immediate cost $c(x, a, y)$.

The behaviour of the decision maker should be non-anticipating, i.e., it is assumed that it can be described by a (deterministic) policy $\pi = (\pi_0, \pi_1, \ldots, \pi_t, \ldots)$, where $\pi_t : (X \times A)^t \times X \to A$ determine the action to be taken at the tth time as a function of the history of the process $((x_0, a_0), (x_1, a_1), \ldots, (x_{t-1}, a_{t-1}))$ and the current state x_t. A policy is called Markovian if the actions taken by the policy depend only on the current state. A policy is stationary if it is Markovian and $\pi_t = \pi_0$ for all t.

Due to the stochastic nature of the decision problem P a policy π together with a starting state x_0 results in a stochastic process (Markovian, if the policy is Markovian) of form $\xi_t^\pi(x_0) = (x_t, a_t)$. The measure generated by $\xi_t^\pi(x_0)$ over the space of possible trajectories $U^{\mathbb{N}}$ is denoted by $\mu_\pi(x_0)$ [3].

For any trajectory of the decision process $\tau = (\tau_1, \tau_2, \ldots, \tau_t, \ldots)$, $\tau_t \in U$, let $X_{\text{i.o.}}(\tau)$ denote the states that are visited infinitely many times by the trajectory:

$$X_{\text{i.o.}}(\tau) = \{ x \in X \mid \tau_t = (x, a_t) \text{ infinitely often } \}.$$

---

2   We identify the set $U \times X$ with the set $\{ (x, a, y) \in X \times A \times X \mid (x, a) \in U, y \in X \}$.

Similarly, for all $x \in X_{\text{i.o.}}(\tau)$ let us define $A_{\text{i.o.}}{}^{\tau}(x) \subseteq A(x)$ as the set of actions that are chosen infinitely many times during the trajectory τ:

$$A_{\text{i.o.}}{}^{\tau}(x) = \{ a \in A \mid \tau_t = (x_t, a) \text{ infinitely often } \}.$$

The total cost incurred by the decision maker can be defined as follows: For any trajectory $\tau = ((x_0, a_0), (x_1, a_1), \ldots, (x_t, a_t), \ldots)$ of the process the immediate costs incurred during the process define the stochastic variable $C_{\pi}^{\tau}(x_0) = \sum_{t=0}^{\infty} \gamma^t c(x_t, a_t, x_{t+1})$, where $0 < \gamma < 1$ is a fixed discount factor. $C_{\pi}^{\tau}(x_0)$ is called the total discounted cost along trajectory τ. Since the variable $C_{\pi}^{\tau}(x_0)$ is random it does not determine an ordering of the policies – "decision functions", which map random variables to values must be used if one would like to arrive at an ordering [4]. One possibility is to use the ess sup operator when the cost of a policy π for a given starting state x_0 is determined as the worst probable value of $C_{\pi}^{\tau}(x_0)$:

$$v_{\pi}(x_0) = \sup_{\tau \in \text{support}(\mu_{\pi}(x_0))} C_{\pi}^{\tau}(x_0).$$

This gives rise to the minimax criterion, since the optimal cost funcion defined by $v_P^*(x) = \inf_{\pi} v_{\pi}(x)$ can now be written as

$$v_P^*(x) = \inf_{\pi} \sup_{\tau \in \text{support}(\mu_{\pi}(x_0))} C_{\pi}^{\tau}(x).$$

The optimal cost function can be shown to satisfy the Bellman Optimality Equation (BOE) [4, 11]:

$$v_P^*(x) = \min_{a \in A(x)} \max_{(y \in X, p(x,a,y) > 0)} \left(c(x, a, y) + \gamma v_P^*(y) \right), \qquad x \in X. \qquad (1)$$

Since this criterion does not depend on the exact numerical values of the transition probabilities we introduce the sets

$$T(x, a) = \{ y \in X \mid p(x, a, y) > 0 \}, \quad (x, a) \in U$$

and for convenience we will call the 5-tuple $P = (X, A, \mathcal{A}, T, c)$ a Markovian Decision Process (MDP), too. *In the following a MDP will be understood with the minimax criterion.*

Once the optimal cost function is identified, the optimal policies of the decision maker are easy to determine: the possible optimal choices for state x are given as the elements of the set $A^P(x, v_P^*)$, where

$$A^P(x, v) = \text{Argmin}_{a \in A(x)} \max_{y \in T(x,a)} \left(c(x, a, y) + \gamma v(y) \right), \qquad v \in B(X).$$

Elements of $A^P(x, v)$ are called greedy w.r.t. v in state x.

Let $B(X)$ denote the set of real-valued bounded functions over the set X and let the operator $G : B(X) \to B(X)$ be defined by

$$(Gf)(x) = \min_{a \in A(x)} \max_{y \in T(x,a)} \left(c(x, a, y) + \gamma f(y) \right), \qquad x \in X.$$

Using G, Equation (1) takes the shorter form $Gv_P^* = v_P^*$, i.e., v_P^* is the fixed point of G. It is easy to prove that G is a contraction with index γ w.r.t. the supremum norm $\|\cdot\|_\infty$, and therefore it has only one fixed point and the sequence $v_{t+1} = Gv_t$, where $v_0 \in B(X)$ is arbitrary, converges to v_P^*. This iteration is called the (synchronous) dynamic programming (SDP) iteration. If it is important to indicate the problem underlying the greedy operator G (often also called the value operator) then this will be denoted by a subscript, such as G_P. If we do not use the subscript, this means that the greedy operator that corresponds to P (the true model of the system under control) is considered.

In this article we consider the adaptive algorithm given in Table 1. The algorithm consists of 3 main parts: a model building part (Step 2), a cost-function estimation part (Step 3 and 4), and the action selection procedure (Step 5). *The algorithm always chooses the greedy action w.r.t. the latest estimate of the cost function.* We will prove that despite this non-explorative choice of actions, the actions generated by this algorithm become optimal in finite time for almost all trajectories, i.e., this algorithm is *eventually optimal.*[3] It is an open question if the expected number of steps until optimality, $E[T]$, is bounded or not. The pointwise contraction property of the greedy operator may provide a starting point to prove the boundedness of $E[T]$.

3 Results

The adaptive algorithm is greatly simplified if one uses the initialization $T_0(x, a) = T(x, a)$ and $c_0(x, a) = c(x, a)$, $(x, a) \in U$ in Step 0 of Algorithm 1 (which means that the decision model is known to the learner). The corresponding algorithm is called the Myopic Real-Time Dynamic Programming (MRTDP) algorithm. Of course, there is no need for Step 2 in this case, since $T_t = T$ and $c_t = c$ for each t. The proof of the convergence of the adaptive version is reduced to the convergence of the non-adaptive version.

Theorem 1 MARTDP Convergence Theorem. *Let $P = (X, A, \mathcal{A}, T, c)$ be an arbitrary MDP where $c \geq 0$. Let $v_0 = 0$ and assume that $c_0 \leq c$ (e.g., $c_0 = 0$). Assume that $\{x_t\} \subseteq F_t$ for all $t = 1, 2, 3, \ldots$. Then for almost all trajectory τ with starting state x_0, v_t converges to v_P^* on the set of states visited infinitely often by τ:*

$$v_P^*|_{X_{i.o.}(\tau)} = \lim_{t \to \infty} v_t|_{X_{i.o.}(\tau)},$$

Further, for these trajectories the algorithm results in an optimal strategy in finite time, i.e., there exists a (random) time T such that if $t > T$ then $a_t \in A^P(x_t, v_P^*)$.

The proof is carried out in several steps. First one proves the theorem in the special case when the immediate costs are known in advance. The idea of this proof is that for any pair $(x, a) \in U$ the set $T_t(x, a)$ monotonically increases in time and since U is finite there exists a time T_0 such that if $t > T_0$ then

---

[3] Note that the time after which the actions generated by the algorithm are optimal depend on the actual trajectory, i.e., it is a stopping time.

0. Let $T_0(x,a) \subseteq T(x,a), c_0(x,a,y) \leq c(x,a,y)$ and $v_0 \leq v_P^*, v_0 \in B(X)$.
repeat forever{
1. Observe the current state x_t and the reinforcement signal c_t.
2. Modify the model $P_t = (X, A, \mathcal{A}, T_t, c_t)$:

$$T_{t+1}(x,a) = \begin{cases} T_t(x,a) \cup \{x_t\}, & \text{if } (x,a) = (x_{t-1}, a_{t-1}); \\ T_t(x,a), & \text{otherwise,} \end{cases}$$

$$c_{t+1}(x,a,y) = \begin{cases} \max(c_t, c_t(x,a,y)), & \text{if } (x,a,y) = (x_{t-1}, a_{t-1}, x_t); \\ c_t(x,a,y), & \text{otherwise.} \end{cases}$$

3. Select the set of states $F_t \subseteq X$ whose estimated cost is to be refreshed.
4. Refresh the cost function estimates:

$$v_{t+1}(x) = \begin{cases} v_t(x), & \text{if } x \notin F_t; \\ (G_{P_{t+1}} v_t)(x), & \text{if } x \in F_t; \end{cases}$$

where $G_{P_{t+1}}$ is the actual estimate of the greedy operator G based on P_{t+1}.
5. Action selection: $a_t \in A^{P_{t+1}}(x_t, v_{t+1})$.
6. Execute the action.
7. $t := t + 1$.
}

Table 1. Myopic Adaptive Real-time Dynamic Programming (MARTDP).

In Step 4 the update of a state x, for which there is no non-empty $T_t(x,a)$, should be understood as the identity operation.

$T_t(x,a) = T_{t+1}(x,a) = T_\infty(x,a)$. It is also clear that $T_\infty(x,a) \subseteq T(x,a)$. If $t > T_0$ then Algorithm 1 thus acts like a myopic RTDP algorithm corresponding to the problem $P_\infty = (X, A, \mathcal{A}, T_\infty, c)$.

The convergence of MRTDP can be shown in the following way: For almost all trajectories of the process τ, v_t can be shown to converge to some function $v = v_\tau \in B(X)$ which satisfies the BOE of P on $X_{\text{i.o.}} = X_{\text{i.o.}}(\tau)$:

$$v(x) = \min_{a \in \mathcal{A}(x)} \max_{y \in T(x,a)} (c(x,a,y) + \gamma v(y)), \quad x \in X_{\text{i.o.}} \tag{2}$$

and if $x \in X_{\text{i.o.}}(\tau)$ then $A_{\text{i.o.}}{}^\tau(x) \subseteq A^P(x,v)$. From these it follows that $v|_{X_{\text{i.o.}}(\tau)} = v_P^*|_{X_{\text{i.o.}}(\tau)}$ and by the following Lemma the eventual optimality of the MRTDP algorithm.

Lemma 2. *Let $P = (X, A, \mathcal{A}, T, c)$ be an arbitrary MDP and π a policy. Let $x_0 \in X$ be fixed. The following statements are equivalent:*

(i) π is eventually optimal, i.e., for almost all trajectory τ generated by π and x_0 there exist a time T such that if $t > T$ then $a(\tau, t)$ is optimal.

(ii) For almost all trajectory τ the optimal cost function of P satisfies

$$v_P^*(x) = \min_{a \in A_{\text{i.o.}}{}^\tau(x)} \max_{y \in T(x,a)} (c(x,a,y) + \gamma v_P^*(y)), \quad x \in X_{\text{i.o.}}(\tau). \tag{3}$$

If the costs are not known in advance then we have a sequence of cost functions, c_t, which is monotonically increasing and (since they are bounded by c) converges to some function c_∞. The rest of the proof follows almost the same lines as the proof when the costs are known in advance. The complete proof can be found in [10].

Note that in order to prove the convergence of the adaptive version we had to prove the convergence of the non-adaptive version. We could not find any simple way to extend the convergence proof of the RTDP theorem by Barto et al. [1] or that of the LRTA* algorithm by Korf [5] to our case. The main differences are that Barto et al. assume that $F_t = \{x_t\}$ in each step which makes it possible to reduce the convergence of the RTDP algorithm to that of the asynchronous dynamic programming in a direct way and that Korf assumed deterministic transitions which enables a non-probabilistic approach simplifying the proof greatly.

4   Consequences for repeated two-player zero-sum deterministic games

We show that repeated two-player zero-sum deterministic games can be viewed as minimax control problems. In such a game one or the other player chooses an action in each state with one player striving to minimize the total cost and the other trying to maximize it. A great deal of RL research has been directed to solving games of this kind [13, 14, 7, 2, 12, 6]. It is possible to define a set of Bellman equations for the optimal minimax value of such a game,

$$V^*(x) = \begin{cases} \min_{a \in A} (C(x,a) + \gamma V^*(t(x,a))), & \text{if minimizer moves in } x \\ \max_{a \in A} (C(x,a) + \gamma V^*(t(x,a))), & \text{if maximizer moves in } x, \end{cases}$$

where $C(x,a)$ is the cost incurred by the minimizing player (and is the reward of the maximizing player since the game is zero sum in each step) and $t(x,a)$ is the next state when action a is executed from x [8]. Without loosing generality one may assume that the two players move one another in each step, i.e., the move of player I is always followed by the move of player II, and vice versa. Now, it is easy to see that the restriction of V^* to those states in which the minimizer moves satisfies the equality $V^*(x) = \min_{a \in A} \max_{y \in T(x,a)}(c(x,a,y) + \gamma^2 V^*(y))$, where $T(x,a) = \{t(t(x,a),b) \mid b \in A\}$ and $c(x,a,y) = C(x,a) + \gamma \max_{b:t(t(x,a),b)=y} C(t(x,a),b)$. This shows that from the point of view of the minimizer the game is of minimax nature.

If the rules of the game are known to the minimizer, i.e., she has access to c and T, then it follows from our results that her policy will become eventually optimal if she plays according to the MRTDP algorithm. It is interesting to note that if the minimizer plays with a maximizer who uses a fixed (although arbitrary) policy then she can do even better if he uses the adaptive version of the MRTDP algorithm. If the maximizer uses an eventually sub-optimal policy then it may happen that $T_\infty(x,a)$ as learned by the MARTDP algorithm will be a proper subset of $T(x,a)$. The optimal cost function associated with the MDP

$(X, A, \mathcal{A}, T_\infty, c)$ may be smaller then V^*, meaning that the adaptive strategy allows the minimizer to take advantage of the sub-optimality of the policy of the maximizer. However, if the maximizer eventually finds the optimal counter-policy then the "adaptive" minimizer may perform worse in terms of the total regret than the non-adaptive version. If both the minimizer and the maximizer use the MARTDP algorithm (the above proofs can be trivially extended to maximin models) then both player will eventually play the optimal policies. In other words, if an agent trained by MARTDP plays against herself then she is guaranteed to find the optimal policy eventually. We have compared the learning curves of ARTDP algorithms with different action selection strategies on the game 'Tic-Tac-Toe'. The results (to be presented elsewhere) show that the myopic strategies (i.e., the MARTDP algorithm) yields the fastest convergence.

It is important to note that our result about the MARTDP algorithm does *not* extend to the case of stochastic games with the *expected* total discounted cost criterion. The reason of this can be understood by considering the following simple case: assume that the state space has only one element and we have two actions, a and b. Let the cost of the actions be random with finite expected values $Q^*(b) < Q^*(a)$ (this problem can also be given in terms of deterministic costs and stochastic transitions over an augmented state space). The problem is the action with the minimal cost. The MARTDP procedure (with the greedy action selection strategy) will choose the action with the smallest estimated cost, i.e., it chooses a if $Q_t(a) < Q_t(b)$. If $Q_0(b) > Q_t(a)$ for all t then the algorithm will fail to find the optimal action, b. This situation may happen with *positive probability* if $Q_0(b) > Q^*(b)$. One may notice that the conditions of Theorem 1 outrule this possibility. Now, if $Q_0 \leq Q^*$ for both a and b, then due to the non-zero variance of the random cost it may still happen with positive probability that $Q_t(b) > Q^*(b) > Q_t(a)$ for some t, and thus we find again that the MARTDP algorithm fails with positive probability. Another problem arises when just part of the state space (in fact state-action space) is visited infinitely often. For expected value models improperly estimated values of finitely visited states may result in improper estimation of infinitly often visited states.

If the stochasticity in the effect of actions is caused by noise then the minimax optimality criterion will tend to find overly "pessimistic" policies which may be undesirable. One may weaken this effect by introducing a positive threshold θ and letting $T(x, a) = \{y \in X \mid P(x, a, y) > \theta\}$. In the adaptive case this calls for the identification of the transition probabilities. Because of the stochasticity of the identification process the inclusions $T_t(x, a) \subseteq T(x, a)$ need no longer holds. This may prevent convergence to the optimal policy. To overcome this problem we propose to introduce state, action and time dependent thresholds, $\theta_t(x, a)$ which should converges to θ from above slowly. We conjecture that by either using the law of iterated logarithm or a two-stage estimation procedure as in [9] asymptotic convergence to an optimal policy can be retained.

References

1. A.G. Barto, S.J. Bradtke, and S.P. Singh. Learning to act using real-time dynamic programming. *Artificial Intelligence*, 72:91–138, 1995. Technical Report 91-57, Computer Science Department, University of Massachusetts, Vol. 59., 1991.
2. Justin A. Boyan. *Modular Neural Networks for Learning Context-Dependent Game Strategies*. Master's thesis, Department of Engineering and Computer Laboratory, University of Cambridge, Cambridge, UK, August 1992.
3. E.B. Dynkin and A.A. Yushkevich. *Controlled Markov Processes*. Springer-Verlag, Berlin, 1979.
4. M. Heger. *Risk-sensitive decision making*. PhD thesis, Zentrum für Kognitionwissenschaften, Universität Bremen, FB3 Informatik, Postfach 330 440, 28334 Bremen, Germany, 1996.
5. R.E. Korf. Real-time heuristic search. *Artificial Intelligence*, 42:189–211, 1990.
6. M.L. Littman and Cs. Szepesvári. A Generalized Reinforcement Learning Model: convergence and applications. In *Int. Conf. on Machine Learning*, 1996. http://iserv.iki.kfki.hu/asl-publs.html.
7. Nicol N. Schraudolph, Peter Dayan, and Terrence J. Sejnowski. Using the TD(λ) algorithm to learn an evaluation function for the game of Go. In *Advances in Neural Information Processing Systems 6*, Morgan Kaufmann, San Mateo, CA, 1994.
8. L.S. Shapley. Stochastic games. *Proceedings of the National Academy of Sciences of the United States of America*, 39:1095–1100, 1953.
9. C. Stein. A two-sample test for a linear hypothesis whose power is independent of variance. *Ann. Math. Statist.*, 16, 1945.
10. Cs. Szepesvári. *Certainty equivalence policies are self-optimizing under minimax optimality*. Technical Report 96-101, Research Group on Artificial Intelligence, JATE-MTA, Szeged 6720, Aradi vrt tere 1., HUNGARY, August 1996. URL: http://www.inf.u-szeged.hu/~rgai.
11. Cs. Szepesvári. *Some basic facts concerning minimax sequential decision problems*. Technical Report 96-100, Research Group on Artificial Intelligence, JATE-MTA, Szeged 6720, Aradi vrt tere 1., HUNGARY, August 1996. URL: http://www.inf.u-szeged.hu/~rgai.
12. Cs. Szepesvári and M. Littman. Generalized Markov Decision Processes: Dynamic programming and reinforcement learning algorithms. *Operations Research*, 1996. in preparation.
13. Gerald Tesauro. Temporal difference learning and TD-Gammon. *Communications of the ACM*, 58–67, March 1995.
14. Sebastian Thrun. Learning to play the game of chess. In *Neural Information Processing Systems 7*, 1995.

Model Combination in the
Multiple-Data-Batches Scenario

Kai Ming Ting[1] and Boon Toh Low[2]

[1] Department of Computer Science,
University of Waikato, Hamilton, New Zealand.
E-mail: kaiming@cs.waikato.ac.nz
[2] Department of Systems Engineering and Engineering Management,
Chinese University of Hong Kong, Shatin, Hong Kong
E-mail: btlow@se.cuhk.edu.hk

Abstract. The approach of combining models learned from multiple batches of data provide an alternative to the common practice of learning one model from all the available data (i.e., the data combination approach). This paper empirically examines the base-line behaviour of the model combination approach in this multiple-data-batches scenario. We find that model combination can lead to better performance even if the disjoint batches of data are drawn randomly from a larger sample, and relate the relative performance of the two approaches to the learning curve of the classifier used.

The practical implication of our results is that one should consider using model combination rather than data combination, especially when multiple batches of data for the same task are readily available.

Another interesting result is that we empirically show that the near-asymptotic performance of a single model, in some classification task, can be significantly improved by combining multiple models (derived from the same algorithm) if the constituent models are substantially different and there is some regularity in the models to be exploited by the combination method used. Comparisons with known theoretical results are also provided.

Keywords: model combination, data combination, empirical evaluation, learning curve, near-asymptotic performance.

1 Introduction

When different batches of data for the same task are available, the usual approach is to combine all available data and produce one classifier. This is an intuitive approach that stems from the conventional wisdom: "more data the better". Here we investigate an approach which differs from the way data is utilised. It learns one classifier for each batch of data (using the same learning algorithm) and then combines the classifiers' predictions. We call the former *"data combination"* and the latter *"model combination"*. Figure 1 shows these two types of combination at the data and model levels.

While there has been a considerable amount of research on methods to combine multiple models reported in the literature (e.g., Brodley, 1993; Breiman,

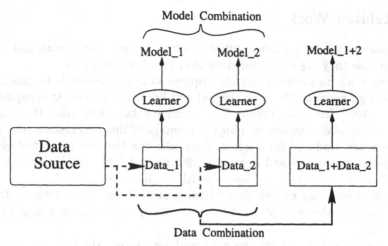

Fig. 1. Combination at different levels – data or model.

1996a,1996b; Freund & Schapire, 1996; Perrone & Cooper, 1993; Krogh & Vedelsby, 1995), investigation into combining models from a single learning algorithm induced using *completely disjoint sets of data* has been limited. Most work shows that combining multiple models induced from either one type or different types of learning algorithm using *a single dataset* performs better than a single model induced from the same dataset.

This paper concentrates on a situation where multiple batches of data are available for a single classification task. The scenario might be collections of data in consecutive years or in different events from the same source. We attempt to determine the conditions under which model combination performs better than data combination in this scenario. Thus, our focus here is not on different types of model combination method. Specifically, we address the question: is model combination a viable option as compared to data combination in classification tasks? If the answer is yes, when should one use it?

The intuition is that different batches of data provide some variation of data representation in the description space. Theories induced separately from these independent batches become "specialists" in different parts of the space. Model combination allows cooperation between these specialists. Data combination destroys the data variation, and forms a global representation.

Some research on multiple model combination focus on varying the *induction bias* of the learning algorithm(s) to generate models of uncorrelated errors. These include varying learning parameters of a single learning algorithm and using different types of learning algorithm. Others use sampling methods to create *multiple overlapping data subsets* from a given dataset. Here we show that *data variation in different data batches*, even if the disjoint batches are drawn randomly from a larger sample, can also produce substantially different models from a single learning algorithm. We review related work on using multiple models to enhance performance in the next section. The experimental design based on a hypothesis is described in Section 3. The results of the experiments are reported in Section 4 and followed by discussion and conclusions.

2 Related Work

We focus our review on how multiple models are generated, with just a minor note on how they are combined since that is not our emphasis.

Some work on multiple models employs sampling methods to generate the models, e.g., bagging (Breiman, 1996a) and boosting (Freund & Schapire, 1996; Quinlan, 1996; Breiman, 1996b). Each sample dataset has either the same data size as the available dataset or a high percentage of the total instances. A set of n classifiers are produced from n sets of samples and they are combined by voting or weighted voting. Ali and Pazzani (1996) use a k-fold partitioning to generate k models by training on all but the ith partition k times. Breiman (1996c) investigates boosting models derived using small bites of the entire dataset. In this formalism, the multiple models are usually produced from a single learning algorithm.

Multiple models can also be produced by varying the learning parameters of a single learning algorithm. Work in generating multiple neural networks (Hansen & Salamon, 1990; Perrone & Cooper, 1993) by using different initial random weight configurations or/and orders of training data; multiple decision trees (Kwok & Carter, 1990; Buntine, 1991; Oliver & Hand, 1995) by selecting different tests at each node, generating option trees, or pruning a tree in different ways; and multiple rules (Kononenko & Kovačič, 1992) by stochastic search guided by heuristics. These works re-order the rank of the classes by (weighted) averaging the outputs of multiple neural networks, or class probabilities of multiple trees, or by using Naive Bayesian combination of different rules.

Chan and Stolfo (1995; 1996) investigate various model combination methods. They show that some combination method (for models learned from disjoint partitions of a dataset) can outperform one single model learned from the entire dataset in some domains. While there is some overlap with our work, their investigation is limited in two ways. First, only two datasets are used. Second, it is unclear when a combination method (for models learned from partitions of data) is better than a single model learned from the entire dataset.

Some methods provide guidance as to how to partition the description space. Some use the information gain criterion (Utgoff, 1989), user-provided information (Tcheng, Lambert & Rendell, 1989), or hand-crafted rules (Brodley, 1993) to guide the recursive partitioning process in a tree structure; and others (Ting, 1994; Wettschereck, 1994) employ a confidence measure provided from one particular learned model, during classification, to decide which one of the two different models shall be used for final prediction. The former methods apply different types of learning algorithm for each of the mutually exclusive partitions, and the latter methods derive different types of model independently using the entire dataset. Baxt (1992) describes a situation where the data is pre-sorted manually into two different groups according to some criterion (i.e., high and low risk groups in a medical diagnostic task), and then separate neural networks are trained using each data group. During classification, the network trained using the low risk group is used if its output is below certain threshold, otherwise the other network is used. This method may only be applicable when the information about the sorting criterion is available.

Provost and Hennessy (1996) describe a distributed approach to learning a single ruleset from several rulesets induced from disjoint partitions of a given dataset. They ensure that the ruleset is a superset of the rules induced from the entire dataset. This is achieved by maintaining the invariant-partitioning property during the rule learning process. This property guarantees that each rule which is satisfactory over the entire dataset will be satisfactory over at least one subset. This approach aims at speeding up the process of learning a set of rules that cover the entire dataset. It is not meant to generate multiple different models to enhance performance. Brazdil and Torgo (1990) also work on converting different models into one unique model.

Most of this work assumes that a single dataset is used for multiple model generation and combination. The exceptions are Chan and Stolfo's (1996), Provost & Hennessy's (1996), Breiman (1996c) and Baxt's (1992) investigations. Only the first two studies have the similar working assumption to ours, i.e., multiple batches of data for the same task are available without any prior information about them.

3 Experimental Design

The basis of the experimental design rests on the hypothesis that

the relative performance of model combination and data combination is related to the learning curve of a learning algorithm used.

At the beginning of the learning curve, where the training data size is relatively small, data combination will usually give a big gain in performance; whereas at the near-asymptotic region of the curve, additional data only improves the performance marginally. The near-asymptotic region is grossly defined here to be the region where doubling the training data size gives little performance gain. The effect of doubling the training data sizes (X & Y) in two different regions of a learning curve is illustrated in Figure 2. The reverse is true for model combination. When little data is available, the estimated measure(s) required for successful model combination can be inaccurate; thus, the performance gain would be marginal. Large amounts of data enable more accurate estimation and therefore a better performance gain. Thus, the experiments are designed to unveil the learning curves of learning algorithms and model combination methods used for each dataset.

We choose to combine two classifiers because it is the simplest combination; its study provides an understanding of its base-line behaviour in model combination. In support of our choice, the empirical study conducted by Chan and Stolfo (1995; 1996) indicates that a combination of two classifiers performs better than those using more than two classifiers in the same working assumption. This is also true when this combination is being stacked up to form a tree, i.e., a binary tree is better than higher order trees (Chan & Stolfo; 1995).

We employ a recent model combination method (Ting, 1996) to conduct our investigation. This is based on the characterisation and estimation of predictive

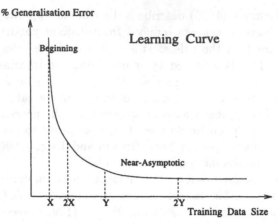

Fig. 2. Performance gain as a result of doubling the training data sizes (X & Y) in two different regions of a learning curve.

accuracy for each prediction of a classifier. Each classifier is trained independently and uses a cross-validation method to perform an estimation of predictive accuracy. During classification, the prediction of a classifier which has the best predictive accuracy is selected among the constituent classifiers as the final prediction. See the Appendix for a more detailed description of the method. An "oracle" combination method is also used for comparison. It always makes the correct prediction from its constituent classifiers, if one exists.

4 Experiments and Results

Two inductive learning algorithms, IB1* and NB* (Ting, 1994; 1997), are used in our experiments. IB1* is a variant of IB1 (Aha, Kibler & Albert, 1991) that incorporates the modified value-difference metric (Cost & Salzberg, 1993) and NB* is an implementation of the Naive Bayes (Cestnik, 1990) algorithm. Both algorithms include a method (Fayyad & Irani, 1993) for discretising continuous-valued attributes in the preprocessing. This preprocessing improved the performance of the two algorithms in most of the continuous-valued attribute domains studied by Ting (1994). We use the nearest neighbour for making prediction in IB1* and the default settings are the same as those used in IB1[3] in all experiments. No parameter settings are required for NB*.

Our studies employ two artificial domains (i.e., waveform and LED24) and four real-world datasets (i.e., euthyroid, nettalk(stress), splice junction and protein coding) obtained from the UCI repository of machine learning databases (Merz & Murphy, 1996). The two noisy artificial domains are introduced by Breiman, Friedman, Olshen and Stone (1984). Each instance of the waveform domain contains twenty-one relevant and nineteen irrelevant continuous-valued attributes. There are three uniformly distributed classes in this domain. Each class consists of a random convex combination of two of the three waveforms

---

[3] IB1 stores all training instances and uses maximum differences for attributes that have missing values, and computes Euclidean distance between any two instances.

with Gaussian noise added. The LED24 domain has seven boolean attributes indicating whether the light-emitting diodes are on or off, plus seventeen irrelevant binary attributes. Each attribute value is inverted with a probability of 0.1. The task is to classify the input as one of the ten digits.

The euthyroid dataset is one of the sets of Thyroid examples from the Garvan Institute of Medical Research in Sydney described in Quinlan, Compton, Horn and Lazarus (1987). It consists of 3163 case data and diagnoses for one of the many thyroid disorders: euthyroidism. Eighteen binary attributes and seven continuous-valued attributes are used in this dataset. The task is to predict whether a patient suffers euthyroid or not.

The goal of the NETtalk task (Sejnowski & Rosenberg, 1987) is to learn to pronounce English words by studying a dictionary of correct pronunciations. Each letter to be pronounced is presented to the classifier together with the three preceding and three succeeding letters in the word. The goal is to produce phoneme and stress that constitute the pronunciation of the letter. The nettalk(stress) dataset of 5438 instances is for the prediction of stress (five classes), produced from the NETtalk Corpus of the 1000 most common English words.

The splice junction dataset, courtesy of Towell, Shavlik and Noordewier (1990), contains 3177 instances of sixty sequential DNA nucleotide positions and each position can have one of the four base values. The task is to recognize, given a DNA sequence, two types of the splice junction or neither.

The protein coding dataset, introduced by Craven and Shavlik (1993), contains DNA nucleotide sequences and its classification task is to differentiate the coding sequences from the non-coding ones. Each sequence has fifteen nucleotides with four different values each. This dataset has 20,000 sequences.

In what follows, we first perform the experiments using the artificial domains and then the real-world datasets.

4.1 Artificial Domains

To simulate different batches of data, different seeds are used to generate the data in the waveform and LED24 domains. We examine data batches of equal size. The training data size is varied but the testing data size is fixed at 5000 instances. For each training data size, two models are induced from a learning algorithm (either IB1* or NB*) from two batches of data. Model combination uses these two models to produce a final prediction. Data combination concatenates the two batches of data to form a single training dataset and produces a model using the same learning algorithm. For each training data size, it is repeated 10 trials using different seeds in data generation, and the average error rate and its standard error are reported. Figures 3 and 4 shows the results of the experiments (i.e., the learning curves). The horizontal-axis shows the training data size of data combination; the single model induced from a batch of half of this training data size is designated as "1/2 Data Size"[4]. The results of model combination and

---

[4] There are two such models that perform very similarly. One of their learning curves is eliminated to provide a better readability of the plot.

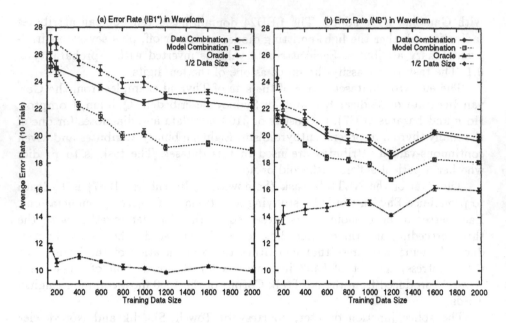

Fig. 3. Learning Curves in the Waveform domain.

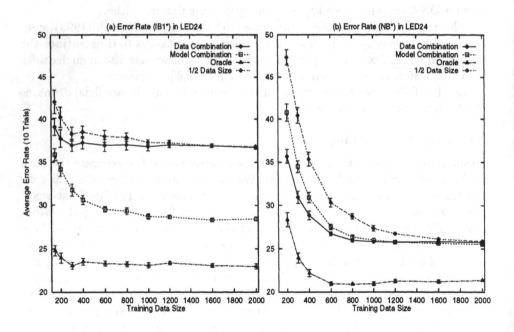

Fig. 4. Learning Curves in the LED-24 domain.

the oracle (which makes incorrect prediction if and only if both models predict incorrectly) are also shown. Plots (a) and (b) in each figure show the results using IB1* and NB*, respectively.

We summarise the results as follows. When using IB1*, model combination performs significantly better than data combination in both the waveform and LED24 domains in almost all the experimental training data sizes. Two average error rates are regarded to be significantly different if they differ by more than or equal to two standard errors (with $\geq$ 95% confidence). Similar performance is observed for NB* in the waveform domain. Note that in these three cases, the performance difference is small between data combination and the single model induced from half of the training data size. The general trend is that the positive performance gain of model combination over data combination becomes bigger towards the near-asymptotic region of the learning curve. This is the region where the classifier's performance gain as a result of doubling the data size does not gain as much as that at the beginning of the curve. For NB* in the LED24 domain, data combination performs significantly better than model combination when using small training data sizes and then becomes marginally worse as the data size gets larger. In all cases, model combination and data combination are always better than model combination's constituent models. The oracle shows the optimal performance for model combination and it is the best among the four methods.

One interesting phenomenon is that, in the LED24 domain, IB1* seems to reach its (near-)asymptotic performance from data size 800 onwards. But, the approach to combine models learned from half of these data sizes can still significantly improve the algorithm's (near-)asymptotic performance! The performance of the oracle indicates that the two models are significantly different since the performance difference between the oracle and its constituent models is as large as 15%! We will come back to this point in Section 5.

4.2 Real-World Datasets

In this experiment, we employ four real-world datasets; and for each dataset, we simulate two different batches by random subsampling of the training data for data combination into two disjoint subsets of equal size. The size of training data size is varied from 10% to 90% of the entire dataset. Each data size is repeated over 20 trials, except in the protein coding dataset for its huge data size and only 10 trials are used. The testing dataset is from the remaining portion of the entire dataset not used for training.

Figures 5 to 8 show the results for the four datasets. In the euthyroid, nettalk(stress) and splice junction datasets, the performance trends of model combination and data combination generally in accordance to the results observed the artificial domains. Model combination performs worse than data combination at the beginning of the learning curve in all three datasets. At the near-asymptotic region of the curves, model combination performs better using NB* and comparably using IB1* in the euthyroid dataset; model combination performs better using IB1* and comparably using NB* in the other two datasets.

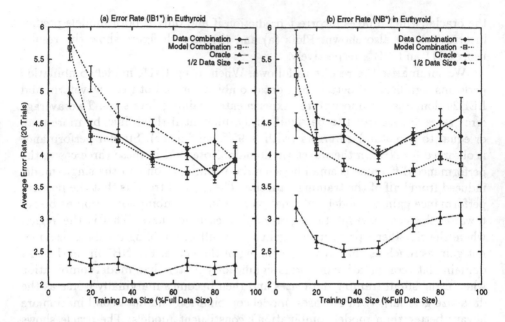

Fig. 5. Learning Curves in the Euthyroid dataset.

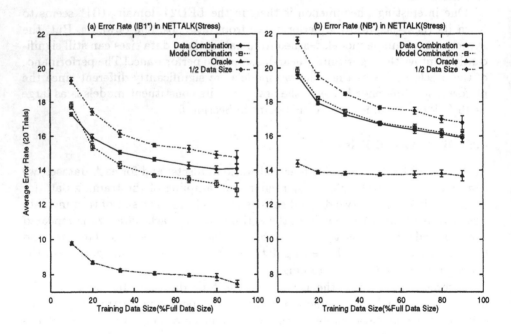

Fig. 6. Learning Curves in the Nettalk(Stress) dataset.

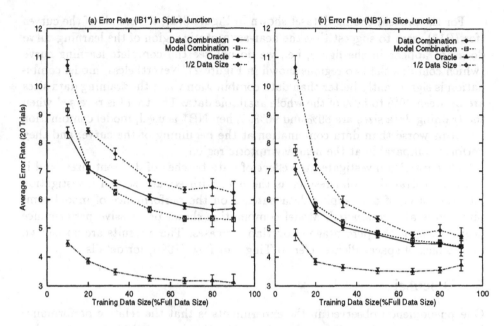

Fig. 7. Learning Curves in the splice junction dataset.

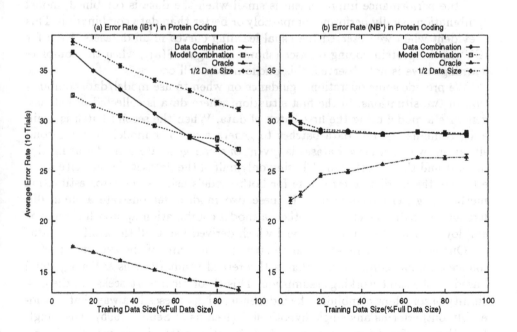

Fig. 8. Learning Curves in the protein coding dataset.

For the protein coding dataset shown in Figure 8(a), the trends of the curves (for IB1*) seem to suggest that the near-asymptotic region of the learning curve does not appear in the figure, i.e., we do not see the complete learning curve (which contains the two regions shown in Figure 2). Nevertheless, model combination is significantly better than data combination when the training data sizes are between 10% to 50% of the whole available data. The trend is reversed when the training data sizes are 80% and 90%. When NB* is used, model combination performs worse than data combination at the beginning of the curve, and they perform comparably at the near-asymptotic region.

We have also investigated the effect of data batches of different sizes, and it has demonstrated similar results as the ones with equal size. An investigation into the effect of overlapping data batches on the performance of model combination is also conducted. Model combination shows progressive performance degradation as the percentage of overlap increases. These results are not shown due to lack of space. Please refer to Ting and Low (1996) for details.

5 Discussion

One phenomenon observed in the experiments is that the relative performance between model combination and data combination is related to the learning behaviour of the classifier. This is consistent with our hypothesis stated in Section 3. If the performance improvement is small when the data is combined, model combination usually performs comparably or better than data combination. This is evident when we observed the usual learning curves in all datasets. Even for IB1* in the protein coding dataset (shown in Figure 8(a)), when the complete learning curve is not observed, this phenomenon still occurs.

We provide some operational guidance on when to use model/data combination in two situations. In the first situation, where data is collected in batches, generate a model using the first batch of data. When the second batch is available, combine the two data batches to generate another model. In the second situation, where a large dataset is given, one can generate a model using this dataset and then another model using only half of the dataset. In each situation, estimate the predictive error rate for both models using some error estimation method (e.g., cross-validation). If these two models demonstrate a small difference in predictive error rate, then a model combination approach should be employed. Otherwise, use the model which derived using all the available data.

Our empirical result seems to be stronger, in terms of the expected performance of model combination, than a theoretical result (Kearns & Seung, 1995) based on the same working assumption. This theoretical work seeks "... the possibility of somehow combining the independent hypotheses in a way that considerably outperforms any single hypothesis" (Kearns & Seung, 1995). The 'single hypothesis' refers to any of the model combination's constituent models. Our result indicates that model combination can significantly outperform not only its constituent models but the model learned from aggregating the available data; in spite of the the fact that this result only shows the base-line behaviour of model combination, i.e., combining two models.

It might be assumed that the models learned in the near-asymptotic region would be very similar as shown by their indistinguishable performance. However, our experimental results suggest that the two models learned from separate data batches in this region are substantially different even though they demonstrate the same performance. This is evident in most of the experimental datasets, where the performance of the oracle is significantly better than those of its constituent models and data combination in the near-asymptotic region. This indicates that the assumption is incorrect, at least in the near-asymptotic region.

What surprises us is that *the near-asymptotic performance of a single model can be significantly improved by combining multiple models of the same learning algorithm.* This can only happen if the constituent models are substantially different and there is still some regularity in the models to be exploited by any combination methods. Figure 4(a) shows an example of performance improvement as a result of model combination's exploitation in the near-asymptotic region. This empirical evidence of further significant improvement on the near-asymptotic performance of a learning algorithm using multiple models is new to us, to the best of our knowledge. Previous work (e.g., Hansen & Salamon, 1990; Perrone & Cooper, 1993; Oliver & Hand, 1995; Chan & Stolfo, 1995; Breiman, 1996a,1996b; Freund & Schapire, 1996; Ali & Pazzani, 1996) only show the possibility of improving the performance using multiple models in some datasets, without considering the (near-)asymptotic performance; despite the theoretical result of boosting (Schapire, 1990) shows that this is possible.

Though our investigation is limited to one type of model combination method, we believe that the results are applicable to other reasonable combination methods (e.g., Ali & Pazzani, 1996) judging from the performance of the "oracle" combination method. In all datasets, the oracle performs significantly better than data combination, sometimes with huge margins. This shows there is plenty of room for any reasonable combination method to gain advantage. We also believe that the results would also hold when other types of learning algorithm are used (e.g., decision trees and neural networks). Indeed, in a subsequent work, Ting and Witten (1997) confirm our conjecture here by showing that stacked generalisation (i.e., a different model combination method (Wolpert, 1992)) also behaves similarly in the same scenario by using either NB, IB1 or C4.5 (a decision tree learning algorithm (Quinlan, 1993)).

6 Conclusions

A comparison of the base-line behaviour of model combination and data combination using two randomly drawn disjoint data batches reveals that model combination compares favourably when the performance gain due to data combination is small, or the performances of the models induced from the data batches are at the near-asymptotic region of the learning curve. The empirical evidence presented in this paper and subsequently by Ting & Witten (1997) show that this result is not sensitive to the particular learning algorithm or model combination method employed.

The practical implication of our results is that one should consider using model combination rather than the common method of data combination, especially when multiple batches of data for the same task are readily available.

Another interesting result is that we empirically show that it is possible to significantly improve the near-asymptotic performance of a single model by combining multiple models of the same algorithm if the models are substantially different, and there is some regularity in the models to be exploited by the combination method used.

Acknowledgment

Ross Quinlan and Robert Schapire help to clarify the issue on (near-)asymptotic performance. Z. Zheng, B. Pfahringer, M. Cameron-Jones, I. Witten and members of the machine learning group and the anonymous reviewers provide helpful comments during the early draft of this paper. Ronny Meir provides some pointer to the related work in NIPS. This paper is prepared with supports from a grant from the Chinese University of Hong Kong and Department of Computer Science, University of Waikato.

Appendix – The Method of Model Combination

We use the composite learner framework (Ting, 1996) as the method for model combination in our experiments. Ting uses the term *the characterisation of predictive accuracy* to mean the use of a measure in an induced model as an indicator for its predictive accuracy. The posterior probability and the measure of typicality (defined as inter-concept distance divided by intra-concept distance) are employed as the characterisation of predictive accuracy for NB* and IB1*, respectively.

During training, the algorithm (either NB* or IB1*) performs a k-fold cross-validation to estimate predictive accuracy from the characterisations for each batch of data independently. In a k-fold cross-validation, a dataset is partitioned into k equal-size subsets and perform training using all subsets except the ith subset k times. At each fold, the ith subset is used as the testing set. Thus, each instance will be tested only once; and a training set of size n will have the testing results of size n at the end of the cross-validation. We set k to three in our experiments.

For each predicted class, the individual test results from the k-fold cross-validation are then sorted according to the values of the characterisation (i.e., posterior probability, or typicality on the x-axis), shown in the left plot of Figure A. The aim is to produce a binned graph that relates the average value of the characterisation to its binned predictive accuracy for each class, shown in the right plot of Figure A. The transformation process, from the left plot to the right plot, goes as follows. First, use a bin/window which contains a fixed number of instances in the left plot. This bin is transformed to a point in the right plot by averaging the values of the characterisation for all instances in the bin on the x-axis and converting the number of correct/incorrect classifications into accuracy on the y-axis. This process is repeated in the style of a "moving window", i.e., the next bin is obtained by dropping the leftmost instance and adding an instance adjacent to the rightmost instance of the current bin. At the end of the training process, a model induced from all the n training instances and the binned graphs for all classes are stored for future classification. The above procedure is conducted for each model derived using one batch of data. There are two models in the model combination used in our experiments.

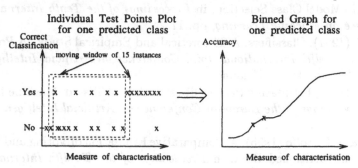

Fig. A. Transforming individual cross-validation test points to a binned graph for one predicted class.

To classify an instance X, it is inputed into both models and the model which has the higher estimated predictive accuracy for its output is chosen to make the final prediction. The predictive accuracy, $PA(C, H|X)$, is obtained by referring to the predicted class' (C) binned graph with the corresponding value of the characterisation (H). Formally, the selection process can be defined as follows.

$$C_f = C_{M1} \text{ if } PA(C_{M1}, H_{M1}|X) > PA(C_{M2}, H_{M2}|X),$$
$$= C_{M2} \text{ if } PA(C_{M1}, H_{M1}|X) < PA(C_{M2}, H_{M2}|X),$$
$$\text{else random select.}$$

where C_f : final prediction;
C_M & H_M : Model M's prediction & characterisation;
$PA(C, H|X)$: predictive accuracy of C and H given instance X.

References

Aha, D.W., D. Kibler & M.K. Albert (1991), Instance-Based Learning Algorithms, *Machine Learning, 6*, pp. 37-66.

Ali, K.M. & M.J. Pazzani (1996), Error Reduction through Learning Multiple Descriptions, *Machine Learning*, Vol. 24, No. 3, pp. 173-206.

Baxt, W.G. (1992), Improving the Accuracy of an Artificial Neural Network using Multiple Differently Trained Networks, *Neural Computation*, Vol. 4, No. 5, pp. 772-780, The MIT Press.

Brazdil,P. & Torgo,L. (1990), Knowledge Acquisition via Knowledge Integration. In *Current Trends in Knowledge Acquisition*, Wielinga, B. et al.(eds.).

Breiman, L. (1996a), Bagging Predictors, *Machine Learning*, Vol. 24, No. 2, pp. 123-140.

Breiman, L. (1996b), Bias, Variance, and Arcing Classifiers, *Technical Report 460*, Department of Statistics, University of California, Berkeley, CA.

Breiman, L. (1996c), Pasting Bites Together for Prediction in Large Data Sets and On-Line, [ftp.stat.berkeley.edu/users/pub/breiman/pasting.ps].

Breiman, L., J.H. Friedman, R.A. Olshen & C.J. Stone (1984), *Classification And Regression Trees*, Belmont, CA: Wadsworth.

Brodley, C.E. (1993), Addressing the Selective Superiority Problem: Automatic Algorithm/Model Class Selection, in *Proceedings of the Tenth International Conference on Machine Learning*, pp. 17-24.

Buntine, W. (1991), Classifiers: A Theoretical and Empirical Study, in *Proceedings of the Twelfth International Joint Conference on Artificial Intelligence*, pp. 638-644, Morgan-Kaufmann.

Cestnik, B. (1990), Estimating Probabilities: A Crucial Task in Machine Learning, in *Proceedings of the European Conference on Artificial Intelligence*, pp. 147-149.

Chan, P.K. & S.J. Stolfo (1995), A Comparative Evaluation of Voting and Meta-learning on Partitioned Data, in *Proceedings of the Twelfth International Conference on Machine Learning*, pp. 90-98, Morgan Kaufmann.

Chan, P.K. & S.J. Stolfo (1996), On the Accuracy of Meta-learning for Scalable Data Mining, in *Journal of Intelligent System*, to appear.

Cost, S & S. Salzberg (1993), A Weighted Nearest Neighbor Algorithm for Learning with Symbolic Features, *Machine Learning, 10*, pp. 57-78.

Craven, M.W. & J.W. Shavlik (1993), Learning to Represent Codons: A Challenge Problem for Constructive Induction, *Proceedings of the Thirteenth International Joint Conference on Artificial Intelligence*, pp. 1319-1324.

Fayyad, U.M. & K.B. Irani (1993), Multi-Interval Discretization of Continuous-Valued Attributes for Classification Learning, in *Proceedings of 13th International Joint Conference on Artificial Intelligence*, pp. 1022-1027.

Freund, Y. & R.E. Schapire (1996), Experiments with a New Boosting Algorithm, in *Proceedings of the Thirteenth International Conference on Machine Learning*, pp. 148-156, Morgan Kaufmann.

Hansen, L.K. & P. Salamon (1990), Neural Network Ensembles, in *IEEE Transactions of Pattern Analysis and Machine Intelligence, 12*, pp. 993-1001.

Kearns, M. & H.S. Seung (1995), Learning from a Population of Hypotheses, *Machine Learning, 18*, pp. 255-276, Kluwer Academic Publishers.

Kononenko, I. & M. Kovačič (1992), Learning as Optimization: Stochastic Generation of Multiple Knowledge, in *Proceedings of the Ninth International Conference on Machine Learning*, pp. 257-262, Morgan Kaufmann.

Krogh, A. & J. Vedelsby (1995), Neural Network Ensembles, Cross Validation, and Active Learning, in *Advances in Neural Information Processing Systems 7*, G. Tesauro, D.S. Touretsky & T.K. Leen (Editors), pp. 231-238.

Kwok, S. & C. Carter (1990), Multiple Decision Trees, *Uncertainty in Artificial Intelligence 4*, R. Shachter, T. Levitt, L. Kanal and J. Lemmer (Editors), pp. 327-335, North-Holland.

Merz, C.J. & Murphy, P.M. (1996), *UCI Repository of machine learning databases* [http:// www.ics.uci.edu/ mlearn/MLRepository.html]. Irvine, CA: University of California, Department of Information and Computer Science.

Oliver, J.J. & D.J. Hand (1995), On Pruning and Averaging Decision Trees, in *Proceedings of the Twelfth International Conference on Machine Learning*, pp. 430-437. Morgan Kaufmann.

Perrone, M.P. & L.N. Cooper (1993), When Networks Disagree: Ensemble Methods for Hybrid Neural Networks, in *Artificial Neural Networks for Speech and Vision*, R.J. Mammone (Editor), Chapman-Hall.

Provost, F.J. & D.N. Hennessy (1996), Scaling Up: Distributed Machine Learning with Cooperation, in Proceedings of the Thirteen National Conference on Artificial Intelligence, pp. 74-79, Menlo Park, CA: AAAI Press.

Quinlan, J.R. (1993), *C4.5: Program for machine learning*, Morgan Kaufmann.

Quinlan, J.R. (1996), Boosting, Bagging, and C4.5, in *Proceedings of the 13th National Conference on Artificial Intelligence*, pp. 725-730, AAAI Press.

Quinlan, J.R., P.J. Compton, K.A. Horn & L. Lazarus (1987), Inductive Knowledge Acquisition: A Case Study, in *Applications of Expert Systems*, J.R. Quinlan (Editor). Turing Institute Press with Addison Wesley.

Schapire, R.E. (1990), The Strength of Weak Learnability, *Machine Learning*, 5, pp. 197-227, Kluwer Academic Publishers.

Sejnowski, T.J. & C.R. Rosenberg (1987), Parallel networks that learn to pronounce English text, *Complex Systems*, 1, pp. 145-168.

Tcheng, D., B. Lambert, C-Y. Lu & L. Rendell (1989), Building Robust Learning Systems by Combining Induction and Optimization, in *Proceedings of the 11th International Joint Conference on Artificial Intelligence*, pp. 806-812.

Ting, K.M. (1994), Discretization of Continuous-Valued Attributes and Instance-Based Learning, *TR 491*, Basser Department of Computer Science, University of Sydney.

Ting, K.M. (1996), The Characterisation of Predictive Accuracy and Decision Combination, in *Proceedings of the Thirteenth International Conference on Machine Learning*, pp. 498-506, Morgan Kaufmann.

Ting, K.M. (1997), Discretisation in Lazy Learning Algorithms, to appear in the special issue on Lazy Learning in *Artificial Intelligence Review Journal*.

Ting, K.M. & B.T. Low (1996), Theory Combination: an alternative to Data Combination, *Working Paper 96/19*, Department of Computer Science, University of Waikato. [http://www.cs.waikato.ac.nz/cs/Staff/kaiming.html].

Ting, K.M. & I. H. Witten (1997), Stacked Generalization: when does it work?, *Working Paper 97/1*, Dept of Computer Science, University of Waikato.

Towell, G., J. Shavlik & M. Noordewier (1990), Refinement of Approximate Domain Theories by Knowledge-Based Artificial Neural Networks, in *Proceedings of the Eighth National Conference on Artificial Intelligence*.

Utgoff, P.E. (1989), Perceptron Trees: A case study in hybrid concept representations, *Connection Science, 1*, pp. 337-391.

Wettschereck, D. (1994), A Hybrid Nearest-Neighbor and Nearest-Hyperrectangle Algorithm, in *Proceedings of the Seventh European Conference on Machine Learning, LNAI-784*, pp. 323-335, Springer Verlag.

Wolpert, D.H. (1992), Stacked Generalization, *Neural Networks*, Vol. 5, pp. 241-259, Pergamon Press.

Search-Based Class Discretization

Luís Torgo
email : ltorgo@ncc.up.pt

João Gama
email : jgama@ncc.up.pt

LIACC - University of Porto
R. Campo Alegre, 823 - 4150 Porto - Portugal
Phone : (+351) 2 6001672   Fax : (+351) 2 6003654
WWW : http://www.ncc.up.pt/liacc/ML

Abstract. We present a methodology that enables the use of classification algorithms on regression tasks. We implement this method in system RECLA that transforms a regression problem into a classification one and then uses an existent classification system to solve this new problem. The transformation consists of mapping a continuous variable into an ordinal variable by grouping its values into an appropriate set of intervals. We use misclassification costs as a means to reflect the implicit ordering among the ordinal values of the new variable. We describe a set of alternative discretization methods and, based on our experimental results, justify the need for a search-based approach to choose the best method. Our experimental results confirm the validity of our search-based approach to class discretization, and reveal the accuracy benefits of adding misclassification costs.

Keywords : Regression, Classification, Discretization methods.

1   Introduction

Machine learning (ML) researchers have traditionally concentrated their efforts on classification problems. However, many interesting real world domains demand for regression tools. In this paper we present and evaluate a discretization method that extends the applicability of existing classification systems to regression domains. The discretization of the target variable values provides a different granularity of predictions that can be considered more comprehensible. In effect, it is a common practice in statistical data analysis to group the observed values of a continuous variable into class intervals and work with this grouped data (Bhattacharyya & Johnson, 1977). The choice of these intervals is a critical issue as too many intervals impair the comprehensibility of the models and too few hide important features of the variable distribution. The methods we propose provide means to automatically find the optimal number and width of these intervals. The motivation for transforming regression into classification is to obtain a different tradeoff between comprehensibility and accuracy of regression models. As a by-product of our methods we also broaden the applicability of classification systems.

We argue that mapping regression into classification is a two-step process. First we have to transform the observed values of the goal variable into a set of intervals. These intervals may be considered values of an ordinal variable (i.e. discrete values with an implicit ordering among them). Classification systems deal with discrete target variables. They are not able to take advantage of the given ordering. We propose a second step whose objective is to overcome this difficulty. We use misclassification costs which are carefully chosen to reflect the ordering of the intervals as a means to compensate for the information loss regarding the ordering.

We describe several alternative ways of transforming a set of continuous values into a set of intervals. Initial experiments revealed that there was no clear winner among them. This fact lead us to try a search-based approach to this task of finding an adequate set of intervals. We use a wrapper technique (John et al., 1994; Kohavi, 1995) as a method for finding near-optimal settings for this mapping task.

We have tested our methodology on four regression domains with three different classification systems : C4.5 (Quinlan, 1993); CN2 (Clark & Nibblet, 1988); and a linear discriminant (Fisher, 1936; Dillon & Goldstein, 1984). The results show the validity of our search-based approach and the gains in accuracy obtained by adding misclassification costs to classification algorithms.

The next section describes how to transform a continuous target variable into a set of intervals. In section 3 we describe our proposal of using misclassification costs to deal with ordinal variables. The experiments we carried out done are described on section 4. Finally, we comment the relations to other work and present the conclusions of this paper.

2 Obtaining a Set of Intervals

In regression problems we are given samples of a set of independent (predictor) variables $x_1, x_2, ..., x_n$, and the value of the respective dependent (output) variable y . Our goal is to obtain a model that captures the mapping $y = f(x_1, x_2, ..., x_n)$ based on the given samples. Classification differs from this setup in that y is a discrete variable instead of continuous one.

Mapping regression into classification can be seen as a kind of pre-processing technique that enables the use of classification algorithms on regression problems. Our method starts by creating a data set with discrete target variable values. This step involves examining the original continuous values of the target variable and suitably dividing them into a series of intervals. Every example whose output variable value lies within the boundaries of an interval will be assigned the respective "discrete class"[1] .

Grouping the range of observed continuous values of the target variable into a set of intervals involves two main decisions : how many intervals to create; and how to choose the interval boundaries. As for this later issue we use three methods that for a given a set of continuous values and the number of intervals return their defining boundaries :

- *Equally probable intervals (EP):* This creates a set of N intervals with the same number of elements.
- *Equal width intervals (EW):* The original range of values is divided into N intervals with equal width.

---

[1] We use the median of the values lying within the interval as class label.

- *K-means clustering (KM):* In this method the aim is to build N intervals that minimize the sum of the distances of each element of an interval to its *gravity center* (Dillon & Goldstein, 1984). This method starts with the EW approximation and then moves the elements of each interval to contiguous intervals whenever these changes reduce the referred sum of distances.

The number of intervals used (i.e. the number of classes) will have a direct effect on the accuracy of the subsequent learned theory. This means that they can be seen as a parameter of the learning algorithm. Our goal is to set the value of this "parameter" such that the system performance is optimized. As the number of possible ways of dividing a set of continuous values into a set of intervals is potentially infinite a search algorithm is necessary. The *wrapper* approach (John et al., 1994; Kohavi, 1995) is a well known strategy has been mainly used for feature subset selection (John et al., 1994) and parameter estimation (Kohavi, 1995). The use of this iterative approach to estimate a parameter of a learning algorithm can be described by the following figure:

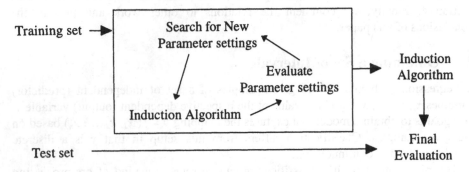

Figure 1 - The wrapper approach.

The two main components of the wrapper approach are the way new parameter settings are generated and how their results are evaluated in the context of the target learning algorithm. The basic idea is to try different parameter settings and choose the one that gives the best estimated accuracy. This best setting found by the wrapper process will then be used in the learning algorithm in the *real* evaluation using an independent test set. As for the search component we have used a hill-climbing search coupled with a settable lookahead parameter to minimize the well-known problem of local minima. Given a tentative solution and the respective evaluation the search component is responsible for generating a new tentative. We provide the following two alternative search operators :

- *Varying the number of intervals (VNI):* This simple alternative consists of incrementing the previously tried number of intervals by a constant value.
- *Incrementally improving the number of intervals (INI) :* The idea of this alternative is to try to improve the previous set of intervals taking into account their individual evaluation. The next set of intervals is built using the median of

these individual error estimates. All intervals whose error is above the median are further split by dividing them in two. All the other intervals remain unchanged.

These two alternatives together with the three given splitting strategies make six alternative discretization methods which can be tuned to the given task using a wrapper approach. The RECLA system allows the user to explicitly select one of these methods. If this is not done the system automatically selects the one that gives better estimated results.

The other important component of the wrapper approach is the evaluation strategy. We use a N-fold Cross Validation (Stone, 1974) estimation technique which is well-known for its reliable estimates of prediction error. This means that each time a new tentative set of intervals is generated RECLA uses an internal N-fold Cross Validation (CV) process to evaluate it. In the next subsection we provide a small example of a discretization process to better illustrate our search-based approach.

2.1 An illustrative example

In this example we use the *servo* data set (see details in section 4). We have coupled RECLA with C4.5 and evaluated the learned model with the MAE statistic (see section 3). We have performed two experiments with different discretization methods. In the first experiment we use the VNI search operator with the KM splitting algorithm. Table 1 presents the discretizations of this first experiment (KM+VNI). The first column shows the number of intervals tried in each iteration[2]. The second column shows the obtained intervals by the KM splitting method. The second line of this column includes the median of the values within the intervals (the used "classes"). The last column gives the internal 5-fold CV error estimate of each tentative set of intervals. In this example we have used the value 1 for the "Lookahead" parameter mentioned before. The solution of this method is thus 4 intervals (the trial with best estimated error).

N.Ints	Intervals / Discrete Class Values	Error
2	[0.13-2.60] [2.60-7.10] 0.58 4.50	0.510
4	[0.13-0.45] [0.45-0.75] [0.75-3.20] [3.20-7.10] 0.34 0.54 1.03 4.50	0.374
6	[0.13-0.38] [0.38-0.52] [0.52-0.75] [0.75-1.08] [1.08-3.20] [3.20-7.10] 0.28 0.47 0.58 0.90 1.30 4.50	0.429

Table 1 - Trace of KM+VNI method.

In the second experiment we use the same splitting algorithm but with the INI search operator. The results are given in Table 2. We also include the estimated error of each interval (the value in parenthesis). The next tried iteration is dependent on these estimates. The intervals whose error is greater than the median of the estimates are split in two intervals. For instance, in the third iteration we can observe that the third interval was maintained from the second trial, while the other were obtained by splitting a previous interval.

---

[2] The fact that starts with 2 and goes in increments of 2 is just an adjustable parameter of RECLA.

N.Ints	Intervals / Discrete Class Values	Error
1	[0.13-7.10] 0.73 (0.91)	0.91
2	[0.13-2.60] [2.60-7.10] 0.58 (0.41) 4.50 (0.32)	0.42
3	[0.13-0.73] [0.73-2.60] [2.60-7.10] 0.5 (0.35) 1.90 (0.35) 4.50 (0.33)	0.35
5	[0.13-0.4] [0.46-0.73] [0.73-1.07] [1.1-2.60] [2.60-7.10] 0.35 (0.29) 0.54 (0.38) 0.9 (0.51) 1.4 (0.49) 4.50 (0.4)	0.41

Table 2 - Trace of KM+INI method.

The two methods follow different strategies for grouping the values. In this example the second alternative lead to lower error estimates and consequently this alternative was preferred by RECLA.

An interesting effect of increasing the number of intervals is that after some threshold the algorithm's performance decreases. This may be caused by the decrease of the number of cases per class leading to unreliable estimates due to overfitting the data.

3 Using Misclassification Costs with Ordinal Variables

Classification systems search for theories that have minimal estimated prediction error according to a 0/1 loss function, thus making all errors equally important. In regression, prediction error is a function of the difference between the observed and predicted values (i.e. errors are metric). Accuracy in regression is dependent on the amplitude of the error. In our experiments we use the Mean Absolute Error (MAE) and the Mean Absolute Percentage Error (MAPE) as regression accuracy measures :

$$MAE = \frac{\sum |y_i - y_i'|}{N} \qquad MAPE = \frac{\sum |(y_i - y_i')/y_i| \times 100}{N} \qquad (1)$$

In order to differentiate among different errors our method incorporates misclassification costs in the prediction procedure. If we take $c_{i,j}$ as the cost of classifying a class j instance as being class i, and if we take $p(j|X)$ as the probability given by our classifier that instance X is of class j, we can take the task of classifying instance X as finding the class i that minimizes the expression

$$\sum_{j \in \{classes\}} c_{i,j}\, p(j|X) \qquad (2)$$

Here we associate classes with intervals and we take as class labels the intervals medians. In our methodology we propose to estimate the cost of misclassifying two intervals by using the absolute difference between their representatives, i.e.

$$c_{i,j} = |\tilde{y}_i - \tilde{y}_j| \qquad (3)$$

where $\tilde{y}_i$ is the median of the values that where "discretized" into the interval i.

By proceeding this way we ensure that the system predictions minimize the expected absolute distance between the predicted and observed values.

4   Experimental Evaluation

We have carried out several experiments with four real world domains. These data sets were obtained from the UCI machine learning repository (Merz & Murphy, 1996). Some of the characteristics of the data sets used are summarized in Table 3.

Data Set	N. Examples	N. Attributes
housing	506	13 (13C)
servo	167	4 (4D)
auto-mpg	398	7 (4C+3D)
machine	209	6 (6D)

Table 3- The used data sets (C - continuous attribute; D - discrete attribute).

RECLA system was coupled with C4.5 (a decision tree learner), CN2 (a rule-based system) and Discrim (a linear discriminant). MAE and MAPE were used as regression accuracy measures. The error estimates presented in Table 4 are obtained by a 5-fold cross validation test[3]. We also include the standard deviation of the estimates and the discretization methodology chosen by RECLA.

DataSet	Algorithm	MAE		MAPE	
Servo	Cn2	0.38 ± 0.13	(ep-INI)	36.0 ± 9.03	(ep-INI)
	C4.5	0.36 ± 0.06	(ep-INI)	32.6 ± 8.6	(ep-INI)
	Discrim	0.39 ± 0.10	(km-VNI)	37.5 ± 4.0	(km-INI)
Auto-Mpg	Cn2	3.0 ± 0.3	(km-INI)	13.8 ± 2.07	(km-INI)
	C4.5	3.1 ± 1.6	(ep-VNI)	13.1 ± 3.6	(ep-VNI)
	Discrim	2.6 ± 1.1	(ep-VNI)	11.5 ± 2.3	(ep-VNI)
Housing	Cn2	3.68 ± 0.5	(ew-INI)	18.09 ± 3.8	(km-INI)
	C4.5	4.2 ± 0.66	(ew-VNI)	21.9 ± 5.7	(km-VNI)
	Discrim	3.8 ± 1.14	(km-VNI)	18.0 ± 4.85	(ep-VNI)
Machine	Cn2	46.8 ± 11.8	(km-INI)	43.3 ± 9.2	(ew-INI)
	C4.5	47.1 ± 24.5	(ep-INI)	47.4 ± 8.5	(ep-VNI)
	Discrim	38.8 ± 23.7	(km-VNI)	42.0 ± 11.6	(km-VNI)

Table 4 - Best results of Classification algorithms using RECLA.

The observed variability of the chosen discretization method provides an empirical justification for our search-based approach. We can also notice that the best method is dependent not only on the domain but also on the used induction tool (and less frequently on the error statistic). This justifies the use of a wrapper approach that chooses the best number of intervals taking these factors into account.

In another set of experiments we have omitted the use of misclassification costs. This lead to a significant drop on regression accuracy in most of the setups thus providing empirical evidence of the value of adding misclassification costs. However, it should be mentioned that misclassification costs cannot be used with all classification systems. In effect, if the system is not able to output class probability

---

[3] Notice that this test is independent from the internal cross validation that is performed by RECLA to estimate the best discretization.

distributions when classifying unseen instances, we are not able to use misclassification costs. The consequence will probably be a lower accuracy as our experiments indicate.

RECLA provides means of using different types of classification systems in regression tasks. The regression models obtained by this methodological approach are in a way more comprehensible to the user as the predictions have higher granularity. However, the loss of detail due to the abstraction of continuous values into intervals has some consequences on regression accuracy. We have tried to find out this effect by obtaining the results of some "pure" regression tools on the same data sets using the same experimental methodology. Table 5 shows the results obtained by a regression tree similar to CART (Breiman et al., 1984), a 3-nearest neighbor algorithm (Fix & Hodges, 1951) and a standard linear regression method :

Dataset	Algorithm	MAE	MAPE
Servo	Regression tree	0.43 ± 0.4	34.0 ± 9.9
	3-NN	0.52 ± 0.11	57.1 ± 17.3
	Linear Regression	0.87 ± 0.07	104.5 ± 22.7
Auto-Mpg	Regression tree	2.6 ± 0.3	11.22 ± 0.9
	3-NN	2.4 ± 0.25	10.05 ± 1.5
	Linear Regression	2.5 ± 0.23	11.06 ± 0.9
Housing	Regression tree	2.8 ± 0.2	14.5 ± 2.2
	3-NN	2.9 ± 0.4	13.7 ± 1.08
	Linear Regression	3.4 ± 0.4	16.5 ± 2.7
Machine	Regression tree	46.8 ± 12.6	54.5 ± 9.47
	3-NN	34.1 ± 11.1	47.45 ± 8.8
	Linear Regression	36.8 ± 6.7	58.9 ± 14.6

Table 5 - Performance of Regression Tools.

These results are comparable with the ones given in Table 4. This means that our approach can provide an interesting alternative when a different trade-off between accuracy and comprehensibility is needed.

5   Related Work

Mapping regression into classification was first proposed by Weiss & Indurkhya (1993, 1995). These authors incorporate the mapping within their regression system. They use an algorithm called P-class that splits the continuous values into a set of K intervals, and use cross validation to estimate the number of intervals. Their methodology is similar to our KM+VNI discretization. Compared to this work we added other alternative discretization methods and empirically proved the necessity of a search-based approach to class discretization. Moreover, by separating the discretization process from the learning algorithm we extend this approach to other systems. Finally, we have introduced the use of misclassification costs to overcome the inadequacy of classification systems to deal with ordinal target variables.

Previous work on continuous attribute discretization usually proceeds by trying to maximize the mutual information between the resulting discrete attribute and the classes (Fayyad & Irani, 1993). This strategy is applicable only when the classes are given. Ours is a different problem, as we are determining which classes to consider.

6 Conclusions

The method described in this paper enables the use of classification systems on regression tasks. The significance of this work is two-fold. First, we have managed to extend the applicability of a wide range of ML systems. Second, our methodology provides an alternative trade-off between regression accuracy and comprehensibility of the learned models. Our method also provides a better insight about the target variable by dividing its values in significant intervals, which extends our understanding of the domain.

We have presented a set of alternative discretization methods and demonstrated their validity through experimental evaluation. Moreover, we have added misclassifications costs which provide a better theoretical justification for using classification systems on regression tasks. We have used a search-based approach which is justified by our experimental results which show that the best discretization is often dependent on both the domain and the induction tool.

References

Breiman,L. , Friedman,J.H., Olshen,R.A. & Stone,C.J. (1984): *Classification and Regression Trees*, Wadsworth Int. Group, Belmont, California, USA, 1984.

Bhattacharyya,G., Johnson,R. (1977) : *Statistical Concepts and Methods*. John Wiley & Sons.

Clark, P. and Niblett, T. (1988) : The CN2 induction algorithm. In *Machine Learning*, **3**.

Dillon,W. and Goldstein,M. (1984) : *Multivariate Analysis*. John Wiley & Sons, Inc.

Fayyad, U.M., and Irani, K.B. (1993) : Multi-interval Discretization of Continuous-valued Attributes for Classification Learning. In *Proceedings of the 13th International Joint Conference on Artificial Intelligence (IJCAI-93)*. Morgan Kaufmann Publishers.

Fisher, R.A. (1936) : The use of multiple measurements in taxonomic problems. *Annals of Eugenics*, **7**, 179-188.

Fix, E., Hodges, J.L. (1951) : Discriminatory analysis, nonparametric discrimination consistency properties. Technical Report 4, Randolph Field, TX: US Air Force, School of Aviation Medicine.

John,G.H., Kohavi,R. and Pfleger, K. (1994) : Irrelevant features and the subset selection problem. In *Proceedings of the 11th IML*. Morgan Kaufmann.

Kohavi, R. (1995) : Wrappers for performance enhancement and oblivious decision graphs. PhD Thesis.

Merz,C.J., Murphy,P.M. (1996) : UCI repository of machine learning databases [http://www.ics.uci.edu/MLReposiroty.html]. Irvine, CA. University of California, Department of Information and Computer Science.

Quinlan, J. R. (1993) : *C4.5 : programs for machine learning*. Morgan Kaufmann Publishers.

Stone, M. (1974) : Cross-validatory choice and assessment of statistical predictions. *Journal of the Royal Statistical Society*, B **36**, 111-147.

Weiss, S. and Indurkhya, N. (1993) : Rule-base Regression. In *Proceedings of the 13th International Joint Conference on Artificial Intelligence*, pp. 1072-1078.

Weiss, S. and Indurkhya, N. (1995) : Rule-based Machine Learning Methods for Functional Prediction. In Journal Of Artificial Intelligence Research (JAIR), volume 3, pp.383-403.

Natural Ideal Operators
in Inductive Logic Programming

Fabien Torre and Céline Rouveirol

Inference and Learning Group,
Laboratoire de Recherche en Informatique
Bâtiment 490, Université Paris-Sud
91405 - Orsay Cedex (France)
{fabien,celine}@lri.fr

Abstract. We present in this paper the original notion of *natural relation*, a quasi order that extends the idea of generality order: it allows the sound and dynamic pruning of hypotheses that do not satisfy a property, be it completeness or correctness with respect to the training examples, or hypothesis language restriction.

Natural relations for conjunctions of such properties are characterized. Learning operators that satisfy these complex natural relations allow pruning with respect to this set of properties to take place before inappropriate hypotheses are generated.

Once the natural relation is defined that optimally prunes the search space with respect to a set of properties, we discuss the existence of ideal operators for the search space ordered by this natural relation. We have adapted the results from [vdLNC94a] on the non-existence of ideal operators to those complex natural relations. We prove those non-existence conditions do not apply to some of those natural relations, thus overcoming the previous negative results about ideal operators for space ordered by θ-subsumption only.

1 Introduction

A search problem consists of a set of states (the search space), a set of operators, an initial state and a goal state. The goal state may not be explicitly described, but may rather be specified through a set of properties it must satisfy.

After [Mit82], *"generalization problem is essentially a search problem"*. In the framework of definite semantics, the search space is a set of definite clauses, the initial state is given by a positive example of the target concept and the operators are learning operators that alter a hypothesis clause for the target concept into a set of new and possibly better hypotheses. The learning goal is classically defined in Inductive Logic Programming (ILP) as follows [MR94]: given a set E^+ of positive examples and a set E^- of negative examples for the target concept, a background knowledge B, find a hypothesis H such that

$$\forall e^+ \in E^+ : \quad B \cup H \models e^+ \quad (H \text{ is complete}) ,$$
$$\forall e^- \in E^- : \quad B \cup H \not\models e^- \quad (H \text{ is correct}) .$$

In ILP, the cost of exhaustively exploring the search space in order to find a hypothesis that satisfies the completeness and correctness criteria is prohibitive, and several techniques have been developed to prune the search space, either statically (before search) or dynamically (during search).

On the one hand, a well-known pruning technique [Mit82] is to exploit the generality ordering on the learning search space. For instance, given that the search proceeds bottom up with respect to a generality ordering, and that a given hypothesis H in the search space covers a negative example, it is not necessary to develop any of its generalizations, as none of them will ever meet the correctness criterion anymore.

On the other hand, pruning techniques exploiting additional constraints on the expected target concept definition known as *learning bias*, have also been extensively studied in ILP (see [NRA$^+$96] for a survey). In particular, *language bias* allows constraint setting on the syntax of the target concept definition. Handling language bias, by pruning hypotheses which are irrelevant with respect to a specific learning problem, adapts the learning process to the problem at hand, and enhances both the quality and the efficiency of learning.

However, in learning systems that search a hypothesis space ordered by a generality relation, the handling of language bias may be expensive: hypotheses generated by the learning operator may not always satisfy the language bias, which therefore have to be tested at each learning step. Even worse, it may well be that a hypothesis does not satisfy a language bias, and that some of its descendants through the learning operator satisfy it: even if a hypothesis fails against the language bias test, its descendants nevertheless have to be generated and tested.

In this paper, we study a smoother and more efficient way to integrate language bias handling in learning. As opposed to systems that only use a generality ordering to explore and prune the search space, the idea is to also take into account the language bias to order the search space. In that aim, we propose an extended definition for the learning task: given a set of properties $\mathcal{P} = \{P_1, \ldots, P_n\}$, find a hypothesis H such that $P_1(H) \wedge \ldots \wedge P_n(H)$. The P_i necessarily include at least completeness or correctness with respect to the examples of the target concept. To deal with this new definition, new quasi-orders called *natural relations* are designed that allow optimal pruning with respect to training example coverage *and* a subset $\mathcal{P}_{ord}$ of $\mathcal{P}$. This pruning is dynamic : when a generated hypothesis H does not satisfy $\mathcal{P}_{ord}$, all the descendants of H can be safely pruned. Roughly speaking, this amounts to pruning the search space with respect to both a generality relation and some language bias, as done previously with respect to a generality order only. This saves the cost of generating and testing inappropriate hypotheses.

On a more theoretical basis, ILP related works have studied different quasi-orderings for First Order Logic (FOL) search spaces: θ-subsumption [Plo70], generalized subsumption [Bun88], T-implication [IA95], or logical implication [NCdW96], and have formalized learning operators as *refinement operators* that go through a quasi-ordered space of clauses [Sha81, Nib93, vdL95]. Given a quasi-ordered space, [vdLNC94a] has defined the notion of *ideal* operator. Intuitively, the ideality property for an operator ensures that given any hypothesis H of the search space, the set of alterations of H is finite, that none of such alterations of H is equivalent to H, and that the operator is complete. Ideality seems reasonable to expect from a learning operator, but it has been proved that no ideal operator exists for unrestricted search spaces ordered by θ-subsumption [vdLNC94a] or by logical implication [vdLNC94b]. Given our natural relations, we then check whether some ideal operators may exist for the search space ordered by a natural relation, by adapting the conditions introduced in [vdLNC94a, vdLNC94b]. We find a number of favorable cases, in which those non-existence conditions do not apply. Finally, we exhibit an ideal operator for the search space ordered by a given natural relation.

The paper is organized as follows. In section 2, we give general definitions necessary to introduce our framework. In section 3, we define $\geq_P$, the *natural relation* for a property set P. We discuss in section 4 the necessary conditions for the existence of ideal learning operators for sets ordered by a natural relation and, in section 5. As an illustration, in a specific case for which these conditions are met, a new ideal operator is proposed. We conclude by situating this work with respect to previous approaches in ILP and by describing its perspectives. For the sake of brevity, proofs have been omitted from this paper, but full proofs for all propositions can be found in [TR97].

2 Definitions

2.1 Refinement Operator

In this paper, we consider a *refinement operator* as a binary relation on the search space. An operator $\mathcal{O}$ is then represented by the set of pairs (H, H'), such that $H' \in \mathcal{O}(H)$. Typically, the search space is a set of clauses S ordered by a generality relation $\geq$. A binary relation $\mathcal{O}$ is an *upward refinement operator* for $\langle S, \geq \rangle$ iff $\forall C, D \in S : C \mathcal{O} D \Rightarrow C \geq D$. In other words, $\mathcal{O}$ is a refinement operator iff

$$\forall C \in S : \{ D \in S \mid C \mathcal{O} D \} \subseteq \{ D \in S \mid C \geq D \} \ .$$

In the same way, a binary relation $\mathcal{O}$ is a *downward refinement operator* for $\langle S, \geq \rangle$ iff $\forall C, D \in S : C \mathcal{O} D \Rightarrow D \geq C$. We note $\mathcal{O}(C)$ the set $\{ D \in S \mid C \mathcal{O} D \}$. Then, we will say that an operator $\mathcal{O}$ *satisfies* a relation $\mathcal{R}$ iff $\mathcal{O} \subseteq \mathcal{R}$. [vdLNC94a] has introduced a class of theoretically interesting operators, *ideal* operators.

2.2 Ideality

We present here a summary of definitions and results on ideal operators from [vdLNC94a, vdLNC94b, vdL95].

A refinement operator $\mathcal{O}$ is said *ideal* for $\langle S, \geq \rangle$ if it is locally finite, complete and proper for $\langle S, \geq \rangle$.

1. A refinement operator $\mathcal{O}$ is said *locally finite* for $\langle S, \geq \rangle$ iff $\forall C \in S : \mathcal{O}(C)$ is finite and computable, i.e., for any hypothesis H of $\langle S, \geq \rangle$, the set of refinements of H through $\mathcal{O}$ is finite and computable, which is the least we can expect for any practical implementation of $\mathcal{O}$.

2. A downward refinement operator $\mathcal{O}$ is said *complete* for $\langle S, \geq \rangle$ iff $\forall C, D \in S : C \geq D \Rightarrow \exists E \in S : E \in \mathcal{O}^*(C) \wedge E \sim D$, where $\mathcal{O}^*$ denotes the transitive closure of $\mathcal{O}$, and $\sim$ denotes the equivalence relation of $\geq$. An upward refinement operator $\mathcal{O}$ is said *complete* for $\langle S, \geq \rangle$ iff $\forall C, D \in S : D \geq C \Rightarrow \exists E \in S : E \in \mathcal{O}^*(C) \wedge E \sim D$. This means that, given any two comparable hypotheses C and D of $\langle S, \geq \rangle$, there exists a refinement chain from C to D. In other words, if the target concept definition belongs to $\langle S, \geq \rangle$, a complete learning operator will reach it.

3. A refinement operator $\mathcal{O}$ is said *proper* for $\langle S, \geq \rangle$ iff $\forall C, D \in S : D \in \mathcal{O}(C) \Rightarrow C \not\sim D$. This last property ensures that set of refinements of H does not contain any hypothesis equivalent to H. Intuitively, at each application of $\mathcal{O}$, the rank of hypotheses with respect to the quasi-order increases.

There are two situations in which ideal operators do not exist: there exist *uncovered infinite chains* or infinite *cover set* in the search space.

The notion of *cover* is used to represent the immediate successors or predecessors of a hypothesis with respect to $\geq$.

Definition 2.1 (cover). C covers D iff $C > D$ and there is no E such that $C > E > D$. We call C an *upward cover* of D and D a *downward cover* of C.

Definition 2.2 (cover sets). A *downward* (resp. *upward*) *cover set* of a clause C in $\langle S, \geq \rangle$ is a maximal set of non-equivalent downward (resp. upward) covers of C.

Example 2.3 (downward cover sets). Let us consider a set $\{a, b, c, d, e\}$ ordered as shown on figure 1. a has two possible downward cover sets: $\{b, d\}$ or $\{c, d\}$ (b and c are equivalent and so, they cannot appear in the same cover set).

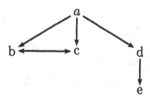

Figure 1. Example of quasi-ordered set.

It has been proved that a cover set of a hypothesis has to be included in its set of refinements through an ideal operator. As a consequence, two problems may raise:

- the cover set cannot be computed: given two hypotheses C and D, such that D is more general than C, there is an infinite number of hypotheses in between C and D, therefore completeness is lost[1];
- the cover set is infinite, which implies, that the production of an ideal operator would be infinite also and hence, the operator uncomputable.

The first case is formalized through the notion of *uncovered infinite chain*.

Definition 2.4 (uncovered infinite chains). An *uncovered infinite (strictly) descending chain* for $\langle S, \geq \rangle$ is an infinite set $\{D_i\}_{i \geq 1}$ where $D_i \in S$ such that $D_1 > D_2 > \ldots > D_n > D_{n+1} > \ldots > C$ and C has no upward cover E in S covered by all D_i. An *uncovered infinite (strictly) ascending chain* for $\langle S, \geq \rangle$ is an infinite set $\{A_i\}_{i \geq 1}, A_i \in S$ such that $C > \ldots > A_{n+1} > A_n > \ldots > A_2 > A_1$ and C has no downward cover F in S covering all A_i.

Example 2.5 (uncovered infinite descending chain). Figure 2 illustrates the descending chain definition on an example: under θ-subsumption, $\{D_i\}_{i \geq 2}$ is an uncovered infinite descending chain of C with:

$$\begin{cases} C : q(X_1) \leftarrow p(X_1, X_1) \ , \\ D_n : q(X_1) \leftarrow \{p(X_i, X_j) | 1 \leq i, j \leq n, i \neq j\} \ . \end{cases}$$

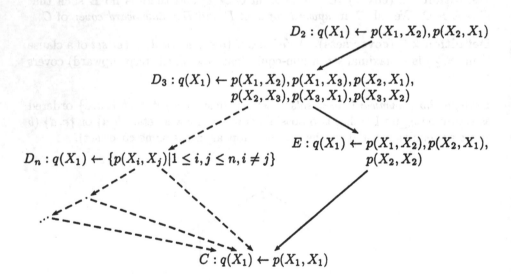

Figure 2. Uncovered infinite descending chain.

---

[1] One may think, for instance, of the set $\mathbb{R}$ of reals: for a given real, it is impossible to build a real immediately greater.

2.3 Properties

As quoted in the introduction, we indifferently include in the set of expected properties for the target concept completeness and correctness with respect to training examples and language bias constraints. As quoted in the introduction, we can find in ML and ILP literature a large range of language restrictions that a target concept definition should satisfy. We detail in the following the ones we have focused our study on. This list is largely representative of language biases classically used in ILP. Besides, as we will see in next section, it can be considered as indicative, as our framework is general enough to integrate new properties.

- A hypothesis must, or must not cover a given example.
- One may impose a (upper or lower) bound on

  - number of existential variables (variables not occurring in the head of the clause),
  - number of literals in the body of the clause,
  - depth [MF90]. The depth of a clause is the maximal depth of its terms. Variables and constants have depth zero. A term $f(\ldots, t_i, \ldots)$ has depth one plus the maximal depth of t_i.
  - level [DMR92]. The level of a clause is the maximum of the level of its variables. Variables of the head have level zero. The level of an existential variable V is one plus the minimal level of variables appearing in the first literal containing V.

- One may impose a hypothesis to be

  - range-restricted (variables of the head must appear in the body),
  - connected [Qui90] (level is defined for all variables of the hypothesis),
  - reduced for θ-subsumption (C is reduced iff $\nexists \theta : C\theta \subset C$).

In the above list, some of the language biases have been specifically developed for FOL languages. On the one hand, those language biases have an interest as they allow to express meaningful information about the expected form of the concept. For instance, the range-restriction property states that a meaningful definition for the concept "X is the grandfather of Y", should contain constraints on X and Y. On the other hand, those language biases define subsets of FOL for which the coverage test of hypotheses with respect to examples is (relatively) efficient. Finally, any hypothesis that fails against a language bias does not have to be checked against examples, which may save a lot of computation efforts.

Now the use of bias in ILP is motivated, we show in next section that the only way to prune the search space with respect to a given property is to explore it with an operator that satisfies a relation "induced" by this property, namely, its natural relation.

3 Natural Relations

Idestam-Almquist [IA95] says *"Implication is the most natural and straightforward basis for generalization in inductive learning, since the concept of induction can be defined as the inverse of logical entailment"*. We give here a more formal justification of why logical implication is the most natural relation to order a search space of hypotheses when solutions are defined with respect to at least completeness or correctness criteria. We extend the notion of natural relation to other properties.

3.1 Private property

The aim is to explore a small search space without risking to miss a solution. It is safe to stop the refinement of a given H that does not satisfy the expected properties (and therefore to prune the search space), iff no descendant of H will ever satisfy those properties. This intuition is illustrated on figure 3, and formalized in the following definition.

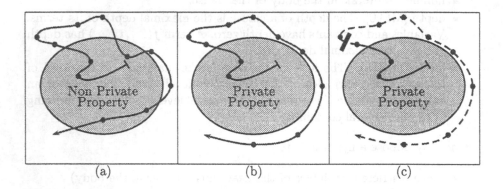

(a)	(b)	(c)

Figure 3. Private and non private properties. Figure (a) illustrates that safe pruning is not possible with respect to non private property. In case (b), pruning is sound and (c) shows how pruning operates.

Definition 3.1 (private property). A property P is said *private* with respect to the relation $\mathcal{R}$ iff

$$\forall H, H' \in S : \quad \forall \left(H \, \mathcal{R} \, H' \wedge \overline{P(H)} \Rightarrow \overline{P(H')} \right) \; {}^{2}.$$

Let us assume the property P is expressed by a FOL formula. The parameters of the property are the free variables in this formula.

---

^{2} If F is a formula, then $\forall F$ denotes the universal closure of F, which is the closed formula obtained by adding a universal quantifier for every variable having a free occurrence in F [Llo87]. The semantic of $\overline{F}$ is the negation of F.

Example 3.2 (length of clause). Let us consider the property that bounds the length of clause to k literals, expressed as $|H| \leq k$. The property LENGTH$_k$ is private with respect to the relation $\mathcal{R}$ iff

$$\forall H, H' \in S: \quad \forall k \in \mathbb{N} : (H \mathcal{R} H' \wedge |H| > k \Rightarrow |H'| > k) \ .$$

A relation $\mathcal{R}$ that satisfies this property is, for instance, the one defined by: $H \mathcal{R} H'$ iff there exists a literal L such that $H' = H \cup \{L\}$.

3.2 Natural relation

A property is private for many relations. For instance, the empty and identity relations make any property private and are, as a consequence, of little interest, as far as the pruning of the search space is concerned. Indeed, an operator satisfying the identity relation applied to a given hypothesis H, generates at most H itself. We will consider in the following that a natural relation for a given property is one of the largest relations that make this property private.

Definition 3.3 (natural relation). $\mathcal{R}$ is a *natural relation* for the property P iff

1. P is private with respect to the relation $\mathcal{R}$;
2. if a relation $\mathcal{R}'$ exists such that P is private with respect to the relation $\mathcal{R}'$ and $\mathcal{R} \Rightarrow \mathcal{R}'$, then $\mathcal{R} = \mathcal{R}'$.

Let us try to give a more precise characterization of this natural relation. We will see in the following that the natural relation of a property is indeed unique. Two hypotheses are "naturally" related if, for all possible instantiations of the property parameters, either the first hypothesis satisfies the property or the second one does not.

Proposition 3.4. *A property P has a single natural relation, denoted $\geq_P$. $\geq_P$ is defined by*

$$\forall C, D \in S: \quad C \geq_P D \Leftrightarrow \forall \left(P(C) \vee \overline{P(D)} \right) \ .$$

Therefore, a property P is private with respect to the relation $\mathcal{R}$ iff $\mathcal{R} \Rightarrow \geq_P$. This result justifies why we have chosen the largest relation as natural relation: a relation makes a property private iff this relation is included in the natural relation of the property. Therefore, safe and dynamic pruning of the search space with respect to a given property can only be achieved through an operator which satisfies its natural relation.

Remark 3.5. Given the definition of downward refinement operator (section 2.1), if $\mathcal{O}$ is downward with respect to $\geq_P$ then P is private with respect to $\mathcal{O}$.

We assume, in the remainder of this paper, that any property can be expressed as $f(H) \mathcal{R} k$ where

- f is a function from the search space S to a domain $\mathcal{D}_f$;
- $\mathcal{R}$ is a quasi-order on $\mathcal{D}_f \times \mathcal{D}_f$;
- $k \in \mathcal{D}_f$ (k represents the parameter of the property P).

Table 1 shows our properties expressed in this framework. For each property of this table, the dual property can be considered[3].

Table 1. Properties expressed in our framework.

COVER$_e$	$H \models e$
RANGE-RESTRICTED$_b$	$RR(H) = b$
CONNECTED$_b$	$Connected(H) = b$
REDUCED$_b$	$Reduced(H) = b$
LENGTH$_n$	$|H| \leq_{\mathbb{N}} n$
VARS$_n$	$Nv(H) \leq_{\mathbb{N}} n$
DEPTH$_d$	$Depth(H) \leq_{\mathbb{N}} d$
LEVEL$_l$	$Level(H) \leq_{\mathbb{N}} l$

This assumption on the form of the property allows the simplification of the expression of natural relation.

Proposition 3.6. *Let P be a property defined by $\forall C \in S : P(C) \Leftrightarrow f(C) \mathcal{R} k$. The natural relation of P is also defined by*

$$\forall C, D \in S : \quad C \geq_P D \Leftrightarrow f(C) \mathcal{R} f(D)$$

Example 3.7. Let us consider the property COVER$_e$ stating that a hypothesis H covers an example e, $H \models e$. Function f is here identity, $\mathcal{R}$ is identified to $\models$, the parameter of the function is e. By direct application of the above proposition, the natural relation for COVER$_e$ is defined by $\forall C, D \in S : C \geq_{\text{Cover}} D \Leftrightarrow C \models D$.

Thus, saying that an operator makes COVER$_e$ private is equivalent to imposing that this operator satisfies a generality ordering. This justifies that a refinement operator must satisfy a generality ordering. The notion of natural relation extends that of generality order to all properties a target concept must satisfy. Table 2 lists the natural relations for all the target concept properties we address.

Now that the natural relation for a single property has been characterized, we explore how to compute the natural relation of its dual property and then, and the natural relation of a conjunction of properties, as there are usually more than one imposed on the target concept definition.

---

[3] For a given property P, we call the dual P, the property $\overline{P}$.

Table 2. Natural relations.

Property P	Relation $\forall C, D \in S : C \geq_P D \Leftrightarrow$
COVER$_e$	$C \models D$
RANGE-RESTRICTED	$\text{RR}(C) = \text{RR}(D)$
CONNECTED	$\text{Connected}(C) = \text{Connected}(D)$
REDUCED	$\text{Reduced}(C) = \text{Reduced}(D)$
LENGTH$_n$	$|C| \leq_{\text{IN}} |D|$
VARS$_n$	$\text{Nv}(C) \leq_{\text{IN}} \text{Nv}(D)$
DEPTH$_p$	$\text{Depth}(C) \leq_{\text{IN}} \text{Depth}(D)$
LEVEL$_l$	$\text{Level}(C) \leq_{\text{IN}} \text{Level}(D)$

Proposition 3.8 (dual property). *Let P be a property and, $\geq_P$, its natural relation, $\forall C, D \in S :$ $D \geq_P C \Leftrightarrow C \geq_{\overline{P}} D$.*

The natural relation of a dual property is the inverse relation of the natural relation. After remark 3.5, a downward operator with respect to $\geq_P$ makes this property private and allows the dynamic pruning of hypotheses that do not satisfy this property. Therefore, the corresponding upward operator deals with the dual property.

Example 3.9. The natural relation for the dual of the property COVER$_e$ $\forall C, D \in S : C \geq_{\overline{\text{Cover}}} D \Leftrightarrow D \models C$.

Proposition 3.10 (conjunction of properties). *Let P_1 and P_2 be two properties, $\geq_{P_1}$ and $\geq_{P_2}$, their respective natural relation,*

$$\forall C, D \in S : \quad C \geq_{P_1 \wedge P_2} D \Leftrightarrow C \geq_{P_1} D \wedge C \geq_{P_2} D .$$

Example 3.11. By the expression of the completeness criterion as a conjunction of COVER$_{e_i}$ for e_i ranging over the set of positive examples of the target concept, the natural relation for completeness is logical entailment, as expected.

4 Ideal Operators for naturally ordered sets

In the previous section, we have defined the notion of natural relation for a property. This natural relation characterizes the set of operators that allow dynamic pruning of the search space with respect to this property. As quoted in the introduction, there is no ideal operator for unrestricted search space ordered by θ-subsumption or logical implication. The open question is now whether some of those complex natural relations are a sound basis for ideal operators, i.e., whether we may overcome the previous negative results about the existence of ideal operator for unrestricted search space ordered by a natural relation.

Notation 4.1. We denote by $\geq_f^{\mathcal{G}}$ the natural relation obtained by combining the generality ordering $\mathcal{G}$ with the property represented as $f(H)\,\mathcal{R}\,k$.

For instance, $\geq_{||}^{\theta}$ denotes the conjunction of θ-subsumption and natural relation of LENGTH$_k$. In the following, we restrict the natural relation for correctness/completeness (logical implication) to θ-subsumption, which is equivalent to logical implication for most of the practical problems (see [Got87]).

When looking for an ideal operator for a conjunction of properties P_a and P_b, a simple case is when their respective natural relations are included (i.e., when one property implies the other).

Proposition 4.2. *Let $\geq_a$ and $\geq_b$ be quasi-orders such that $\forall C, D \in S : C \geq_a D \Rightarrow C \geq_b D$. An operator is ideal for $\langle S, \geq_a \cap \geq_b \rangle$ iff it is an ideal operator for $\langle S, \geq_a \rangle$.*

There are two direct applications for this proposition. Firstly, if there is no ideal operator for $\langle S, \geq_a \rangle$, then looking for an ideal operator for $\langle S, \geq_a \cap \geq_b \rangle$ is pointless. Secondly, if we find an ideal operator for $\langle S, \geq_a \cap \geq_c \rangle$ for a given $\geq_c$, then this one is ideal for $\langle S, \geq_a \cap \geq_b \cap \geq_c \rangle$ too.

In both cases, we do not have to consider $\geq_b$, since it has no incidence on the construction of ideal operators for $\langle S, \geq_a \cap \geq_b \rangle$.

Example 4.3. Since $C \geq^{\theta} D \Rightarrow \mathrm{Depth}(C) \leq_{\mathbb{N}} \mathrm{Depth}(D)$, there exists no ideal operator for $\langle S, \geq_{depth}^{\theta} \rangle$.

Now that this simple case is solved, let us adapt the non-existence conditions for ideal operators (section 2.2) to natural relations defined in the previous section. By doing so, we aim at finding a general method for discriminating favorable cases, i.e., natural relations for which an ideal operator may exist, from others. Theorem 4.7 and proposition 4.8 are the sufficient non-existence conditions of an ideal operator (existence of an uncovered infinite chain and infinite cover sets).

The first result is a general observation about uncovered infinite chains for θ-subsumption.

Lemma 4.4. *Let $\{D_i\}_{i \geq 1}$ be an uncovered infinite chain of a clause C for θ-subsumption. In $\{D_i\}_{i \geq 1}$, the number of variables increases infinitely.*

Remark 4.5. This lemma points out that some simple quantities infinitely increase in an uncovered infinite chain, that chain being ascending or descending: number of variables, length, and number of occurrences of at least one predicate symbol. Intuitively, the only way to have an uncovered infinite chain is to add to a clause new literals with new variables.

We now focus on relations defined by conjunctions of two relations with one of them being the natural relation $\geq_f$ of a property expressed as $f(C)\,\mathcal{R}\,k$ where f is a function from the search space to a countable (possibly infinite) set.

Lemma 4.6. *Let $\{D_i\}_{i\geq 1}$ be an uncovered infinite chain of C for $\langle S, \geq_? \cap \geq_f \rangle$. There exists a n such that, for all i great enough, $f(D_i) = n$.*

We are now able to identify quasi-ordered sets which do not contain uncovered infinite chains.

Theorem 4.7. *If $\langle S, \geq_f^\theta \rangle$ contains uncovered infinite chains then there is a subset of S in which hypotheses have the same value by f and their number of variables is not bounded.*

Unfortunately, the absence of such chains does not necessarily imply the existence of ideal operators: a quasi-ordered set without uncovered infinite chain may contain some clauses which have an infinite cover set (definition 2.2). We give here a sufficient condition to have an infinite cover set.

Proposition 4.8 (infinite cover sets). *If, for a given clause C of S (ordered by $\geq_f^\theta$), we have an infinite number of clauses D which are incomparable under θ-subsumption and such that $C >^\theta D$ and there is no E such that $C >^\theta E >^\theta D$, and $f(C) = f(D)$, then the downward cover set of C is infinite.*

5 Natural Operators

We are now able to characterize natural relations for which we may expect to construct an ideal operator. The next step is to identify such relations among the ones we have considered before. Finally, we may then exhibit one ideal operator.

Notation 5.1. The notation for operators associated to natural orderings is similar to that of natural orderings (notation 4.1). G denotes the generality ordering the natural relation is based on, and f refers to the property denoted as $f(H)\mathcal{R}k$ (see table 1 for the possible values of f). $\rho_f^\mathcal{G}$ denotes a downward refinement operator, $\lambda_f^\mathcal{G}$ denotes a upward operator with respect to $\langle S, \geq_f^\mathcal{G} \rangle$. The operator $\rho_f^\mathcal{G}$ searches through a space ordered by $\geq_f^\mathcal{G}$. Stating that $\rho_f^\mathcal{G}$ is ideal means that $\rho_f^\mathcal{G}$ is ideal for $\langle S, \geq_f^\mathcal{G} \rangle$.

After example 4.3, there exists no ideal operator for $\langle S, \geq_{depth}^\theta \rangle$. As θ-subsumption ordering does not imply any of the other natural relations of table 2, we therefore look for ideal operators for conjunctions of θ-subsumption and one such relation.

Remark 4.5 provides guidelines on how to abort uncovered infinite chains for θ-subsumption: breaking those chains amounts to bounding the number of variables (with VARS_v), the number of literals (with LENGTH_n) or the number of occurrences of predicate symbols.

No language bias allows the bounding of the latter quantity. This leads us to introduce the new following language bias: for each predicate symbol p of a given alphabet $\mathcal{A}$, and a given clause C, we define $\mathrm{Occ}(p,C)$ as the number of occurrences of the predicate symbol p in clause C. This language bias, called MAX-OCC, consists in bounding the following value: $\mu(C) = \max\{\mathrm{Occ}(p,C)\}_{p\in\mathcal{A}}$. This bound can be global for all predicate symbols in $\mathcal{A}$, or specific bounds can be defined for each predicate symbol. For instance, one may specify that at most three benzene rings should appear in the body of a clause describing an active molecule in the mutagenesis application.

Given these three properties, we will now apply theoretical results of the previous section in order to identify relevant combinations to break uncovered infinite chains of θ-subsumption.

Proposition 5.2. *Neither $\langle S, \geq^{\theta}_{||}\rangle$, nor $\langle S, \geq^{\theta}_{Nv}\rangle$, nor $\langle S, \geq^{\theta}_{\mu}\rangle$ contain uncovered infinite chains.*

Theorem 4.7 cannot be applied for range-restriction, connection, reduction, depth and level: for these properties, the number of variables may increase infinitely. So, the existence of uncovered infinite chains is possible and, indeed, the uncovered infinite chain of example 2.5 is also an uncovered infinite chain for those properties.

Now that we may ensure that no uncovered infinite chain may occur neither for $\langle S, \geq^{\theta}_{||}\rangle$, nor for $\langle S, \geq^{\theta}_{Nv}\rangle$ and $\langle S, \geq^{\theta}_{\mu}\rangle$, we still have to consider the possible existence of infinite cover sets.

Proposition 5.3. *Some clauses in $\langle S, \geq^{\theta}_{Nv}\rangle$ have an infinite downward cover set.*

By exploiting the previous results, we may now build ideal operators for all three orders $\geq^{\theta}_{||}$, $\geq^{\theta}_{Nv}$, $\geq^{\theta}_{\mu}$. In the following, we will only provide the characterization of operator ρ^{θ}_{μ}. A similar technique may give us $\rho^{\theta}_{||}$ (which is similar to Shapiro's operator ρ_0), $\lambda^{\theta}_{||}$, λ^{θ}_{Nv}, λ^{θ}_{μ} and others operators associated to more complex combination of properties (see [TR97] for a full description of those ideal operators).

We introduce terms or literals which are *most general* (see [Sha81] for a similar approach).

Definition 5.4. t is a *most general term* with respect to a clause C and a variable X iff $C >^{\theta} C\{X/t\}$ and there is no u such that $u >^{\theta} t$ and $C >^{\theta} C\{X/u\}$; L is a *most general literal* with respect to a clause C, iff $C >^{\theta} C \cup \{L\}$.

One may notice that a most general literal with respect to a clause C does not unify with any literal in C (adding L to C that unifies with a literal in C would produce a clause which is θ-equivalent).

We may now introduce as an illustration the downward refinement operator ρ^{θ}_{μ}, based on θ-subsumption and MAX-OCC.

Definition 5.5 (operator ρ^{θ}_{μ}). Let C be a clause of S. Then, $D \in \rho^{\theta}_{\mu}(C)$ when exactly one of the following holds:

1. $D = C\{X/t\}$ where X is a variable of C and t is a most general term with respect to C and X.
2. $D = C\{X_1/X_2\}$ and $|C| = |D|$, where X_1 and X_2 are variables of C.
3. $D = C \cup \{p\}$, where p is a predicate symbol of arity zero and p does not occur in C.
4. $D = C \cup \{p(\ldots, Y_i, \ldots)\}$, where p is a predicate symbol (which is not a symbol without argument) such that $\text{Occ}(p, C) = 0$.
5. $D = C \cup \{p(\ldots, Y_i, \ldots)\}$, where p is a predicate symbol (which is not a symbol without argument) such that $\text{Occ}(p, C) = \mu(C) > 0$, and Y_i are new variables.
6. $D = C \cup \{L\}$, where L has a predicate symbol p such that $0 < \text{Occ}(p, C) < \mu(C)$ and L is a most general literal with respect to C.

This operator is ideal [TR97]. Let us informally illustrate some of its features on the clause C: $q \leftarrow p(X_1, X_2), p(X_2, X_1)$. C is known as a clause with an uncovered infinite ascending chain under θ-subsumption (see [vdLNC94a] for further details). First in this chain is the clause D_1:

$$q \leftarrow p(X_1, X_2), p(X_2, X_1), p(Y_1, Y_2), p(Y_2, Y_3), p(Y_3, Y_1)$$

Along this chain, $D_{i+1} >^\theta D_i$ (by definition of uncovered infinite ascending chain) and $\mu(D_{i+1}) \geq_{\text{IN}} \mu(D_i)$ (see remark 4.5). Therefore, these clauses are incomparable for $\geq_\mu^\theta$: uncovered infinite chains are broken. D_i are still more specific than C and should be computable from C by our ideal operator. Assuming that p is the only predicate symbol and the constant a is the only function symbol, ρ_μ^θ applied on C will compute the following clauses:

$$
\begin{aligned}
&q \leftarrow p(a, X_2), p(X_2, a) && \text{(applying subcase 1)} \\
&q \leftarrow p(X_1, a), p(a, X_1) && \text{(applying subcase 1)} \\
&q \leftarrow p(X_1, X_2), p(X_2, X_1), p(Y_1, Y_2) && \text{(applying subcase 5)}
\end{aligned}
$$

Further applications of ρ_μ^θ on the third refinement will yield the clause D_1.

To sum up, the search space ordered by $\geq_\mu^\theta$ does not have uncovered infinite chains any more and our operator is complete. Note that, by construction, ρ_μ^θ satisfies the natural relation of MAX-OCC, and the search space can be indifferently pruned with respect to MAX-OCCor coverage of positive examples.

Remark 5.6. These operators exactly compute the cover set with respect to the associated natural relation. This does not prove ideality [vdL95], but they are as efficient as possible, since the minimal number of refinements is computed: in order to have an ideal operator $\mathcal{O}$, one must have for every hypotheses of S the cover set of H included in the set of refinements of H, as we compute here the exact cover set of H.

6 Conclusion and Future Research

In this paper, we have introduced new relations, called *natural relations*, that allow the optimal pruning of the search space; we have adapted non-existence conditions of ideal operators to these natural relations. Moreover, we have designed a new language bias, MAX-OCC, which breaks uncovered infinite chains for θ-subsumption. Finally, we have proposed a new ideal operator that ideal for unrestricted search space ordered by combination of θ-subsumption and our natural relation.

The approach of [Sha81] is similar to our. It introduces a language bias, *size*, the aim of which is to make the refinement operator computable. Therefore, strong restrictions are set on *size*: *size* is valued in $\mathbb{N}$, and for a given $n \in \mathbb{N}$, the set of hypotheses such that $size(H) = n$ is finite. As opposed, we do not set any restriction on the language bias used, except that the property should be expressed as $f(H) \mathcal{R} k$.

We have adopted the framework introduced in [vdLNC94a], as [CBS95] ("empirical ordering") and [ELMS96] (quasi-ordering on DATALOG clauses). Our approach differs in that we have extended generality orderings in order to take into account the necessity to prune the search space with respect to language biases. This leads us to exhibit ideal operators for unrestricted search spaces.

Future work will extend our results for θ-subsumption to logical entailment. We also plan to overcome negative results of this paper by considering more complex conjunctions of properties.

Ideality has been defined initially to guarantee sound exploration of the search space. Our claim in that paper is that operators that dynamically prune their search space with respect to a set of properties may be ideal. We expect that this pruning capacity will yield efficient and adapted learning procedures. By any means, we will consider our natural relations with respect to other class of operators, such as optimal operators.

Finally, our aim is to produce an interactive learning system which provides most interesting operators given a learning task expressed as the set of properties which must be satisfied by the target concept. Such a system is in the line of generic learning architectures such as $\mathcal{HAIKU}$ [NRA+96], in which a prelimary version of private bias handling has been implemented.

Acknowledgments. This work is partially supported by the Esprit LTR Project n°20237 (ILP²). The authors wish to thank C. Nédellec, M.E. Goncalves and Q. Elhaik for their helpful and constructive comments on previous versions of this paper.

References

Bun88.   W. Buntine. Generalized subsumption and its application to induction and redundancy. *Artificial Intelligence*, 36:375–399, 1988.

CBS95.   M. Champesme, P. Brézellec, and H. Soldano. Empirically conservative search space reductions. In L. De Raedt, editor, *Proceedings of the 5th International Workshop on Inductive Logic Programming*, pages 387–402. Department of Computer Science, Katholieke Universiteit Leuven, 1995.

DMR92.   S. Džeroski, S. Muggleton, and S. Russel. PAC-Learnability of Determinate Logic Programs. In *Proceedings of 5th ACM Workshop on Computational Learning Theory*, pages 128–135. ACM Press, 1992.

ELMS96. F. Esposito, A. Laterza, D. Malerba, and G. Semeraro. Refinement of datalog programs. In *Proceedings of the MLnet Familiarization Workshop on Data Mining with Inductive Logic Programming (ILP for KDD)*, pages 73–94, July 1996.

Got87. Georg Gottlob. Subsumption and implication. *Information Processing Letters*, 24(2):109–111, January 1987.

IA95. P. Idestam-Almquist. Generalization of clauses under implication. *Journal of Artificial Intelligence Research*, 3:467–489, 1995.

Llo87. J. W. Lloyd. *Foundations of Logic Programming*. Springer, Berlin, 2 edition, 1987.

MF90. S. Muggleton and C. Feng. Efficient induction of logic programs. In *Proceedings of the 1st Conference on Algorithmic Learning Theory*, pages 368–381. Ohmsma, Tokyo, Japan, 1990.

Mit82. T. M. Mitchell. Generalization as search. *Artificial Intelligence*, 18:203–226, 1982.

MR94. S. Muggleton and L. De Raedt. Inductive logic programming: Theory and methods. *Journal of Logic Programming*, 19:629–679, 1994.

NCdW96. S.H. Nienhuys-Cheng and R. de Wolf. Least generalizations and greatest specializations of sets of clauses. *Journal of Artificial Intelligence Research*, 4:341–363, 1996.

Nib93. T. Niblett. A note on refinement operators. In P. B. Brazdil, editor, *Proceedings of the 6th European Conference on Machine Learning*, volume 667 of *Lecture Notes in Artificial Intelligence*, pages 329–335. Springer-Verlag, April 1993.

NRA+96. C. Nédellec, C. Rouveirol, H. Adé, F. Bergadano, and B. Tausend. Declarative bias in ILP. In L. De Raedt, editor, *Advances in Inductive Logic Programming*, pages 82–103. IOS Press, 1996.

Plo70. G. Plotkin. A note on inductive generalization. In *Machine Intelligence*, volume 5. Edinburgh University Press, 1970.

Qui90. J. R. Quinlan. Learning logical definitions from relations. *Machine Learning*, 5(3):239–266, 1990.

Sha81. E. Y. Shapiro. Inductive inference of theories from facts. Technical Report 192, Yale University Department of Computer Science, February 1981.

TR97. F. Torre and C. Rouveirol. Natural ideal operators in inductive logic programming. Technical report, Laboratoire de Recherche en Informatique, Université Paris Sud, 1997. To appear.

vdL95. P.R.J. van der Laag. *An Analysis of Refinement Operators in Inductive Logic Programming*. PhD thesis, Erasmus Universiteit, Rotterdam, the Netherlands, 1995.

vdLNC94a. P.R.J van der Laag and S.H. Nienhuys-Cheng. Existence and nonexistence of complete refinement operators. In F. Bergadano and L. de Raedt, editors, *Proceedings of the 7th European Conference on Machine Learning*, volume 784 of *Lecture Notes in Artificial Intelligence*, pages 307–322. Springer-Verlag, April 1994.

vdLNC94b. P.R.J. van der Laag and S.H. Nienhuys-Cheng. A note on ideal refinement operators in ILP. In S. Wrobel, editor, *Proceedings of the 4th International Workshop on Inductive Logic Programming*, volume 237 of *GMD-Studien*, pages 247–262. Gesellschaft für Mathematik und Datenverarbeitung MBH, September 1994.

A Case Study in Loyalty and Satisfaction Research

K. Vanhoof, Josee Bloemer and K. Pauwels

Limburgs Universitair Centrum
Departement Bedrijfskunde
Universitaire Campus
B-3590 Diepenbeek
Belgium
Telephone : +31-11-268608
Fax : +31-11-268700
E-mail : vanhoof@rsftew.luc.ac.be

Abstract. Over the years, research in the field of the relationship between satisfaction and loyalty has been confronted with a number of conceptual, methodological, analytical as well as operational drawbacks. We introduce an analysis method, based on machine learning techniques. The method provides insight into the nature of the relationship between satisfaction and loyalty. In this article, building on previous research concerning brand and dealer loyalty, the relationship between satisfaction with the car, satisfaction with the dealer (sales and after-sales), brand loyalty and dealer loyalty (sales and after-sales) has been investigated. The method has been evaluated and the results are compared with the results of a frequently used method.

Keywords: loyalty and satisfaction research, relevance measure, classification rules

1 Introduction

Over the years, research in the field of the relationship between satisfaction and loyalty has been confronted with a number of conceptual, methodological, analytical as well as operational drawbacks. This article will concentrate on the analytical difficulties.

First, most of the time, the distribution of satisfaction scores is rather skewed (Fornell, 1992; Reichheld, 1996). Many respondents indicate that they are 'very satisfied' or at least 'satisfied' and only a few indicate that they are 'not so satisfied' or 'not satisfied at all'. Second, the most widely used analyzing techniques assume linear relations between satisfaction and loyalty. However, there are indications that these types of relations may not be typical for this research domain. It has been suggested for instance that the relationship between low levels of satisfaction and loyalty may differ from the relationship between high levels of satisfaction and loyalty. Coyne (1989) hypothizes the existence of thresholds of satisfaction for affecting customer behavior. Heskett et al (1994) and Jones and Sasser (1995) argue that only extremely satisfied customers demonstrate loyal behavior.

This picture becomes even more complicated if not just one type of loyalty is taken into account but different types. For instance, brand loyalty and store loyalty or dealer loyalty. Studies generally indicate that store or dealer loyalty is an intervening variable between satisfaction with the product and brand loyalty, but the nature of the relationship remains unclear.

Concentrating on these analytical problems within the field of the relationship between customer satisfaction and loyalty,we introduce in this article a framework of analysis methods, which helps to resolve some of the above mentioned issues. In the framework no linear relationships are presumed and different relations between different factors are allowed for. Moreover, it allows to take into account the skewness of the original data-set. Last but not least, it also helps to provide insight into the nature of the relationship between satisfaction and loyalty. In this article, building on previous research concerning brand and dealer loyalty, the relationship between satisfaction with the car, satisfaction with the dealer (sales and after-sales), brand loyalty and dealer loyalty (sales and after-sales) will be investigated.

2 Method of analysis

The primary goal of the proposed method is the discovery, representation and analysis of 'interesting' data regularities and dependencies between attributes (such as satisfaction) and the concept or goal variable (such as loyalty). In this application interesting' means that we are able to confirm or reject hypotheses from previous research. More concrete, the following hypotheses are of special interest :

A. the relationship between low levels of satisfaction and loyalty may differ from the relationship between high levels of satisfaction and loyalty;

B. the existence of thresholds of satisfaction;

C. only extremely satisfied customers demonstrate loyal behavior.

For reaching our goal we used from the machine learning community class-sensitive discretization, a context-sensitive relevance measurement technique and the analysis of classification rules as research methods.

2.1 Discretization

When the discretization algorithm is concept-sensitive, it is possible to construct intervals of consecutive attribute values which feature a concept distribution that is uniform and homogeneous but, at the same time, contrasts the distributions of adjacent intervals significantly.

A top-down method for discretizing continuous attributes based on a minimal entropy heuristic, presented in Catlett (1991) and Fayyad & Irani (1993), is also used in our experimental study. This supervised algorithm uses the concept information entropy of candidate partitions to select intervals for discretization. By using this concept sensitive discretesation algorithm, we are able to detect threshold values of satisfaction (hypotheses B).

For discretizing the concept (goal variable) we used the monothetic contrast criterion (Van de Merckt 1993):

$$Contrast(N_1, N_2, A) = \frac{N_1 N_2}{N_1 + N_2}(m_1 - m_2)^2$$

where N_1, N_2 are the number of cases of the resulting binary split and m_i is the mean value for attribute A of N_i instances. The desirable split is the cut point that produces the highest contrast. As a stopping criterion we used the MDLP criterion.

2.2 Contextual merit and determination of satisfiers, dissatisfiers and performers

Contextual merits (Hong 1994, Vanhoof 1995) capture relative importance of attributes in distinguishing the concept values in the context of other attributes. Using this measure has one main advantage: we have one common selection criterium to determine the most interesting attributes in different contexts.

So it is possible to find the most important attributes, in the context of the other attributes, separately for every loyalty value. This allows us to define our definitions. An attribute is called a dissatisfier when it has a high contextual merit for a low loyalty level an a low contextual merit for a high loyalty level. An attribute is called a satisfier when it has a low contextual merit for a low loyalty level and a high contextual merit for a high loyalty level. An attribute is a performer when it has a high contentual merit for a low and high loyalty level. An attribute is a less-relevant attribute when it is nor a satisfier nor a dissatisfier nor a performer.

2.3 Analysis of the corresponding classification rules

The previous definitions(satisfiers,dissatisfiers,..) can be strengthened by analysing the most interesting corresponding classification rules. A corresponding rule is a rule where the level of the independent attribute is the same as the level of the concept. A confidence ar coverage level is considered as high when it is above 70%. For a dissatisfier A, the most interesting corresponding rule is 'IF satisfaction = low Then loyalty = low'. When this rule shows a high confidence and a low coverage level, this attribute is considered as a penalty attribute. For a satisfier the most interesting corresponding rule is 'IF satisfaction= high Then loyalty = high'. When this rule shows a high confidence and a low coverage level, this attribute is considered as a reward attribute. When the confidence level is low and the coverage level is high, the attribute is a characteristic descriptor. When both confidence and coverage level are high, we may conclude that the attribute level and the concept level are strongly related.

For a performer C, the most interesting corresponding rules are: *'IF satisfaction = low Then loyalty = low'* and *'IF satisfaction= high Then loyalty = high'*. Attribute C is called a basic attribute when the first rule indicates a penalty and the second rule a characteristic pattern. The attribute C is called an excitement attribute when the first rule shows a characteristic and the second rule a reward pattern. Finally, the combination of a penalty pattern and a reward pattern indicates a strongly related performer.

3 Research design

Since we choose the automobile market as the research setting, the concepts included in the analysis are: satisfaction with a car, satisfaction with the sales service, satisfaction with the after sale service, brand loyalty, dealer sales loyalty and dealer after-sales loyalty.

The respondents in the empirical part of the study are customers of different automobile dealers (n= 407) of two related German brands in the Netherlands. These two brands belong to the same holding and are therefore often sold by the same dealer. However, brand A is generally regarded as more exclusive and expensive than brand B. The market shares of both brands differ remarkably; brand A has a smaller share than brand B. Because the respondents had to express their feelings about the sales service, the car had to be bought less than two years before. Furthermore, the customer had to have some experience with the after sales service, which leads us to impose a minimum of a one year ownership. Previous research (Bloemer and Lemmink, 1992) found significant differences with respect to loyalty between new and used cars and between automobiles for private and for business use. In order to avoid difficulties here and prevent them from confusing our findings, we decided to concentrate on new cars for private use. Therefore, a homogeneous group of car owners will be researched here.

4 Results, discussion and managerial implications

Overviewing our findings (table 1), the mutual dependence between the loyalty constructs becomes clear. Especially brand loyalty and dealer sales loyalty are closely linked. A second look at the results for each brand seperately, reveals important differences however. Table 1 summarizes the findings about the independent attributes and the loyalty concept (in bold) for both brands. The classifaction results (satisfier, dissatisfier,...) and the patterns of the corresponding classification rules, based on the contextual merit analyses, are shown in seperate columns.

Table 1: Summary of the general findings for brand A and brand B

Brand Loyalty	Brand A	Role	Brand B	Role
Dissatisfiers	Satisfaction Sales	P	/	
Satisfiers	Dealer AS loyalty	C	Dealer AS loyalty	R
Performers	Dealer S loyalty	E	Dealer S loyalty	SR
	Satisfaction Car	B	Satisfaction Car	B
less relevant	Satisfaction AS		Satisfaction AS	
			Satisfaction Sales	
Dealer Sales Loyalty				
Dissatisfiers	Satisfaction Car	P		
	Satisfaction Sales	SR	Satisfaction Sales	P
	Satisfaction AS	P		
Satisfiers	/		/	
Performers	Brand loyalty	SR	Brand Loyalty	B
	Dealer AS loyalty	SR	Dealer AS loyalty	B
less relevant	/		Satisfaction Car	
			Satisfaction AS	
Dealer after-sales loyalty				
Dissatisfiers	Satisfaction Sales	P	Satisfaction AS	P
Satisfiers	/		/	
Performers	Dealer S loyalty		Dealer S loyalty	B
	Brand loyalty	B	Brand loyality	B
less relevant	Satisfaction Car		Satisfaction Car	
	Satisfaction AS		Satisfaction Sales	

Legend: AS = After Sales, S = Sales,P = Penalty; C= characteristic, R = Reward, SR = strongly related, B = basic, E = exciter.

In the case of the exclusive brand A, it is obvious that the satisfaction with the car must be high for brand loyalty to occur. Our findings confirm satisfaction with the car being a performer factor for brand loyalty. However, satisfaction with the car is neither the only nor the most important attribute for brand loyalty. The contextual merit of dealer sales loyalty is twice as high, indicating that customer who are loyal to the dealer, also demonstrate brand loyalty. Another attribute influenced by dealers, satisfaction with the sales service, is a penalty factor. A customer dissatisfied with the sales service is not likely to stay loyal to the brand. When the minimum requirements for brand loyalty are met, dealer after-sales loyalty starts to play a role. Customers who return to the same dealer for after-sales service are likely to buy the same kind of brand on the next purchase occasion.

For brand B, the direct impact of satisfaction on loyalty is more pronounced. First of all, satisfaction with the car is the only relevant satisfaction measure. Improving satisfaction with the car is likely to result in proportionately higher levels of brand loyalty (basic performer). Manufacturers and dealers should therefore focus on sound car quality, taking into account that brand B customers feel capable of judging the quality of the car, since they base their loyalty decision on this judgement.

Dealers interested in improving low dealer sales loyalty, should above all concentrate on its penalty attribute; satisfaction with the sales service. The findings for dealer after-sales loyalty mirror those for dealer sales loyalty. Satisfaction with the after-sales service is a penalty dissatisfier. In contrast to brand A customers, for which this attribute was less relevant, brand B customers base their loyalty decision on the quality of the after-sales service. An excellent technical staff that can also communicate on the level of the brand B customer, will help the dealer in improving satisfaction and enhancing after-sales loyalty. Dissatisfied customers will use alternative service options. Again, excellent technical expertise and customer satisfaction is only the first step. Brand loyalty and dealer sales loyalty are basic performers and should be monitored as well. Finally, high levels of dealer after-sales loyalty can not be garantueed. Building on previous discussion, a transactional approach to dealing with brand B customers could be the best alternative.

5 Comparison of the used method with Two-Stage-Least-Squares analysis

Comparing the 2SLS analysis with the machine learning method, we notice identical results concerning the existence of relationships. In the 2SLS analysis for both brands, all the hypotheses about the direct link between a satisfaction and the corresponding loyalty construct were confirmed. The only exception was the non-significance of the relation between satisfaction with the after-sales service and dealer after-sales loyalty for brand A. These findings correspond to the results of the presented analysis method: whereas the satisfaction measure always shows to be a relevant attribute for the corresponding loyalty factor, satisfaction with the after-sales service is a less relevant attribute for dealer after-sales loyalty. In other words, the existence of relationships is correctly identified by means of the analysis method.

6 Conclusion

We presented an analysis method customized for our application and showed that this method can be used as a complementar method for the frequently (in this application domain) used two-stage-least-square analysis method. The 2SLS-method assumes linear relationships and lacks the richness of attribute classification. For instance, satisfaction with the car has an impact on dealer sales loyalty for both brands (significant correlation in 2SLS), but there is no means of establishing whether this satisfaction influences mainly the lower or the upper scores of dealer sales loyalty. In contrast, the analysis method classifies satisfaction with the car as a dissatisfier for brand A and as a satisfier for brand B. On the other hand, the absence of significance tests is a disadvantage of this method compared to the 2SLS-analysis.

In the context of the identified mutual dependence between the loyalty constructs, neither 2SLS nor the presented method can identify the direction of the relationship. Nevertheless, the method does break down these relations in terms of satisfiers,dissatisfiers and performers, providing additional insight in the nature of the relationship. This allows us to confirm or reject hypotheses from literature. The generated output is more comprehensible than a 2SLS model, so it was relatively easy for the domain experts to extract managerial conclusions and to link the results with previous results.

We conclude that the proposed method offers several advantages satisfaction-loyalty research. However, additional research is needed to address its weaknesses and explore its possibilities in other research settings.

References

1. Bloemer, J.M.M., Lemmink, J.G.A.M.: The importance of customer satisfaction in explaining brand and dealer loyalty. Journal of Marketing Management **8** (1992) 351-364.
2. Coyne, Kevin P.: Beyond Service Fads: Meaningful Strategies for the Real World. Sloan Management Review (Summer) (1989) 69-76.
3. Catlett, J.: On changin continuous attributes into ordered discrete attributes. In: European working session on learning (1991).
4. Fayyad, U.M., Irani, K.B.: Multi-interval discretizatioin of continouos-valued attributes for classification learning. In: M. Kaufmann (ed.) Proccedings of the 13th Internaltional Joint Conference on Artificial Intelligence (1993) 1022-1027.

5. Fornell, C.: A national customer satisfaction barometer: the Swedish experience. Journal of Marketing 56 (1992) 6-21.
6. Heskett, J., Jones, T., Lovemer, G., Sasser, W., Schlesinger, L.: Putting the Service-Profit Chain to work. Harvard Business Review (March-April) (1994) 164-171.
7. Hong, S. J.: Use of contextual information for feature ranking and discretization. Technical report RC 19664, IBM Research Division (1994).
8. Jones, T.O., Sasser, W.E.: Why Satisfied Customers Defect. Harvard Business Review (November-December) (1995) 88-99.
9. Merkckt, T. van de: Desion trees in numerical attributes spaces. In: M. Kaufmann (ed.), Proceedings of the 13th International Joint Conference on Artificial Intelligence (1993) 1016-1021.
10. Reichheld F.: The Loyalty Effect. The Hidden Force Behind Growth, Profits, and Lasting Value. Bain Company Inc. Harvard Business School Press. Boston, Massachusetts (1996).
11. Vanhoof, K., Swinnen, G.: Comparing different measures of relevance. In: New techniques and technologies for statistics (Eurostat seminar) (1995) 520-533, Bonn.

Ibots Learn Genuine Team Solutions

Cristina Versino and Luca Maria Gambardella

IDSIA, Corso Elvezia 36, CH-6900 Lugano, Switzerland
{cristina,luca}@idsia.ch, http://www.idsia.ch

Abstract. "Ibots" (Integrating roBOTS) is a computer experiment in group learning. It is designed to understand how to use *reinforcement learning* to program automatically a team of robots with a shared mission. Moreover, we are interested in deriving *genuine team solutions*. These are policies whose form strongly depends on the number of robots composing the team, on their individual skills and weaknesses, and on any other mission boundary condition which makes it worth to prefer "at a team level" certain solutions to others. The Ibots learn to accomplish the integration mission by means of a reinforcement signal which measures their performance as a team. This form of payoff leads to genuine team solutions. Benefits and drawbacks of using a single team payoff as opposed to individual robot payoffs are discussed.

1 Introduction

Reinforcement learning [1] provides us with a framework to achieve self-programming, adaptive robots. In *single robot* missions, the reinforcement signal directly evaluates the behavior of the only robot in charge of the task. The picture changes as *many robots* are acting synchronously, with no knowledge about teammate activities. In this scenario, if the reinforcement signal reflects the whole team performance, each single robot is faced with the problem of deciding to what extent its own behavior has contributed to the overall team's good or bad score: this is the *robot credit assignment problem*.

The robot credit assignment problem can be bypassed in at least two ways.

A *first* way is to enable *communication* between teammates [2, 3, 4]. If a robot is *aware* of other robots' perceptions and actions, then it is in a position to make sense out of a global team payoff. But communication is not always possible technically and it tends to become a bottleneck as the team size increases [5].

A *second* way of avoiding the robot credit assignment problem is to measure *each robot's individual performance* instead of team performance. In [6, 7] this idea is applied to the training of a group of real robots in a puck collection task. Each robot in the team learns a personal policy through individual payoff. For example, a robot is rewarded whenever it either grasps a puck or drops a puck at a home area. In this framework, a single robot is not interested in the performance of its teammates, because it addresses the mission in an individualistic sense. We see *two* drawbacks in this approach. *First:* its assumption is that team performance indirectly increases because individual performance increases. However, if the robots do not learn the task at a *similar pace*, it cannot be guaranteed that each robot will learn and participate to the mission. If not all robots learn how to contribute to the mission, the team performance will be suboptimal. As an example, suppose that in the puck collection task one robot in the team manages to learn the individually optimal policy after a few trials. This "super-robot" will collect most of the pucks by itself, diminishing the learning opportunities of its teammates because pucks are a *limited, shared resource*. *Second:* where do the policies learnt by the robots converge? They will converge to the optimal policy for a robot carrying out the mission by itself. The robots will behave as "clones" of *a robot designed to work alone*. We feel this violates the spirit of team learning, which should be aimed instead at producing *genuine team solutions*.

Genuine team solutions are policies whose shape is strongly influenced by the number of robots composing the team, by each robot's skills and weaknesses, and by any other mission boundary condition which is relevant for discriminating "at a team level" some good solutions against some others.

To obtain truly team solutions, one should use team payoffs at the price of dealing with the ambiguity posed by the robot credit assignment problem.

Experiments along this line are illustrated in recent works [8, 9, 10]. In [8] a team of simulated agents learns signaling behaviors to efficiently solve an object-gathering task in an unknown and changing environment. The reinforcement signal is based on the total time needed by the team to gather all the objects in the workspace. Experiments are carried out under several conditions: with teams of different size, with a variable number of objects, and with different object distributions. Statistical analysis of the results shows that the team is able to discover a near-to-optimal signaling policy given specific mission conditions. In [9] a team of Q-learning agents is engaged in the real-world problem of elevator dispatching. Each agent is responsible for controlling one elevator car. Two different control architectures are tested. In the *parallel* architecture, the agents share a single neural network which models a common policy: this allows the agents to learn from each others experiences but forces them to use identical policies. In the *decentralized* architecture, the agents learn personal networks, which allow them to specialize their control policies. In both architectures, the team receives as global payoff the sum of squared wait times of passengers. Results obtained in simulation surpass the best known heuristic elevator control algorithm.

This paper presents "Ibots" (Integrating roBOTS) [10], a computer experiment in collective robotics designed to understand how to use reinforcement learning to program automatically a team of robots with a shared mission. The "integration" mission is an artificial task for robots, but it addresses several issues commonly arising in group learning, such as: *sharing a limited resource* in a way which is beneficial for the team; learning *public* or *private* policies; learning by trial-and-error from a *global team payoff*. Experimental results show that the Ibots learn to adapt their behavior to the actual team size and to different mission boundary conditions, as well as to each robots's special skill or limitation. The robot credit assignment problem (which arises when the Ibots learn private policies *without communication*) is handled with rules analogous to those used

 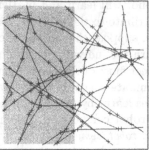 

Fig. 1. (Left) The squared arena and the "half-full" *Region*: $I = 0.49$. The arena side is 500 unit long. (Middle) Trajectory of one Ibot running a solitary trial with $N_{max} = 100$ and $Prog = (30°, 200)$. Crosses indicate sampled points. The result is $N_{in} = 52$, $\hat{I} = 0.52$. (Right) Trajectories of two Ibots running a shared trial with $N_{max} = 100$, starting from a scattered configuration and running private control programs: $Prog^1 = (180°, 50)$ (gray trace), $Prog^2 = (20°, 150)$ (black trace). The result is $N_{in}^1 = 55$, $N_{in}^2 = 30$, $\hat{I} = 0.85$. Ibot 1 took $N_{sam}^1 = 61$ samples, Ibot 2 took $N_{sam}^2 = 39$.

in connectionist reinforcement learning to solve the network structural credit assignment problem [11]. After all, a neural net is a good example of a set of partially independent agents which learn to act well as a team. In a similar way, the Ibots manage to learn genuine team solutions.

2 Ibots

The *mission* for the Ibots is to guess the integral I ($0 \leq I \leq 1$) of an arbitrary gray *Region* drawn on the white ground of a squared arena (Fig. 1, left).

How are robots turned into Ibots? Let us first consider the case of a team composed of one Ibot.

2.1 One Ibot

The Ibot's *control program Prog* lets it explore the arena while sampling the ground color. By activating *Prog*, the Ibot performs a *trial* run (Fig. 1, middle).

A trial starts from a random location in the arena. It is a sequence of N_{max} *elementary movements* separated by stops. Whenever the Ibot stops, it samples the ground color. A "gray" reading gives evidence for the sample to be "inside *Region*", a "white" reading is interpreted as "outside *Region*". At the end of the trial, the Ibot returns the number N_{in} of samples inside *Region*. $\hat{I} = N_{in}/N_{max}$ is its estimate of I at this trial. $E = |I - \hat{I}|$ is the error in the estimate.

How are elementary movements generated? The Ibot control program *Prog* depends stochastically on two parameters $(\alpha_{prog}, \delta_{prog})$ which remain fixed during a trial. α_{prog} is used to generate a rotation instruction for the Ibot, while δ_{prog} induces a translation. The semantics of α_{prog} and δ_{prog} is as follows. First, a number α is drawn from a uniform distribution in $[-\alpha_{prog}, +\alpha_{prog}]$. This is interpreted by the Ibot as: "Rotate α degrees.". Second, a number δ is drawn from a uniform distribution in $[0, \delta_{prog}]$. The interpretation for δ is: "Translate δ units in your current heading direction, calling the *bumping rule* if necessary.". The bumping rule is called when the Ibot meets the arena border before having covered the whole distance δ. In this case, the Ibot rotates 180° and covers the remaining distance. The bumping rule can be called recursively.

In our computer experiment, a rotation instruction is executed by the Ibot in one time unit whatever the rotation angle α; the execution time of a translation instruction is directly proportional to the distance δ.

Finally, both program parameters α_{prog} and δ_{prog} take values in a finite range: $0 \leq \alpha_{prog} \leq \alpha_{max}$ and $0 \leq \delta_{prog} \leq \delta_{max}$.

2.2 A Team of Ibots

Each Ibot i $(i = 1, \ldots, N_{ibots})$ being equipped with a control program $Prog^i = (\alpha^i_{prog}, \delta^i_{prog})$, there are several ways of generalizing from the single Ibot case to the team case (Fig. 1, right). We have considered both the cases where the $Prog^i$s may be *public* or *private*. Public means that all Ibots share the same $Prog$ (i.e., all $Prog^i$ are equal), while private means that each Ibot works with a personal, different $Prog^i$.

The Ibots activate the $Prog^i$s in parallel to run a team trial. At the beginning of the trial, the Ibot locations are chosen at random in the arena, and these are either *clustered* or *scattered*. In the clustered configuration, all Ibots have the same initial position and orientation; in the scattered configuration, they have different positions and orientations. During a trial, the Ibots are granted a total of N_{max} elementary movements to collect N_{max} samples of the ground color *overall: samples are the team limited and shared resource.* Whenever an Ibot stops to take a sample, it is allowed to do so only if less than N_{max} samples have been taken by the team so far. Notice that when the Ibots work with private $Prog^i$s, each Ibot i collects a different number of samples N^i_{sam}: Ibots with small δ^i_{prog}s traslate for short distances and take, on the average, more samples than Ibots with larger δ^i_{prog}s. At the end of the trial, each Ibot i returns the number N^i_{in} of samples it counted inside *Region*. These contributions are summed in $N_{in} = \sum_i N^i_{in}$, leading to the team integral estimate $\hat{I} = N_{in}/N_{max}$, the error being $E = |I - \hat{I}|$.

Finally, Ibots are *immaterial*, they do not collide when their trajectories intersect.

3 Programmed Ibots vs. Learning Ibots

The goal of group learning is to find control programs $Prog^i$s which lead to estimates $\hat{I}$ close to I. As each program depends on its parameters α^i_{prog} and δ^i_{prog}, the target of learning is to discover "good" pairs $(\alpha^i_{prog}, \delta^i_{prog})$.

Notice that we know a *general* solution, namely:

$$\forall i : \begin{cases} \alpha^i_{prog} = 180° \\ \delta^i_{prog} = \text{"length of arena diagonal"} \end{cases} \tag{1}$$

With this choice of parameters, the Ibots perform a pseudo-random motion and take samples *uniformly distributed* in the arena. This brings us to the hypothesis of the Monte Carlo method [12] for integration. This states that, by drawing N_{max} points from a uniform distribution in the arena, the error E in the estimate of the integral is probabilistically bounded by N_{max}:

$$P\left\{ E \leq \frac{1}{\sqrt{N_{max}}} \right\} \geq 0.9999 \tag{2}$$

For example, by drawing 100 points, the error in the estimate will not exceed 0.1. Given N_{max}, this result quantifies the *admissible error* for the Ibots mission. We call the control programs defined by Eq. 1 the "programmer solution", because it reflects, in our opinion, the way a programmer would address this robot programming task: by looking for a *general* solution, which will work whatever the number of Ibots in the team, independently of their starting configuration in the arena. Though appealing, we are not interested in this *a priori* solution. Rather, we are looking for *real team solutions* established through experience. These should depend on the number of Ibots, on their initial configuration, and on their specific skills when these latter are no longer homogeneous.

4 Learning to Be Good Ibots

"Good" *Prog*^{i}s are programs which lead to *admissible* and *stable* estimates of I. The Ibots learn good *Prog*^{i}s by reinforcement through a sequence of trials. Each time instant t corresponds to a team trial. Let $Prog^i(t) = (\alpha^i_{prog}(t), \delta^i_{prog}(t))$ be Ibot i control program at time t. The following 4 steps are repeated forever.

1. *Each Ibot "i" independently generates a new, tentative control program* $New^i(t) = (\alpha^i_{new}(t), \delta^i_{new}(t))$ *by slightly modifying* $Prog^i(t)$.

    Given:

    $$\alpha^i_{temp}(t) = \alpha^i_{prog}(t) + \alpha^i_{rand}(t) \cdot \alpha_{step}$$
    $$\delta^i_{temp}(t) = \delta^i_{prog}(t) + \delta^i_{rand}(t) \cdot \delta_{step}$$

    it is:

    $$\alpha^i_{new}(t) = \begin{cases} 0° & \text{if } \alpha^i_{temp}(t) < 0° \\ \alpha_{max} & \text{if } \alpha^i_{temp}(t) > \alpha_{max} \\ \alpha^i_{temp}(t) & \text{otherwise} \end{cases}$$

$$\delta^i_{new}(t) = \begin{cases} 0 & \text{if } \delta^i_{temp}(t) < 0 \\ \delta_{max} & \text{if } \delta^i_{temp}(t) > \delta_{max} \\ \delta^i_{temp}(t) & \text{otherwise} \end{cases}$$

where:

- $\alpha^i_{rand}(t)$ and $\delta^i_{rand}(t)$ are uniform random numbers in $[-\rho(t), +\rho(t)]$ (see below for the definition of $\rho(t)$);
- α_{step} and δ_{step} are constants.

2. *The Ibots collectively carry out a trial with the newly generated programs $New^i(t)s$.*

At the beginning of the trial, the Ibots are positioned at a random configuration. At the end of the trial, each Ibot returns $N^i_{in}(t)$. The team integral estimate is $\hat{I}(t) = N_{in}(t)/N_{max}$, with $N_{in} = \sum_i N^i_{in}$. The error in the estimate $E(t)$ is:

$$E(t) = \frac{|I - \hat{I}(t)|}{\max(I, 1 - I)}$$

3. *The team reinforcement signal $R(t)$ is computed and communicated to each Ibot.*

$R(t)$ is defined as the difference between the team errors in two successive trials:

$$R(t) = E(t - 1) - E(t) \qquad (3)$$

$E(t - 1)$ can be thought of as a naïve predictor of $E(t)$.

4. *Each Ibot "i" independently computes a modification for its control program and updates it.*

The modification is:

$$\Delta\alpha^i_{prog}(t) = \epsilon \cdot R(t) \cdot (\alpha^i_{new}(t) - \alpha^i_{new}(t - 1)) \qquad (4)$$
$$\Delta\delta^i_{prog}(t) = \epsilon \cdot R(t) \cdot (\delta^i_{new}(t) - \delta^i_{new}(t - 1)) \qquad (5)$$

where ϵ, a real parameter, is the learning rate.
Given:

$$\alpha^i_{temp}(t + 1) = \alpha^i_{prog}(t) + \Delta\alpha^i_{prog}(t)$$
$$\delta^i_{temp}(t + 1) = \delta^i_{prog}(t) + \Delta\delta^i_{prog}(t)$$

the updated control programs is:

$$\alpha^i_{prog}(t+1) = \begin{cases} 0° & \text{if } \alpha^i_{temp}(t+1) < 0° \\ \alpha_{max} & \text{if } \alpha^i_{temp}(t+1) > \alpha_{max} \\ \alpha^i_{temp}(t+1) & \text{otherwise} \end{cases}$$

$$\delta^i_{prog}(t+1) = \begin{cases} 0 & \text{if } \delta^i_{temp}(t+1) < 0 \\ \delta_{max} & \text{if } \delta^i_{temp}(t+1) > \delta_{max} \\ \delta^i_{temp}(t+1) & \text{otherwise} \end{cases}$$

The description of the algorithm is completed by the following remarks and definitions.

- When the Ibots work with public control programs, only one Ibot generates the tentative program $New^i(t)$ at step 1; then, $New^i(t)$ is communicated to the other team members.
- About the error measure $E(t)$: by dividing $|I - \hat{I}(t)|$ by $max(I, 1 - I)$, $E(t)$ varies between 0 and 1, no matter what the value of I. As a consequence, the reinforcement signal also varies in a fixed interval, namely $[-1, +1]$.
- $E(-1) = E(0)$. At trial 0, we assume that the expected error $E(-1)$ is equal to the measured error $E(0)$. This implies $R(0) = 0$, so no change is made to $Prog(0)$.
- $\rho(t) = max(|R(t-1)|, \rho_c)$. The amount of variation in the new control programs is proportional to the absolute value of the reinforcement signal at previous trial. This is to enhance the tendency of escaping from programs with unpredictable performance, and, viceversa, to favor the convergence towards programs with stable performance. ρ_c is a positive constant which maintains a minimal level of exploration in program space when $R(t-1) = 0$.

In the reinforcement learning panorama, this set-up corresponds to a *nonassociative, immediate* reward learning problem running on a distributed system. The closest analogy is with a neural net [11] with no inputs from the environment other than the performance signal itself, and using an adaptive critic to predict its performance. The learning algorithm is expected to guide the team towards admissible and stable control programs.

5   Experiments

On the "half-full" *Region* ($I = 0.49$) of Fig. 1, we have run repeated learning experiments with Ibots' teams of increasing size ($N_{ibots} = 1, \ldots, 14$), with public or private $Prog^i$s, and starting from clustered or scattered configurations. We have also considered Ibots with heterogeneous skills due to differences in sensing and acting capabilities. In all experiments we have set: $N_{max} = 100$ (the corresponding admissible error being 0.1), $\alpha_{max} = 180°$ and $\delta_{max} = 500$ (length of arena side), $\alpha_{step} = \alpha_{max}/10$ and $\delta_{step} = \delta_{max}/10$, and, for each Ibot i, $Prog^i(0) = (\alpha^i_{prog}(0), \delta^i_{prog}(0)) = (0°, 0)$.

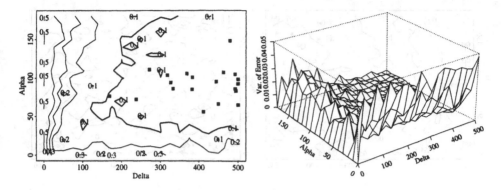

Fig. 2. One Ibot. (Left) $\mu_{prog}(E)$ and convergence points for 20 learning experiments. (Right) $\sigma^2_{prog}(E)$.

To examine the form of learnt programs, a learning experiment was stopped either after having obtained 10 consecutive admissible estimates, or after a predefined number of trials, depending on which of these two events occured first. Programs learnt by applying this stopping criterion are called the *convergence points* of the learning experiment.

5.1 One Ibot

The single Ibot experiment is a point of reference for comparing results obtained with teams of Ibots. It requires to discover a pair $(\alpha_{prog}, \delta_{prog})$ which produces admissible and stable integral estimates. As in this case the program space is bidimensional, one can explore it in a systematic way to test the quality of a significant number of programs. Thus, before starting the learning experiments, we have run background trials with different combinations of α_{prog} and δ_{prog} values. Each combination program was tested on N_{trials} different trials to have a sample of integral estimates $\hat{I}_k$. Then, for each program we computed the *mean of errors* $\mu_{prog}(E)$ and the *variance of errors* $\sigma^2_{prog}(E)$:

$$\mu_{prog}(E) = \frac{1}{N_{trials}} \sum_k |I - \hat{I}_k| = \frac{1}{N_{trials}} \sum_k E_k$$

$$\sigma^2_{prog}(E) = \frac{1}{N_{trials}} \sum_k (E_k - \mu_{prog}(E))^2$$

$\mu_{prog}(E)$ measures the accuracy of the estimates, while $\sigma^2_{prog}(E)$ measures their stability.

Figure 2 shows plots of $\mu_{prog}(E)$ (left) and $\sigma^2_{prog}(E)$ (right) in the Ibot program space. On the $\mu_{prog}(E)$ plot we have highlighted the contour lines of level 0.1: these lines identify the space of admissible programs. Notice that these programs are also stable. Most of them are distant from the "programmer solution"

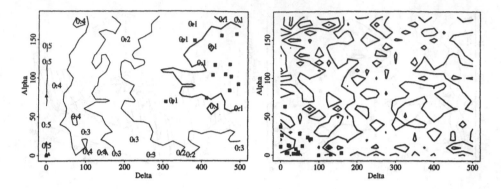

Fig. 3. A team of 14 Ibots with public control programs. $\mu_{prog}(E)$ and convergence points for 20 learning experiments for clustered configurations (left) and for scattered configurations (right).

$(180°, 700)$. From the $\sigma^2_{prog}(E)$ plot we also remark that not only admissible programs are stable. For example, all "staying in place" programs ($\delta_{prog} = 0$) have a very predictable performance. This makes the learning task more difficult.

The convergence points of 20 learning experiments have been indicated as squares on the left plot of Fig. 2. Learning stopped in all cases before the limit of 1000 trials. All experiments ended inside the space of admissible and stable programs.

5.2 Teams of Ibots

The form of admissible and stable programs completely changes for teams of Ibots.

Public Control Programs. The first case study we have addressed is that of Ibots equipped with public control programs. As in the single Ibot case, the program space is bidimensional, so we first ran background trials (with no learning) for teams of increasing size, both for the clustered and the scattered configuration. The results for the largest team of 14 Ibots are shown in Fig. 3. The left plot is the contour plot of $\mu_{prog}(E)$ for the clustered configuration, while the right plot shows $\mu_{prog}(E)$ for the scattered configuration. On the left plot, the bold line delimits the space of admissible programs; for the scattered configuration, all programs are admissible.

By comparing these results with those of Fig. 2 (left), one observes how the single Ibot's solution space "shrinks" or "expands" depending on whether the Ibots are started in the clustered or in the scattered way. Why?

First, consider the clustered configuration starting condition. As the Ibots begin a trial from the same position and with the same orientation, they have to disperse in the arena in order to explore it. Moreover, the number of samples they are allowed to take as individuals decreases as the team size increases,

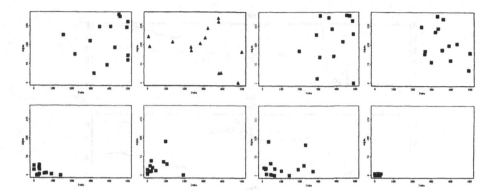

Fig. 4. A team of 14 Ibots with private control programs. Convergence points for 4 learning experiments for clustered configurations (first row) and for scattered configurations (second row). In each plot, the vertical axis is indexed by α_{prog}, the horizontal axis by δ_{prog}.

because the samples budget N_{max} remains the same whatever the team size. As a consequence, in a large team, each Ibot is granted fewer samples and fewer elementary movements to disperse in the arena. Given this constraint, the only way of achieving dispersion in few movements is through control programs with large variability both in translation and in rotation. *In conclusion, most of the solutions which are valid for the single Ibot would not work for this team.*

Second, consider the opposite case where the Ibots start a trial from scattered positions. As they are already uniformly distributed in the arena, any kind of motion program would lead to admissible estimates. *Most of this team solutions would not be admissible for the single Ibot.*

Figure 3 also reports the convergence points of 20 learning experiments for both initial configuration types. Programs which did not converge to admissible and stable estimates within the time limit of 2000 trials are represented by triangles. Not surprisingly, all the experiments for the scattered configuration converged very rapidly (right). On the contrary, for the clustered configuration, not all experiments managed to converge to admissible programs within the pre-defined time limit (left). This is due to the fact that the Ibots initial program is $Prog^i(0) = (0°, 0)$, a bad but very stable program.

Private Control Programs. Figure 4 shows a representative set of learning experiments performed with a team of 14 Ibots working with private control programs and started from clustered (first row) or scattered configurations (second row). Each plot shows the programs learnt by the team within the time limit of 20000 trials. Essentialy, these solutions are similar to those obtained with public control programs: clustered Ibots need large variability in angle and translation, while scattered Ibots don't. This uniformity is not surprising, because the integration task does not require differentiation in behavior as long as the Ibots have homogeneous skills.

From the point of view of learning, the main difference between dealing with

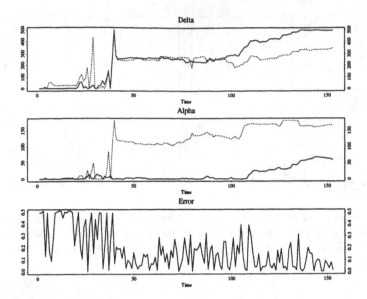

Fig. 5. Robot credit assignment problem for a team of two Ibots: Ibot 1 (dashed line) and Ibot 2 (solid line). Time evolution of δ^i_{prog}s (first plot), of α^i_{prog}s (second plot), and of the error E (third plot).

a single public program or with many private programs is the robot credit assignment problem. Figure 5 illustrates the robot credit assignment problem for a team of two Ibots. The first and the second time plot present the evolution of the Ibots' δ^i_{prog}s and α^i_{prog}s parameters, respectively; the third time plot shows the error E in the integral estimate. Around time 30, Ibot 1 (dashed line) has already acquired an admissible program ($Prog^1 = (49°, 437)$), but this does not appear at level of team performance because Ibot 2 (solid line) is still locked to the initial "staying in place" program. Consider also that Ibot 2's contribution to the team integral weighs more than Ibot 1's contribution, because Ibot 2 takes more samples. This is also the cause for the non-converging experiment of Fig. 4 (first row, second plot), where a minority of Ibots translating for short distances damage the team performance. To improve this state of affairs, Ibot 1 (Fig. 5), first backtracks from its admissible program, then relearns at a similar pace with Ibot 2.

Private Control Programs for Heterogeneous Ibots. As a last experiment, we forced the learnt control programs to specialization by differentiating the Ibots' skills. Figure 6 refers to a learning experiment with a team of two heterogeneous Ibots running private control programs. Ibot 1 (dashed line) translates four times as fast as Ibot 2 (solid line). Moreover, Ibot 2 is *blind*: its ground color sensor reads "white" whatever its position in the arena.

The strategy discovered by the team to provide admissible and stable estimates is clear from the δ^i_{prog}s and α^i_{prog}s plots of Fig. 6. The blind Ibot minimizes its catastrophic contribution to the team integral estimates by travelling long

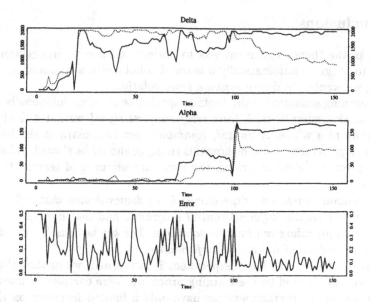

Fig. 6. A team of two heterogeneous Ibots: Ibot 1 (dashed line) and Ibot 2 (solid line). Time evolution of δ^i_{prog}s (first plot), of α^i_{prog}s (second plot), and of the error E (third plot).

δ^1_{prog}	α^1_{prog}	δ^2_{prog}	α^2_{prog}	$\mu(N^1_{sam})$	$\sigma(N^1_{sam})$
565	95	1528	179	85.5	1.5
876	95	2000	171	85.9	1.7
361	176	1549	2	88.9	1.3
537	165	1646	102	86.9	2.0
422	75	1061	66	84.1	0.5

Table 1. (Columns 1–4) Programs learnt by the heterogeneous team in 5 repeated experiments (one experiment per row). (Columns 5 and 6) Mean and standard deviation of the number of samples taken by Ibot 1 over 10 trials.

distances ($\delta^2_{prog} = 2000$, having set $\delta_{max} = 2000$ for this particular experiment). Observe that the error E stabilizes to low values only when the difference between δ^1_{prog} and δ^2_{prog} is sufficiently large. Still, Ibot 1 can afford a parameter of $\delta^2_{prog} = 800$ because it moves very fast.

Table 1 reports more programs learnt by this team in 5 repeated experiments. Ibot 1 always travels for shorter distances than Ibot 2. In all experiments, the balance between δ^1_{prog} and δ^2_{prog} is such that Ibot 1 consistently manages to collect at least 85 out of the 100 samples available to the team.

6 Conclusions

The aim of the Ibots experiment was to understand how to use reinforcement learning to program automatically a team of robots with a common mission. In addition, we wanted to derive *genuine team solutions*.

The learning scenario for the Ibots is applicable to other missions because it relies on weak assumptions. A *team reinforcement signal* evaluates the behavior of the group as a whole. A *limited, common resource* constrains the Ibots, but there is no a priori rule to decide how this resource should be shared. When working with private control programs, the Ibots are *unaware* of teammate control programs.

As a general conclusion, experiments have demonstrated that different mission conditions require different control programs, and that a simple reinforcement learning procedure can find the solutions. The key issue is to optimize team performance instead of individual performance.

As far as the specific Ibots experiment is concerned, we cannot claim that the solutions discovered by the learning procedure were completely unexpected. However, as robot programmers, we have only a limited intuition on the form of the solutions which are more appropriate for specific mission conditions. This motivates the use of learning as an alternative to handcrafting the programs for the team. *Second*: in general, a program which is admissible for a single Ibot is not admissible for a team of Ibots, and viceversa. Thus, we cannot simply find a solution for one Ibot and clone it n times, n being the team size. The form of the solution to a problem changes as the number of "problem solvers" changes. Moreover, the robots become aware of this fact only if they are confronted with their performance as a team. On the contrary, a group of robots learning from individual payoffs would ignore opportunities which become evident only if the task is considered at a team level. *Third*, the space of admissible programs strongly depends on the number of Ibots involved in the mission and on their initial configuration in the arena. The admissibility space "shrinks" when the team size grows and the Ibots are started in a clustered configuration. On the contrary, the admissibility space "enlarges" when the Ibots are started in a scattered configuration. The mission becomes easier in this case because, by initially distributing the Ibots at random in the arena, we bring them close to the problem solution; a team of individualistic robots would not be aware of this opportunity. *Fourth*, when the Ibots work with private control programs, the robot credit assignment problem arises, resulting in longer learning time. Interestingly, the robot credit assignment problem forces the Ibots to learn admissible programs at a similar pace, to prevent "slow" learners from jeopardizing the team mission. *Fifth*, the robot credit assignment problem vanishes when the Ibots learn a public policy, and the learnt policy is still a genuine team solution. The possibility of learning a single public program instead of several private programs should be not overlooked in missions where specialization of robot behavior is not required: the time necessary for the team to learn a public program is much shorter. Finally, *sixth*, the Ibots with their heterogeneous acting and sensing capabilities manage to specialize private control programs. They take advantage of individual skills and minimize the impact of individual weaknesses. In this way, the "blind" Ibot and the "fast" Ibot find a solution which is good for the team. This is possible because Ibots do not care about individual performance.

Acknowledgements

Cristina Versino is supported by the project No. 2129-042413.94/1 of the Fonds National de la Recherche Scientifique, Berne, Suisse. We thank an anonymous reviewer for helpful comments.

References

1. A.G. Barto, R.S. Sutton, and C.J.C.H. Watkins. Learning and sequential decision making. Technical Report COINS-89-95, Dept. of Computer and Information Science, University of Massachusets, Amherst, 1989.
2. L.E. Parker. The effect of action recognition and robot awareness in cooperative robotic teams. In *IROS95, IEEE/RSJ International Conference on Intelligent Robots and Systems, Pittsburgh, PA, August*, volume 1, pages 212–219, 1995.
3. L.E. Parker. ALLIANCE: An architecture for fault tolerant, cooperative control of heterogeneous mobile robots. In *IROS94, IEEE/RSJ International Conference on Intelligent Robots and Systems, Munich, Germany, September*, pages 776–783, 1994.
4. M.J. Matarić, M. Nilsson, and K.T. Simsarian. Cooperative multi-robot box-pushing. In *IROS95, IEEE/RSJ International Conference on Intelligent Robots and Systems, Pittsburgh, PA, August*, 1995.
5. C.R. Kube and H. Zhang. Collective robotics: From social insects to robots. *Adaptive Behavior*, 2(2):189–218, 1994.
6. M.J. Matarić. Interaction and intelligent behavior. Technical Report AI-TR-1495, MIT Artificial Intelligence Lab, Boston, 1994.
7. M.J. Matarić. Learning in multi-robot systems. In G. Weiss and S. Sen, editors, *Adaptation and Learning in Multi-Agent Systems*, volume 1042, pages 152–163. Springer-Verlag, Lecture Notes in Artificial Intelligence, 1996.
8. A. Murciano and J. del R. Millán. Learning signaling behaviors and specialization in cooperative agents. *Adaptive Behavior*, 5(1):5–28, 1997.
9. R.H. Crites and A.G. Barto. Improving elevator performance using reinforcement learning. In D.S. Touretzky, M.C. Mozer, and M.E. Hasselmo, editors, *Advances in Neural Information Processing Systems 8*, pages 1017–1023, Cambridge MA, 1996. MIT Press.
10. C. Versino and L.M. Gambardella. Learning real team solutions. In G. Weiss, editor, *DAI Meets Machine Learning*, Lecture Notes in Artificial Intelligence. Springer-Verlag, 1997. In press.
11. A.G. Barto, R.S. Sutton, and C.W. Anderson. Neuronlike adaptive elements that can solve difficult learning control problems. *IEEE Transactions on Systems, Man, and Cybernetics*, 13:835–846, 1983.
12. J.M. Hammersley and D.C. Handscomb. *Monte Carlo Methods*. Methnen & Co., London, 1964.

Global Data Analysis and the Fragmentation Problem in Decision Tree Induction

Ricardo Vilalta, Gunnar Blix, and Larry Rendell

Beckman Institute and Computer Science Department
University of Illinois at Urbana-Champaign
405 North Mathews Avenue, Urbana, IL 61801 USA
phone: (217) 244-1620
fax: (217) 244-8371
email: vilalta@cs.uiuc.edu

Abstract. We investigate an inherent limitation of top-down decision tree induction in which the continuous partitioning of the instance space progressively lessens the statistical support of every partial (i.e. disjunctive) hypothesis, known as the *fragmentation problem*. We show, both theoretically and empirically, how the fragmentation problem adversely affects predictive accuracy as variation ∇ (a measure of concept difficulty) increases. Applying feature-construction techniques at every tree node, which we implement on a decision tree inducer *DALI*, is proved to only partially solve the fragmentation problem. Our study illustrates how a more robust solution must also assess the value of each partial hypothesis by recurring to all available training data, an approach we name *global data analysis*, which decision tree induction alone is unable to accomplish. The value of global data analysis is evaluated by comparing modified versions of *C4.5rules* with *C4.5trees* and *DALI*, on both artificial and real-world domains. Empirical results suggest the importance of combining both feature construction and global data analysis to solve the fragmentation problem.

1 Introduction

In this study, we investigate the internal mechanism of top-down decision tree inducers [14, 1]. We focus on the fragmentation problem: a limitation of the divide-and-conquer strategy in which the continuous partitioning of the training set at every tree node reduces the number of examples (i.e. the statistical support) at lower-level nodes. One noticeable effect of this problem is the replication of subtrees along the output tree [12, 9], also known as the *replication problem*. The fragmentation problem has been attacked in different ways: by constructing compound features at every tree node [12, 18]; by reducing the number of possible partitions [5, 16]; and by using alternative concept representations, e.g., sets of rules [15], decision graphs [6, 11], SE-Trees [22], decision lists [12, 21]. Nonetheless, no clear solution has emerged.

Our analysis of the causes and effects of the fragmentation problem elucidates relevant issues: the fragmentation problem is not coined to decision tree induction alone, but might affect other inductive learning models; replication and fragmentation are not separate problems, but rather the former is simply an effect of the latter. We use concept variation, ∇ (a measure of concept difficulty [20, 13]), to prove that as ∇ increases, the fragmentation problem is further aggravated, partly explaining the inadequacy of decision tree induction when applied to *difficult* domains.

We test a new decision-tree inducer, *DALI*, to show that constructing new features at every tree node mitigates the fragmentation problem, but does not completely eliminate it. For a more robust solution, our study reveals the importance of analyzing all training data when assessing the value of every induced hypothesis, an approach we name *global data analysis*. Decision tree induction does not analyze data in this manner, neither alone nor when augmented with feature construction. Our experiments compare $C4.5$rules, $C4.5$trees, and *DALI*, empirically evaluating the importance of global data analysis by isolating this component in $C4.5$rules. Our results suggest the importance of combining both feature construction and global data analysis to solve the fragmentation problem.

This paper is organized as follows. Section 2 provides an overview of decision tree induction; Sect. 3 defines the fragmentation problem; Sect. 4 explains the scenarios in which the fragmentation problem is critical, and details on the importance of global data analysis during learning; Sect. 5 shows experimental results. Lastly, Sect. 6 gives a summary and conclusions.

2 Preliminaries

For simplicity, we focus on domains where each example X is described by n boolean features (i.e., attributes, variables), $x_1, x_2, \cdots, x_n$, and where an underlying target concept $C : \{0,1\}^n \mapsto \{-,+\}$ classifies the space of all 2^n examples, also referred to as the *instance space*, into 2 classes. A learning mechanism (i.e., inducer) attempts to discover C by analyzing the information given by a training set $S : \{(X_i, c_i)\}_{i=1}^m$, where c_i is the class assigned by C to X_i, i.e., $C(X_i) = c_i$. The result of the analysis is a hypothesis/classifier H approximating C. Our main interest is in the ability of H to correctly *predict* the class of examples outside S. We look for hypotheses not only consistent with S, but that *generalize* beyond that set.

A decision tree inducer uses a divide-and-conquer strategy for learning. Proceeding top-down, the root of the tree is formed by selecting a function $f : \{0,1\}^n \mapsto \{0,1\}$ that splits the training set into mutually exclusive subsets S_0, S_1, such that $S_0 = \{X \in S \mid f(X) = 0\}$, $S_1 = \{X \in S \mid f(X) = 1\}$, $S = S_0 \cup S_1$, and $S_0 \cap S_1 = \emptyset$. Commonly f is a single feature – selected via some impurity measure, e.g., entropy, gini, Laplace, χ^2 –, which yields axis-parallel partitions over the instance space, but other combinations are possible [2, 8]. The same methodology is recursively applied on S_0 and S_1 to construct the left and right subtrees respectively. A subset S' represents a leaf if all examples in S' belong to the same class, or if $|S'| < \beta$, where β is user defined; the majority class in S' is associated with that leaf. An example X is classified, starting from the root of the tree, by following the branch that matches the output of every splitting function (i.e., by iteratively following the left branch if $f(X) = 0$, or the right branch if $f(X) = 1$). At the end of the path, the class attached to that leaf is assigned to X.

3 The Fragmentation Problem

Under a DNF representation, a target concept C is expressed as the disjunction of several subconcepts, such that $C = C_1 + C_2 + \cdots + C_l$. A hypothesis H approximating C can be expressed as a set of disjunctive hypotheses $H_1, H_2, \cdots, H_l$, where H_i approximates C_i. The set of examples covered by hypothesis H_i on training set S, $\mathrm{COV}(H_i) = \{X \in S \mid H_i(X) = +\}$, is referred to as the source of support or evidential credibility for H_i [23].

A decision tree inducer adopts a DNF concept representation: each branch from the root of the tree to a positive leaf is equivalent to a disjunctive hypothesis H_i. The final set of disjunctive hypotheses must be mutually exclusive, i.e., $\mathrm{COV}(H_1) \cap \mathrm{COV}(H_2) \cap \cdots \cap \mathrm{COV}(H_l) = \emptyset$. The method to find every H_i carries out a continuous partition-refinement over the instance space; every tree branch is grown until a terminal node or leaf delineates a single-class region. A limitation inherent to this approach is that, while searching for a disjunctive hypothesis H_i, each splitting of the training data may separate or pull apart examples in support of a different hypothesis H_j – due to the irrelevancy of the splitting function to H_j. This situation not only requires that several approximations $H_j{}', H_j{}'', H_j{}'''$ etc., be found on dispersed regions of the instance space, giving rise to replicated subtrees along the output tree, but also reduces the support or evidential credibility of each individual hypothesis, eventually complicating its identification. This problem is known as the *fragmentation problem*.

The fragmentation problem stems from two main causes:

1. The requirement that the coverage of disjunctive hypotheses be mutually exclusive precludes the representation of any H_i and H_j such that $\mathrm{COV}(H_i) \cap \mathrm{COV}(H_j) \neq \emptyset$. The examples in $\mathrm{COV}(H_i) \cap \mathrm{COV}(H_j)$ are directed towards H_i or H_j, but not both. This is illustrated in the following example. Assume a 3-dimensional boolean space where each point represents an example $X = (x_1, x_2, x_3)$, with target function $C = x_1 x_2 + x_1 x_3$, as shown in Fig. 1a. Concept C can be decomposed into two subconcepts: $C_1 = x_1 x_2$, with examples $(1, 1, 0)$ and $(1, 1, 1)$, and $C_2 = x_1 x_3$, with $(1, 0, 1)$ and $(1, 1, 1)$. Let H_1 and H_2 be the disjunctive hypotheses approximating C_1 and C_2 respectively. With all examples available, $\beta = 1$, and single features as splitting functions, two possible decision trees are depicted in Figs. 1b and 1c. In the tree for Fig. 1b, splitting on feature x_2 directs two positive examples to the right branch in support of H_1, but only one positive example (out of two) to the left branch in support of H_2. As a consequence, $H_1 = C_1$ but $H_2 \neq C_2$, since the irrelevant condition $\bar{x}_2$ is incorporated: $H_2 = x_1 \bar{x}_2 x_3$. This was caused because $\mathrm{COV}(C_1) \cap \mathrm{COV}(C_2) = \{(1, 1, 1)\}$, which could only be covered

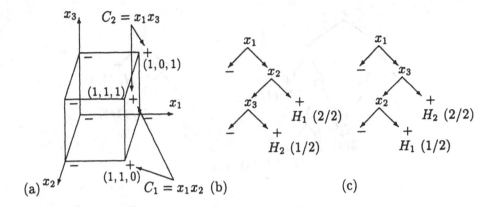

Fig. 1. (a) A 3-dimensional boolean space for target concept $C = C_1 + C_2$, where $C_1 = x_1 x_2$ and $C_2 = x_1 x_3$. (b) and (c) Two decision trees for (a) where the fragmentation problem reduces the support of either H_1 or H_2, as shown by the fraction of examples that belong to C_1 and C_2 arriving at each positive leaf.

by H_1 or H_2. The same phenomenon occurs in the tree on Fig. 1c, except here the loss of support occurs to H_1.

2. Each partition over the instance space is too coarse, such that many steps are required to delimit a single-class region. The search for a disjunctive hypothesis H_i inevitably results in the fragmentation of a different disjunctive hypothesis H_j. Consider the tree in Fig. 2a for boolean concept $C = x_1 x_2 + x_3 x_4$, where $C_1 = x_1 x_2$ and $C_2 = x_3 x_4$. Assume all possible examples available, $\beta = 1$, H_1 the approximation to C_1, and H_2' and H_2'' the approximations to C_2. Splitting on feature x_1 separates the examples in C_2, directing two positive examples (out of four) to the left branch in support of H_2', and two examples to the right branch. Splitting on feature x_2 reduces the support of H_2'' to only one example. Since C_2 is represented by H_2' and H_2'', the final tree replicates subtrees. This replication effect originates from the fragmentation of H_2 (into H_2' and H_2'') at the root of the tree.

One approach to combat the fragmentation problem is to conjoin several features at every tree node, which results in more refined partitions over the instance space. As shown in Fig. 2b, using the conjunction of single features as splitting functions eliminates the replication of the subtree approximating C_2. Nevertheless, H_2 continues experiencing loss of support, since $COV(H_1) \cap COV(H_2) = \{(1,1,1,1)\} \neq \emptyset$. Hence, using multiple-feature tests at every tree node can reduce the number of partition-steps required to delimit single-class regions (cause 2), but cannot avoid pulling apart examples lying in the intersection of several partial subconcepts (cause 1).

The fragmentation problem is not exclusive to decision tree inducers but to any learning mechanism that progressively lessens the evidential credibility of its

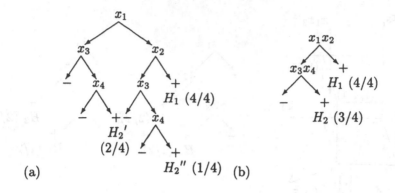

Fig. 2. (a) A decision tree for $C = C_1 + C_2$, where $C_1 = x_1 x_2$ and $C_2 = x_3 x_4$. Examples in C_2 are separated into two regions after splitting on feature x_1. (b) A decision tree for (a) with multiple-feature tests. The replication of subtrees is eliminated, but H_2 experiences loss of support when splitting on $x_1 x_2$.

induced hypotheses. Consider the separate-and-conquer strategy common to the construction of rule-based systems [10, 4, 28]. In this case, an iterative process starts by selecting a positive example or *seed* on the training data; this example is generalized to produce the next disjunctive hypothesis H_i. The set of examples covered by H_i, COV(H_i), is *removed* before another seed is selected, potentially weakening the support of other disjunctive hypotheses. A similar effect occurs in the mechanism for building decision lists [12, 21].

4 Detrimental Effects and Global Data Analysis

One may argue against the significance of the fragmentation problem based on the success of decision tree inducers on many real-world applications. As explained shortly (and demonstrated in Sect. 5), a detrimental effect is evident only among domains with high variation ∇.

Decision tree inducers, as well as many other inductive mechanisms, adopt a *similarity-based bias*, which assumes any pair of examples X_i, X_j lying close to each other in the instance space (i.e., sharing many similar feature-values) generally belong to the same class, i.e., $C(X_i) = C(X_j)$. This bias is adequate when a concept is characterized by few disjunctive subconcepts, each subconcept covering many examples, because proximity in the instance space correlates to class similarity [19]; these domains we denote as *simple*. By contrast, domains with instance spaces populated by many dispersed regions, each disjunctive subconcept covering few examples, violate this assumption, and thus become inadequate; these domains we denote as *difficult*.

The degree of difficulty of a concept can be known through concept variation ∇ [20, 13], which provides an estimate of the probability that any two neighbor

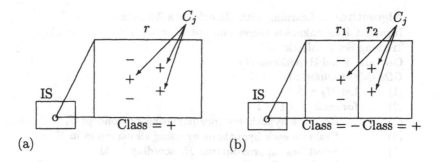

Fig. 3. (a) A region r of an instance space (IS) where the support for the prediction of class $+$ is unstable. (b) After partitioning r into r_1 and r_2, C_j is fragmented. The majority of negative examples in r_1 changes the prediction to class $-$.

examples differ in class value, roughly measuring the amount of irregularity in the distribution of examples along the instance space. ∇ is defined as follows. Let $X_1, X_2, \cdots, X_n$ be the n closest neighbors – at Hamming distance one – of an example X in an n-dimensional boolean space. The degree of class *dissimilarity* of the neighborhood around X can be estimated simply as

$$\sigma(X) = \sum_{j=1}^{n} \text{diff}(C(X), C(X_j)) , \qquad (1)$$

where $\text{diff}(C(X, X_i)) = 1$ if $C(X) \neq C(X_i)$ and 0 otherwise. A normalization factor $\overline{\sigma}(X) = \frac{\sigma(X)}{n}$ gives a value in $[0, 1]$. Concept variation is defined as the average of this factor when applied to every example in the instance space:

$$\nabla = \frac{1}{2^n} \times \sum_{i=1}^{2^n} \overline{\sigma}(X_i) \in [0, 1] . \qquad (2)$$

The effect of the fragmentation problem relates to ∇ (i.e. to concept variation) in the following way. The terminal node or leaf of a tree branch, corresponding to a disjunctive hypothesis H_i, classifies a region r of examples according to a majority-class vote on the training examples in r. Let θ be defined as the difference between the number of training positive and negative examples in r; then for any $X \in r$,

$$C(X) = \begin{cases} + & \text{if } \theta \geq 0 \\ - & \text{otherwise} \end{cases} \qquad (3)$$

The fragmentation problem is irrelevant over domains with low ∇ (i.e. over simple domains), because, in the presence of disjunctive subconcepts covering many examples of similar class value, each hypothesis (i.e. tree branch) delimits a region of examples r for which $\theta >> 0$ (i.e. for which θ is stable). But when dissimilarity in the vicinity of any example is high, as is characteristic in domains with high ∇ (i.e., in difficult domains), then separating the few examples covered by each disjunctive subconcept reduces the support of its hypothesis(es). If $\theta \sim 0$

Algorithm 1: Learning with Global Data Analysis
Input: Given unknown target concept $C = C_1 + C_2 + \cdots + C_l$,
Training Set S, Metric M
Output: Final Hypothesis H_f
GDA-MECHANISM(S)
(1)   Let $H_f = \emptyset$
(2)   **foreach** $i = 1 \cdots l$
(3)   Generate hypotheses approximating subconcept C_i
(4)   Evaluate each hypothesis by using all examples in S
(5)   Select best approximation H_i acording to M
(6)   Let $H_f = H_f + H_i$
(7)   **end for**
(8)   Refine/Prune H_f by using all examples in S
(9)   **return** H_f

Fig. 4. General learning mechanism with global data analysis.

(i.e. θ is unstable), then removing examples from r may cause θ shift sign, thereby causing the misclassification of all $X \in r$. In addition, observe that if $\nabla > 0.5$, a similarity-based bias becomes totally inadequate, even without the presence of the fragmentation problem, because, on average, more than 50% of the vicinity of any example X would differ in class value with X.

To illustrate these ideas, Fig. 3a shows a region r of an instance space where $\theta \geq 0$, such that for any $X \in r$, class + is predicted. If the set of training positive examples in r belong to a subconcept C_j (and possibly other subconcepts as well), then finding an approximation to a subconcept C_i before C_j may lead to a partitioning of r into r_1 and r_2, as shown in Fig. 3b. The positive training example representing C_j in r_1 may be mistakenly perceived as a noise signal. The instability of θ in r causes $\theta < 0$ in r_1, forcing a change of classification to every example $X \in r_1$; this is unlikely to occur if ∇ is low because all examples in a small region are expected to belong to the same class.

We claim an important step to solve the fragmentation problem consists of building/refining each partial hypothesis independently, by assessing its value against all training examples together, in this way avoiding misclassification of regions of examples for which little support is found. Figure 4 depicts a general learning mechanism that incorporates a *global data analysis*. The main idea is to better estimate the value of each partial hypothesis by avoiding the effects of previously induced hypotheses. Under this learning framework, an approximation H_i to a subconcept C_i is built under the support of all available data (lines 4-5, Fig. 4). The final hypothesis H_f may also be refined (e.g., pruned) in this way (line 8, Fig. 4).

In contrast, the search for disjunctive hypotheses in decision tree induction is not global but local: often a hypothesis is supported by only a fraction of the examples of the subconcept being approximated. This holds irrespective of the modifications exerted on the learning mechanism (e.g., splitting function, pruning mechanism, stopping criteria, etc.), because such search is limited by the learning strategy. Henceforth, we identify two major operations during the development of learning systems: 1) the search for partial hypotheses, and 2) the refinement of the final hypothesis comprising all best partial hypotheses. Both steps can be attained through a global data analysis, but the inherent mechanism of decision tree induction *omits* this operation. In the next section we evaluate the importance of a global data analysis over the refinement of the final hypothesis (step 2); better results are expected if the same methodology is carried on over the construction of all partial hypotheses (step 1).

5 Experiments

5.1 The Learning Systems Used for Testing

We use $C4.5$trees [16] to represent a decision tree inducer where each splitting function tests on a single feature. The importance of global data analysis is underlined in modified versions of $C4.5$rules [15, 16], as explained in Sect. 5.3. For a decision tree inducer with multiple-feature tests, we developed a new version of the LFC system [18]; the new version is called $DALI$ [26] (Dynamic Adaptive Lookahead Induction). In both $DALI$ and LFC, a splitting function is defined as the conjunction of several boolean features (see Fig. 2b), which allows for more refined partitions over the instance space. Unlike LFC, $DALI$ obviates user-defined parameters (e.g., lookahead depth and beam width), with a faster response time, and similar performance in terms of predictive accuracy. We now briefly compare $DALI$ and LFC, but the reader can safely skip to the next subsection if uninterested in such differences.

Figure 5 outlines $DALI$'s search mechanism. At each tree node, both $DALI$ and LFC conduct a beam search over the space of all boolean-feature conjuncts, or *monomials*. In LFC, the search space is limited by user-defined width and depth; the search continues until the maximum depth d is attained, at which point the best monomial – of any size in $[1 - d]$ – is returned as the next splitting function. By contrast, $DALI$ extends the search depth until no more monomials can be generated, and selects the beam width dynamically. $DALI$ mainly differs from LFC on two steps:

1. A systematic search to avoid redundant combinations [22, 27], Lines 3-4, Fig. 5. Each monomial F_i conjoins several boolean features (or their complements), e.g., $F_i = x_1 \bar{x}_3 x_5$. Because conjunction is commutative, the search space is defined by avoiding any state F_j that is identical to a state F_i except for the order in which features appear, e.g., $F_j = \bar{x}_3 x_5 x_1$.
2. A global-pruning technique [27, 17], Line 5, Fig. 5. Define F_{best} as the best explored monomial according to some impurity measure H (e.g., entropy), such that, for all currently explored monomials F_i, $H(F_{\text{best}}) < H(F_i)$. As long as H is monotonic, a monomial F_i can be eliminated if the best value F_i can ever attain along its search path – according to H – is worse than F_{best}.

Algorithm 2: Search Mechanism in *DALI*
Input: A list of literals (i.e., boolean features and
their complements) $L_{bool} \leftarrow \{x_1, \bar{x}_1, x_2, \bar{x}_2, \cdots x_n, \bar{x}_n\}$
Output: Best monomial F_{best}
DALI-SEARCH(L_{bool})
(1) $L_{beam} \leftarrow$ best literals in L_{bool} according to entropy
(2)   **while (true)**
(3) $L_{new} \leftarrow$ Systematically form the conjunction
(4)   of every $F_i \in L_{beam}$ with every $F_j \in L_{bool}$
(5)   Apply global-pruning into L_{new}
(6)   **if** $L_{new} = \emptyset$
(7)   **return** best monomial F_{best}
(8) $L_{beam} \leftarrow$ best combinations in L_{new} according
            to entropy
(9)   **end while**

Fig. 5. *DALI*'s search mechanism at every tree node. The best constructed feature (i.e., best monomial), is used as the next splitting function.

The combination of systematic search and global pruning makes the search space sufficiently manageable so that a limitation on depth or breadth of search is no longer necessary. The ease of use of *DALI* favors this system over *LFC* for our experimental purposes.

5.2 Methodology

Since variation ∇ can be computed only when the target concept is known, our experiments mainly focus on artificial boolean concepts (defined on both 9 and 12-features; see Appendix A). The concepts include DNF formulae, CNF formulae, Multiplexor (MUX), Majority (MAJ), and Parity (PAR), covering a range of varying ∇.

Learning curves[1], not presented here for space considerations, show that greater differences in accuracy occur when small samples are used for training. Our results reflect the largest effects found at 20% training-set size for 9-feature concepts and 10% training-set size for 12-feature concepts. Each reported value is the average over 50 runs; predictive accuracy is computed as the percentage of correct classifications for all examples outside the training set. Experiments on real-world domains estimate predictive accuracy by using stratified 10-fold cross-validation [7], averaged over five repetitions. Since *DALI* is limited to boolean domains, we performed an initial discretization step on all numeric (following [3]) and nominal features (constructing a boolean feature for each nominal value). All systems were set to default parameters. Significant differences are computed using a two-sided t-test. Runs were performed on a SPARCstation 10/31.

---

[1] Graphs for all learning curves are accessible upon request to the authors.

5.3 The Value of Global Data Analysis

To measure the gains obtained when global data analysis is used to tackle the fragmentation problem, we first compared modified versions of C4.5rules with C4.5trees as explained next. The mechanism for C4.5rules (see [16] for details) can be summarized in three steps:

1. Given a decision tree T, form a rule R from every branch in T that starts at the root node and ends on a leaf node; R is an implication: if $cond_1$ and $cond_2$ and $\cdots$ and $cond_{d-1} \rightarrow c$, where $cond_i$ is the feature-value (i.e. splitting-function value) encountered on every node along a branch of length d, and c the class assigned to the leaf node.
2. Eliminate all irrelevant conditions from every rule R in step 1. Let R' equals R except for condition $cond_i$ being removed. Based on the information given by all training data, R and R' are both globally evaluated – and only one retained – according to a pessimistic estimation of their corresponding error rates.
3. Apply the minimum description principle, according to a particular bit-encoding scheme, to remove rules from the rule set in step 2.

While each individual rule is originally obtained from a previously constructed decision tree, Step 2 refines the final set of rules through a global data analysis: each rule is analyzed independently and modified according to its credibility on all training data. This differs from step 3 where rules are assessed in terms of description lengths. To isolate each learning component, we defined three system versions: C4.5rules-Std, comprising steps 1, 2, and 3 (i.e., Standard); C4.5rules-GDA, comprising steps 1 and 2 (i.e., isolating the Global Data Analysis component); and C4.5rules-MDL, comprising steps 1 and 3 (i.e. isolating the Minimum Description Length component). We also compared the effects of tree pruning as a form of refinement operation; it mainly differs from a global data analysis in that each disjunctive hypothesis – or tree branch – is not analyzed independently, but remains intertwined to the tree structure.

Table 1 illustrates results for predictive accuracy on all artificial and real-world domains. Each group of 9- and 12-feature concepts is ordered by increasing variation ∇. Columns for the different versions of C4.5rules and C4.5trees-pruned show the increase/decrease of accuracy against C4.5trees-unpruned. On the set of artificial concepts, both C4.5rules-Std and C4.5rules-GDA increasingly outperform C4.5trees-unpruned as ∇ grows higher (the effect being more evident for 12-feature than for 9-feature concepts), except when $\nabla > 50\%$ (explained in Sect. 4) This trend is not observed on C4.5rules-MDL. The use of pruning exhibits a significant gain only until ∇ is high. The same results are depicted in Figs. 6a and 6b for 9- and 12- feature concepts respectively, where we computed a regression line for each version of C4.5rules and C4.5trees-pruned against ∇. An overall comparison for C4.5rules reveals C4.5rules-Std attains the highest advantage, proving the benefit of combining both C4.5rules-GDA and C4.5rules-MDL, and that C4.5rules-GDA is the component providing the most

Table 1. Tests on predictive accuracy for both artificial and real-world domains. Columns for the different versions of C4.5rules and C4.5trees-pruned show the increase/decrease of accuracy against C4.5trees-unpruned. The column for DALIrules is relative to DALItrees. Significant differences (at the p = 0.05 level) are marked with an asterisk.

Concept	∇ (%)	C4.5trees-		C4.5rules-			DALI-	
		unpruned	pruned	Std	GDA	MDL	trees	rules
DNF9a	14	99.2	−0.7	+0.5	+0.3	+0.0	100.0	+0.0
CNF9a	17	99.5	−0.6	+0.5*	+0.5*	+0.0	100.0	+0.0
MAJ9a	17	100.0	+0.0	+0.0	−0.8	+0.0	100.0	+0.0
MAJ9b	21	82.1	−0.1	+2.1*	+1.4*	−0.2	85.3	+0.0
CNF9b	22	94.0	+2.3*	+6.0*	+3.8*	+0.0	100.0	−0.2
MUX9	22	86.8	0.9	+8.5*	+7.0*	−0.8	99.0	−0.2
DNF9b	24	83.0	+0.6	+10.7*	+5.0*	−0.7	99.4	+0.0
PAR9a	33	62.5	+13.5*	+27.7*	+21.7*	−2.2	98.4	+1.3*
PAR9b	67	43.1	+1.9*	+2.6*	+0.6*	+3.6*	43.6	+0.1
MAJ12a	13	100.0	+0.0	+0.0	+0.0	+0.0	100.0	+0.0
DNF12a	15	99.7	+0.0	+0.3*	+0.3*	+0.0	99.9	+0.0
CNF12a	15	99.6	−0.1	+0.4*	+0.2*	+0.0	100.0	+0.0
MAJ12b	18	84.5	−0.1	+3.0*	+2.7*	−0.6*	87.9	+0.7*
CNF12b	19	89.8	+0.7	+9.8*	+5.1*	−1.3	99.7	−0.1
DNF12b	20	89.5	+3.2*	+9.6*	+6.6*	−0.6	99.2	+0.0
MUX12	21	84.9	+0.1	+12.9*	+8.7*	−2.9*	99.4	−0.2
PAR12a	33	58.6	+11.9*	+33.7*	+24.0*	−3.8*	92.9	+6.4*
PAR12b	67	46.5	+0.7*	+1.6*	+0.2*	+2.5*	46.0	+0.5*
TicTacToe		85.8	−0.3*	+13.3*	+10.4*	+0.5*	98.4	−0.4
Lympho[2]		80.2	+3.3*	+3.0*	+2.1*	−0.5*	87.9	−0.2
Lympho[3]		74.4	+3.1*	+6.1*	+5.4*	+1.7*	84.6	−0.4
Promoters		81.9	−0.6	+5.0*	+3.5*	−0.9	83.4	+0.0
Cancer		95.1	−0.6*	+0.8*	+0.5*	−0.3*	95.7	+0.3
Hepatitis		82.3	−1.2*	−0.4	−0.6	−0.5	80.2	−0.6
ABS AVRG		83.46	85.0	90.0	86.5	83.2	90.9	91.2

significant contribution. For real-world domains, the improvement of C4.5rules-Std and C4.5rules-GDA over C4.5trees-unpruned is observed on the Tic-Tac-Toe, Lymphography, and Promoters domains, where ∇ may be relatively high due to interaction among features bearing a low representation to the target concept (e.g., board-configurations used to determine win or loose), but not so evident on the Hepatitis domain, which may be characterized by comprising highly representative features (i.e. denoting low ∇).

To test the effect of using a global data analysis over a decision tree with multiple-feature tests on every node, we compared the difference in predictive accuracy between DALI (Sect. 5.1) and a modified version of C4.5rules that accepts as input a decision tree from DALI. The new version, named DALIrules, operates as follows:

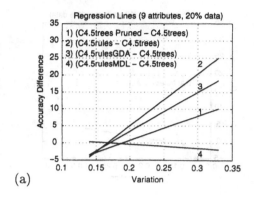
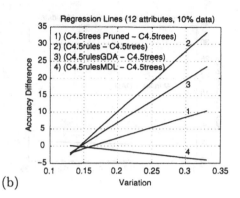

(a) (b)

Fig. 6. Regression lines for the columns of *C4.5* (all different versions) on Table 1 vs. Variation ∇ on (a) 9- and (b) 12-attribute concepts. Numbers enclosed in parentheses show the mean of the residuals between the linear model and the actual values (the same applies to Fig. 5.3).

1. Given a tree, T_m, with multiple feature tests on each node, define a new training sample S_m, such that every feature x_{m_i} in S_m corresponds to a tree node in T_m (i.e., every new feature is a combination of the original-feature set, used as a splitting function on T_m).

2. Apply *C4.5rules-Std* to the tree T_m output by *DALI*, and to the corresponding new training sample S_m, which is now described in terms of feature set $(x_{m_1}, x_{m_2} \cdots, x_{m_r})$.

Table 1 shows the results of comparing *DALIrules* with *DALI* in terms of predictive accuracy. The trend of accuracy increase as ∇ grows is apparently delayed until ∇ gets close to 50%. We note the use of more refined partitions over the instance space alleviates the effects of the fragmentation problem but does not eliminate it (Sect. 4), as evidenced by the results on parity concepts PAR9a and PAR12a (see [25]), where the advantage for *DALIrules* is significant. None of the real-world domains may achieve this high ∇, where no significant difference is observed between these two systems. Figures 7a and 7b depict regression lines for the differences on predictive accuracy between *DALIrules* and *DALI*. An increase of predictive accuracy is evident for *DALIrules* on 12-feature concepts.

We finally compared absolute predictive accuracy averaged over all artificial and real-world domains, as shown on the last row of Table 1. The performance of *DALIrules* supports the claims of the importance of combining 1) feature-construction techniques (see *DALItrees*' performance), and 2) a global evaluation of each disjunctive hypothesis (see *C4.5rules-Std*' and *C4.5rules-GDA*' performance), to solve the fragmentation problem.

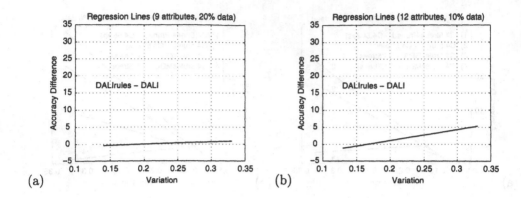

Fig. 7. Regression lines for the column of *DALI*-rules on Table 1 vs. Variation ∇ on (a) 9- and (b) 12-attribute concepts.

6 Summary and Conclusions

The divide-and-conquer implementation of decision tree induction is responsible for a progressive loss of statistical support at every new partition, as the number of examples giving credibility to every disjunctive hypothesis progressively diminishes. This fragmentation problem has little effect on domains with low variation ∇ (i.e., on simple domains), because every disjunctive hypothesis is supported by large regions of positive examples; but the same problem is severely aggravated by the instability imposed by high variation over the instance space.

We experimented with a new decision tree inducer, *DALI*, to prove the benefit of using refined partitions over the instance space in combating the fragmentation problem. We identified an additional important step to solve this problem consisting of independently assessing the value of each disjunctive hypothesis against all training data. This "global data analysis", embedded in *C4.5*rules, proved effective in improving the classifications made by *C4.5*trees (single-feature tests), and *DALI* (multiple-feature tests), with a positive correlation to ∇ (i.e. predictive accuracy increased as ∇ grew higher), except when $\nabla > 50\%$ because of the similarity-based assumption. We suggest combining feature construction with global data analysis as a robust solution against the fragmentation problem.

One important conclusion can be drawn from this study: that a better understanding of what causes a learning algorithm to succeed or fail can be attained if the algorithm is viewed as the combination of multiple components, each component exerting a particular effect during learning. The development of learning algorithms could be guided by the combination of those – well understood – learning components known to provide the correct generalizations under the class of domains of study (e.g., all structured real-world domains, since no universal learner is attainable [24]).

Acknowledgments

We are grateful to the anonymous reviewers for their helpful suggestions. Our work was supported in part by National Science Foundation (IRI 92–04473), Consejo Nacional de Ciencia y Tecnología (México), and Norges Forskningsråd (Norway).

A. Definitions for Artificial Concepts

Let: $X = (x_1, x_2, \ldots, x_n)$,
$\quad \text{address}(x_1, x_2, \ldots, x_m) = 2^0 x_1 + 2^1 x_2 + \ldots + 2^{m-1} x_m$

Definitions:

DNF9a : $x_2 x_3 + \bar{x}_2 x_3 x_7 + x_2 \bar{x}_3 x_8 + x_2 \bar{x}_7 \bar{x}_8 + \bar{x}_3 x_7 x_8$

DNF9b : $x_1 x_2 x_3 + \bar{x}_1 \bar{x}_2 + x_7 x_8 x_9 + \bar{x}_7 \bar{x}_9$

DNF12a : $x_1 x_2 x_9 x_{12} + x_1 x_2 \bar{x}_9 x_{11} + \bar{x}_1 x_2 x_5 x_9 + \bar{x}_1 \bar{x}_2 x_8 \bar{x}_9$

DNF12b : $x_1 x_2 \bar{x}_7 \bar{x}_8 + x_1 x_2 x_{11} x_{12} + x_1 \bar{x}_2 \bar{x}_{11} x_{12} +$
$\quad \bar{x}_1 x_2 x_{11} \bar{x}_{12} + \bar{x}_1 \bar{x}_2 \bar{x}_{11} \bar{x}_{12} + x_7 x_8 x_{11} x_{12}$

CNF9a : $(x_4 + x_6)(\bar{x}_4 + \bar{x}_5 + x_7)$

CNF9b : $(x_1 + \bar{x}_2 + x_3)(\bar{x}_1 + x_2 + x_5)(x_1 + x_2 + \bar{x}_3)$

CNF12a : $(x_8 + x_9)(x_7 + x_6 + x_5)(\bar{x}_8 + \bar{x}_6 + x_2)$

CNF12b : $(x_1 + x_2 + x_6)(\bar{x}_1 + \bar{x}_2 + x_7)(x_9 + x_{10} + x_{12})$
$\quad (\bar{x}_6 + \bar{x}_7 + x_8)(x_9 + x_{10} + x_{12})(\bar{x}_8 + \bar{x}_9 + \bar{x}_7)$

MAJ9a : $\{X \mid (\sum_{i=1}^{9} x_i) \geq 3\}$

MAJ9b : $\{X \mid (\sum_{i=1}^{9} x_i) \geq 6\}$

MAJ12a : $\{X \mid (\sum_{i=1}^{12} x_i) \geq 4\}$

MAJ12b : $\{X \mid (\sum_{i=1}^{12} x_i) \geq 8\}$

PAR9a : $\{X \mid ((\sum_{i=1}^{3} x_i) \bmod 2) > 0\}$

PAR9b : $\{X \mid ((\sum_{i=1}^{6} x_i) \bmod 2) > 0\}$

PAR12a : $\{X \mid ((\sum_{i=1}^{4} x_i) \bmod 2) > 0\}$

PAR12b : $\{X \mid ((\sum_{i=1}^{8} x_i) \bmod 2) > 0\}$

MUX9 : $\{X \mid x_{(\text{address}(x_1, x_2)+3)} = 1\}$

MUX12 : $\{X \mid x_{(\text{address}(x_1, x_2, x_3)+4)} = 1\}$

References

1. Breiman L., Friedman J. H., Olshen R. A., Stone C. J.: Classification And Regression Trees. Wadsworth, Belmont, CA. (1984)
2. Brodley C. E., Utgoff P. E.: Multivariate Decision Trees. Machine Learning, 19:1, (1995) 45–78
3. Catlett J.: On Changing Continuous Attributes into Ordered Discrete Attributes. In Proceedings of the European Working Session on Learning, (1991) 164–178
4. Clark P., Niblett T.: The CN2 Induction Algorithm. Machine Learning, 3:4, (1989) 261–284.
5. Fayyad U.: Branching on Attribute Values in Decision Tree Generation. In Proceedings of the 12th National Conference on Artificial Intelligence, (1994) 601–606
6. Kohavi R.: Bottom-Up Induction of Oblivious Read-Once Decision Graphs. In Proceedings of the European Conference on Machine Learning, (1994) 154–169

7. Kohavi R.: A Study of Cross Validation and bootstrap for Accuracy Estimation and Model Selection. In Proceedings of the 24th International Joint Conference on Artificial Intelligence, (1995) 1137-1145

8. Luc D., László G., Gábor L.: A Probabilistic Theory of Pattern Recognition. Springer-Verlag, New York (1996)

9. Matheus C. J.: Feature Construction: An Analytical Framework and an Application to Decision Trees. Ph.D. thesis. University of Illinois at Urbana-Champaign.

10. Michalsky R., et al.: The Multipurpose Incremental Learning System AQ15 and its Testing Application to Three Medical Domains. In Proceedings of the 5th National Conference on Artificial Intelligence, (1986) 1041-1045

11. Oliveira A. L.: Inferring Reduced Ordered Decision Graphs of Minimum Description Length. In Proceedings of the 12th International Conference on Machine Learning, (1995) 421-429

12. Pagallo G., Haussler D.: Boolean Feature Discovery in Empirical Learning. Machine Learning, 5:1, (1990) 71-99

13. Pérez E., Rendell L. A.: Learning Despite Concept Variation by Finding Structure in Attribute-based Data. In Proceedings of the 13th International Conference on Machine Learning, (1996) 391-399

14. Quinlan J. R.: Induction of Decision Trees. Machine Learning, 1:1, (1986) 81-106

15. Quinlan, J. R.: Generating Production Rules from Decision Trees. In Proceedings of the 10th International Joint Conference on Artificial Intelligence, (1987) 304-307

16. Quinlan J. R.: C4.5 Programs for Machine Learning. Morgan Kaufmann Publishers, Inc., Palo Alto, CA. (1994)

17. Quinlan J. R., Cameron J.: Oversearching and Layered Search in Empirical Learning. In Proceedings of the 24th International Joint Conference on Artificial Intelligence, (1995) 1019-1024

18. Ragavan H., Rendell L. A.: Lookahead Feature Construction for Learning Hard Concepts. In Proceedings of the 10th International Conference on Machine Learning, (1993) 252-259

19. Rendell L. A.: A General Framework for Induction and a Study of Selective Induction. Machine Learning, 1:2, (1986) 177-226

20. Rendell L. A., Seshu R.: Learning Hard Concepts through Constructive Induction: Framework and Rationale. Computational Intelligence, 6, (1990) 247-270

21. Rivest L.R.: Learning Decision Lists. Machine Learning, 2:3, (1987) 229-246

22. Rymon, R.: An SE-tree Based Characterization of the Induction Problem. In Proceedings of the 10th International Conference on Machine Learning, (1993) 268-275

23. Satosi W.: Knowing and Guessing. John Wiley & Sons, New York (1969)

24. Schaffer J.: A Conservation Law for Generalization Performance. In Proceedings of the 11th International Conference on Machine Learning (1994), 259-265

25. Thornton C.: Parity: The Problem that Won't Go Away. In Proceedings of the 11th Biennial Conference of the Canadian Society for Computational Studies of Intelligence, Toronto Ontario, Canada, (1996) 362-374

26. Vilalta R., Blix G., Rendell L.: Techniques for Efficient Feature Construction in Decision Tree Induction. Document in Preparation. Beckman Institute, University of Illinois at Urbana-Champaign (1997)

27. Webb G.I.: OPUS: An Efficient Admissible Algorithm for Unordered Search. Journal of Artificial Intelligence Research, 3 (1995), 431-465

28. Weiss S., Indurkhya N.: Optimized Rule Induction. IEEE Expert, 8:6, (1993) 61-69

Part III:

Workshop Position Papers

Case-Based Learning:
Beyond Classification of Feature Vectors*

David W. Aha[1] and Dietrich Wettschereck[2]

[1] Navy Center for Applied Research in Artificial Intelligence, Naval Research
Laboratory, Washington, DC USA, aha@aic.nrl.navy.mil
[2] FIT.KI, GMD (German National Research Center for Information Technology),
Schloß Birlinghoven, 53754 Sankt Augustin, Germany, dietrich.wettschereck@gmd.de

Abstract. The dominant theme of case-based research at recent ML
conferences has been on classifying cases represented by feature vectors.
However, other useful tasks can be targeted, and other representations
are often preferable. We review the recent literature on case-based learning, focusing on alternative performance tasks and more expressive case
representations. We also highlight topics in need of additional research.

1   Introduction

The majority of machine learning (ML) research has focussed on *supervised
learning* tasks in which class-labeled cases, each represented as a vector of *features*, are given to a learning algorithm that induces a *concept description*. This
description can then be used to predict the class labels of unlabeled cases. One
approach for solving supervised learning tasks, called *case-based*,[3] involves storing cases, often as ⟨problem,solution⟩ pairs, and retrieving them to solve similar
problems. This distinguishes their behavior from approaches that greedily replace cases with abstract data structures (e.g., decision trees, rule sets, artificial
neural networks, and Bayesian nets).

ML research on case-based approaches frequently focuses on classifying feature vectors (e.g., Aha et al., 1991; Cost & Salzberg, 1993; Wettschereck &
Dietterich, 1995). This is not surprising given that several classes of related algorithms also focus on classifying feature vectors, including *k-nearest neighbor classifiers*, *locally weighted learners*, *radial basis function networks*, and *exemplar-
based models* of human concept formation. However, this restriction tends to slow
scientific progress on other case-based learning (CBL) issues.

We advocate greater emphasis on alternative performance tasks and case
representations, where several significant problems remain unsolved. Section 2
reviews the case-based reasoning (CBR) problem solving cycle, identifies several
of its learning issues, and reviews related research. Because this cycle is rife
with other interesting research topics, few CBR researchers focus on developing
learning algorithms, and ML researchers may be unfamiliar with some of its

---

* This is a companion paper for the ECML-97 MLNet Workshop with the same title.
  See http://nathan.gmd.de/persons/dietrich.wettschereck/ecml97ws.html.
[3] Popular synonyms include *instance-based*, *memory-based*, and *exemplar-based*.

other learning opportunities. Therefore, we outline some open CBL research issues in Section 3. Space constraints prevent us from reviewing CBL research on classifying feature vectors here, which is the focus of (Aha, 1997a).

2 Case representation and case-based learning

We begin by describing the CBR problem solving cycle and its knowledge sources, and then use them to organize our brief description of relevant CBL research. The CBR problem solving cycle (Aamodt & Plaza, 1994) contains four steps:

1. *Retrieval*: Retrieve a set of cases whose problems are similar to the query.
2. *Reuse*: Apply the retrieved cases' solutions to solve the query.
3. *Revision*: Evaluate this solution, and revise it as necessary.
4. *Retention*: Add the new ⟨query problem,solution⟩ pair to the case library.

Most CBL research on classifying feature vectors has focussed on modifying retrieval knowledge (e.g., new similarity functions, fast indexing strategies). Other issues concerning retrieval (e.g., modifying retrieval behavior by applying ease-of-revision constraints) are usually not reported at ML conferences. This also applies to the other steps in this cycle, primarily because solutions in classification tasks are class labels, which do not require complex reuse and revision strategies. However, solutions in cases can be plans, designs, or other complex structures, which complicates case reuse and revision.

According to Richter (1995), four *containers* of knowledge interact with these steps in the CBR cycle:

1. the case description language,
2. the similarity measure (for case retrieval),
3. the solution transformation (for adaptation during case revision), and
4. the cases themselves.

The following subsections summarize CBL research that targets one or more of these containers. We focus on research that either uses alternatives to feature vector representations for cases and/or addresses tasks other than classification.

2.1 Alternative representations for describing cases

Several representations for cases have been investigated (Gebhardt, 1996). For example, cases in case-based design systems (Maher et al., 1996; Börner, 1995; Surma & Braunschweig, 1996) are complex design artifacts. These require structural similarity functions, and the performance task is typically design construction rather than classification.

Other performance tasks also typically influence choices for representing cases. For example, CIBL (Branting & Broos, 1997) learns the concept of a *preference pair*, where each case is an ordered pair of states (feature vectors) in which the first is preferable to the second. Given a new pair of states, it predicts which is preferable. Langley and Pfleger (1995) instead represented cases as *evidence grids* (i.e., two-dimensional matrices, where each element is a probability estimate that its location contains a tangible object). Their algorithm learns to classify a given location as one of a set of known places.

Sequential problem-solving tasks, such as two person games, often demand complex case representations. Kerner's (1995) chess player represents cases as frames that serve as *explanation patterns* to evaluate game patterns. He described several learning operators for modifying them. CABOT (Callan et al., 1991), an Othello player, represents cases as ⟨state,move⟩ pairs. Given a query, it retrieves a most similar (game) state, and then uses a second similarity computation to select the move that best mimics the retrieved case's implicit state changes. If an oracle indicates a selection error occurred, then CABOT updates one of its two similarity functions or stores a new case. Finally, Elliot and Scott's (1991) algorithm solves integration problems, where cases (expressions) are nodes in a tree-structured hierarchy and similarity is a function of hierarchy distance. Learning involves modifying counts indicating whether operators were successfully applied, and associating an operator for each expression.

Horn clauses have also been used to represent cases. Grolimund and Ganascia (1995) used them for an optimization task. Their learning algorithm stores and reuses operator selection experience during a tabu search. RIBL (Emde & Wettschereck, 1996), a first-order classifier, instead constructs cases from multirelational data and computes the similarities between arbitrarily complex cases. Finally, Malek and Rialle (1994) described a medical diagnosis task and learning procedures for modifying Horn clause cases.

Other case representations that have been used include graphs, which require attention to the subgraph isomorphism problem. Messmer and Bunke (1995) described a TDIDT approach that allows graph-structured cases to be retrieved in polynomial time, but it trades off exponential space. Applying tree simplification strategies (e.g., pruning) can decrease space requirements, but they also reduce gains in computational efficiency. In contrast, cases in CABINS (Miyashita & Sycara, 1993) are schedules; it improves their quality using an iterative refinement process. Ramsey and Grefenstette (1994) defined a case as a (genetically induced) rule population. Their CBL algorithm uses environmental cues to select which population to use in response to concept drifts. Finally, *case retrieval nets* represent cases as sets of entities in a joint semantic network. Lenz (1996) described their application to classification tasks.

2.2 Learning retrieval knowledge

Complex representations and tasks (e.g., planning) require learning algorithms tailored to their needs for case retrieval and revision. For example, CAPLAN/CBC (Muñoz-Avila & Hüllen, 1996) learns feature weights to index plan descriptions, and RUNNER (Seifert et al., 1994) learns operator application conditions and uses them to index cases represented by semantic networks. HAMLET (Borrajo & Veloso, 1997) learns to improve its search efficiency and resulting plan quality by incrementally refining its control rules using a CBL approach. META-AQUA

(Cox & Ram, 1994) uses explicit learning goals to select strategies for recovering from planning failures. Krovvidy and Wee's (1993) CBL system saves partial planning solutions and learns heuristics for selecting them during problem solving. Knowledge on the adaptability of retrieved cases can also be used to successfully bias retrieval behavior (Smyth & Keane, 1995a).

2.3 Learning adaptation knowledge

Learned adaptation knowledge can be used to bias the case vocabulary. For example, ROBBIE (Fox & Leake, 1995) uses constructive induction to learn new indices by estimating their ability to retrieve more easily adapted cases. Adaptation knowledge can also be learned by integrating case- and rule-based approaches (Leake et al., 1996), by evolutionary algorithms (Hunt, 1995), or by analyzing case comparisons (Hanney & Keane, 1996). CARMA (Hastings et al., 1995) instead learns weights on adaptation operators.

Approaches that annotate case solutions with explicit justification knowledge for guiding reuse and revision employ a form of adaptation known as *derivational analogy*. This is most often used in planning tasks. Veloso and Carbonell (1993) described a derivational approach that learns to improve case indices and speed problem solving. Bhansali and Harandi (1993) used derivational analogy to learn how to synthesize UNIX programs. In both cases, several learning opportunities arose, including how to use justification knowledge to direct the search for selecting goals, operators, and bindings.

2.4 Learning and case libraries

The final knowledge container is the case library itself. Because new cases do not always contribute sufficient information to warrant their retention, several case-based systems selectively retain cases. For example, Smyth and Keane (1995b) described algorithms that delete cases whose solutions are covered by other cases. Aha (1997b) instead proposed how learning algorithms can be used to modify cases rather than delete them.

3 Some suggested research topics

Several CBL research issues require attention, both in the context of specific performance tasks and as components in integrated learning frameworks. The following subsections briefly describe some of these issues.

3.1 Data mining

Data mining is a step in the *knowledge discovery process* in which inferences are generated from large databases (Fayyad et al., 1996). Case-based learning systems can assist in data mining activities in several ways. For example, CBL can be used to locate extreme cases (i.e., *gems*) that are of particular interest. Also,

CBL is a promising approach for mining in multi-relational databases (Emde & Wettschereck, 1996), which has not yet been extensively investigated even though many large databases employ relational representations. Data mining requires attention to efficiency concerns, which could spur research on designing typicality-guided retrieval strategies (Porter et al., 1990), parallel case retrieval (Kettler et al., 1994), and software support for case construction (Kitano et al., 1993). Also needed are techniques for validating the behavior of case revision operators, and further research on how abstraction can be used to reduce search without requiring that solutions be downward refinable (Branting & Aha, 1995).

3.2 Synthesis performance tasks

Most CBL research has focussed on analysis (e.g., classification) rather than synthesis (e.g., design, planning) tasks. It is not clear what modifications of techniques for classifying feature vectors are needed for synthesis tasks. For example, for problems described by feature collections, Muñoz-Avila and Hüllen (1996) showed how feature weighting can be used in planning tasks, but it is unclear how weighting algorithms should be designed for problems represented by graphs. Similarly, adaptation has a more complex role in synthesis than in most classification tasks. More robust techniques are needed for learning and modifying constraints in case-based planning and design systems (Avesani et al., 1993; Purvis & Pu, 1995).

Several case-based systems, especially those that target legal analysis, learn to synthesize *explanatory arguments* for (and sometimes also against) specific decisions (e.g., Branting, 1990). Additional CBL research is needed on inducing rules to supplement case-based argumentation, such as by identifying case retrieval contexts for given legal situations, and by updating indexing topologies to ensure that the retrieved case solutions are appropriate.

3.3 Components in integrated learning frameworks

CBL algorithms have been integrated with learning algorithms that target a variety of performance tasks, including knowledge acquisition (Tecuci, 1993), analytic problem solving (Borrajo & Veloso, 1997), reinforcement learning (McCallum, 1995), and Bayesian reasoning (Tirri et al., 1996). These integrations frequently use CBL in innovative fashions. For example, McCallum's cases provide historical information that allow agents to distinguish perceptually identical locations, while Borrajo and Veloso used several lazy explanation-based learning techniques to improve plan quality and reduce planning time. However, these integrations often introduce several novel research issues. For example, Tecuci showed how simple determinations can help induce structured explanations for observations, but leaves open the question of whether and how more elaborate CBL techniques (e.g., derivational analogy) can be used to dynamically formulate cases and acquire knowledge. Similarly, additional research is needed to investigate how CBL techniques can assist in inducing Bayes networks, where cases are individual networks. Many other opportunities for novel research contributions exist in the context of integrating CBL with other learning approaches.

4 Conclusion

Previous machine learning research on case-based approaches has typically focussed on classifying feature vectors. Although much progress has been made, attention to several other case-based learning issues is needed. This paper briefly outlines existing research on case-base learning that goes beyond classifying feature vectors, and suggests directions for future research.

Acknowledgements

Thanks to Len Breslow, Héctor Muñoz-Avila, Jerzy Surma, and Henry Tirri for their comments on an earlier draft of this paper. This research was supported by the Office of Naval Research.

References

Aamodt, A., & Plaza, E. (1994). Case-based reasoning: Foundational issues, methodological variations, and system approaches. *AI Communications, 7*, 39–59.

Aha, D. W. (1997a). A brief history of case-based classification. Unpublished manuscript. http://www.aic.nrl.navy.mil/~aha.

Aha, D. W. (1997b). A proposal for refining case libraries. To appear in *Proceedings of the Fifth German Workshop on Case-Based Reasoning.*

Aha, D. W., Kibler, D., & Albert, M. K. (1991). Instance-based learning algorithms. *Machine Learning, 6*, 37–66.

Avesani, P., Perini, A., & Ricci, F. (1993). Combining CBR and constraint reasoning in planning forest fire fighting. *Proceedings of the First European Workshop on Case-Based Reasoning* (pp. 235–239). Kaiserslautern, Germany: Unpublished.

Bhansali, S., & Harandi, M. T. (1993). Synthesis of UNIX programs using derivational analogy. *Machine Learning, 10*, 7–55.

Borrajo, D., & Veloso, M. (1997). Lazy incremental learning of control knowledge for efficiently obtaining quality plans. To appear in *Artificial Intelligence Review.*

Börner, K. (Ed.) (1995). *Modules for design support* (Technical Report 35). Freiburg, Germany: University of Freiburg, Center for Cognitive Science.

Branting, L. K. (1990). *Integrating rules and precedents for classification and explanation: Automating legal analysis* (Technical Report AI90-146). Austin, TX: University of Texas, Artificial Intelligence Laboratory.

Branting, L. K., & Aha, D. W. (1995). Stratified case-based reasoning: Reusing hierarchical problem solving episodes. *Proceedings of the 14th International Joint Conference on Artificial Intelligence* (pp. 384–390). Montreal: Morgan Kaufmann.

Branting, L. K., & Broos, P. (1997). Automated acquisition of user preferences. *International Journal of Human-Computer Studies, 46*, 55–77.

Callan, J. P., Fawcett, T. E., & Rissland, E. L. (1991). CABOT: An adaptive approach to case-based search. *Proceedings of the Twelfth International Joint Conference on Artificial Intelligence* (pp. 803–808). Sydney: Morgan Kaufmann.

Cost, S., & Salzberg, S. (1993). A weighted nearest neighbor algorithm for learning with symbolic features. *Machine Learning*, *10*, 57–78.

Cox, M., & Ram, A. (1994). Managing learning goals in strategy-selection problems. In *Working Papers of the Second European Workshop on Case-Based Reasoning* (pp. 85–93). Chantilly, France: Unpublished.

Elliot, T., & Scott, P. D. (1991). Instance-based and generalization-based learning procedures applied to solving integration problems. *Proceedings of the 8th Conference of the Society for the Study of AI* (pp. 256–265). Leeds, UK: Springer.

Emde, W., & Wettschereck, D. (1996). Relational instance-based learning. *Proceedings of the Thirteenth International Conference on Machine Learning* (pp. 122–130). Bari, Italy: Morgan Kaufman.

Fayyad, U. M., Piatetsky-Shapiro, G., Smyth, P., & Uthurusamy, R. (Eds.), *Advances in Knowledge Discovery and Data Mining*. Cambridge, Massachusetts: MIT Press.

Fox, S., & Leake, D. L. (1995). Using introspective reasoning to refine indexing. *Proceedings of the 14th International Joint Conference on Artificial Intelligence* (pp. 391–397). Montreal: Morgan Kaufmann.

Gebhardt, F. (1996). Structure oriented case retrieval. *Fourth German Workshop on Case-Based Reasoning: System Development and Evaluation* (pp. 95–102). Technical Report, Humbold University, Informatik-Bericht Number 55.

Grolimund, S., & Ganascia, J.-L. (1995). Integrating case-based reasoning and tabu search for solving optimisation problems. *Proceedings of the First International Conference on Case-Based Reasoning* (pp. 451–460). Sesimbra, Portugal: Springer.

Hanney, K., & Keane, M. T. (1996). Learning adaptation rules from a case-base. *Proceedings of the 3rd European Workshop on CBR* (pp. 179–192). Lausanne: Springer.

Hastings, J., D., Branting, L. K., & Lockwood, J. A. (1995). Case adaptation using an incomplete causal model. *Proceedings of the First International Conference on Case-Based Reasoning* (pp. 181–192). Sesimbra, Portugal: Springer.

Hunt, J. (1995). Evolutionary case based design. In I. D. Watson (Ed.), *Progress in Case-Based Reasoning: First United Kingdom Workshop*. Salford, UK: Springer.

Kerner, Y. (1995). Learning strategies for explanation patterns: Basic game patterns with application to chess. In *Proceedings of the First International Conference on Case-Based Reasoning* (pp. 491–500). Sesimbra, Portugal: Springer.

Kettler, B. P., Hendler, J. A., Andersen, W. A., & Evett, M. P. (1994). Massively parallel support for case-based planning. *IEEE Expert*, *2*, 8–14.

Kitano H., Shimazu H., & Shibata A. (1993). Case-method: A methodology for building large-scale case-based systems. *Proceedings of the Eleventh National Conference on Artificial Intelligence* (pp. 303–308). Washington, DC: AAAI Press.

Krovvidy, S., & Wee, W. G. (1993). Wastewater treatment systems from case-based reasoning. *Machine Learning*, *10*, 341–363.

Langley, P., & Pfleger, K. (1995). Case-based acquisition of place knowledge. *Proceedings of the Twelfth International Conference on Machine Learning* (pp. 344–352). Tahoe City, CA: Morgan Kaufmann.

Leake, D. B., Kinley, A., & Wilson, D. (1996). Acquiring case adaptation knowledge: A hybrid approach. *Proceedings of the Thirteenth National Conference on Artificial Intelligence* (pp. 684–689). Portland, OR: AAAI Press.

Lenz, M. (1996). Case retrieval nets applied to large case bases. *Fourth German Workshop on Case-Based Reasoning: System Development and Evaluation* (pp. 111–118). Technical Report, Humbold University, Informatik-Bericht Number 55.

Maher, M. L., Balachandran, M. B., & Zhang, D. M. (1995). *Case-Based Reasoning in Design*. Mahwah, NJ: Erlbaum.

Malek, M., & Rialle, V. (1994). A case-based reasoning system applied to neuropathy diagnosis. *Proceedings of the Second European Workshop on Case-Based Reasoning* (pp. 329–336). Chantilly, France: Unpublished.

McCallum, R. A. (1995). Instance-based utile distinctions for reinforcement learning. *Proceedings of the Twelfth International Conference on Machine Learning*. Lake Tahoe, CA: Morgan Kaufmann.

Messmer, B. T., & Bunke, H. (1995). *Subgraph isomorphism in polynomial time* (Technical Report IAM 95-003). Bern, Switzerland: University of Bern, Institute of Computer Science and Applied Mathematics.

Miyashita, K., & Sycara, K. (1993). Improving schedule quality through case-based reasoning. In D. Leake (Ed.), *Case-Based Reasoning: Papers from the 1993 Workshop* (Technical Report WS-93-01). Menlo Park, CA: AAAI Press.

Muñoz-Avila, H., & Hüllen, J. (1996). Feature weighting by explaining case-based problem solving episodes. *Proceedings of the Third European Workshop on Case-Based Reasoning* (pp. 280–294). Lausanne, Switzerland: Springer.

Porter, B. W., Bareiss, R., & Holte, R. C. (1990). Knowledge acquisition and heuristic classification in weak-theory domains. *Artificial Intelligence, 45*, 229–263.

Purvis, L. & Pu, P. (1995). Adaptation using constraint satisfaction techniques. *Proceedings of the First International Conference on Case Based Reasoning* (pp. 289–300). Sesimbra, Portugal: Springer Verlag.

Ramsey, C. L., & Grefenstette, J. J. (1994). Case-based anytime learning. In D. W. Aha (Ed.), *Case-Based Reasoning: Papers from the 1994 Workshop* (Technical Report WS-94-01). Menlo Park, CA: AAAI Press.

Richter, M. (1995). The knowledge contained in similarity measures. http://wwwagr.informatik.uni-kl.de/ lsa/CBR/Richtericcbr95remarks.html.

Seifert, C. M., Hammond, K. J., Johnson, H. M., Converse, T. M., McDougal, T. F., & Vanderstoep, S. W. (1994). Case-based learning: Predictive features in indexing. *Machine Learning, 16*, 37–56.

Smyth, B. & Keane, M. T. (1995a). Experiments on adaptation-guided retrieval in case-based design. *Proceedings of the First International Conference on Case-Based Reasoning* (pp. 313–324). Sesimbra, Portugal: Springer.

Smyth, B. & Keane, M. T. (1995b). Remembering to forget: A competence-preserving deletion policy for case-based systems. *Proceedings of the 14th International Joint Conference on Artificial Intelligence* (pp. 377–383). Montreal: Morgan Kaufmann.

Surma, J., & Braunschweig, B. (1996). REPRO: Supporting flowsheet design by case-based retrieval. *Proceedings of the Third European Workshop on Case-Based Reasoning* (pp. 400–412). Lausanne, Switzerland: Springer.

Tecuci G., (1993). Plausible justification trees: A framework for deep and dynamic integration of learning strategies. *Machine Learning, 11*, 237–261.

Tirri, H., Kontkanen, P., & Myllmäki, P. (1996). A Bayesian framework for case-based reasoning. *Proceedings of the Third European Workshop on Case-Based Reasoning* (pp. 413–427). Lausanne, Switzerland: Springer.

Veloso, M. M., & Carbonell, J. G. (1993). Derivational analogy in PRODIGY: Automating case acquisition, storage, and utilization. *Machine Learning, 10*, 249–278.

Wettschereck, D., & Dietterich, T. G. (1995). An experimental comparison of the nearest neighbor and nearest hyperrectangle algorithms. *Machine Learning, 19*, 5–28.

Empirical Learning of Natural Language Processing Tasks

Walter Daelemans[1], Antal van den Bosch[2], Ton Weijters[2]

[1] Computational Linguistics, Tilburg University, The Netherlands
[2] Dept. of Computer Science / MATRIKS, Universiteit Maastricht, The Netherlands

Abstract. Language learning has thus far not been a hot application for machine-learning (ML) research. This limited attention for work on empirical learning of language knowledge and behaviour from text and speech data seems unjustified. After all, it is becoming apparent that empirical learning of Natural Language Processing (NLP) can alleviate NLP's all-time main problem, viz. the knowledge acquisition bottleneck: empirical ML methods such as rule induction, top down induction of decision trees, lazy learning, inductive logic programming, and some types of neural network learning, seem to be excellently suited to automatically induce exactly that knowledge that is hard to gather by hand. In this paper we address the question why NLP is an interesting application for empirical ML, and provide a brief overview of current work in this area.

1 Empirical Learning of Natural Language

Looking at the ML literature of the last decade, it is clear that language learning has not been an important application area of ML techniques. Especially the absence of more research on the *empirical learning of language knowledge and behaviour from text and speech data* is strange. After all, a main problem of the AI discipline of Natural Language Processing (NLP) is the *knowledge-acquisition bottleneck*: for each new language, domain, theoretical framework, and application, linguistic knowledge bases (lexicons, rule sets, grammars) have to be built basically from scratch.

In our opinion, there are at least three reasons why ML researchers should become more interested in NLP as an application area:

- **Complexity of tasks.** Data sets describing language problems exhibit a complex interaction of regularities, sub-regularities, pockets of exceptions, idiosyncratic exceptions, and noise. As such, they are a perfect model for a large class of other poorly-understood real-world problems (e.g. medical diagnosis) for which it is less easy to find large amounts of data. A better understanding of which algorithms work best for this class of problems will transfer to many other problem classes.
- **Real-world applications.** The market pull for applications in NLP (especially text analysis and machine translation) is enormous, but has not been matched by current language technology. ML techniques may help in realising the enormous market potential for NLP applications.

- **Availability of large datasets.** Datasets of NLP tasks containing tens or hundreds of thousands of examples are readily available. Traditional benchmark datasets usually contain far less examples. Experimenting with linguistic datasets will force algorithm designers to work on the issue of scaling abilities.

Examples of linguistic data available on electronic media exist across the board. Corpora that have been made available for research purposes and which can be or already have been used for empirical learning of NLP tasks include the following[3]:

- **CELEX** is a lexical data base containing word lists of English, German, and Dutch: for each word, detailed phonological and morphological information is provided. For each language, information on a hundred thousand words or more is available;
- **Penn Treebank II** is a data base of parsed and tagged sentences, stemming mainly from the Wallstreet Journal, containing about a million words;
- **WordNet** is a lexical data base for English, in which relations between words are implemented as links in a semantic network.

Our optimism about the marriage of empirical learning and NLP is based on our claim that NLP tasks fit the classification paradigm of supervised ML very well. Empirical learning (inductive learning from examples) is fundamentally a *classification* paradigm. Given a description of an object in terms of a propositional or first-order language, a category label is produced. This category should normally be taken from a finite inventory of possibilities, known beforehand. It is our claim that *all* linguistic tasks can be redefined this way and can thus be taken on in a ML context. All linguistic problems can be described as a mapping of one of two types of classification (Daelemans, 1995):

- **Disambiguation.** Given a set of possible categories and a relevant context in terms of attribute values, determine the correct category for this context. An example from text-to-speech conversion: given a letter in its context (a word), determine its pronunciation. An example from parsing: given a word in a sentence, determine the syntactic role of the word.
- **Segmentation.** Given a target and a context, determine whether a boundary is associated with this target, and if so which one. An example from word processing: given a position in a word, determine whether the word can be hyphenated there. An example from parsing: given two words in a sentence, determine whether a syntactic constituent boundary lies between the words.

---

[3] The three corpora can be reached at URLs http://www.kun.nl/celex/ (CELEX); ftp://ftp.cis.upenn.edu/pub/treebank/public_html/home.html
(Penn Treebank); and http://www.cogsci.princeton.edu/~wn/ (WordNet). Cf. http://www.cs.unimaas.nl/signll/signll-www.html for more links to home pages of corpora.

To redefine linguistic tasks as classification tasks appears straightforward for tasks such as text-to-speech conversion and hyphenation (i.e., tasks in the *morpho-phonological* domain), but may appear less so for complex NLP tasks such as word-sense disambiguation or parsing (i.e., tasks in the *syntactic-semantic* domain). Such complex tasks should not be redefined as one-pass classification tasks (e.g., given a sentence of written words, determine whether it is grammatical), but they can be defined as *cascades* of disambiguation and segmentation tasks. For example, parsing can be decomposed into deciding on the morpho-syntactic role of words (disambiguation), finding constituent boundaries (segmentation), resolving attachment ambiguities, determining the label of constituents, and determining grammaticality of sequences of constituents (all three disambiguation). Besides studying the learnability of identified linguistic tasks (which is what most current work is aimed at), an additional research goal of empirical learning of NLP tasks is therefore to search and test appropriate decompositions of complex tasks into tasks which are more easily learnable.

In the remainder of this paper, we provide an overview of current research on the empirical learning of NLP tasks. While the amount of work in some domains is limited, the results are often impressive. We structure the overview in four sections. This structure reflects what we view as an important dimension in empirical learning of NLP tasks, of which *lazy learning* on the one hand, and *greedy learning* on the other hand are the extremes. The essential difference between the two extremes is that in lazy learning, information encountered in training is not abstracted, whereas in greedy learning information is abstracted by restructing and removing redundant or unimportant information. Applications of lazy-learning algorithms are given in Section 2. The next three sections describe three approaches to greedy learning, viz. decision-tree learning and rule induction (section 3, artificial neural networks (section 4, and inductive logic programming (section 5).

2 Lazy Learning

The lazy learning learning paradigm is founded on the hypothesis that performance in cognitive tasks (in our case language processing) is based on reasoning on the basis of analogy of new situations to *stored representations of earlier experiences*, rather than on the application of *mental rules* abstracted from earlier experiences (as in rule induction and rule-based processing). The concept has appeared in different AI disciplines (from computer vision to robotics) several times, using alternative terms such as similarity-based, example-based, exemplar-based, analogical, case-based, nearest-neighbour, instance-based, and memory-based (Stanfill and Waltz, 1986; Kolodner, 1993; Aha *et al.*, 1991). Learning is 'lazy' as it involves adding training examples (feature-value vectors with associated categories) to memory without abstraction or restructuring. During classification, a previously unseen test example is presented to the system. Its similarity to all examples in memory is computed using a *similarity metric*, and the category of the most similar example(s) is used as a basis for predicting the category of the test example.

From the early nineties onwards, lazy-learning approaches to NLP tasks have been explored intensively by the partners of the ATILA project (University of Tilburg, Antwerp University, Universiteit Maastricht). Daelemans (1995) provides an overview of early work of this group on phonological and morphological tasks (grapheme-to-phoneme conversion, syllabification, hyphenation, morphological synthesis, word stress assignment). More recently, the approach has been applied to part-of-speech tagging (morphosyntactic disambiguation), morphological analysis, and the resolution of structural ambiguity (PP-attachment) (Daelemans et al., 1996; Van den Bosch et al., 1996). Cardie (1994, 1996) suggests a lazy-learning approach for both (morpho)syntactic and semantic disambiguation and shows excellent results compared to alternative approaches. Ng and Lee (1996) report results superior to previous statistical methods when applying a lazy learning method to word sense disambiguation. The exemplar-based reasoning aspects of lazy learning are also prominent in the large literature on example-based machine translation (see Jones, 1996, for an overview).

3 Decision-Tree Learning and Rule Induction

The *decision-tree learning* paradigm is based on the assumption that similarities between examples can be used to automatically extract decision-trees and categories with explanatory and generalisation power. In this paradigm, learning is *greedy*, and abstraction occurs at learning time. Decision-tree learning is a well-developed field within AI, see e.g. Quinlan (1993) for a synthesis of major research findings. The goal of *rule induction* (e.g., C4.5rules, Quinlan, 1993; CN2, Clark and Boswell, 1991) is, more than it is with decision-tree learning, to induce limited sets of interpretable rules from examples or decision trees.

Work on parsing (including tagging) of text with decision trees was pioneered at IBM (Black et al., 1992, Magerman, 1995). SPATTER (Magerman, 1995) starts from the premise that a parse tree can be viewed as the result of a series of classification problems. The most probable sequence of decisions for a sentence, given a training corpus, is its most probable analysis. Schmid (1994) describes TREETAGGER, in which transition probabilities between tags in a tag sequence are estimated using a decision tree induced from a set of n-grams occurring in the Penn treebank corpus. The features are the tags of the words preceding the word to be tagged. Schmid reports robustness relative to training set size: TREETAGGER 'degrades gracefully' with smaller training set sizes.

An example application of rule induction to the semantic domain is the classification of dialogue acts (Andernach, 1996). In this work, rule induction is employed to automatically generate and test theories on what are useful cues in texts for classifying them as dialogue acts. The output of rule induction offers interesting alternative insights to what existing theories consider relevant (Andernach, 1996). The use of rule induction to find heuristics for disambiguating between discourse use and sentential use of cue phrases in text was investigated by Litman (1996).

In the morpho-phonological domain the decision-tree learning algorithm IG-Tree (Daelemans *et al.*, to appear) has been applied successfully to grapheme-phoneme conversion (Van den Bosch and Daelemans, 1993) and morphological analysis (Van den Bosch *et al.*, 1996). An example application of rule induction to a morpho-phonological task is the application of C4.5rules to Dutch diminutive formation (Daelemans *et al.*, 1996).

4 Artificial Neural Networks

During the last decade, the study of connectionist models or *Artificial Neural Networks* (ANNs), has also led to applications in the NLP domain. The type of ANN learning most commonly used for NLP tasks, viz. supervised learning of classification tasks, contrasts with symbolic approaches with respect to its non-symbolic knowledge representation. The functionality of trained ANNs nonetheless displays the same interesting properties as that of lazy learning and decision-tree learning: an ANN can represent abstractions as well as store specific input-output mappings. A commonly-used learning algorithm for supervised learning of classification tasks in ANNs is back-propagation (BP) (Rumelhart, Hinton, and Williams, 1986).

In the current development of applying ANNs in NLP, one finds a stress on the issue of *representation* in syntactic and semantic applications, and on *generalisation* in morpho-phonological applications. Successful applications to syntax and semantics include modelling state machines discriminating between grammatical and ungrammatical sentences (e.g., Lawrence, Fong, and Giles, 1995). For excellent overviews of ANN applications to syntax and semantics, the reader is referred to Reilly and Sharkey (1992), and Wermter, Riloff, and Scheler (1996).

In the morpho-phonological domain, successes are claimed for ANNs as good generalisation models for classification tasks, e.g., grapheme-phoneme conversion (Dietterich *et al.*, 1995; Wolters, 1995). However, work by Weijters (1991), Van den Bosch and Daelemans (1993), and Van den Bosch (forthcoming), consistently shows a significantly lower performance on a range of morpho-phonological subtasks by BP as compared to decision-tree learning and lazy learning. Apparently, the amount of abstraction in a BP-trained ANN is accounting for a similar harmful effect on generalisation performance witnessed in decision-tree learning as opposed to lazy learning.

5 Inductive Logic Programming

Inductive Logic Programming (ILP) is one of the newest subfields in AI. For a general introduction to ILP, see Lavrac and Dzeroski (1994), or the contribution of Muggleton and De Raedt (1994) in an anniversary issue of the Journal of Logic Programming. ILP algorithms induce first-order hypotheses from examples. By using first-order logic as representation language, ILP can successfully learn problems for which feature-value-based algorithms fail.

First-order logic plays a crucial role in ILP. The general aim is to induce a hypothesis such that the classification of each learning example is entailed by the combination of background knowledge, the induced hypothesis, and the example. First-order (clausal) logic is used for the description of the background knowledge, the learning examples, and the hypothesis.

Despite the limited number of applications in which the relatively novel method of ILP is used for NLP tasks, the results are impressive: the rich representation language and the use of background knowledge in ILP enables the learning of complex NLP tasks such as (semantic) parsing (Zelle and Mooney, 1994; Muggleton *et al.* 1996), and tagging (Cussens, 1996). Dehaspe *et al.* (1996) uses ILP for small-scale linguistic tasks: grammaticality checking and Dutch diminutive forming.

6 Conclusion

Some general trends become clear when analysing the results of these studies. First, the most striking result is that the accuracy of induced systems is always comparable and often better than state-of-the-art hand-crafted systems, at a fraction of the development effort and time. This proves the point that ML techniques may help considerably in solving knowledge acquisition bottlenecks in NLP.

Second, it depends on the goal of the system whether lazy learning or greedy learning algorithms at an advantage. If the goal is optimal accuracy, lazy learning is preferable (Daelemans, 1996). We find that simple lazy-learning algorithms, extended with feature weighting and probabilistic decision rules, consistently obtain the best generalisation accuracy on a large collection of linguistic tasks (e.g., within the morpho-phonological domain, Van den Bosch, forthcoming). A possible explanation for this is the structure of NLP tasks discussed earlier: apart from a number of clear generalisations, a lot of subregularities and exceptions exist in the data. Exceptions tend to come in 'families'; it is therefore advantageous to *keep exceptions* (some family members may turn up during testing) rather than abstracting away from them: *being there is preferable to being probable*. If the goal of learning is creating inspectable, understandable generalisations about the data, however, the greedy-learning algorithms are obviously at an advantage: greedy learning techniques, such as ILP and Rule Induction, induce structures which may add to the understanding of the domain, and indeed sometimes generate new linguistic descriptions of the domain.

Third, the learning techniques described are well-suited for *integrating* different information sources (e.g. syntactic and semantic features may be combined in a single feature vector). Especially in lazy learning, feature-weighting techniques in the similarity metric achieve an optimal fusion and integration of these information sources in many applications.

The study of the usefulness of empirical ML for NLP has only just begun, but the results already achieved certainly warrant further systematic investigation.

References

Aha, D., Kibler, D., and Albert, M. (1991). Instance-based learning algorithms. *Machine Learning*, 7:37–66.

Andernach, T. (1996) A machine learning approach to the classification of dialogue utterances. In K. Oflazer and H. Somers (Eds.), *Proceedings of the Second International Conference on New Methods in Language Processing*, NeMLaP, pp. 98–109.

Black, E., Jelinek, F., Lafferty, J, Mercer, R., and Roukos, S. (1992). Decision tree models applied to the labeling of text with parts-of-speech Darpa Workshop on Speech and Natural Language.

Cardie, C. (1994). *Domain-Specific Knowledge Acquisition for Conceptual Sentence Analysis*. Ph.D. Thesis, University of Massachusetts, Amherst, MA.

Cardie, C. (1996). Embedded Machine Learning Systems for Natural Language Processing: A General Framework. In S. Wermter, E. Riloff, and G. Scheler, (Eds.), *Connectionist, Statistical and Symbolic Approaches to Learning for Natural Language Processing*, pp. 315–328. Berlin: Springer-Verlag.

Clark, P., and Boswell, R. (1991). Rule induction with CN2: Some recent improvements. In *Machine Learning: Proceedings of the Fifth European Conference*, pp. 151-163.

Cussens, J. (1996). Part-of-speech disambiguation using ILP. Technical report PRG-TR-25-96, Oxford University Computing Laboratory.

Daelemans, W. (1995). Memory-based lexical acquisition and processing. In P. Steffens (Ed.), *Machine Translation and the Lexicon*, pp. 85–98. Berlin: Springer-Verlag.

Daelemans, W. (1996). Abstraction considered harmful: Lazy learning of language processing. In H. J. van den Herik and A. Weijters (Eds.), *Proceedings of the 6th Belgian-Dutch Conference on Machine Learning*, Maastricht, The Netherlands, pp. 3–12.

Daelemans, W., Berck, P, and Gillis, S. (1996). Unsupervised discovery of phonological categories through supervised learning of morphological rules. In *Proceedings of the 16th International Conference on Computational Linguistics*, Copenhagen, Denmark, pp. 95-100.

Daelemans, W., Van den Bosch, A., and Weijters, A. (to appear). IGTree: using trees for classification in lazy learning algorithms. *Artificial Intelligence Review*, special issue on Lazy Learning. To appear.

Dehaspe, L., Blockeel, H., and De Raedt, L. (1996). Induction, logic and natural language processing. In *Proceedings of the Joint ELSNET/COMPULOG-NET/EAGLES Workshop on Computational Logic for Natural Language Processing*, South Queensferry, Scotland.

Dietterich, T. G., Hild, H., and Bakiri, G. (1990). A comparison of ID3 and Backpropagation for English text-to-speech mapping. Technical Report 90–20–4, Oregon State University.

Jones, D. *Analogical Natural Language Processing*. London: UCL Press, 1996.

Kolodner, J. (1992). *Case-Based Reasoning*. San Mateo, CA: Morgan Kaufmann.

Lavrac, N. and Dzeroski, S. (1994). *Inductive Logic Programming*. Chichester, UK: Ellis Horwood.

Lawrence, S., Fong, S., and Giles, C. Lee (1991) Natural language grammatical inference: A comparison of recurrent neural networks and machine learning methods. In S. Wermter, E. Riloff, and G. Scheler (Eds.), *Connectionist, Statistical, and Symbolic Approaches to Learning for Natural Language Processing*, pp. 33–47. Berlin: Springer-Verlag.

Litman, D. J. (1996). Cue phrase classification using machine learning. *Journal of Artificial Intelligence Research*, 5:53-94, 1996.

Magerman, D. (1995). Statistical decision tree models for parsing. In *Proceedings of the Association for Computational Linguistics.*, 1995.

Muggleton, S., and De Raedt, L. (1994). Inductive logic programming: Theory and methods. *Journal of Logic Programming*, 19,20:629-679.

Muggleton, S., Page, D., and Srinivasan, A. (1996). Learning to read by theory revision. Technical Report PRG-TR-26-96, Oxford University Computing Laboratory.

Ng, H. T. and H. B. Lee (1996). Integrating multiple knowledge sources to disambiguate word sense: an exemplar-based approach. In *Proceedings of the annual meeting of the ACL*, ACL-96.

Quinlan, J. R. (1993). c4.5: *Programs for Machine Learning*. San Mateo, CA: Morgan Kaufmann.

Reilley, R. G. and Sharkey, N. E., Eds. (1992). *Connectionist Approaches to Natural Language Processing*. Hillsdale, NJ: Lawrence Erlbaum Associates.

Rumelhart, D. E., Hinton, G. E., and Williams, R. J. (1986). Learning internal representations by error propagation. In D. E. Rumelhart & J. L. McClelland (Eds.), *Parallel Distributed Processing: Explorations in the Microstructure of Cognition*, volume 1, pp. 318-362. Cambridge, MA: The MIT Press.

Schmid, H. (1994). Probabilistic Part-of-Speech Tagging Using Decision Trees. *Proceedings of the International Conference on New Methods in Language Processing*, NeMLaP, Manchester, 44-49.

Van den Bosch, A., and Daelemans, W. (1993). Data-oriented methods for grapheme-to-phoneme conversion. In *Proceedings of the 6th Conference of the EACL*, pp. 45-53.

Van den Bosch, A., Daelemans, W., and Weijters, A. (1996). Morphological analysis as classification: an inductive-learning approach In K. Oflazer and H. Somers (Eds.), *Proceedings of the Second International Conference on New Methods in Language Processing*, NeMLaP, Ankara, Turkey, pp. 79-89.

Van den Bosch, A. (forthcoming). *Machines Learning to Pronounce Words: Empirical Learning and Modularisation of Morpho-Phonology*. PhD-Thesis, Universiteit Maastricht.

Weijters, A. (1991). A simple look-up procedure superior to NETtalk? In *Proceedings of the International Conference on Artificial Neural Networks*, Espoo, Finland.

Wermter, S., Riloff, E., and Scheler, G. (1996). *Connectionist, Statistical, and Symbolic Approaches to Learning for Natural Language Processing*. Berlin: Springer-Verlag.

Wettschereck, D., Aha, D. W. & Mohri, T. (1996). A review and comparative valuation of feature weighting methods for lazy learning algorithms. Technical Report AIC-95-012. Washington, DC: NRL Navy Center for Applied Research in AI.

Wolters, M. (1995). A dual-route approach to grapheme-to-phoneme conversion. In *Proceedings of the International Conference on Artificial Neural Networks*.

Zelle, J. M., and Mooney, R. J. (1994). Inducing deterministic Prolog parsers from treebanks: A machine learning approach. In *Proceedings of the Twelfth National Conference on Artificial Intelligence*, Seattle, WA, pp. 748-753.

Human-Agent Interaction and Machine Learning

Michael Kaiser[1]*, Volker Klingspor,[2] and Holger Friedrich[1]

[1] University of Karlsruhe, Institute for Real-Time Computer Systems & Robotics,
D-76128 Karlsruhe, Germany
[2] University of Dortmund, Lehrstuhl Informatik VIII, D-44221 Dortmund, Germany

Abstract. Human-Agent Interaction as a specific area of Human-Computer Interaction is of primary importance for the development of systems that should cooperate with humans. The ability to learn, i.e., to adapt to preferences, abilities and behaviour of a user and to peculiarities of the task at hand, should provide for both a wider range of application and a higher degree of acceptance of agent technology. In this paper, we discuss the role of Machine Learning as a basic technology for human-agent interaction and motivate the need for interdisciplinary approaches to solve problems related to communication with artificial agents for task specification, teaching, or information retrieval purposes.

1 Introduction

The concept of "intelligent agents" has recently found growing interest both in theory-oriented research as well as in applications such as robotics, manufacturing, information retrieval, and human-computer interaction. Especially, the idea of agents as "intelligent systems" that act in cooperation with or on behalf of a human user becomes increasingly important in today's information-oriented society. Research issues in this context comprise, among others:

1. Which tasks are really suited for agents (robots and softbots)?
2. How can artificial agents be designed and developed in a systematic manner?
3. How can humans communicate with artificial agents (and vice versa)?
4. How can artificial agents adapt to changing user preferences, a changing environment, etc.?

For Machine Learning, the field of intelligent agents offers a wide area of both research and applications. Specifically, the following questions ought to be answered if intelligent agents are to become useful for everyday users:

1. What and how can artificial agents learn from humans?
2. What and how can artificial agents learn from each other?

---

* Now with ABB Corporate Research Ltd., CHCRC.C, CH-5405 Baden-Dättwil, Switzerland.

3. What and how can artificial agents learn without external guidance or instruction, i.e., on their own?

Throughout this paper, we will try to set the stage for an interdisciplinary treatment of these questions. To this aim, we will shortly discuss the basics of human-agent interaction, and identify learning tasks that are to be solved. Afterwards, we will give a brief overview on the role current Machine Learning techniques can play to solve these tasks. Finally, some examples will be presented that illustrate the application of Machine Learning in Interaction tasks. The examples are related to adaptive user interfaces, user-adaptive information retrieval, and human-robot interaction.

2 The Psychology of Human-Agent Interaction

Agents should act in cooperation with or on behalf of a user. They should aid her to perform a difficult task, or take over a task completely which she doesn't want to do or isn't capable of. The more knowing and autonomous an agent gets, the closer the relationship between user and agent approaches that of two equal partners. However, in all cases the underlying relationship can be characterized as the human user **making use** of the artificial agent. For the agent, the user is the reference w.r.t. task specification and evaluation of performance.

Especially w.r.t. the actual communication (for task specification, monitoring, and performance evaluation), agent designers (and the agents themselves) should therefore take a quite objectivistic point of view, assuming that the reference for the meaning of symbols used for communication will be the user's understanding of these symbols. The agent should not – at least for communication purposes – construct its own symbols, but should ground user-defined symbols onto its own perceptions and actions.

Within this setting, the need for an agent to be adaptive w.r.t. the input it receives from its human user is obvious. The specific learning tasks, which are related to both communication and task execution, are discussed in the next section.

3 Learning Tasks in Human-Agent Interaction

Principally, an agent may have to adapt to two different things: the preferences of the user and variations in its tasks, including variations in its operating environment[3]. In the first case, we can distinguish learning **for** communication (i.e., to learn how to communicate with the human user) and learning **from** communication (which includes, for example, learning by observation).

To learn for communication requires the agent to build relations between user-supplied symbols to its own knowledge representation and, finally, to ground

---

[3] One might even say that an "agent-worthy task" should **require** an agent to adapt itself to it [Beale and Wood, 1994].

these symbols on its own perceptions and actions. This symbol grounding problem [Harnad, 1990] has found explicit treatment especially in human-robot interaction [Klingspor et al., 1996] and distributed AI [Kaiser et al., 1996b], but it is inherent in any learning task that requires the agent to relate its own behaviour to a user-defined concept, just as *usefulness* or *interestingness*. To solve this task, supervised inductive techniques are mostly being used, ranging from neural networks to ILP [Klingspor et al., 1996].

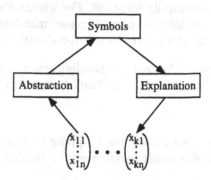

Fig. 1. Duality of abstraction and explanation.

The basic idea is always the same (Fig. 1): The meaning of language symbols is **explained** to the agents without using the language. The task of the agent is to abstract from the observations made during the explanation to the general concept represented by the user-given language symbol.

When learning from communication, the agent receives instructions from the user that are related to its behaviour. To understand these instructions, a common language between the agent and the user is mandatory, learning for communication may be required to provide it.

In the most simple case, instructions given to the agent are complete in that sense that they relate each possible state the agent may encounter to an appropriate action. Then, no induction is necessary. However, in the more general case only for some states information about how to behave are given to the agent, such that **incremental supervised learning** has to take place. The user may also be able to supply additional information to guide the agent's learning process, such that learning needs not to be purely inductive. This is the typical setting of Programming by Demonstration (see section 4.1).

Another prototypical setting is that of **reinforcement learning,** in which the agent receives a possibly delayed qualitative feedback from the user. Hence, the agent doesn't get explicit instructions. Therefore, the agent must explore the space of possible actions, in order to adapt to the user's performance criteria.

In any case, if learning takes place in a supervised manner, such that the given feedback consists of an optimal action or a quantitative indication of the error made by the agent, either

- the teacher must know the action space of the instructed agent and formulate the advice appropriately,

or

- the instructed agent must be able to map the teacher's advice onto its own action space.

Both requirements are not trivial, especially if agents should learn from other agents that are not structurally identical. For agents that should learn from human users, appropriate interfaces are therefore mandatory.

For learning on the basis of a scalar reward, the situation is very similar. Either

- the teacher must know the range of possible rewards used by the instructed agent (i.e., what is the "good" and "bad" in terms of the pupil),

or

- the instructed agent must know the mapping between the teacher's reward and its own range of rewards (what does the teacher mean by "good" and "bad").

In all cases, teacher or pupil must initiate the learning process. An important requirement is also that the teacher knows the limits of the instructed agent, since it makes no sense to try to teach an agent to go beyond its maximum capabilities. To enable the teacher to take care of this aspect requires the teacher to query these limits from an agent and to correctly interpret the agent's answer. Similarly, the instructed agent must understand the teacher's request and relate its capabilities properly to the task specified by the teacher.

4 Applications of Machine Learning in Human-Agent Interaction

4.1 Interface Agents

By interface agents, we mean agents that assist users with computer-based tasks. Simple examples are guides that have been given a fixed behaviour (such as Microsoft's "Wizards"). More sophisticated agents that learn by watching a human user are being developed under the heading of Programming by Demonstration (PbD)[Cypher, 1993].

PbD has been applied successfully several domains such as graphic editors like the MONDRIAN [Lieberman, 1993] system that learns new graphical editing procedures using a form of explanation based generalization. Instructible software agents [Maulsby, 1994] learn tasks like autonomous text formating or graph editing by observing the user doing the task. he knowledge is adapted and corrected by processing corrections issued by the user during automatic task execution. Intelligent specification interfaces such as the ViCCS interface

[Minton et al., 1995] and the interface agent assisting with completion of repetitive forms of Hermens and Schlimmer [Hermens and Schlimmer, 1994] are other examples of PbD applications.

Finally, an interface agent may also directly control the feedback given to a human user, even in an application-independent manner. An example of this is the system described in [Münch and Stangenberg, 1996], which provides selective haptic feedback to users of an X-Windows application.

4.2 Agents for Information Retrieval

The quickly growing World Wide Web demands for agents collecting and presenting interesting information to a user. NewsWeeder [Lang, 1995] is an agent that learns which Netnews are interesting for the reader. It learns from explicit specifications of the user preferences (the reader rates each read article), and NewsWeeder clusters highly rated articles by calculating the frequency of the words occurring in the article. It do not use, however, the linguistic structur of the articles.

WebWatcher [Armstrong et al., 1995] learns, which pages in the WWW are related to each other by observing the user when surfing in the Web. It generalizes the structural information contained in the sequence of pages being visited. Similarly, Lieberman's Letizia [Lieberman, 1995] aims at hypothesizing on the user's interests by observing the user's actions, in order to find possibly interesting pages, starting from the current page.

Knowledge Discovery in Databases (KDD) is another information retrieval task in which the human user can greatly benefit from support by an intelligent agent. Apart from performance issues [Kargupta et al., 1997], we also find that the main task for such agents is to perform information filtering, such that only those patterns are being presented that are really of interest for the human user [Davies and Edwards, 1995]. In addition, the user may also communicate with the actual mining agent, in order to guide its search [Wrobel et al., 1996].

4.3 Human-Robot Interaction

In robotics, the idea of the "personal robot" or "personal robotic assistant" (e.g., for aiding the elderly or disabled) is lately receiving a lot of attention. However, to enable new robot applications with emphasis on service tasks, it is necessary to develop techniques which allow untrained users to make efficient and safe use of a robot. In brief, what is required is

1. an interface that allows a user to intuitively instruct the robot, and
2. informative feedback such that the user can immediately understand what's happening on the robot's side.

Especially for users who are not experts in robot programming, **Robot Programming by Demonstration (RPD, [Heise, 1989])** has a considerable potential to become a suitable programming technique. Demonstrations of the robot's tasks are used as the primary input and can be used to transfer different kinds of knowledge to a robot.

- Demonstrations were proven to be suitable for the acquisition of *new program schemata on task level* [Segre, 1989]. In [Kuniyoshi et al., 1994], sequences of video images were analyzed in order to generate assembly plans. [Andreae, 1984] presented NODDY, a system which generates generalized programs by fusing several demonstrations. Single demonstrations and acquired user intentions are the basis for the robot programs generated by the system described in [Friedrich et al., 1996].
- On the *control level*, demonstrations can be used as the basis for learning both, *open-loop and closed-loop elementary skills*. The acquisition of open-loop skills is mostly focused on the reconstruction of trajectories from a sequence of demonstrated states (positions) [Delson and West, 1994, Ude, 1993]. Systems supporting the acquisition of closed-loop elementary skills comprise acquisition techniques for manipulation tasks such as deburring operations [Asada and Liu, 1991] and assembly [Kaiser and Dillmann, 1996] as well as for vehicle control [Pomerleau, 1991] and autonomous robot navigation [Reignier et al., 1995, Kaiser et al., 1996a].
- Learning new perceptive skills for object and landmark recognition can also take place on several system control levels. [Accame and Natale, 1995] present an approach to learn sensor parameterizations from demonstrations. Learning operational concepts, i.e., the combination of actions and sensing for the purposes of object recognition, reactive planning, and communication, is the topic of work presented in [Klingspor et al., 1996].

In Machine Learning, **behavioural cloning** has become popular as a synonym for "skill acquisition via human demonstration." Typical applications are the cart-pole balancing tasks [Guez and Selinsky, 1988], as well as the work on "Learning to fly" [Sammut et al., 1992] and recent work on crane control [Urbancic and Bratko, 1994], [Bratko et al., 1995]. In contrast to work in robotics, these approaches focus on the evaluation of a specific learning technique for cloning. Also **imitation learning** [Demiris and Hayes, 1996] must be considered in the context of Robot Programming by Demonstration. It is concerned with learning by imitating another agent (another robot), and as thus can be considered a special case of PbD. An important difference is that the actions that the robot performs due to the imitation mechanism form the basis for learning. While this technique puts less demands on the actual interaction interfaces, the learning agent must be much more skilled in interpreting its observations.

5 Summary and Conclusion

Throughout this paper, we discussed the importance of Machine Learning for human-agent interaction. We identified the basic learning tasks that need to be solved and indicated possible solutions to these tasks. Several application examples have shown that learning capabilities are really required, and that agents can exhibit such capabilities by using state of the art ML techniques. However, we have also seen that to design learning agents is a task that should be solved in a strongly user-oriented manner. Therefore, the discussion of technical issues must be complemented by treatment of the underlying interaction mechanisms and actual usability concerns. To provide a forum for this kind of interdisciplinary approach to human-agent interaction and especially the learning issues in this area, has been the major motivation for proposing the workshop.

References

[Accame and Natale, 1995] Accame, M. and Natale, F. D. (1995). Neural tuned edge extraction in visual sensing. In *3rd Europ. Workshop on Learning Robots*, Heraklion.

[Andreae, 1984] Andreae, P. M. (1984). Constraint limited generalization: Aquiring procedures from examples. In *Proc. of the Nat. Conf. on AI*, pages 6 – 10.

[Armstrong et al., 1995] Armstrong, R., Freitag, D., Joachims, T., and Mitchell, T. (1995). Webwatcher: A learning apprentice for the world wide web. In *1995 AAAI Spring Symp. on Information Gathering from Heterogeneous, Distributed Environments*.

[Asada and Liu, 1991] Asada, H. and Liu, S. (1991). Transfer of human skills to neural net robot controllers. In *IEEE International Conference on Robotics and Automation*, pages 2442 – 2448, Sacramento.

[Beale and Wood, 1994] Beale, R. and Wood, A. (1994). Agent-based interaction. In *Proceedings of the HCI 94*, Glasgow, UK.

[Bratko et al., 1995] Bratko, I., Urbancic, T., and Sammut, C. (1995). Behavioural cloning: Phenomena, results, and problems. In *5th IFAC Symposium on Automated Systems based on Human Skill*, Berlin.

[Cypher, 1993] Cypher, A. I. (1993). *Watch what I do – Programming by Demonstration*. MIT Press, Cambridge.

[Davies and Edwards, 1995] Davies, W. H. E. and Edwards, P. (1995). Distributed learning: An agent-based approach to data-mining. In *11th Int. Conf. on Machine Learning, Workshop on Agents that learn from other agents*, Tahoe City, California.

[Delson and West, 1994] Delson, N. and West, H. (1994). The use of human inconsistency in improving 3D robot trajectories. In *IEEE/RSJ International Conference on Intelligent Robots and Systems*, pages 1248 – 1255, München.

[Demiris and Hayes, 1996] Demiris, J. and Hayes, G. (1996). Imitative learning mechanisms in robots and humans. In *Fifth European Workshop on Learning Robots*, pages 9 – 16, Bari.

[Friedrich et al., 1996] Friedrich, H., Münch, S., Dillmann, R., Bocionek, S., and Sassin, M. (1996). Robot programming by demonstration: Supporting the induction by human interaction. *Machine Learning*, 23:163 – 189.

[Guez and Selinsky, 1988] Guez, A. and Selinsky, J. (1988). A neuromorphic controller with a human teacher. In *IEEE International Conference on Neural Networks*, pages 595 – 602, San Diego.

[Harnad, 1990] Harnad, S. (1990). The symbol grounding problem. *Physica D*, 42.

[Heise, 1989] Heise, R. (1989). Demonstration instead of programming: Focussing attention in robot task acquisition. Technical Report 89/360/22, Department of Computer Science, University of Calgary.

[Hermens and Schlimmer, 1994] Hermens, L. A. and Schlimmer, J. C. (1994). A machine-learning apprentice for the completion of repetitive forms. *IEEE Expert.*

[Kaiser et al., 1996a] Kaiser, M., Deck, M., and Dillmann, R. (1996a). Acquisition of basic mobility skills from human demonstrations. *Studies in Informatics and Control*, 5(3):223 – 234.

[Kaiser and Dillmann, 1996] Kaiser, M. and Dillmann, R. (1996). Building elementary robot skills from human demonstration. In *IEEE International Conference on Robotics and Automation*, Minneapolis, Minnesota, USA.

[Kaiser et al., 1996b] Kaiser, M., Rogalla, O., and Dillmann, R. (1996b). Communication as the basis for learning in multi-agent systems. In *ECAI '96 Workshop on Learning in Distributed AI Systems*, pages 50 – 59, Budapest.

[Kargupta et al., 1997] Kargupta, H., Hamzaoglu, I., Stafford, B., Hanagandi, V., and Buescher, K. (1997). PADMA: An architecture for scalable text classification. In *High Performance Computing.* to appear.

[Klingspor et al., 1996] Klingspor, V., Morik, K., and Rieger, A. (1996). Learning concepts from sensor data of a mobile robot. *Machine Learning*, 23(2/3):305 – 332.

[Kuniyoshi et al., 1994] Kuniyoshi, Y., Inaba, M., and Inoue, H. (1994). Learning by watching: Extracting reusable task knowledge from visual observation of human performance.

[Lang, 1995] Lang, K. (1995). Newsweeder: Learning to filter net news. In *Proceedings of the 12th International Conference on Machine Learning.* Morgan Kaufmann.

[Lieberman, 1993] Lieberman, H. (1993). *Watch what I do*, chapter MONDRIAN: A teachable graphical editor.

[Lieberman, 1995] Lieberman, H. (1995). Letizia: An agent that assists web browsing. In *Proc. of the Int. Joint Conf. on Artificial Intelligence*, Montreal, Canada.

[Maulsby, 1994] Maulsby, D. (1994). *Instructible agents.* PhD thesis, University of Calgary, Canada.

[Minton et al., 1995] Minton, S., Philpot, A., and Wolfe, S. (1995). Specification by demonstration: The ViCCS interface. In *International Conference on Machine Learning, Workshop on Programming by Demonstration*, Tahoe City.

[Münch and Stangenberg, 1996] Münch, S. and Stangenberg, M. (1996). Intelligent control for haptic displays. In *Eurographics '96*, Poitiers, France.

[Pomerleau, 1991] Pomerleau, D. A. (1991). Efficient training of artificial neural networks for autonomous navigation. *Neural Computation*, 15:88 – 97.

[Reignier et al., 1995] Reignier, P., Hansen, V., and Crowley, J. (1995). Incremental supervised learning for mobile robot reactive control. In *Intelligent Autonomous Systems 4*, pages 287 – 294, Karlsruhe.

[Sammut et al., 1992] Sammut, C., Hurst, S., Kedzier, D., and Michie, D. (1992). Learning to fly. In *9th Int. Conf. on Machine Learning*, pages 385 – 393, Aberdeen.

[Segre, 1989] Segre, A. M. (1989). *Machine Learning of Robot Assembly Plans.* Kluwer Academic Publishers.

[Ude, 1993] Ude, A. (1993). Trajectory generation from noisy positions of object features for teaching robot paths. *Robotics and Autonomous Systems*, 11:113 – 127.

[Urbancic and Bratko, 1994] Urbancic, T. and Bratko, I. (1994). Reconstructing human skill with machine learning. In *European Conf. on AI*, Amsterdam.

[Wrobel et al., 1996] Wrobel, S., Wettschereck, D., Verkamo, I., Siebes, A., Mannila, H., Kwakkel, F., and Klösken, W. (1996). User interactivity in very large scale data mining. In *9. Fachgruppentreffen Maschinelles Lernen*, Chemnitz, Germany.

Learning in Dynamically Changing Domains: Theory Revision and Context Dependence Issues

Charles Taylor[1] and Gholamreza Nakhaeizadeh[2]

[1] University of Leeds, Leeds LS2 9JT, UK
[2] Daimler-Benz Research and Technology, 89013 Ulm, Germany

Abstract. Dealing with dynamically changing domains is a very important topic in Machine Learning (ML) which has very interesting practical applications. Some attempts have already been made both in the statistical and machine learning communities to address some of the issues. In this paper we give a state of the art from the available literature in this area. We argue that a lot of further research is still needed, outline the directions that such research should go and describe the expected results. We argue also that most of the problems in this area can be solved only by interaction between the researchers of both the statistical and ML-communities.

1 Introduction

The ability to "learn" (or discover) knowledge from data in a more directed framework has had a long history both in Machine Learning (ML) and in Statistics; see [9] for a review and a list of references. In classification the data are generally of the form (*attributes*, *class*), and the objective is simply to learn a "rule" whereby a new observation can be classified into one of the classes using the information in the attributes.

For any rule, however, difficulties arise when the data are not static, and so the validity of patterns and rules (discovered 'knowledge') depends, in some unspecified way, on **time**, and it changes with time. In this case, learning and classification (or prediction) procedures need robust mechanisms for detecting and adapting to changes.

In the machine learning literature, the generic term for such time-dependent changes is **concept drift**. Concept drift may be caused by continuous changes of the world and the environment – for example, in economic problems, the presence of inflation causes a continual drift in the real value of money which means that rules based on absolute monetary values will quickly become out of date – or it may occur when the attribute values or the concepts depend on a certain (possibly unknown) *context*. For example, the relative proportions of vehicles made by each manufacturer will depend on the region (or country) of observation. Thus, the location can be seen as the context in which the data are collected – knowledge of the context (or a change of context) will aid the knowledge discovery process.

There are various ways in which concept drift can manifest itself: the distribution of the attributes in a class can change; new attributes become available or existing attributes can no longer be measured (for example due to changes in the law); or a subset of the variables can change in their importance or ability to predict the class.

In the case of supervised learning (classification or prediction), the extracted rules or dependencies can be no longer valid over time due to different changes which can occur. However, this statement is probably valid for unsupervised and reinforcement learning as well.

Learning in dynamically changing domains has a very high industrial relevance. During 1990-1993, the authors of this paper were involved in the ESPRIT Project StatLog which completed an evaluation of the performance of Machine Learning, neural and statistical algorithms on complex commercial and industrial problems. The overall aim was to give an objective assessment of the potential for classification algorithms in solving significant commercial and industrial problems, and to widen the foundation for commercial exploitation of these and related algorithms [9]. This project showed the shortcomings of ML-algorithms in dealing with real industrial and commercial large-scale applications [10]. Specifically, it turned out that one serious shortcoming is that the readily available ML-algorithms can not be applied to dynamically changing domains. Two such examples were examined:

The first is about a complex problem (introduced by Daimler-Benz) dealing with fault diagnosis of automatic transmissions. The goal was to show the practicability of symbolic ML algorithms to the end users and to convince them that ML would be a cheaper and faster approach to develop the next generation of the fault diagnosis systems. A classification system based on a decision tree approach was implemented which provided the desired accuracy rates. The results are reported in [9] in detail. After a while, however, it turned out that the generated rules had become completely invalid due to the changes of the parameters of the diagnosis device.

The second example deals with a complex problem from the credit industry. Using data about the users of mobile telephone cards [4], it was observed that the payment behaviour of customers changes over time and learned classification systems based on static approaches could not handle such dynamic changes.

Clearly, learning in dynamically changing domains is relevant to a wide range of industrial and commercial applications. Further examples which are based on time-dependent data and involve **prediction or classification** include:

- the analysis and prediction or various time series, such as the stock market and currency exchange;
- the analysis of data concerning buyers of new cars or other articles, in order to determine changing patterns in customer behaviour;
- development of different HELP-DESK applications, specially for technical diagnosis

There have been some attempts in the literature to address the problem of structural change in concepts and the dynamic aspects of data in Machine Learning. But most of the ML-algorithms can still not deal with this problem.

As described above, research in this direction has very important practical implications because structural change in concepts occurs often in the real-world domain. By considering this issue Machine Learning has a better chance of acceptance in industry and commerce.

There are many contributions that Statisticians have (already) made to this field, but their communication is hampered by a different terminology. For example, ML uses "unfamiliar" terms such as context learning, dynamic learning and theory revision, whereas statistical approaches to these problems include significance tests, structural change (used by econometricians) and multivariate regression methods. The question which remains is:

Have the Statisticians done everything; What is the challenge for ML? In which directions the research should go?

In the rest of the paper we try to discuss some of these issues. In Sect. 2 we give a short summary of available approaches in the literature. In Sect. 3 we discuss the challenge and need for further research in dealing with dynamically changing domains. In Sect. 4 we suggest some ideas which could be useful in performing further research in this area and we outline the expected results.

2   The State of the Art

Most of the literature on on-line, incremental learning has more or less tacitly assumed *stationary* environments; dynamic long- or short-term changes were not considered. For example, [17], [18] has developed an incremental algorithm that produces the same decision tree as would be found if all the examples had been available at once. In this case the sequence of the observations does not affect the final outcome.

It is only rather recently that the notions of concept drift and the influence of changing contexts have been directly addressed in the machine learning and statistics communities. Some specialized methods have been developed that try to detect and track changes under certain circumstances (see [20] and the references therein). Approaches so far developed include:

- using Statistical Process Control (SPC) methods to detect changes and adapt or modify rules as appropriate [13];
- using machine learning and statistical methods to learn to detect contextual clues and react accordingly when a change in context is suspected [20];
- using a "forgetting factor" whereby the rule is constantly updated using the most recently available observations [12].
- *incremental* (or *on-line*) learning with flexible 'forgetting operators' [21, 20, 19];

There are also links with exemplar and predictor evaluation methods in instance-based learning [1] [2] and to well-known updating methods of stochastic approximation as well as more standard time series models which use exponential smoothing.

To deal with dynamic aspects there are essentially two problems (in addition to those normally associated with classification). The first problem is to *detect* any change in the situation. In econometrics this is known as *structural change* and there are a variety of methods to test for changepoints (at least in the univariate case), and most of these approaches are model-based. For a recent review of developments in this area see [5], references therein and other papers in that volume. The second problem is how to react to any detected change. At one extreme it could be that the current rule must be completely re-learned since the population drift has been quite sudden; at the other extreme we may conclude that there has been no change, in which case an optimal approach may be to improve the current rule using incremental learning, for example. However, between these extremes we should be able to update the existing rule by giving giving appropriate weight to the more recent observations.

A closely related topic is that of *drifting concepts*. For example, early work was done by [16] with his STAGGER system. See also [15] and more recent work by [7]. When formulated in a logical framework [3] argue that incremental concept-learning can be understood as an instance of the more general problem of belief updating. This insight allows for potential interesting cross-fertilization between these areas. Some general principles were given by [6] for the development of classification systems for dynamic objects with variable properties that are observed under changing conditions. He outlines the following requirements for dynamic classification systems: to handle changing composition of features, different feature types, and varying accuracy and statistical characteristics of observations; to give precedence in time and quantitatively change proximity of the object to a particular class; to rely on a single prior description of objects or processes. The approach, which is fairly general, uses conditional probabilities. He concludes by recommending a hierarchical system for classification of dynamic objects, retaining a catalogue that stores the results of past observations, and generalized distributions of features on one of the classification levels.

3 The Need for Further Research

There is so far no comprehensive evaluation that shows if available algorithms can handle real industrial and commercial applications. Questions of robustness have not been sufficiently addressed. Moreover, *batch* incremental learning (in which new observations are naturally grouped in some way) has hardly been studied at all in this context, although it plays a very important role specially in the case of large-scale datasets.

Also, reliable and robust formal *measures* of change and concept drift are still largely missing. A recent step in this direction is the developed metric in [14] for "structural instability", a measure of the change in the decision rule as a result of incremental learning updates due to new observations. More general criteria are needed that can measure the different relevant dimensions of concept drift (extent, speed, etc.), that can reliably distinguish real changes from *noise*, and that can also recognize potential *structure* in changes (*e.g.*, oscillations, cyclic recurrence of contexts, and other regularities).

Finally, and perhaps most importantly, the available literature does not provide a *general framework* that would provide reliable guidelines for dealing with dynamic aspects. There is no substantial body of practical experience with drift and context effects in realistic application environments, nor is there a comprehensive collection of general or specialized methods with well-understood characteristics. Due to this reason, it is necessary to both develop generally applicable methods and integrate them into a general framework which covers the dynamic aspects not only of symbolic learning algorithms but also of statistical and neural learning as well as knowledge discovery. Furthermore, further research is needed to realize some of the ideas presented in [11], [20] and [8].

4 Some Ideas for Performing Further Research and the Expected Results

4.1 Suggested Directions for Further Research

The above discussion shows that although some attempts have ben made to handle the problem of learning in dynamically changing domains, there still remains a lot of questions which are open to both the statistical and ML-communities. In this section, we suggest some ideas to handle some of these issues.

Generally speaking, the main goal of the further research should be developing practical methods for classification, prediction, forecasting, and knowledge discovery that effectively deal with both gradual concept drift and more abrupt context changes. The common core of these tasks is inductive generalization, and the methods to be developed (or extended) belong to the fields of **machine learning** and **statistics**. Further research should aim at methods that are as general as possible, so that they will be useful to such diverse (though related) tasks as

- induction of classification rules;
- prediction (including forecasting) of numerical values;
- detection of logical patterns via ILP;
- detection of (other) associations (e.g., functional dependencies, clustering, interesting projections) within the data;
- description of interesting classes, clusters and their inter-relationships.

Generally, adapting to changing circumstances can be done by on-line learning and/or by updating our knowledge at appropriate times, *i.e.* when a change (in context) has been detected. One can identify various subproblems for which appropriate methods and algorithms could be developed:

Drift/change detection: An obvious way to detect concept drift is to use a form of Statistical Process Control (SPC). The methodology typically assumes that the data are grouped into "batches" which are monitored over time, and appropriate *warning* and *action* limits must be obtained for a parameter of interest. In the case of monitoring the class means it is necessary to take account of the correlations amongst the attributes. In the case of non-Normal data standard distribution results will not be available and nonparametric methods will be needed to set appropriate limits.

Adaptation / classifier update: Once a change has been detected, adaptation of the classifier (or predictor) is needed. At this stage it may be helpful to discover in which attributes the distribution is changing, and/or discover the change in context which is the underlying cause. The adaptation can take the form of complete re-learning (in the case that the change has been "large") or a modification of some of the existing rules (in the case that the change has been "small"). The precise meaning of "large" and "small" needs to be determined. Methods for assessing this from characteristics of the learning task will have to be developed. Adaptation and classifier updating functions need to be developed both for batch-incremental and truly incremental (on-line) learning.

Characterization and/or explanation of change: An important component in any adaptation is that there are suitable diagnostics to enable the description of the changes which have occurred. The explicit description or characterization of changes by the learning system makes it possible to detect "meta-level" patterns such as recurring contexts. When this is achieved then a second layer of learning could be formulated in which the appropriate updating method can be selected based on the type of change. The explicit description of changes is also desirable in applications directed towards knowledge discovery, where the goal is not so much to have an efficient classifier as to gain an understanding of the data or process under study. Inductive 'meta-learning' algorithms as described in [20] might be a first step in this direction and should be further developed.

Tackling all these subproblems in a comprehensive way will require a nontrivial combination of statistical methods with symbolic machine learning and knowledge discovery approaches. This should be one of the explicit premises of further research. One possible starting point might be the use of memory-based learning methods like *k-Nearest-Neighbor (k-NN)*, which are well-known from the statistical literature and are now being studied with increased interest in machine learning. Such "locally weighted learning" algorithms [2] have been shown to have the potential to track concept drift. In further research this direction should be explored.

It should be mentioned that in some cases the further development or adaptation of existing methods is necessary. These methods should be tested on a variety of real industrial and commercial complex problems with the aim of determining which aspects are best suited for each type of data. The developed framework should enable a fair comparison of the different approaches. It is likely that certain mathematical properties can be derived which characterize the data for which these methods are applicable. In addition, characteristics which indicate the preferred method should be found. The testing and assessment of methods should use agreed criteria which will include objective measures (error rates, time to learn, ability to adapt) as well as theoretical considerations.

4.2 Anticipated Results of Further Research

The types of results and output which can be expected from further research:

General tests and measures: (statistical) tests and criteria for detecting concept drift or potential context changes as well as measures of characteristics like extent, speed, etc. of concept drift;

Algorithms for classifier adaptation / update / knowledge revision: in particular, methods that optimize learned rules or concepts to fit a changed environment;

On-line algorithms for continual drift tracking: especially for prediction and forecasting tasks, on-line learning algorithms will be provided which adapt to changing concepts incrementally;

Diagnostics: formalisms and algorithms for the characterization and explanation of context changes;

General framework and procedures: this will include the integration of various components described in the previous section; within this general framework a range of new algorithms which incorporate the processes of monitoring, adaptation, and diagnostics will be completed;

Informative results of comparative experiments: competing algorithms will be evaluated systematically on complex data sets from real applications;

Characterization of domains of applicability of developed methods; general guidelines as to the application of learning methods in tasks involving concept drift will be developed;

5 Conclusions

An important component in further research is the interaction of researchers working in the fields of statistics and computer science. Previous attempts to bring these groups together (in the non-dynamic setting) have been very fruitful; see for example [9] and [11].

Acknowledgements: The authors would like to thank Pavel Brazdil and Gerhard Widmer for useful discussion on some issues described in this paper.

References

1. Aha, D., Kibler, D., & Albert, M.K. (1991). Instance-Based Learning Algorithms. *Machine Learning, 6(1)*, 37–66.
2. Atkeson, C.G., Moore, A.W. and Schaal, S. (1997) Locally Weighted Learning. To appear in a special issue of Artificial Intelligence Review on Lazy Learning.
3. De Raedt, L. and Bruynooghe, M. (1992). Belief updating from integrity constraints and queries. *Artificial Intelligence* **53**, 291–307.

4. Dübon, K. (1997). Dynamic Aspects in Risk Classification. To appear.
5. Dufour, J. M. and Ghysels, E. (1996) Editors' introduction: Recent developments in the econometrics of structural change. *Journal of Econometrics* **70**, 1-8.
6. Filosofov, L. V. (1992). Dynamic classification systems with learning from observation catalogs. *Cybernetics and Systems Analysis* **28**, 368-376.
7. Kubat, M. and Widmer, G. (1995). Adapting to drift in continuous domains. In *Lecture Notes in Artificial Intelligence*, Volume 912, pp. 307-310.
8. Mannila, H. (1995) Aspects of Data Mining. Keynote talk in: *Statistics, Machine Learning and Knowledge Discovery in Databases*, Kodratoff, Y., Nakhaeizadeh, G. and Taylor, C.C. (eds.), Heraklion, Crete. pp. 1-12.
9. Michie, D., Spiegelhalter, D. J. and Taylor, C. C. (eds) (1994) *Machine Learning, Neural and Statistical Classification*, Ellis Horwood, Chichester.
10. Nakhaeizadeh, G. (1995) What Daimler-Benz has learned as an Industrial Partner from the Machine Learning Project StatLog? In: Aha, D. and Riddle P. (Eds.). Proceedings of the Workshop on Applying Machine Learning in Practice at the Twelfth International Machine Learning Conference.
11. Nakhaeizadeh, G. and Taylor, C. C. (eds) (1997) *Machine Learning and Statistics: the Interface*. Wiley, New York.
12. Nakhaeizadeh, G., Taylor, C. C. and Kunisch, G. (1996) Dynamic Aspects of Statistical Classification. In *Intelligent Adaptive Agents, AAAI Technical report No. WS-96-04*, pp. 55-64. AAAI Press, Menlo Park, CA.
13. Nakhaeizadeh, G., Taylor, C. C. and Kunisch, G. (1997) Dynamic Supervised Learning: Some Basic Issues and Application Aspects. In *Classification, Data Analysis, and Knowledge Organisation*, Klar, B. & Opitz, O. (eds.). Springer Verlag.
14. Rissland, E. E., Brodley, C. E. and Friedman, M. T. (1995) Measuring structural change in concepts. Technical report, Department of Computer Science, University of Massachusetts, Amherst, MA 01003.
15. Schlimmer, J. C. (1987). Incremental adjustment of representations for learning. In *Fourth International Workshop on Machine Learning*, pp. 79-90. Irvine, CA:Morgan Kaufmann.
16. Schlimmer, J. C. and Granger, R. (1986). Incremental learning from noisy data. *Machine Learning* **1**, 317-354.
17. Utgoff, P. E. (1989) Incremental learning of decision trees. *Machine Learning* **4**, 161-186.
18. Utgoff, P. E. (1994) An improved algorithm for incremental induction of decision trees. In *Proceedings of Eleventh Machine Learning Conference*, Rutgers University. Morgan Kaufmann.
19. Widmer, G. (1994) Combining Robustness and Flexibility in Learning Drifting Concepts. *Proceedings of the Eleventh European Conference on Artificial Intelligence* (pp. 468-472). Wiley, Chichester.
20. Widmer, G. (1997) Tracking Context Changes through Meta-Learning *Machine Learning* (to appear). Draft version available electronically at ftp://ftp.ai.univie.ac.at/papers/oefai-tr-96-22.ps.Z.
21. Widmer, G. and Kubat, M. (1993) Effective Learning in Dynamic Environments by Explicit Context Tracking. *Proceedings of the Sixth European Conference on Machine Learning* (pp. 227-243). Berlin: Springer-Verlag.

Author Index

Lecture Notes in Artificial Intelligence (LNAI)

Lecture Notes in Computer Science